91-0461

Essays on the
Price History of Eighteenth-Century
Latin America

Essays on

the Price History of

Eighteenth-Century

Latin America

Edited by
Lyman L. Johnson
and
Enrique Tandeter

University of New Mexico Press

Albuquerque

Library of Congress Cataloging-in-Publication Data

Essays on the price history of eighteenth-century Latin America /
edited by Lyman L. Johnson and Enrique Tandeter.—1st ed.
p.   cm.
Includes bibliographical references and index.
ISBN 0-8263-1163-6.—ISBN 0-8263-1164-4 (pbk.)
1. Prices—Latin America—History—18th century.   2. Latin
America—Economic conditions.   I. Johnson, Lyman L.
II. Tandeter, Enrique.
HB235.L25E85   1989
338.5'2'09809033—dc20
89-36043
CIP

Translation of chapters 3 and 5 © 1990
by Meredith D. Dodge.

For Our Children

Eliza, Ben and Ned Johnson
and
Freddie and Leah Tandeter

CONTENTS

INTRODUCTION

THE DISCUSSIONS THAT LED TO THIS PROJECT BEGAN IN 1981 WHEN THE editors were both visiting lecturers in Great Britain. Each of us was working on the price history of a major city in the Viceroyalty of Río de la Plata—Tandeter on Potosí and Johnson on Buenos Aires—and each of us was eager to find a way to integrate our research with the work of other economic historians interested in the eighteenth century. As a result, we sought out colleagues involved in similar projects. This book is the first result of this collective effort. The essays collected here represent a substantial new contribution to the price history of colonial Latin America, a field that has attracted relatively little scholarly attention. It is our hope that by publishing these essays in a single volume we will encourage comparative analyses of eighteenth-century economic performance.

This relative lack of scholarly attention is particularly surprising given the lasting impact of E. J. Hamilton's work on wages and prices in metropolitan Spain.[1] Although many of his conclusions and some of his methods have been criticized by Pierre Vilar, Nadal Oller, and others, Hamilton's research promoted a valuable and lively debate over the long-term economic consequences of New World bullion production.[2] Given the scale of subsequent studies, the geographic and chronological breadth of Hamilton's work remains impressive. Colonial Latin America has not yet found its Hamilton, although some excellent price histories have been published. The best price histories for the region have avoided the problems of method and interpretation identified in Hamilton's work. Nevertheless, historians interested in the economy of Spanish and Portuguese America still lack reliably comparable price series for most of the colonial period.

In the early 1960s, Ruggiero Romano brought his considerable skill and experience as an economic historian to this task and published a series of essays that set out his preliminary conclusions.[3] After examining some surviving eighteenth-century ecclesiastical records in Santiago, Chile, and Buenos Aires, Argentina, Romano concluded that the late colonial period in Latin America was characterized by a general stagnation in prices and by a chronic shortage of currency. These characteristics he termed a "natural economy." As a result, he assumed that the accumulation of capital in colonial Latin America was retarded and local investment in both rural and urban production remained at low levels relative to the expanding societies of Europe in that era. Romano suggested that these characteristics of the colonial economy played an important role in establishing the direction of Latin America's later development.

One important result of Romano's pioneering work was the promotion of serious price research by Latin Americans. Enrique Florescano's study of corn prices in colonial New Spain is the best-known and most important representative of this generation of price history.[4] The price records of municipal grain warehouses in Mexico City proved more reliable and more uniform over a longer period of time than the manuscripts consulted in Chile and Argentina by Romano. Florescano was able to examine a much longer period (nearly the entire last century of Spanish rule), and thus reduced the likelihood that some short-term anomaly in economic performance would distort his conclusions. More importantly still, he published his data in the conventional tabular form developed by European economic historians, thereby allowing other historians to use his results in their own research.

Florescano found that corn prices fluctuated widely during the eighteenth century, but argued that no clear trend in corn prices existed. His analysis did show that the last years of the colonial period were characterized by a dramatic increase in corn prices. He argued convincingly that the effect of high prices for the preeminent Mexican staple must have been devastating for the working masses. However, the basic elements of Romano's model were compatible with Florescano's conclusions, despite the emergence of a price history characterized by a much greater short-term volatility than one would have anticipated from Romano's discussion of Santiago and Buenos Aires. Of particular interest to historians of New Spain, Florescano appeared to find chronological connections between periods of violent price inflation and civil unrest. The coincidence of high corn prices and the Hidalgo revolt being of obvious importance. Here in the Mexican case, we seemed to have concrete evidence of the fundamental role played by economic forces in the determination of political events.

Harold Johnson's careful study of commodity prices in Rio de Janeiro from 1763 to 1823 indicated that there were substantial regional economic differences in late colonial Latin America.[5] With the exception of a short list of domestically produced agricultural and grazing products, Johnson found a steady upward trend in prices during this important period in Brazil's economic history. He also examined urban wages and estimated an increase of between 150 and 166 percent had occurred by the 1820s. As a result, he concluded that "the economy of the city of Rio and of the surrounding region was clearly a market economy, thoroughly monetarized (although coin may have been scarce), and linked by trade (however irregular) with Europe and later North America." Rather than dismissing the model of Romano, Johnson suggested that the late colonial period was perhaps characterized by a "dual economy" with Santiago and Buenos Aires as representatives of a natural economy and Rio as representative of the price inflation and capital accumulation found in the North American and European sectors of the Atlantic economy in the eighteenth century.

The authors presented in this collection were drawn to price history along diverse paths. Among the authors who present substantial new time series for the colonial period, Richard L. Garner, José Larraín, Dauril Alden, Enrique Tandeter, and Nathan Wachtel set out from the beginning to examine prices in the tradition represented by Florescano and Harold Johnson. All the others became interested in prices and wages as a means of illuminating some other area of social or economic history. Brooke Larson's primary concern was the connection in the countryside of Alto Peru between the workings of the market and the effects of speculation during the eighteenth century. Kendall Brown sought to assess the impact of Bourbon fiscal policy on the rural producers of Arequipa. Lyman Johnson undertook an analysis of late colonial wages and prices because he concluded that the history of the urban working class required an effort to measure accurately changes in income and consumption and in particular to establish the material basis for an assessment of social justice. Robert Ferry developed his price series on Venezuelan cacao as one component of his study of political resistance to the Caracas Company. Javier Cuenca was drawn to price history by his interest in eighteenth-century commercial relationships. Here he examines the effects of colonial price differentials on Atlantic trading patterns. Ruggiero Romano offers an interpretive essay that pulls together previously published data and theory on colonial prices and examines some of his earlier work in the light of new research.

One of the important issues that has not received adequate attention from Latin American economic historians is the inflationary effect of the region's many mining booms. This is particularly surprising given Hamilton's hypothesis of a linkage of New World mining production and Old World inflation. Dauril Alden offers here an important contribution to this area of scholarly concern. His analysis begins before the Brazilian mining boom and ends after its conclusion. Although the analysis is concentrated on the important market of Salvador, Professor Alden includes comparative price data from other Brazilian cities as well. The prices of a broad range of basic consumption goods are examined in this essay, including sugar, manioc, beans, and, significantly for the study of the Brazilian economy, slaves.

Richard Garner's essay represents a major addition to the price history of colonial Mexico. His analysis includes data from important secondary cities as well as Mexico City to present a broader picture of late colonial economic performance than that offered by Florescano. In addition to corn prices, Professor Garner has included price series for other products of primary consumption—wheat, flour, and *frijoles*. Finally, he has compared the growth rate of prices with those of population, mining, and agriculture to more effectively measure real economic growth. Of particular importance to historians of late eighteenth-century Mexico is Garner's conclusion that a slight inflationary trend underlay the violent price fluctuations identified earlier by Florescano.

Buenos Aires was one of the most dynamic Spanish American cities in the late colonial period. This was the second colonial city studied by Romano. Here he also found stagnant prices during the period after 1776. Lyman Johnson examined eight basic consumption goods as well as urban rents and found substantial price inflation, particularly for wheat. Imported foods and rents, on the other hand, appear to have followed the pattern asserted by Romano. Johnson also compared a consumer price index with an index of urban wages. This comparison indicates that working class wages rose steeply at the end of the colonial period, but that consumer prices rose even faster. The last decade of the colonial period witnessed a decline in real wages.

Romano began the modern analysis of colonial price history with his work on Santiago, Chile. During the past ten years, José Larraín has undertaken a detailed study of Santiago's price history that provided a much more reliable and better illustrated summary than that provided earlier by Romano.[6] Although this research demonstrates that colonial prices were more volatile than suggested in Romano's early work, the evidence did not completely resolve the debate over the long-term trend in prices. The essay included in this volume is an important new contribution to his illumination of this topic. Larraín examines the consumption of both imported and domestic goods during the period 1680–1808. He also provides an analysis of changing consumption patterns in the city that resulted from the Bourbon monarchy's increasingly liberal import policy. Finally, Larraín uses price series to estimate gross domestic product.

Arequipa was an important secondary city in late colonial Peru. It produced goods for local subsistence and also wine and its processed derivative *aguardiente* for the Potosí market. Kendall Brown based this study of Arequipan prices on the account books of the local Jesuit college and on the tax records of the local custom house. He presents prices for locally produced goods (wine, brandy, corn, wheat, and potatoes) and a mix of colonial and European goods (olive oil, sugar, pepper, paper, and iron among others). Finally, the effect of price changes on the consuming public is measured through the construction of a cost of living index.

Enrique Tandeter and Nathan Wachtel have provided the first reliable price series for the important mining city of Potosí. Using the rich records of the Franciscan monastery of San Antonio de Padua, they were able to generate price series for an exceptional list of both domestic and imported goods. The length of this series, 1680–1816, makes it a particularly valuable contribution to the economic history of Alto Peru. All students of the Andean region will find useful their analysis of the differential effects of price changes on the indigenous and European communities.

Javier Cuenca-Esteban's essay focuses on the price component of Spanish American export values to the rest of the world in the years from 1790 to 1820. He identifies and explains the major trends and cycles in the prices of six colonial commodities during the period in terms of relative market size, world supply and demand, and other variables. This essay is the most methodologically sophisticated and theoretically explicit in this volume. Cuenca's essay indicates the fundamental utility of the other essays found in this work. The separate price series produced by these authors are important contributions to the necessary evidentiary foundation required to forge an analysis of late colonial economic performance, indeed to understand at a level higher than anecdote the development of the Atlantic economy.

The history of the Caracas Company (Real Compañía Guipuzcoana) has attracted a number of students. The organization of the cacao industry by this monopoly company and the political energies engendered by its policies are a part of almost every discussion of the origins of Venezuelan nationalism. Robert Ferry's essay probes the roots of local dissatisfaction with the Guipuzcoana Company by analyzing the price history of cacao. Cacao prices are also tied to slave importations and the expanding agricultural frontier.

It is fitting to include here an essay by Ruggiero Romano, a scholar who helped initiate the study of Latin American colonial price history. Romano provides an overview that pulls together much of the recent work in this field, including the essays in this volume. He also places his analysis of regional price history in a broader geographic context by comparing American and European prices for representative tropical export products. Romano's conclusions remain controversial, disagreeing with some of the results and interpretations reported by other contributors to this project, but his strong integrative instinct remains an important focus in a field still characterized by a narrow positivist strain.

Herbert Klein and Stanley Engerman and John Coatsworth were invited to comment on the essays collected in this volume. The essay by Klein and Engerman places these contributions within the context of current debate over methods and sources. They also offer some help in evaluating the strengths and weaknesses of the disparate sources used to construct these studies of price history, reminding us, among other things, that a comprehensive price history would require the elaboration of series for money, exchange rates, wages, and interest rates. The author's discussion of levels of market integration and money supply indicate two areas that must be directly addressed as we move from price history to an analysis of economic performance for eighteenth-century Latin America.

John Coatsworth critically reviews these essays and discusses general problems of methods and sources. He also offers concrete suggestions for future research. In addition, Coatsworth summarizes the results of an effort to test for market integration. As one would expect, strongest evidence of integration was found for goods with a high value to bulk ratio. The results of this effort were inconclusive and Coatsworth reminds us of the many problems inherent in the application of modern statistical techniques to eighteenth-century data.

The editors hope that this publication proves useful to other students of the colonial economy. The conclusions offered here are often tentative; more work needs to be done. We look forward to the day when these early efforts will be revised by our colleagues.

NOTES

1. Among Earl Hamilton's more valuable publications see *American Treasure and the Price Revolution in Spain* (Cambridge, Mass., 1934), *War and Prices in Spain* (Cambridge, Mass., 1947), and "American Treasure and Andalusian Prices, 1503–1660," *Journal of Economic and Business History,* I (November, 1928), 1–35.

2. Pierre Vilar, "Problems of the Formation of Capitalism," *Past and Present,* 10 (November, 1956), 15–38; Jorge Nadal Oller, "La revolución de los precios españoles en el siglo XVI," *Hispania,* 19 (1959), 503–529; and Docent Ingrid Hammarström, "The Price Revolution of the Sixteenth Century," *Scandinavian Economic History Review,* V (1957), 118–154. For a valuable recent contribution to this debate see Michel Morineau, *Incroyables gazettes et fabuleux metaux. Les rétours du trésor américain d'après les gazettes hollandaises (XVI–XVIII siècles)* (Paris, 1985).

3. Ruggiero Romano, "Movimiento de los Precios y Desarrollo Económico: el Caso de Sudamérica en el Siglo XVIII," *Desarrollo Económico,* vol. 3, No. 1–2 (April-September, 1963), pp. 31–43. See especially pp. 32–34.

4. Enrique Florescano, *Precios del maíz y crisis agrícolas en México, 1708–1810* (Mexico, 1971).

5. Harold B. Johnson, "A Preliminary Inquiry into Money, Prices and Wages in Rio de Janeiro, 1763–1823" in Dauril Alden (ed.), *Colonial Roots of Modern Brazil* (Berkeley, 1973).

6. For the most complete presentation of this research see Armando de Ramón and José de Larraín, *Origenes de la vida económica chilena, 1659–1808* (Santiago, 1982).

METHODS AND MEANINGS IN PRICE HISTORY

Herbert S. Klein and Stanley J. Engerman

OUR AIM IN THIS ESSAY IS TO EXPLORE SOME OF THE LARGER ISSUES RELATED to the historical study of prices. This involves questions both as to methods and interpretations of prices as well as to their significance for understanding larger historical issues. As the essays in this volume indicate, such price data go well beyond answering fundamental questions about the local and international economies and can be used as well to explore a number of important questions in social and political history. At the same time, the study of prices has generated a large body of literature concerning methods, procedures of analysis, and the interpretation of the consequent findings. It is from this point of view about methods, procedures, and interpretations that we would like to discuss the essays in this volume.

Prices are the basic data of the economic system, the outcome of transactions in the market, and are therefore frequently recorded in surviving historical records. They exist for many times and places throughout recorded history and, as indicated by the essays here, are found in many diverse sources. This very abundance of price data can often provide a basis for the useful comparisons of price movements and market behavior, although there do remain important difficulties in their collection and analysis. Frequently prices are not available for prolonged periods of time or the frequency of observations varies, posing difficulties for the preparation of reliable time series. Further, as in any historical study, there are a number of problems that make precise price comparisons difficult. For example, the specific details of transactions may vary as to period of payment, credit terms, and interest costs for future payment; the quality of goods may vary; and even the unit of measure can change over time.

The first formal, international organization for the historical study of prices—the International Scientific Committee on Price History—was established in the late 1920s and led to numerous publications from the 1930s to the 1950s. The most familiar collections that were published included those of Sir William Beveridge for England; Arthur H. Cole, Anne Bezanson, G. F. Warren and F. A. Pearson, Thomas S. Berry, George R. Taylor, and Ruth Crandall for the United States; and Nicolaas W. Posthumus for the Netherlands. There were also series prepared for Austria, France, Germany, Poland, and Spain.[1] Of most direct importance for this volume is the series on Spanish prices prepared by Earl J. Hamilton. These enormous compendia involved principally the collection of price data by commodities from various primary sources and the preparation of simple price indices. Relatively less was done by these original scholars in terms of analysis of the resulting series. Recently there has been a revival of interest in the field, as can be seen in more advanced statistical studies, in several conferences, and even in the recent publication of a *Price History Newsletter*.[2]

All this concern with prices is justified by the singular importance price series can have for examining the behavior of past societies. It can be argued that much of economic history is encompassed by price history. In the study of changing market structure and behavior, the growth of various industries, and the measurements of standards of living, the examination of changes in prices is fundamental. Prices alone, however, provide insufficient data to describe these larger economic processes or structures, and therefore to write price history requires that scholars obtain detailed supplementary data to make clear the meanings of the price changes they have found in the historical record. Thus, for example, it is generally necessary to obtain information on levels and changes in outputs of specific commodities so that it is possible to distinguish the relative importance of supply and demand forces in price change. Further, in the attempts made in preparing the cost of living indices to measure changing real wages and living standards over time, it is necessary to obtain appropriate consumption weights for individual expenditure categories (as has been done by several of the authors). The information for the construction of these weights generates, as an interesting side product, important information on the social history of diets and of other necessary consumer goods.[3]

Aside from the obvious consumer and producer products whose prices have been studied, the construction of a systematic price history requires the elaboration of price series for other items such as money (interest rates), foreign currencies (exchange rates), and labor (wages). Interest rates are important for internal market comparisons, since prices may be affected by the relative scarcity or abundance of specie and other forms of money. Similarly, changes in the rate of exchange of the currencies of two countries could explain differences observed in the price movements between these two countries. Thus, to compare differing price trends in two countries it is important to determine the influence—positive, negative, or neutral—of the movements in the exchange rate between the two.[4] Of these three areas of concern, the only one examined in these essays is wages, with little said about either interest or exchange rates.

It is also essential to remember that prices are a quantitative concept, and their analysis requires the application of modern statistical procedures, such as are currently used for analyzing price movements and their significance in contemporary market economies. This later requirement has often created a certain resistance among traditional historians who are opposed to statistical reasoning applied to historical problems. This in turn has sometimes led to a reluctance of those who study historical prices from carrying out the appropriate analyses. Yet, as we shall later argue in this essay, such analyses are fundamental for the successful interpretation of the nature and meaning of the prices found in historical documents.

We can divide the essays in this volume into roughly four categories. In the first are those studies in which prices serve as the basis of technical measures of items of economic and social interest, for example, real output and real wages.[5] In the second, prices are variables to be explained by supply and demand analysis, leading to an understanding of economic and other changes.[6] The third presents prices seen as an incentive to behavior and as a determinant of the rewards of economic behavior.[7] In the fourth, prices are used as the basis for testing hypotheses, such as the relationship between price-level changes and economic growth and price-level changes and the nature and magnitude of social protest.[8] Given these diverse interests, there is no one method of price history appropriate for all questions. It reminds us, though, of the great range of social and political as well as economic questions that can be examined through these quantitative series.

A fundamental concern with prices is the distinction that must be made between movements in the absolute level of prices and movements in the relative prices of different commodities. As we shall point out, this distinction becomes critical to the analysis of any individual price change. The interpretation of the change in the price of any commodity, for example wheat, differs significantly if it can be shown that all other prices change to the same degree, or if it is the case that wheat has changed in price compared to other available commodities.

The absolute level of prices is a statistical artifact of individual prices used to compute a price index with some weighting scheme to allow for the relative importance of different commodities. When discussing inflationary or deflationary movements, the basic measure is one based upon a composite of relevant commodity prices. Although it is generally presumed that in inflationary movements most prices do move in the same direction, inflation need not imply that all prices change to the same extent or even in the same direction, but that the overall average measure of all prices has changed. The fact that not all prices change in the same order of magnitude is not by itself an argument that can be used against a relationship of monetary changes and price changes, since even with a zero-mean change (that is, constant price level), there can be relative price changes.

This overall price index is generally used to deflate either nominal wages to obtain a measure of real wages or nominal output to obtain measures of real output. By comparisons of real wages and real output over time, it is possible to determine changes in the actual physical amounts consumed and produced. Without accounting for changes in the overall price level, comparisons of nominal wages and nominal output over time will include changes both in the actual physical amounts and changes in the level of prices.

Changes in the level of prices are usually explained by economists as the outcome of changes in the quantity of money and/or its velocity (that is, the frequency with which each unit of money is used to purchase goods). Most familiar for the study of Latin American and European price history is Hamilton's argument relating the magnitude of specie flows from Latin America to the level of prices within Spain and elsewhere in Europe in the sixteenth and seventeenth centuries. An important aspect of these specie flows is that they link the prices in different countries and markets for traded goods. An implication of this is that changes in the absolute price level within one country cannot generally be explained without consideration of prices elsewhere.[9]

It should be noted that the model used to explain overall price level changes differs from that used to explain changes in the relative prices for different commodities. To a certain extent, particularly in the long term, changes in total output may be consistent with a large range of overall price level changes, both positive and negative. Societies have had rapid growth in output in times of rising prices as well as in times of falling prices.[10] This means that there is no necessary relationship between an overall rise in prices and a limited productive capacity, since a constant or falling price level will also be consistent with full employment of resources.[11]

The most familiar use of price-level and real-wage data has been Hamilton's, which linked rising prices to falling real wages, increasing profits, higher investments, and thus increased growth, and consequently the European Industrial Revolution. The Hamilton proposition has long been the subject of historical and economic debate, and several of Hamilton's estimates and interpretations have been criticized by a number of scholars.[12] Nevertheless, in general, it is often believed that rising price levels lead to economic growth, though there are now a number of counterexamples for Latin America, as seen in this volume, and many such counterexamples exist elsewhere. Indeed, as a number of essays here suggest, it may be that too rapid a rise in the price level (without adequate redistribution of purchasing power) may cause economically destabilizing social unrest and rebellion.[13] There is, in short, no predetermined result in terms of output that will necessarily follow a systematic rise or fall in the price level.

A very important set of problems can be studied by examining the changes in the relative prices of different commodities. Many commodities are bought and sold in most markets, and the price of one relative to the prices of others may rise or fall. It is important to determine if the price change for a specific commodity is part of an overall change in the level of all prices or is a change in its relative price compared to a specific set of other commodities.[14] Therefore, it is not sufficient to explain price changes, even when looking at the price of one commodity, without making comparisons with those prices for other goods traded in this market.

Basic to the explanation of relative price (and output) changes is the use of supply and demand analysis. Economists use the apparatus of supply and demand to determine basic underlying elements causing changes in prices and quantities. For example, among those circumstances influencing changing demand would be population change, income change, prices of substitutes and complements, and changes in tastes for different commodities. Those variables influencing supply would include the availability and costs of factors of production and the technical efficiency of production. It should be noted that some of these items are regarded as strictly economic in nature, while others reflect broad social and cultural changes whose economic impact can be analyzed.

To satisfactorily analyze the causes of relative price changes, it is generally necessary to have information about both relative price changes and changes in quantities. A relative price rise may reflect either a reduction in supply (the result, for example, of famine or crop shortage) or else an increase in demand (resulting, for example, from an increase in population). In the former case, the price increase reflects a decline in quantity; in the latter case, the price increase is consistent with an increase in quantity.[15] Unfortunately, in many cases there is direct evidence only on the price change, and it is necessary to discuss the impact of supply and of demand on the basis of supplementary information. At times, the supplementary data permit reasonable inferences, such as information about the presence of famine conditions and/or the changes in population; at other times, such inferences can only be made on a more limited and less certain basis.

Interpretation of relative price changes will also vary depending upon the nature of the market in which the goods are produced and sold. The essays in this volume generally distinguish among goods produced and sold only within a local area; goods produced locally, but sold within a larger market, be it within the country, within the Americas, or in Europe; and goods produced in an external market that are consumed locally. For those goods that are nonlocal in nature, price changes will be influenced (if not determined) in external markets and therefore may not by themselves reflect local market conditions.[16] Further, for those goods in which prices and quantities are determined locally, it is important to note that the relative changes in the two may not be equivalent. The economist's concepts of the elasticities of demand and of supply relate percentage changes in quantities to percentage changes in prices, reminding us that sharp price changes may mean less dramatic changes in quantities. If, for example, the demand for a commodity is inelastic (as is generally the case with most basic foodstuffs), the percentage decline in consumption will be less than the measured percentage increase in price.

Relative prices are also of interest, because in most societies, clearly including those discussed here, prices can determine the rewards people obtain from economic activity and thus influence behavior. The study of past prices also helps us to understand the impact of expected changes in prices and quantities upon behavior; thus, the nature of the formation of price expectations is a central part in understanding the process of economic change.[17] High relative prices in one period, if expected to continue, should generally generate higher levels of output in future years. Therefore, it is argued, shortages in one period will lead to adjustments with increased output in the future.

Prices as rewards of the economic system influence the distribution of income. Changes in the level of prices by themselves will generally aid one group in the market at the expense of another.[18] Noting that there are two sides to the market, it is usually true that some group is hurt by price change or, at the least, could have been made better off with some alternative price changes. Thus, high and rising prices will generally hurt consumers (and benefit producers), while low and falling prices will benefit consumers (often at the expense of producers). "Overproduction" (usually indicated by falling prices) is always assumed to be harmful to producers, but it should be noted that the economic benefits to those who consume these goods are too often ignored. Lower prices, however, may not in themselves mean a worsening of producer conditions over time, if low prices reflect improvements in methods of production and/or reduction in the costs of necessary inputs.[19] Since there are two sides to a market, one can always find discontent no matter what direction the price moves in and no matter what the change in income position compared to an earlier period of time.

In looking at the conclusions of these essays, several general patterns emerge. First, concerning a historic perennial raised by Hamilton as well as Ruggiero Romano, is the relationship between changing prices and rates of economic growth. While the results examined are somewhat mixed, in a number of studies (for example, eighteenth-century Peru and Chile), economic growth was apparently more rapid when prices were declining.[20] This pattern, it should be noted, is also found in many other cases, such as in the period of rapid industrialization of the United States and elsewhere in the late nineteenth century.

The findings concerning the relationship between price changes and social unrest are also rather mixed. Though existence of social unrest has been found with high relative prices of foodstuffs in times of scarcity, as well as in times of high, overall price levels as the result of inflation, examples of unrest caused by low prices have been pointed out by some authors.[21] To again use the example of the United States, the period of the late nineteenth-century price fall was one in which important protest movements developed among farmers and laborers. Clearly then, in and of itself, a rise or fall in the price level alone cannot explain social conflict. The arguments presented for the role of low prices also emphasize problems confronted by special producer groups, as in the case of Cochabamba, where the response to low prices resulting from "overproduction" led to a concern for landlord action against peasants,[22] or as in the case of Caracas, where the lowering of the price paid for cacao in the period of company monopoly created unrest among the producers of the commodity.[23]

Patterns of change in real wages and material life varied, of course, by country and by time period, the result of obvious, significant differences in economic conditions. The use of real-wage measures, accurate and reliable for the population studied, may not, of course, truly reflect overall economic conditions in the specific country. It is important to know the percentage of the labor force affected, and particularly in rural areas, to know the relative importance of incomes in kind and in money.[24] The impact will also vary with the extent to which substitution in consumption among commodities is desirable or possible, since this may help to offset the impact of specific relative-price rises. In examining the magnitude of the declines in living standards indicated, it is useful to understand the implication that previously there were higher levels of wages and of living standards that permitted a reduction to occur without, in general, pronounced demographic effects. Also, falls in real wages may reflect declines in overall output and not just redistribution among the members of the population. Determining the relative importance of declines in output and income redistribution can be an important contribution of price history to the understanding of political issues.

Many of the essays have very suggestive discussions of the relationship between prices and trading patterns. As pointed out earlier, there are different patterns of price change for goods that are traded across international and market boundaries and those that are not. For traded goods, there seems to be some general uniformity of price movement across regions and markets, and the most systematic study of international price movements indicates that for these traded goods, there was a similarity of movement in various markets with periodic exceptions resulting from extramarket phenomenon, such as embargoes, blockades, and wars. Thus, according to Javier Cuenca-Esteban, there was some international equalization of the prices of traded goods.[25] Similarly, the general uniformity of price-level changes indicated for Mexico, Chile, and Peru suggests that movements in specie as well as in goods affected different markets at the same time.

The comparison of prices in different areas and regions also permits some estimation of the degree of market integration. Since markets are linked by transportation costs, large interregional variation in prices, such as those shown by Dauril Alden for Brazil, suggest limited degrees of interpenetration.[26]

The discussions of the linking of prices across areas, as well as the responses to price variations within given regions, indicate that responsiveness to market signals and market rewards did occur across a wide spectrum. Indeed, all the essays contain this premise and indicate that prices and markets were developed, acted upon, and were an influential element in determining the course of political and social as well as economic change.

To an economist it is surprising how little is said in these essays about money and monetary sources in the economic system as an influence upon the price level.[27] One need not be the stereotypical monetarist to realize that, at least as a direct determinant, the amount of the medium of exchange should have had an impact on price-level changes. Perhaps the lack of attention to monetary influences reflects the frequent focus on a particular set of problems, but even then this is not the necessary outcome. Several of the essays focus primarily on one commodity, or one market, before it is made clear to the reader the extent to which price changes for this one commodity or market were relative to prices of other commodities in that market, and/or the extent to which they might reflect conditions outside that market area. More explicit description of the similarity of movement of prices for a number of commodities within a regional market, as well as a more detailed comparison of the movements of prices of tradable goods across countries, would help place these findings in perspective. Furthermore, information about specie and money supplies is important to help to separate out the magnitude of inflation from relative price changes.

Two essays point to a relationship between population increase and rising price levels.[28] This point is given heavy emphasis in the debates about price increases in sixteenth-century Europe, by contemporaries as well as subsequent scholars.[29] It remains difficult, however, to follow the linking of a fully understandable relative-price change for agricultural commodities to an increase in the absolute-price level without attention being paid to changes in either the quantity of money or its velocity. This is particularly difficult, since several recent attempts to explain a change in velocity (dependent upon increased urbanization and expanded market activity) remain generally unconvincing for the times and places discussed in this volume.[30] Population increase is obviously an essential part of the explanation of a rise in relative agricultural prices, but more remains to be done before it provides a satisfactory explanation for an overall inflation. Focus on specie and money alone may not be adequate, but certainly they cannot be ignored in trying to understand the behavior of the economic system. By weighing both sides of the exchange—what goods are sold as well as what is accepted in exchange for them—we shall learn a great deal more about the social and economic interactions in a society.

There are a number of cases where a more explicit attention to the use of supply and demand analysis to explain relative price changes may have a substantial intellectual dividend. Examples of such approaches to explain changing prices and quantities are Robert Zevin's analysis of the growth of the United States cotton textile industry from 1815 to 1860;[31] the suggestive application of demand elasticities in Robert William Fogel's analysis of the impact of English famines on mortality;[32] and Andrew Appleby's study of the differential substitutability among various grains by consumers in England and France in the seventeenth and eighteenth centuries.[33] These studies suggest that explicit incorporation of these models and the asking of different questions can offer a useful interpretive framework to discuss many of the issues raised in the essays here presented.

As we have seen above, the problems related to the study of prices in historical contexts are many, but as this volume demonstrates, the potential rewards for historical analysis are great. Despite difficulties inevitable in such studies, all contribute to a new level of understanding of the local economic, social, and political evolution of Latin American colonial societies. It is hoped that this initial survey will open the way for many more advanced studies in the future and that others will be encouraged to begin the long, difficult, but ultimately rewarding task of reconstructing and interpreting historical price series for Latin America.

NOTES

1. See Arthur H. Cole and Ruth Crandall, "The International Scientific Committee on Price History," *Journal of Economic History* (1964).

2. Published since 1984 by John McCusker.

3. See, e.g., the studies by Dauril Alden, Kendall W. Brown, and, for the most detail, Lyman L. Johnson.

4. For a recent discussion of purchasing-power parity relating changes in price levels in two countries and the exchange rate, see the chapter on "The Monetary Approach to the Balance of Payments," in Richard E. Caves, Ronald W. Jones, and Jeffrey A. Frankel, *World Trade and Payments* (5th ed.; Boston, 1988). The impact of a devaluation upon price level changes in Brazil is described by Alden.

5. See, e.g., Brooke Larson, José Larraín, Johnson, Brown, and Richard L. Garner.

6. See, e.g., Alden, and Enrique Tandeter and Nathan Wachtel.

7. See, e.g., Robert J. Ferry.

8. See, e.g., Larson and Javier Cuenca-Esteban.

9. This point underscores the differential treatment in most essays of the price behavior of goods traded internationally from those traded only locally, a distinction examined below, as well as the frequent similarity in the movement of price levels in different regions, as indicated by Garner.

10. See, e.g., essays by Garner, Brown, and Larraín in this volume.

11. This point was suggested by Alden, Garner, and Johnson for differing reasons. That a limitation to the productive capacity of an economy will exist is not disputed. At issue is whether this limit is more pronounced with rising or high prices as it is with falling or low prices.

12. See, e.g., R. A. Kessel and A. A. Alchian, "The Meaning and Validity of the Inflation-Inducted Lag of Wages Behind Prices," *American Economic Review* (1960). For recent brief reviews of this debate by macroeconomists, see Barry Eichengreen, "Macroeconomics and History," in Alexander J. Field, ed., *The Future of Economic History* (Boston, 1987), and Michael D. Bordo, "Explorations in Monetary History: A Survey of the Literature," *Explorations in Economic History* [Journal] (1986). See also Peter H. Ramsey, ed., *The Price Revolution in Sixteenth-Century England* (London, 1971).

13. Economic growth with constant or falling price levels is indicated by Garner, Brown, and Larraín, while the possible disturbing social effects of rising prices is argued for by Garner, Larson, and Johnson.

14. It may be argued that the change in the price of a commodity can serve as "an index to the cost of a whole range of articles," thus sidestepping this question. See the discussion in Larson.

15. This point is noted by Garner.

16. For examinations of price changes differentiating goods along these lines, see Johnson, Larraín, Tandeter and Wachtel, Brown, and Alden. Cuenca-Esteban, of course, restricts his analysis to goods that are internationally traded.

17. For an explicit discussion of this, see Garner.

18. See, in particular, the discussion by Larson.

19. A related difficulty is seen in Alden's comparisons of slave and sugar prices to argue for a growing unprofitability of slavery. This overlooks the possibility of a greater productivity of slave labor or of longer life expectations for slaves, which would justify the increased relative prices for slaves. It might be noted that U. B. Phillips used the changing prices of cotton and of slaves to argue for a growing unprofitability of U.S. slavery in the nineteenth century. See U. B. Phillips, "The Economic Cost of Slaveholding in the Cotton Belt," *Political Science Quarterly* (1905).

20. See Brown, Larson, and Larraín.

21. See, e.g., Larson and Tandeter and Wachtel.

22. See Larson.

23. See Ferry. The Ferry essay poses a number of interesting questions about the nature of price changes and political protest. Would the political reaction have differed if it had been believed that the lowered price reflected administrative decisions or if these reflected overall market changes over which the company had no control? Why was the reaction so strong to a price reduction that returned prices to previous levels from an unusually high peak, rather than a decline to a uniquely low level? It might be noted that several essays (Larson, Brown, and Johnson) point

to attempts by municipalities and other institutions to control prices for political reasons, with rather mixed outcomes.

24. See Johnson, Brown, and Garner.

25. See Cuenca-Esteban. For a more explicit application of a supply and a demand framework, see his article "Trends and Cycles in U.S. Trade with Spain and the Spanish Empire, 1790–1819," *Journal of Economic History* (1984).

26. See Alden. For a useful discussion of the effect of a major transportation improvement—in this case, the railroad—in reducing the dispersion of prices among regions, see Jacob Metzer, "Railroad Development and Market Integration: The Case of Tsarist Russia," *Journal of Economic History* (1974). See also Nicolás Sánchez-Albornoz, "Congruence Among Spanish Economic Regions in the Nineteenth Century," *Journal of European Economic History* (1974); and his article with Daniel Peña, "Wheat Prices in Spain, 1857–1890: An Application of the Box-Jenkins Methodology," *Journal of European Economic History* (1984). A further refinement of this material is found in Daniel Peña and George E. P. Box, "Identifying a Simplifying Structure in Time Series," *Journal of the American Statistical Association* (1987).

27. There are only very brief mentions of the impact of monetary changes in Garner, Johnson, and Ferry. For a more formal discussion concerning price changes in Rio, see Harold B. Johnson, Jr., "A Preliminary Inquiry into Money, Prices, and Wages in Rio de Janeiro, 1763–1823," in Dauril Alden, ed., *Colonial Roots of Modern Brazil* (Berkeley, 1973).

28. See Garner and Johnson. See also Garner's recent article "Price Trends in Eighteenth-Century Mexico," in the *Hispanic American Historical Review* (1985).

29. See Ramsey, *The Price Revolution,* and the review of this collection by Donald N. McCloskey in the *Journal of Political Economy* (1972). Also see Harry A. Miskimin, "Population Growth and the Price Revolution in England," *Journal of European Economic History* (1975).

30. See Jack A. Goldstone, "Urbanization and Inflation: Lessons from the English Price Revolution of the Sixteenth and Seventeenth Centuries," *American Journal of Sociology* (1984), and the discussion in Peter H. Lindert, "English Population, Wages, and Prices: 1541–1913," *Journal of Interdisciplinary History* (1985).

31. See Robert Brooke Zevin, "The Growth of Cotton Textile Production After 1815," in Robert William Fogel and Stanley L. Engerman, eds., *The Reinterpretation of American Economic History* (New York, 1971).

32. Robert William Fogel, "Nutrition and the Decline in Mortality since 1700: Some Preliminary Findings," in Stanley L. Engerman and Robert E. Gallman, eds., *Long-Term Factors in American Economic Growth* (Chicago, 1986).

33. Andrew B. Appleby, "Grain Prices and Subsistence Crises in England and France, 1590–1740," *Journal of Economic History* (1979).

2

Economic History and the History of Prices in Colonial Latin America

John H. Coatsworth

Without systematic and reliable price data, it is impossible to describe adequately, let alone analyze, the record of past economic behavior. The relative neglect of price history by historians of Latin America, in contrast to Europe and the United States, has long constituted the single most important obstacle to progress in the field of colonial economic history. Immense collections of quantitative information have been unearthed and published in recent years, particularly fiscal and tithe data, but lack of price indices to convert nominal to "real" values has limited their utility.[1] The same may be said for the growing volume of quantitative data on external and internal trade, on the development of enterprise (haciendas, obrajes, mining, merchant houses) and on other aspects of colonial economic activity.[2] The development of comparative economic history, perhaps the most neglected of all fields of economic historical research on Latin America, continues to wait on the discovery and publication of quantitative indicators of economic activity among which price data are now the most critical.[3]

The essays in this volume thus mark an important step forward. Most provide new price data for single regions over more or less extended periods of time. All contribute significant pieces to a complex puzzle. If they inspire others to replicate their discoveries for other regions of Latin America, in the nineteenth century as well as the colonial period, their publication will have marked an even greater leap.

If this volume demonstrates just how abundant and varied are the sources of price data for the colonial era, especially for the eighteenth century, it also demonstrates the need for data collection on an even larger scale employing standardized techniques for the production of rigorously comparable measurements. Major advances in colonial economic history could be achieved if the publication of this volume spurred the adoption of common measures and standardized techniques for rendering the results of price history research transparently comparable. The essays published here employ an array of methods for reducing multiple price observations to a single yearly observation, for constructing indices, and for displaying the data. In most cases, the methods are appropriate for the case in hand but do not readily lend themselves to comparison across regions. The next stage in the revival of price history should thus include efforts to transform it from an artisanal into an "industrial" undertaking: what we need now is mass production of a standardized product.

   The price series displayed in the contributions to this volume reveal trends that vary across locations and classes of commodities. For example, the prices of locally produced agricultural products in most regions appear to have declined or risen only slightly through the first half of the eighteenth century. Differences increased after mid-century. In Salvador and Potosí, food prices moved downward for three decades beginning in the late 1750s. In Chile and Mexico, however, grain prices stagnated until the 1760s or 1770s and rose thereafter. The prices of European imports display equally diverse trends, rising for most of the century in Salvador, for example, while falling in Chile. Among Latin American exports to Europe, sugar prices stagnated, cacao fell (except for a sharp rise in the early 1730s) at least to mid-century, and silver fell (in Mexico) or rose (in Potosí) depending on location.[4] Relative uniformity in price movements appears to take hold late in the century; in all cases for which there are data, commodity prices were rising in the 1790s and during most of the war years that followed.

   These diverse results are interesting, not only because of the contribution they make to the economic history of each of the regions from which they were extracted, but also because they raise the more general issue of market organization and integration. Price trends for different commodities, even within the same market, often diverge because of differently shifting supply and demand schedules. High rates of inflation or deflation can overwhelm such differences for short periods of time, but changes in the relative prices of commodities traded in the same market over the long run are common. In contrast, the prices of identical goods or close substitutes in different locations tend to be highly correlated in today's well-integrated markets, particularly where transport and transactions costs form a small proportion of final price.

   Steven Mange has used price data for five different commodities taken mainly from the essays in this volume to test for market integration in the eighteenth century.[5] Simple bivariate regressions were run using price series (when available) for sugar, yerba mate, potatoes, sheep, and wine in the essays on Chile (Larraín), Potosí (Tandeter and Wachtel), Salvador (Alden), Arequipa (Brown), and Buenos Aires (Johnson). Additional sets of prices from Lima and Arequipa were taken from Macera's pioneering work.[6] Mange's results are interesting, but not conclusive. Sugar prices in Santiago, Arequipa, and Lima tended to be highly correlated with each other. Sugar prices from Salvador, Buenos Aires, and Potosí showed no correlations with other markets at all. Wine prices showed weak to moderate correlations between Arequipa, Lima, and Potosí. Wine prices elsewhere were not correlated. Yerba prices in Potosí and Buenos Aires showed a weak correlation, as did sheep prices from Lima and Arequipa. Potato prices displayed no correlations between any pair of markets.

These results follow expected patterns. Correlations are higher for goods with a relatively high value to bulk ratio between markets communicated by cheap water transport. Correlations are weaker or nonexistent for cheaper and bulkier goods traded, if at all, over longer distances by sea or overland. The results are inconclusive because, as Mange recognized, correlations analysis can serve to confirm the existence of market integration but cannot be used to disprove it. Absence of correlation may occur when local price fluctuations stay within boundaries fixed by the transaction and transportation costs of reaching distant markets. Thus, two distant markets may be well integrated without displaying highly correlated prices for goods that are not normally traded between them.[7]

The lack of correlation between most of the price series Mange tested could also be due to the nature of the data. The price data in this volume come from different kinds of sources in diverse regions of Latin America. All but one of the essays report price data from a single location. The exception is Garner, whose essay contains a "colony-wide" index of maize prices, which combines price series from Zacatecas in the north to Mexico City in the center of the country.[8] In most essays, the reported price appears to represent the unweighted mean of each year's observed prices for each commodity. Again there are exceptions. Larraín's index is more sophisticated while Brown prefers median rather than mean prices.[9] Correlations among these series are no doubt affected by differences in their construction. Moreover, since the prices of many colonial agricultural products varied considerably over the course of a single year (sometimes by as much as a hundred percent or more), variations in the consistency of the sources and lacunae in the data may have affected the reported prices and thus the correlations based on them.

In addition, market responses to price changes across large distances in the eighteenth century were necessarily affected by delays in communication. Even when goods are regularly traded, variable lags in price adjustments due to irregular gaps in communication translate easily into price series that appear to be unrelated. Frequent wartime disruptions of trade also caused irregular fluctuations in the prices of the region's exports and imports throughout the eighteenth century. Moreover, divergent price *trends* in two distant markets could reflect converging price *levels,* and thus demonstrate increasing market integration, while correlation analysis might show little or no relationship in annual price fluctuations. All these possibilities suggest the utility of employing an array of statistical techniques and strategies to analyze the development of market integration in colonial Latin America, as Klein and Engerman propose in their essay.

Several of the essays in this volume contribute, directly or indirectly, to the measurement of trends in economic activity. Economists conventionally measure aggregate economic activity by estimating gross national or domestic product (GNP or GDP), that is, the sum of the value of all the goods and services produced in a given geographic region in a given time period, usually one year. This measure should be roughly equivalent to national income, that is, the sum of all wages, rent, interest, and profits earned by individuals for the same region and time period. For most Latin American countries, there exist no estimates of aggregate economic activity for any date before the twentieth century. The exceptions are Mexico and Brazil.[10] Outside Latin America, estimates are available for Great Britain beginning in the late seventeenth century,[11] and for the United States and some European countries in the eighteenth century.[12] Naturally, national income or product estimates for periods before modern efforts at census-taking or government data-gathering embody greater error margins than would be acceptable for estimates of contemporary income or GNP. Historical estimates are useful, nonetheless, as benchmarks for comparisons across both time and region. In many cases, the trends through time and the differences between regions plotted by relatively crude estimates are more robust and reliable than the precise estimates on which they are based.

Only one of the essays in this volume attempts explicitly to measure aggregate economic activity. Larraín's paper uses data on consumption patterns to estimate the weights to be assigned the price of each product in constructing an index of agricultural prices for central Chile from the mid-seventeenth to the end of the eighteenth century. He then uses this index to deflate tithe revenue data to derive estimates of the value of agricultural output at constant prices. Finally, he argues that his agricultural output series could be used as a proxy for GDP since something like 80 percent of GNP originated in agriculture.[13]

The essays written by Garner and by Tandeter and Wachtel also use long series of tithe revenues. Tandeter and Wachtel use data from the Archbishopric of La Plata, deflating the nominal value of tithe revenues by an index of agricultural prices from Potosí. Their method is thus similar to that of Larraín, though the index they use is somewhat cruder. They do not claim that their tithe-based estimates of agricultural production can serve as a measure of trends in aggregate output, no doubt because of the importance of the mining industry in their region.[14]

For Mexico, Garner uses a different procedure. He is unable to construct an index of agricultural prices because he has complete data only for maize. Since he is reluctant to deflate tithe revenues using maize prices alone, he adopts the more cautious approach of comparing the growth rate of nominal tithe revenues (from the Archbishopric of Michoacán in central Mexico) with the rate of increase in maize prices. The difference in the two rates may be taken as a crude indicator of real growth in output, as Garner claims.

The growth rates for agriculture (or GDP) in these three studies vary substantially. For Chile, Larraín's results show real growth of 1.2 percent per annum between 1681 and 1702, 1.5 percent from 1703 to 1763, and 0.6 percent from 1764 to 1799. Garner's figures show that maize production grew faster than prices (and thus real output grew) by 0.9 percent per year from 1700 to 1750, but then declined at a rate of 0.8 percent from 1750 to 1800. Tandeter and Wachtel do not calculate growth rates, but their data suggest a sharp decline in real output between 1718 and 1734, a substantial recovery from 1735 to 1759, rapid growth from 1760 to 1789, and stagnation between 1790 and 1809.

As growth rates go, most of these are not impressive. Only Chilean growth up to 1763, fueled by grain exports to Peru, appears to have substantially exceeded the rate of population increase. In Mexico, agricultural production in the first half of the eighteenth century may have been rising at slightly above the population trend but in the second half output declined while the population continued to rise. In the Andes, production declined into the 1730s (along with population). In the next quarter century, agricultural production in the La Plata archbishopric rose while Potosí's population continued to fall, but the significance of this result is open to question. Rising production from 1760 to 1790 may have exceeded population growth, but the subsequent stagnation probably wiped out these gains by 1810.

These three studies suggest a close relationship between trends in agricultural output and trends in population growth. In all places and times save one, production and population move up or down together. The exception is central Mexico where maize production turns downward while population continues to grow (though apparently at a decreasing rate) after 1750. A contrary phenomenon appears in the Andean data, though the results are less firm. Tandeter and Wachtel report that Potosí's population declined until the 1760s, though real tithe revenues collected in the La Plata archbishopric began growing as early as the 1730s. This divergence between production and population trends is not conclusive, as the authors point out, because in the larger area covered by the tithe data, population may have begun growing (as elsewhere in the Andes) by the earlier date. Potosí's demographic recovery was delayed because of the prolonged depression in its mining industry. In any case, the relatively low growth rates estimated for Chile and Mexico and the strong link over the long run between production and population trends in all three cases suggests that agricultural (and possibly total) output per capita did not increase much, if at all, over the course of the eighteenth century.[15]

While more explicit and conclusive tests of this hypothesis will be necessary before drawing firm conclusions, it may be worth pushing this point a bit further. If the Latin American economies were growing no faster than population in the eighteenth century, while Britain and the United States were growing at modest rates of 0.5 or so percent per capita, then the relative gap between the two regions would have more than doubled over the course of the eighteenth century. In 1800, the per capita income of the United States was roughly twice that of Mexico. Thus, Mexico could have had an income per capita equal to that of the thirteen British North American colonies in 1700. A century of Mexican stagnation would have been enough to create the income differentials known to exist between Mexico and the United States at the end of the century.[16]

These essays also appear to confirm three significant eighteenth-century trends in the Latin American economies. The first is the widespread shift out of cattle raising and into grain agriculture from central Chile to the Bajío region northwest of Mexico City. In Mexico, this trend is evident as early as the 1750s. It appears somewhat later in Chile and Potosí, according to Larraín and Tandeter and Wachtel. In all three cases, it is linked to population growth and rising demand for food staples (and, in Mexico, for pulque). In Chile, unlike the other two cases, increased grain production was also stimulated by export demand from Peru (chiefly, Lima).

Second, there is evidence, cited by all three authors, of a late eighteenth-century increase in the concentration of landownership and, thus, of income. As land came to be used more intensively, its value rose. Neglected estates good for nothing but cattle grazing were put to the plough (some reviving cultivation abandoned a century earlier). Vacant lands were occupied, tenants expelled or forced to accept higher rents, and conflicts over property rights increased.

Third, after an initial period of revival and growth—more impressive in Chile than in Mexico—agricultural productivity may have begun to decline. In two of these three essays, the authors suggest that agricultural production hit a "ceiling" late in the eighteenth century. In an absolute sense, this hypothesis is not likely to prove fruitful. On the other hand, the suggestion that the supply of agricultural production was becoming less elastic, that new increases in output were achieved at increasing cost, may turn out to have been true in many regions of Spanish America as the eighteenth century wore on. Indeed, the conversion of pasture to arable land in late eighteenth-century Latin America can probably be taken as prima facie evidence of declining marginal productivity in agriculture.

Unlike North America, Spanish America reached independence at a time of crisis and decline in the productivity of agriculture. This conclusion, which now needs more extensive and explicit testing, may help to explain both the prolonged political crises that accompanied independence as well as the failure of the new nations of Spanish America to adopt and incorporate the industrial advances that rising agricultural productivity helped to sustain in the North Atlantic economies.

Aggregate estimates of economic activity can also be constructed on the basis of wage and other factor income data. The essays by Garner, Larson, Brown, and Johnson use price, wage, or consumption data to measure living standards; this kind of data can also be used to derive crude, but nonetheless useful, comparative estimates of per capita income. Estimates of GNP or national income divided by population yield per capita figures that are conventionally used by economists as rough measures of productivity. This indicator cannot be interpreted as a measure of comparative *welfare* because it does not take into account changes in the *distribution* of income and wealth. It is nonetheless the starting point for all international comparisons of productivity.

Garner, for example, cites data taken from Konrad's study of the Jesuit hacienda of Santa Lucia in the eighteenth century showing that wages ranged from three pesos per month (36 pesos per year) for a shepherd (often a child or young teenager) to 46 pesos per month (552 pesos per year) for the best paid mayordomo.[17] The modal (most common) wage for adult male peons in eighteenth-century Mexico was two reales per day (70 pesos for a work year of 280 days). Similar wages prevailed on the other rural estates Garner cites. Most rural employees received a variable ration of maize in addition to their cash wages. Garner also cites wages for urban construction workers in Zacatecas in the second half of the eighteenth century ranging from a low of six to a high of 46 pesos per month (72 to 552 pesos per year).

Larson's study of Cochabamba cites conventional rural wages of two reales per day, exactly equal to the modal wage rate cited by Garner for Mexico. Corn rations normally provided in addition to the cash wage in Mexico could increase the laborer's actual income by as much as a third.[18] Wage levels in the range of 72 (without rations) to 96 pesos per year for unskilled rural labor imply family incomes about half again as high (108 to 144 per annum). Assuming a family size of four, such estimates suggest per capita incomes of 27 to 38 pesos for the rural majority of the population in the eighteenth century. Taking into account the higher incomes of the small portion of the population that earned higher wages or owned income-producing property and adding in government expenditures would raise these figures by perhaps as much as a fifth. Thus, for central Mexico and the Peruvian highlands, per capita incomes of 32 to 47 pesos (compared to roughly 100 for the United States and perhaps 120 for Great Britain) may be taken as plausible.[19]

For Potosí, Tandeter and Wachtel cite a standard wage of four reales per day for unskilled labor. In a work year of 280 days, this amounts to 144 pesos per year, double the annual wages earned by rural labor in Mexico or Cochabamba, but somewhat lower than wages earned by unskilled labor in Mexican mining centers in the eighteenth century.[20] Assuming (as above) that families averaged four members and that wives and children contributed half as much as the male wage earner, per capita income in urban Potosí would come to 54 pesos per year.

Two of the papers, those by Brown and Johnson, provide estimates for major cities. Brown estimates living costs for a mestizo family in Arequipa at between 130 and 200 pesos per annum between 1680 and 1820. For a family of four, his estimates for 1800 suggest a per capita expenditure of 32 pesos per year. By contrast, the more prosperous Hispanic family's living costs in that year amounted to over 60 pesos per capita. Johnson cites wages in Buenos Aires ranging from less than 17 pesos per month (204 pesos per year) for unskilled labor to one peso per day (perhaps 280 pesos or more per year) for a journeyman carpenter. Following earlier assumptions about family size and the earnings of family members, these figures imply urban per capita incomes of 76 to 105 pesos per year. These wage and income levels are well above the living expenses incurred even by Arequipa's wealthier Hispanic families and two to three times higher than the level of mestizo families there as well as rural (and urban) laborers in Mexico and elsewhere in Peru. While drawing firm conclusions from this kind of fragmentary data would be risky at best, it does seem possible to hypothesize that the higher productivity and living standards that characterized the Argentine (or at least the Buenos Aires) economy by the late nineteenth century originated at least a century earlier in the late colonial era.

Blowing up wage and living cost data to produce income estimates, while suggestive, is fraught with statistical perils. Wage data, for example, need to be corrected for differences in the prices of the products on which the wages were spent. While rural unskilled labor in central Mexico and Cochabamba received identical wage rates (two reales per day), maize prices were not identical (Garner puts the Mexican average at just over 15 reales per fanega in 1800, while Larson cites a rough average of 18 for Cochabamba in the late 1790s) and rations varied. Similarly, mine wages may have been somewhat higher in Mexico than in Potosí, but maize prices in Potosí were lower and the diet more varied (so that maize prices were less important to the living standards of Andean miners). In like fashion, data on living costs need to be adjusted for differences in wage levels. It may have cost less in Arequipa, as Brown shows, to consume the same products in 1820 as in 1680, but falling wages could have cancelled or reduced the potential increase in living standards. Similarly, the high wage rates Johnson reports for late eighteenth-century Buenos Aires cannot be compared directly to lower wages elsewhere without taking into account differences in living costs. Future comparative studies must now undertake explicit comparisons which incorporate these variations.

Price history, too long neglected, may now be reaching the point where a major breakthrough is in sight—attainable, if not immediately in prospect. First, a large-scale, collective, international effort is needed to retrieve, summarize, and display price data from the colonial era to the late nineteenth century. This volume suggests that sources of primary data for such an undertaking are more abundant than once thought. At the least, a guide to known sources of price data would help to encourage individual efforts to extract data; at best, a more coordinated undertaking akin to the TePaske-Klein project on the *cajas reales* could build upon and perhaps incorporate previous efforts such as those represented here. Second, a price history manual is needed to provide researchers with a clear notion of standard or preferred techniques for summarizing, indexing, and displaying historical price data. Such a tool could also serve as a guide through the array of statistical manipulations to which historical price data may be subjected for a variety of analytical purposes.

The essays in this volume focus primarily on the prices of non-durable consumer goods; among these products, food prices are most abundant. In some of the essays, scattered wage data are reported. None, however, contains systematic data on the price of services, producers' goods, land, or capital. For some kinds of price data, the relative scarcity or dispersion of sources as well as minor technical difficulties have impeded much-needed new work. Nonetheless, the data are there—in notarial archives, government records and reports, the papers of private enterprise (merchant firms, haciendas, and the like) and quasipublic bodies (churches, convents, consulados, mining guilds) from one end of Latin America to the other—more than enough to keep teams of researchers and research assistants working for a long time.

The utility of price history has to be measured in terms of its contribution to work in other fields of historical research. In economic history, a new boom in historical work on prices is crucial for extending backward in time our knowledge of trends in production, income, and productivity and for making possible a more precise understanding of the origins and history of the modern gap between less developed regions and more developed economies. A revival of price history would also make it possible to construct internationally comparable measures of living standards, to measure and analyze the growth and integration of markets, and to assess the impact of the external sector with greater precision. The essays in this volume suggest how historical price series can contribute to social, demographic, and political history as well. In no other field of economic historical work is the analytical payoff from empirical research so high.

NOTES

1. John J. TePaske and Herbert S. Klein, *The Royal Treasuries of the Spanish Empire in America,* 3 vols. (Durham: N.C.: Duke University Press, 1982); John J. TePaske, *La real hacienda de Nueva España: La real caja de México (1576–1816)* (Mexico:

Instituto Nacional de Antropología e Historia, Departamento de Investigaciones Históricas, Colección Científica, Fuentes, no. 41, 1976); and John J. TePaske and Herbert S. Klein, *Ingresos y egresos de la Real Hacienda en México* (Mexico: Instituto Nacional de Antropología e Historia, forthcoming). Tithe data appear in many recent works; a sophisticated recent example is by Cecilia Andrea Rabell Romero, *Los diezmos de San Luis de la Paz; Economía de una región del Bajío en el siglo XVIII* (Mexico: Universidad Nacional Autónoma de México, 1986).

2. John H. Coatsworth, "Cliometrics and Mexican History," *Historical Methods,* 18:1 (Winter 1985): 31–7.

3. William Glade's comparative economic history, now nearly twenty years old, remains the only major work in this field: *The Latin American Economies: A Study of Their Institutional Evolution* (New York: Van Nostrand, 1969); a new, revised edition is now planned and eagerly awaited.

4. The "price" of silver is the inverse of the price level of the commodities and services purchased with silver coin. The price of silver declined in eighteenth-century Mexico because the prices of everything else went up (see Garner's essay); the price of silver went up in Potosí because other prices were declining for most of the century.

5. Steven A. Mange, "Commodity Price Movements in the Andes and La Plata during the Seventeenth and Eighteenth Centuries" (Unpub. MA thesis, The University of Chicago, 1988).

6. Pablo Macera and Rosario Jiménez, "Precios: Lima, 1667–1738" (Lima: Mimeo, n.d.); Pablo Macera and Rosa Boccolini, "Precios de los Colegios de la Cía de Jesús, Arequipa, 1627–1767" (Lima: Mimeo, 1975).

7. While the prices of locally traded goods, such as maize or potatoes, may not be correlated with prices of locally traded goods in distant markets (for example, Lima and Potosí), they may be highly correlated across a chain of markets stretching between them such that the price of maize in markets A and B, B and C, and C and D are highly correlated, but little or no correlation exists between prices in A and Z. Commonly, market A will export to Z (if at all) only when crop failure in Z drives prices high enough to compensate for high transport costs. Though such events are commonly interpreted as suggesting a lack of integration between markets, they should be seen as confirmation of a high degree of integration.

8. Garner's essay does not contain a detailed description of the procedures followed in computing this index. Ideally, each year's index number would be computed by assigning weights in accordance with the proportion of maize traded at each price across all locations. Data to compute these proportions do not exist for the series Garner used. A second-best procedure would be to compute the (unweighted) mean of the prices observed at each location in each year and combine these by computing a colony-wide mean in which the means from each location are weighted according to the size of the local market (for which population of the market town could serve as a convenient proxy). Even this procedure would be difficult for Mexico because

population data for many localities is missing or crude at best. Garner's colony-wide mean thus appears to be an unweighted mean of the unweighted means reported in the published sources from which most of his data is taken. Given the state of the data, this may be the best that can be done under the circumstances, provided that the "colony-wide" index is based on uninterrupted series from all locations. Lacunae in the data from one or more locations could produce significant distortions in the colony-wide series. For example, with data missing for some years from a location where prices are normally higher (or lower) than elsewhere, the colony-wide index would need to be adjusted to avoid displaying a bogus rise (or fall) during those years.

9. The Larraín index of agricultural prices uses weights based on the proportion of each commodity in the diet of urban consumers. This is the most sophisticated of the price indices reported in this volume. Brown is an exception because he reports the *median* prices of the commodities he tracks rather than the means. This procedure is an alternative to using a weighted mean (like Larraín) or an unweighted mean (as in the other essays) to report the "central tendency" or average of the prices observed over the course of a year. The problem addressed by this procedure is the distortion which results from a skewed distribution: for some products, seasonal variations in prices may be quite sharp, with small amounts of product trading at inflated prices in the off-season and pulling up the unweighted mean. The median price (that is, the price midway between the highest and lowest observed) may reduce the pull of the off-season inflation, but may also introduce other distortions.

10. For Brazil, see Nathaniel Leff, *Underdevelopment and Development in Brazil,* vol. 1, *Economic Structure and Change, 1822–1847* (Boston, 1982), chap. 7. William McGreevey constructed rough estimates for other countries based on trade data and other indicators in "Recent Research on Latin American Economic History," *Latin American Research Review,* 3:2 (1968): 89–118. For Mexico, see John H. Coatsworth, "The Decline of the Mexican Economy, 1800–1860" in *La formación de las economías latinoamericanas y los intereses europeos en la época de Simón Bolivar* edited by Reinhard Lieher (Berlin: Colloquium Verlag, forthcoming).

11. Phyllis Deane, *The First Industrial Revolution* (2nd ed., Cambridge: Cambridge University Press, 1979), 8–9; Phyllis Deane and W. A. Cole, *British Economic Growth, 1688–1959: Trends and Structure* (Cambridge: Cambridge University Press, 1962), 282, 329–30.

12. Paul A. David, "The Growth of Real Product in the United States before 1840: New Evidence, Controlled Conjectures," *Journal of Economic History,* 27 (1967): 151–97; Paul Bairoch, "Europe's Gross National Product: 1800–1975," *Journal of European Economic History,* 5:2 (Fall, 1976): 273–340.

13. The urban food prices used by Larraín include the value added to the commodities by other sectors of the economy (transportation, commerce, finance, government, and even industry where food processing or milling was involved). The tithe revenue data to which Larraín's index was applied may (or may not) have been originally recorded in terms of urban retail prices. If they were, Larraín's claim to

have a good proxy for GDP is strengthened because his index of agricultural output is actually an index of the output of agriculture plus portions of various other sectors of the economy.

14. The Tandeter-Wachtel agricultural price index is an unweighted mean of the price indices calculated for each of seven commodities; in years for which the price data is incomplete, their index is based on the data available, that is, on the price index numbers of one to six commodities. Garner's method for computing his "colony-wide" maize price index is not explained; see above, note 8. The Larraín index, described above, comes closest to modern technical standards.

15. I have suggested elsewhere that Mexican per capita income did not grow over the course of the eighteenth century; John H. Coatsworth, "La historiografía económica de México," *Revista de Historia Económica* (Madrid, forthcoming). On stagnant agricultural productivity, see Eric Van Young, "The Age of Paradoxes: Mexican Agriculture at the End of the Colonial Period, 1750–1810" in *The Economies of Mexico and Peru During the Late Colonial Period, 1760–1810* edited by Nils Jacobsen and Hans-Jürgen Puhle (Berlin: Colloquium Verlag, 1986), 64–90.

16. See Coatsworth, "La historiografía de México." For example, the British and North American economies appear to have grown at a rate just over 0.5 percent per year over the course of the eighteenth century, enough to more than double income per capita in a hundred years. In 1800, U.S. per capita income was roughly double that of Mexico. British income per capita was roughly triple that of Mexico. If Mexican income per capita stagnated between 1700 and 1800, these 1800 comparisons imply a 1700 per capita income equal to that of the thirteen British North American colonies and somewhat below that of Great Britain. Mexico's "golden age" may have witnessed the origins of that country's relative backwardness.

17. See Herman Konrad, *A Jesuit Hacienda in Colonial Mexico: Santa Lucia, 1576–1767* (Stanford: Stanford University Press, 1980), chap. 9.

18. Ibid. Maize rations in the middle of the eighteenth century were commonly set at 12 quartillas (one-fourth a fanega) per month for resident workers (worth perhaps half a peso or so). In addition, such workers had access to hacienda credit. Skilled and supervisory personnel received as much as 48 quartillas (one fanega) of maize in addition to extra (non-maize) rations and a higher credit limit. See also Eric Van Young, "The Rich Get Richer and the Poor Get Skewed: Real Wages and Popular Living Standards in Late Colonial Mexico" (Unpub. paper presented to Workshop on Recent Research in Latin American Studies, University of Chicago, 1987), 27–29.

19. I have estimated Mexican per capita income in 1800 at approximately 40 pesos per capita. See Coatsworth, "The Decline of the Mexican Economy." On the United States and western Europe, see sources cited in notes 11 and 12.

20. See Cuauhtémoc Velasco A., "Los trabajadores mineros de Nueva España, 1750–1810" in *La clase obrera en la historia de México,* vol. 1, *De la colonia al imperio* by Enrique Florescano, et al. (Mexico: Siglo XXI, 1980), 239–301.

SOME CONSIDERATIONS ON THE HISTORY OF PRICES IN COLONIAL LATIN AMERICA

Ruggiero Romano

THE HARVEST OF WORK ABOUT THE HISTORY OF PRICES IN IBERIAN AMERICA developed during recent years is assuredly very important. On the basis of this, I would like to: draw up a balance sheet;[1] lay out a tentative comparative geography of prices on the American continent in the colonial period, and then compare it to the movement of prices in Europe; and present not general criticisms, or—even less—reservations of a methodological nature, but underscore the limits, the thresholds that cannot be exceeded in dealing with the history of prices in the American context.

In order to draw up the balance sheet, I shall, as often as possible, reproduce the very words that various writers have employed to indicate trends (increases, decreases, stagnation) they have perceived. That will prevent any temptation that I might have to alter their ideas.

Let us begin, then, with an examination of the movement in prices of agricultural products:[2]

Central Mexico (1530–1627) (corn): "In a little less than a century, from 1530 to 1627, the average wholesale price of Indian corn rose sixfold";[3]

Central Mexico (1530–73) (wheat): "Our calculation of trend for the forty-four-year period 1530–1573 shows a rise from 4 reales a fanega for wheat in 1530 to 10 reales by 1572 and 10.1 reales by 1573";[4]

Mexico (seventeenth-century corn): C. Guthrie, in his pioneering article, does not provide a view of the whole.[5] His graph (p. 114), however, suggests a substantial stability of prices, interrupted by two violent peaks resulting largely from "riots";

León and Silao (1660–1789) (corn): To judge from Table 37, the curve "of maize prices in León and Silao followed no fixed pattern. Instead, annual prices continually oscillated between troughs of 2–4 reales and crests of 12–15 reales. Within each year seasonal fluctuations tipped summer prices one or two reales beyond the annual average. During a period of 92 recorded years, the median annual price at León was 6 reales a fanega, and in three quarters of these occasions, the average level never surpassed 8 reales. Prior to 1769 the long-term trend was downward, since whereas before 1717 in only 28% of listed years were annual averages pitched at 4 reales or below, after 1723 some 41% failed to rise above this low level. Moreover, the years between 1752 and 1768 were remarkable for their persistently low prices, by reason of its proximity to Guanajuato, prices were usually, although by no means invariably, about two reales higher than in León. Equally important, after 1769 the Silao series manifests an upward movement, with the median close to 10 reales."[6]

Mexico (1708–1810) (corn): "There is no long term upward movement in the prices of corn. Graph 16 is even more eloquent because it points out the differences between the Mexican curve, and the French and European curves for the price of wheat. In the latter two, one can observe, following 1735 and particularly 1745, a continuous increase that in the case of France is prolonged until 1817. In contrast, the curve of prices of corn is seen to be constantly depressed by serious decreases that prevent the formation of a tendency of continual increase. The absence of a long-term increase is confirmed also by reading the numerous indices for the years of the cyclical minimum and of the cyclical averages."[7]

Dolores Hidalgo (1740–90) (corn, wheat, beans): "Corn, in its series of prices, does not register a long-term movement in any manner, doubtless as a consequence of its quite erratic trajectory. As for wheat, one can see, after 1752, a slow but continuous tendency to increase, which on two occasions is interrupted by profound declines that seem on the surface to impede its progress. Beans take a decade more than wheat to demonstrate their movement toward increase, although the latter, like the former, may not show a clear, definite tendency."[8]

San Miguel el Grande (1661–1803) (corn, wheat, beans, barley): S. Galicia's work does not offer global conclusions about long-term movement (it is, however, true that my copy is missing twenty pages), but an examination of the graphs allows us to reach the following conclusions: during the entire period, the four products, especially barley, demonstrate a tendency toward stagnation.[9]

To complete the reading of Mexican prices, the data provided by C. Gibson can be brought in regarding the prices of corn in the Valley of Mexico from 1525 to 1810.[10] This graph appears to be in basic agreement with the movements indicated by E. Borah and S. Cook (sixteenth century), E. Florescano, and Brading (both eighteenth century). For the seventeenth century, in contrast, it appears to me that the prices shown by Gibson are different from those of Guthrie, with a certain tendency toward increase.[11]

San Luis de la Paz (1673–1775 and 1797–1804) (corn): For the first period, the series constructed by C. Rabell shows a stagnant movement. For the years 1797–1804, one has the impression (what can be said about eight years?) that henceforth it has entered into a rising phase.[12]

The whole of the data of which I have already spoken here (and even of others that I have not taken into account) has been collected by R. L. Garner, who has assembled the Mexican prices in the essay published in this volume. Now as for corn, Garner's conclusions are the following: "Maize prices did not move along a straight, upward line. From the end of the first quarter of the sixteenth century to the middle of the seventeenth century, maize prices advanced steadily and energetically at a rate of 2.2 percent per year, but from the middle of the seventeenth century to the end of the colonial period they climbed much more slowly at a rate of 0.5 percent annually." This is too strong a conclusion for such lengthy periods.

Let us proceed to South America.

Santiago de Chile (1650–1810) (wheat flour): "What we believe is important to emphasize is that the prices of flour during the 18th century were much lower than in the previous century."[13]

Buenos Aires (1775–1812) (wheat, rice, chick-peas, dried beans): In the essay by L. Johnson, published in this volume, one can see the data relative to these four products. Now personally I do not see a movement toward increase for either chick-peas, dried beans, or rice where the prices show a sawtooth movement. For wheat, one can see the same finding except for a *curious* increase for the years 1803–1806. I say curious, because I do not understand how it can be possible that, faced with such a violent increase in the price of wheat, there has been a decrease in the prices of rice, chick-peas, and dried beans.

I do not believe, then, that my reading of these prices was in error. Rather there is another problem. Johnson has chiefly reasoned on the basis of a price index constructed on the basis of an equilibrium that seems to give an excessive weight to wheat and that, above all, lacks certain fundamental products of the Porteño diet: meat (chiefly meat), but also fish, not to mention corn. Now, if my memory serves, prices of meat in Buenos Aires are completely stable.

There is more, however. Let us say that my reading is bad, and Johnson is right that prices are rising between 1775 and 1810. The period from 1775 to 1810 does not represent the entire eighteenth century. I mean to say by that that if, for example, one examines the prices of corn in Mexico (after Florescano, 1969) one can say that prices rose during the years 1775–1810. Florescano, however, is correct for the whole of the eighteenth century when he says: "There is no long-term movement toward increase in the prices of corn."

Potosí (1716–1803) (agricultural products): "In summary, we can propose the following periodization for movement in agricultural prices during the 18th century in Potosí:

171(6)–58: rise (?)
1759–89: decrease
1790–180(5): rise."[14]

Potosí (1698–1721) (livestock products: "The following fluctuations can be distinguished: from 169(8) to 172(1), rapid decrease; from 1728 to 1752, more or less regular increase; from 175(4) to 1790, first a brutal increase in terms of the previous phase, with a lacuna in 1753 that hinders the analysis; after 1755, stagnation with some depressions, particularly in 1772 and 1780; from 1791 to 1804, a pronounced decrease; an obvious increase after 1805."

Arequipa (1667–1767) (corn): The documentary work of P. Macera and R. Boccolini allows one to glimpse (but hardly more than glimpse) a tendency toward high prices during the second half of the seventeenth century until the first decade of the eighteenth, followed by a period of decline.[15]

Arequipa (1627–1818) (wheat): That same impression is brought forth as regards wheat in the study of K. Brown published in this volume.

Rio de Janeiro (1760–1820) (flour, dried meat, bacon): "Here two characteristics stand out when one examines these price fluctuations: the seeming irregularity from year to year, with little-discernible longterm trend, and the fact that in the case of wheat flour and bacon the general price level at the end of period (ca. 1820) is no higher than at beginning."[16]

Salvador (1674–79) (manioc, wheat flour): The essay by D. Alden in this volume shows quite clearly an increase in the prices of these two products between 1674 and 1679. Afterward, there is an evident tendency to stagnation and even decrease for manioc flour until 1769; wheat flour, in contrast, reveals a quite prolonged drop from 1720 until 1758. Afterward, it rises continuously, but without ever attaining the level of the first years of the century.

Graph 3.1

Average Price of Wheat in Europe
in Grams of Silver

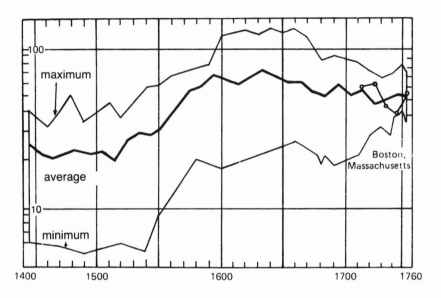

I have presented the movements in the prices of locally produced foodstuffs, in the very words of various authors where this has been possible. They cover different regions of the American continent and do not have a truly homogeneous appearance: to reduce them all to a sort of "American" index would certainly constitute an abuse. Now we shall attempt to analyze them by comparison with a parameter external to America.

For this, let us now take up the price indices of wheat in Europe. When one speaks of European prices, the obligatory point of departure is represented by two graphs (see 3.1 and 3.2) drawn by F. Braudel and F. Spooner.[17]

How are they different? The first is calculated in grams of silver and the second, in money of account. This has very important consequences. For example, regarding the "crisis" of the seventeenth century, if one examines the prices in money of account, one can understand that everything changes after the great short crisis of 1619–22. If one takes into consideration prices in grams of silver, one can choose between two spirals: 1590–1630 to make the seventeenth century "begin" with its once-in-a-century decline.[18]

Graph 3.2

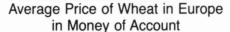

Average Price of Wheat in Europe
in Money of Account

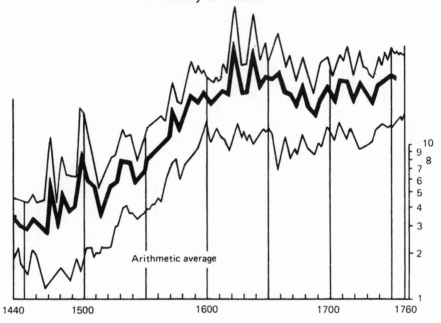

Arithmetic average

10
9
8
7
6
5
4
3
2
1

1440   1500   1600   1700   1760

I prefer prices in money of account. My choice is dictated by the fact that one is dealing with incompletely monetarized economies. The question is the following: how does the purchaser of bread or flour pay for it? Above all, in what terms are the prices calculated?

As for the calculation, the answer is simple and categorical: in pounds, sous, and pennies, in short, in money of account.

As for the manner of payment, the answer is equally simple: coins of copper, bronze, base alloys of silver, or vellon. Just see how clear it is. If one truly wished to amuse himself by making the famous conversion into metal, he would have to carry it out in grams of copper, because, whether he wished it or not, the greater number of transactions were settled precisely in small coin.

Still, however, there is yet another argument that limits our acceptance of prices expressed in grams of precious metals: the curve that one obtains does not express anything other than the reality of the movements of the metals under consideration and totally eliminates all the other elements that

truly make up a price.[19] One is almost ashamed to have to remind oneself
of certain basic truths. The setting of prices is determined essentially by
supply (that is, local production of goods) and demand (the number of persons
who actually go to the market, not by the population understood in a general
fashion even if it does have a certain influence). The supply-demand relation
is expressed by monetary symbols (of account or actual). Even supposing,
though this is a matter of an academic exercise, that the mediation between
supply and demand was realized by the intermediacy of good, metallic coins
of full weight, if one transforms prices into grams of metal, one is doing
away with (there are no other words for it) the two fundamental elements,
supply and demand.

Let us, however, close the parenthesis.

If we analyze movements in the price of wheat and corn in America by
referring to Braudel's and Spooner's graph, what lessons do we learn from
it?

At first glance, one could say, for example, that there is a parallel between
the increase shown by Borah and Cook in the case of Mexico in the sixteenth
century and the increase in Europe. That, however, is only a matter of a
first impression. This is for the good reason that in Europe the rise in prices
in large part has its origin in the increase in population, while in Mexico,
it accompanied an impressive fall in the aboriginal population, who were
precisely the consumers of corn.[20] And what about the increase in the price
of wheat in the sixteenth century? I avow that a fourfold increase in the
price of this product does not convince me. In general, the prices of products
of European origin (wheat, horses, sheep, and cows) tend to decrease in
America during the sixteenth century. Besides, as Borah and Cook indicate,
the fact remains that "from 1528–1542 wheat prices at the very least remained relatively constant and probably declined."[21] There was, then, stability between 1528 and 1572, which is in clear contradiction to everything
that one knows about the history of the acclimatization of European plants
in Spanish America.[22] Thus, the temptation to compare the increase in
Mexican prices with that of Europe is potentially misleading.

If from the sixteenth century we pass to the seventeenth century, we can
follow the movement of the price of corn in Mexico after the work of Guthrie:
a stagnant movement (though one must not forget that it is a question of
the prices being fixed by the cabildo) that is elsewhere partially contradicted
by data provided by Gibson and by D. Brading. Here, then, the comparison
that one will be tempted to make with European prices is risky, since
European prices are only stagnant after 1620—or 1640. Although the data

are less reliable than those for Potosí, Arequipa, and Santiago de Chile, they demonstrate an ascendant profile. Rather than a similarity with the European curve, we find a persistent divergence.

The eighteenth century shows us an even more complicated tableau. As I have already shown, in Santiago, Potosí, Arequipa, and Rio de Janeiro, prices reveal a distinct tendency toward stagnation or to decline. If there is increase, where it exists is only during the last two decades of the century. We find ourselves, then, in the presence of a clearly inverse conjuncture in comparison with Europe. Mexico constitutes a case aside to which I shall return later. Let us say, then, that one has the impression of being confronted with two Americas.[23]

The first, Mexican, seems (but only seems) in the eighteenth century to align its prices with the European model. It is only a matter of false appearances, however, because, as Florescano justly said, if there is alignment, it is only at the level of cyclical movement. As to that tendency, "There is no long-term movement in the prices of corn."[24]

So can one speak of converging conjunctures or must inverse conjunctures be acknowledged?

Before answering that question, let us open a parenthesis and leave the boundaries of Iberian America to deal with the United States and Canada. Regarding the latter, "a long-term movement tending to increase can be seen beginning in the 1750s, is accentuated in 1793–94 and ends abruptly in the years 1811–1816. Canada does not escape the international conjuncture, *but does not truly participate in it after 1793*" (my emphasis).[25] In fact, if one inspects the graph carefully, one verifies that if the cyclical movement in Canadian wheat prices is very similar to the European prices, any tendency toward increase is quite modest.[26] In the same manner as in Mexico, each time the line tends to move up, there is a fall that inexorably makes the underlying tendency decline.[27]

If we take up the case of Philadelphia and examine the movement in the prices of wheat, flour, and meat, one can see that the change is quite similar to that which, for ease of understanding, I would call the Canadian (or Mexican) model.[28] Cincinnati, New York, Charleston, and New Orleans distinctly confirm the same movement.[29] Finally, look at the magnificent graph drawn by A. Cole, where one can see that in the United States as a whole (obviously these were former English colonies before 1774), the eighteenth century is proof of movement that even if they proclaim a tendency to align themselves with European prices, they never manage to do so: a sort of hidden force always seems to drag them down. That occurs at least until the 1780s in that century.[30] We face, then, an isolated continent. What "geography," or "geographies," can we trace from this? There are at least two geographic categories among the different countries of the American continent and between these countries and Europe. (Asia should also enter our accounting, but that is another problem.)

From an intercontinental point of view, it seems to me that, in terms of *locally produced* agricultural products, there are two Americas: the first, comprising the region from Mexico to Canada *seems* to align itself with European prices (at least during the eighteenth century); the other America, the region to the south, never moves in the direction of Europe and proceeds by way of a distinctly inverse conjuncture relative to Europe. This poses a two-fold problem: that of the differences in the movement of prices *within* the continent and, outside it, the difference in the changes of prices between the continent as a whole and Europe.

It is necessary to insist upon these points. It would be useful again to take up the problem, the immense problem, of the eighteenth century. First, what do we mean by "the seventeenth century"? For me, it is the period from 1620 to 1730-40. For others, who love the cyclical peaks, it lasts from 1640 to 1730-40. It is not a question of an academic quarrel over more or less twenty years. The choice of one date rather than another signifies attributing to it the importance of one deed rather than another: 1620 = agriculture the sector that supports the economy of the era; 1640 = merchant "capitalism" (?), an epiphenomenon, if it ever existed. That debate, which, I repeat, is extremely important, is not very significant here, however. Here the problem is situated in the following manner: European prices indicate a decrease, or, at least, a greatly pronounced stagnation, while the American prices that are available for Potosí, Santiago de Chile, Arequipa, and even Lima, according to the sketchy data that exist, show that the American movement is the opposite of the European movement. Is there an exception in the case of Mexico, as Guthrie would have us believe? I repeat that the curve drawn by Guthrie should be corrected with the data of Gibson and Brading. As it is, it remains for him to verify the whole of the problem of the great "crisis" of the seventeenth century in the context of America.[31]

Still, though, at least for South America, one can calmly speak of an inverse conjuncture. Of course, one could (or should) study the nuances, the details, but the core of the problem is the following: during the seventeenth and eighteenth centuries, the movement in prices of agricultural products in Iberian America is inverse in comparison with the European movement.

The seventeenth-century low corresponds to a high in America and vice-versa in the eighteenth century.[32]

From the prices of foodstuffs, we move to the general movement of prices. I have affirmed that I do not like the "general" price movement very much.[33] I know quite well how it was arrived at (for yesterday and today). A brief excursion to the center of the famous "general" price movement can be useful, not so much for the conclusions that one may reach, but in order to trace an intellectual proceeding.

Let us lay out two general price indices from the group from Ibero-America: *Santiago de Chile* (1674–1808): For their part, the periods of lows will be longer and will fill the dates between cycles of highs. The first is between 1674 and 1693 and the second between 1749 and 1793, a complete half-century if we overlook the five-year period 1780–84, when the low price tendency was briefly interrupted.[34] Moreover, that same situation seems confirmed in the essay by J. Larraín, published in this volume.
Bahia (1750–1930): The graph published by Queirós clearly shows a stagnation until the 1790s, followed by a rapid high that lasts until approximately 1805.[35]

These are interesting conclusions, but nothing extraordinary, as in all the famous "general" price indices. They do, however, have the merit of helping us pose what seems to me to be the fundamental question of the entire history of prices in Ibero-America in the colonial era. In a general movement of prices in America, there are three components: prices of locally produced foods; prices of goods produced in America, but not locally (thus, for example, maté consumed in Potosí, sugar consumed in Santiago de Chile); and prices of goods produced in Europe.

In this sense, we have two excellent works available, one for Córdoba, the other for Potosí.

For the period 1711–62, A. Arcondo has given us a very interesting graph (see 3.3).[36]

From all the evidence, those prices reduced to a "general" index will give us a movement toward decrease, but within this decrease we see that local products show a tendency to increase until 1732. In addition, it is only after 1725 that the price of products of European origin reveal not only a tendency to decrease, but also quite frequently drop below the level of local and American products. In Potosí, the problem is posed in a similar fashion: E. Tandeter and N. Wachtel show us clearly in their excellent work that the prices of products of European origin decline most. The prices of American

Graph 3.3

Prices of Local, American, and European Products
in Córdoba

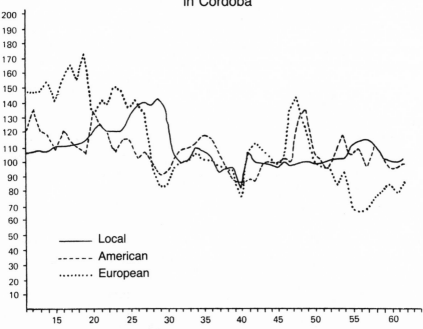

products fall less. Local prices resist the tendency—but stagnate—until the end of the century.

Santiago de Chile appears to confirm this pattern. A. Ramón and J. Larraín in their book are not given to the precision that is, however, fundamental. In spite of that, the fall in prices of imported products is greater than that of agricultural and livestock products.[37] In addition, it is accompanied by a very interesting phenomenon. The index of prices of imported products, which until the end of the seventeenth century was constantly maintained at a level higher than that of agricultural and livestock products, drops below this domestic index at the beginning of the eighteenth century: a veritable pincers movement.

In summary, in the cases that we are able to examine in detail, there are, for the eighteenth century, three price movements: prices of local products that resist change (that is, stagnant); prices of "American" origin that decrease, but less clearly than prices of goods of European origin.

What, however, are the products of "American" origin? It is evident that in the interior of the American continent, the essential part of "commerce" is represented by inter-American commerce, full "circle": wheat, corn, potatoes, animals, chile, and charqui. For those products, though, it is a matter of local and regional circulation.[38] Products that have interregional circulation are different: sugar, tobacco, maté, indigo, and cacao. In sum, fresh products circulate regionally, and "tropical" products circulate interregionally.[39] These last also constitute the essential part of the products exported from America to Europe.

It would be interesting to try to see what the movement of "tropical" products is in America and compare that with the movement of prices of the same products in Europe.

That examination will permit us to arrive at a better understanding of two phenomena: the dependent position of America with regard to Europe; the position of "tropical" products (marketed interregionally) with regard to local products (marketed locally or only marketed regionally).

Let us begin with the first point. European demand for the products is not new for a certain number of them (dyes and sugar, in particular). That demand, however, certainly becomes stronger in the eighteenth century and, above all, is made for a whole series of "new" products (coffee, cacao, tobacco).[40]

Indigo prices offer us a first occasion for certain considerations. A typical product of Guatemala, there was a veritable boom in its exportation between 1772–76 and 1797–1801, from 561,000 pounds to 1,006,000.[41] During that same period, the prices of "excellent" indigo presented the movement seen in Table 3.1.[42]

Prices of indigo from Guatemala (without indication of quality) in Amsterdam during the same period are presented in Table 3.2.[43] We translate the same figures into percentages (1772–76 = 100) in Table 3.3.

It is clear that the movement (and I emphasize *movement*, not *levels*) of indigo prices in Guatemala is low, while in Amsterdam it is stagnant. In spite of everything, however, some problems persist. Why, when between 1782–86 prices in Guatemala rose, did they go down in Amsterdam? Here, one would believe that Europe was dependent in regard to America. There is nothing to this, for at least two reasons:

a) First, we do not know the components that make up the price of indigo in Guatemala. Is the indigo paid for in cash or merchandise? Part in cash, part in merchandise? It is evident that one can accept a loss on the *purchase* price of indigo if one gains on the *sale* price of the merchandise that is given in exchange.

Table 3.1
Indigo Prices

1772–76	12.85 (reales)
1777–81	10.00
1782–86	13.20
1787–91	11.45
1792–96	11.45
1797–1801	10.50

Table 3.2
Indigo Prices in Amsterdam

1772–76	6.70 (guldens)
1777–81	6.73
1782–86	6.54
1787–91	5.95
1792–96	6.42
1797–1801	6.85

Table 3.3
Comparative Indigo Prices

	Prices in Guatemala	Prices in Amsterdam
1772–76	100.00	100.00
1777–81	77.82	100.44
1782–86	102.72	97.61
1787–91	89.10	88.80
1792–96	89.10	95.82
1797–1801	81.71	102.23

b) Another fact is that without believing uselessly in the sterile concept of a supposed "world economy," another element intervenes, since the Dutch (merchants and textile "industrialists" who use indigo) can play on two fronts, indigo from both Guatemala and Java.

Let us go on to another product: cacao. The evolution of its price is seen in Table 3.4.[44]

Once again, translations of those prices into index numbers (1732–36 = 100) are presented in Table 3.5.

During the forty-five years that we have examined, the prices do not manage in either Caracas or Amsterdam to regain the height of the point of departure.[45] In this, the movement of cacao closely approaches that of indigo, which after thirty years had laboriously exceeded in Amsterdam the level at the beginning. This should not be astonishing. In London, Munich, Austria, Poland, and Italy, the movement of prices of "tropical" products is in decline in contrast to those of agricultural products and industrial goods. The latter, although they increase, never catch up with the prices of agricultural products).[46]

This is not astonishing at all, in relationship to the well-known American declines in prices. In the particular case of cacao, the works of E. Farías,[47] R. Hussey,[48] and now R. Ferry in his essay published in this volume have given us valuable explanations for that decline. Without disputing them, however, can one be convinced? Can one only believe in the inauspicious role of the Compañía Guipuzcoana? This latter certainly had a depressing effect on the prices of cacao. The cacao of Caracas, though, from which we get the Amsterdam prices does not arrive in the Low Countries by means of the Compañía Guipuzcoana, but by means of smugglers from Curaçao. Here also, as for indigo, the problem arises of knowing what was the medium of payment used by the cacao smugglers. There is also the problem posed by the arrival in Europe of cacao from Surinam. Once again, European domination plays on multiple fronts.

Another tempting verification can be drawn from the case of sugar. At first, it will be necessary to make an initial declaration. Following the reconstruction that was made by S. Schwartz, the movement of prices shows a clear tendency to increase during the entire seventeenth century and until 1720.[49] This is confirmed by the data presented by Alden in this volume. It shows, between 1675 and 1715–17, a certain tendency toward increase. The work by Alden indicates, for the period after that, a quite clear stagnation of the movement of sugar prices until 1770. Once again, there is an obvious inverse conjuncture in regard with Europe. Let us return, though, to the

Table 3.4
Cacao Prices

	Caracas	Amsterdam
1732–36	131.2	0.93
1737–41	98.4	0.84
1742–46	76.0	0.52
1747–51	75.6	0.45
1752–56	96.0	0.50
1757–61	100.8	0.75
1762–66	112.8	0.72
1767–71	124.8	0.91
1772–76	128.0	0.75

Table 3.5
Comparative Cacao Price Indexes

	Caracas	Amsterdam
1732–36	100.00	100.00
1737–41	75.00	90.32
1742–46	57.92	55.91
1747–51	57.62	48.30
1752–56	73.17	53.76
1757–61	76.82	80.64
1762–66	85.36	77.41
1767–71	95.12	97.84
1772–76	97.55	80.64

problem of comparing the prices of sugar in America and Europe. It appears to me that this comparison is, unfortunately, very difficult, if not impossible. Indeed, H. Johnson, Jr., gives a dual series of prices for "white" sugar and unrefined sugar in his very important work.[50] There remains one problem, though: I do not know what the price of "white" sugar is.

Allow me to explain with an example. In 1755, the price of white sugar in a sugar mill in the Recôncavo of Bahia can be broken down in the following manner:[51] "1$400 reis per arroba of fine white [sugar] with no admixture; 1$200 reis per arroba of round white [sugar], second grade (evidently there was another of first quality); 900 reis per arroba of spiced loaf sugar."

For 1756, I found on the same page only one price, "1$200 reis per arroba of white [sugar]." What can one say about that *white* sugar and its price with no other qualifications? Do those of the different white sugars indicated for 1755 correspond to it? Is it the "round" white? And then, there is the stagnation of prices. Is it the "fine white without admixture"? If so, there is a decrease. In contrast, an increase would exist if it were a matter of "spiced loaf white [sugar]." Not to mention that perhaps it corresponds to "round white [sugar] of first quality," when one does not know the price during the previous year. In short, I do not have the courage to establish a comparison between the Brazilian and Dutch prices.[52] Having said that, however, it seems possible despite everything to affirm that between the seventeenth and eighteenth centuries, the prices of sugar in Brazil show a certain rising tendency although interrupted by falls, while in Amsterdam,[53] decrease is normal, although moderate.[54]

Such uncertain considerations allow us to reach some conclusions. First, one must not forget that in the case of sugar as well as of cacao and indigo in the European markets, there is not only the product from Europe, but also sugar of different origins (Surinam, for example).

That seems to be the fundamental lesson for a study of prices of "tropical" products exported from Ibero-America to Europe: *They are not alone in the international market.* Each of these products has competitors, and thus the pressure that the international market can exert on them is not solely a generic, "colonial" pressure. It is, if you will permit the expression, "pluri-colonial" in the sense that the center of domination can play the different markets off against each other.[55]

Two problems still remain to be looked at: that of the prices of products introduced into an interregional commercial circuit; and that relative to European products in America.

Let us begin with the first. The available series are not numerous. It is, at first, possible to establish a parallel between the prices of sugar in Peru (a center of production)[56] and Chile (a center of consumption).[57]

In Peru, prices fall a great deal between the middle of the sixteenth century and the beginning of the seventeenth. That is normal: a "new" product has the same fate as horses, cows, or wheat. It did not take long for high prices for the "novelty" to become stabilized. What is remarkable, though, is that within that stabilization one can see the pressures of high prices during the seventeenth century, high prices that will never be reached during the eighteenth century.

In Santiago de Chile, the movement of sugar prices follows that of Peruvian sugar, and it seems that the decrease in Santiago in the eighteenth century was, with regard to the seventeenth century, even stronger than one can discover in Peru, though one will know that not to be categorical.

Textiles are among the products circulating interregionally that we can follow. In Potosí, the prices of light woolen cloth and coarse cotton cloth between 1670 and 1810 reveal a continuous decline; for coarse woolen cloth, an increase until around 1700 is followed by a continuous decline. Now, it is necessary to remark that, during the seventeenth century, the prices of textile products are the ones in Europe that show the greatest resistance. Nevertheless, in Potosí, other products such as sugar, soap, maté, wine, and conger reveal a tendency toward stagnation during the entire period between 1676 and 1816.

The last verification it is possible to make is in Córdoba, where the prices of goods produced in America (but not locally) after having shown a certain tendency to increase between 1711 and 1720, show a strong tendency to decrease, as Arcondo's Graph 3 shows. There is also the problem of European products. In the case of Córdoba, the fall in prices is clear.

Let us take up a particular case, though: that of paper. Its price in Spain in the period from 1650 to 1700 demonstrated complete stagnation (from 1650 to 1700) with even a decrease between 1680 and 1700. Then, after the first years of the new century, a quite regular tendency to increase is manifested (interrupted, to be honest, between 1749 and 1752) that is prolonged until 1800.[58] Now, what happens to the prices of paper, certainly of Spanish origin, in Potosí? Once again, there is an inverse conjuncture: from 1676 to 1706, a quite pronounced increase and then stagnation until 1800 (and also strong declines) interrupted by abrupt rises resulting from, according to all the evidence, supply problems.[59]

This is inadequate, I know, but the material that is available does not allow further considerations.

What explanations can one draw from that group of "facts"? I say explanations, because it would be absurd to seek one global explanation. For a bundle of facts, there should be a multiplicity of explanations.

There are at least two problems that must be clarified: Why is there, on the whole, an inverse movement of prices in Ibero-America and Europe? How can one explain that, within a "general" movement of prices in America, there are three submovements associated with the existence of three classes of products: local, "American," and European?

In order to answer the first question, we must take up things at their beginning. The European historiography of prices has reasoned for a long time according to the following schema: the sixteenth century (*grosso modo*, between 1540 and 1640), a time of rising prices, is followed by the seventeenth with stagnant prices or even decreasing prices; only after 1740 do prices begin to rise again. There is no doubt that that schema is not an idle fancy: the great phases of the movement of prices in Europe are those that I have previously indicated. The chronology can change if one wishes to adopt, as I prefer, prices in money of account, but, roughly, the major lines of the European movement of prices remain those that I have indicated above.

Where the error begins is when one passes to the explanations. One can summarize them (except for one glorious exception: W. Abel) in the following monotonous game: the sixteenth century sees massive arrivals of precious metals from America that bring with them an increase in prices; afterward, in the seventeenth century, those arrivals diminish and prices stagnate or decrease; finally, American metals arrive again and prices begin to rise after 1740.

I myself have believed that schema (mea culpa). When I began to doubt the "metallic" aspects of prices, I was soundly criticized.[60] Henceforth, though, there is a great event. Here it is: M. Morineau has completely modified the classic (and arbitrary, because false, *totally false*) schema of the arrivals of precious metals from America.[61] Graph 3.4 shows it clearly:

There is no fall in the amount of silver that arrives during the seventeenth century. Therefore, one must explain the stagnation of prices with regard to other variables (population, climate, harvests, market problems). This obliges one to recognize that the metallic variable (monetary), which assuredly has some importance, is not the determining element and does not explain everything.

While the monetary variable does not explain everything in the European context, it explains even less within the American context. And this, for

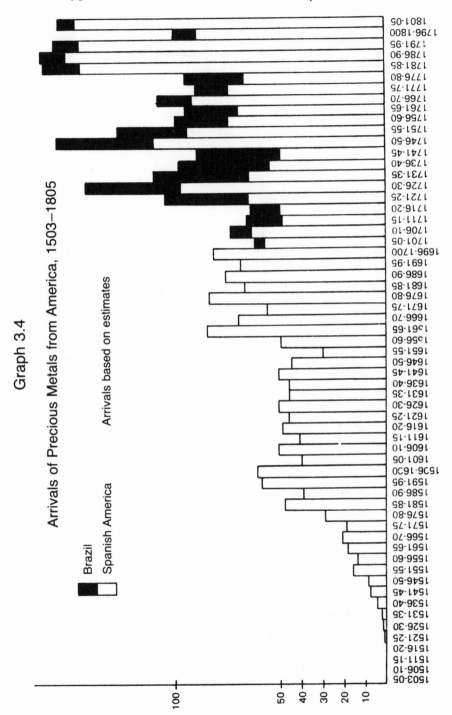

Graph 3.4

Arrivals of Precious Metals from America, 1503–1805

Brazil

Spanish America

Arrivals based on estimates

many reasons, will be much clearer if one abandons any monetarianist interpretation and takes recourse in other elements for the explanation. First, there is population. In a schematic fashion, what can we say? After the dizzying fall of the sixteenth century, the American population again begins to grow after roughly the middle of (or even slightly before) the seventeenth century. To be more specific about this point, it is not only a matter of insisting upon a complete, general increase in population, which, however, exists, but the specific fact of an increase in the white and mestizo population, essentially urban, who constitute the two groups that frequent the market most often and who, for that reason, come to influence the setting of prices. The increase in prices in the seventeenth century, in that sense, is thus "normal."

How can one explain the stagnation and even decrease of prices during the eighteenth century, when population continues to increase? Very probably (if not certainly) this results from overproduction. On those last two points (population and excess production), however, I shall say more later. For the present, I wish to indicate that I do not want to reduce it all to the demographic and/or agricultural component, even though I think these are very important elements because they are structural, much more structural than matters of mining production. Another element in the explanation (and quite structural, as well) appears to me to be constituted by an extremely banal fact that one tends to forget: Ibero-America is a "colony." Now, a colony is more or less subject, according to the era, to seizure from the metropolis. Doubtless, it enjoyed more freedom during the seventeenth than during the eighteenth century: in the seventeenth century, Spain, as well as Portugal, constrained by the problems of its own crisis had to ease the pressure on the colony, which in turn profited by its own economic expansion, which would be brought into line when the metropolis, in the eighteenth century, caught its breath. From this point of view, the high prices of the seventeenth century, like the low prices of the following century, "signify" something: they first express a moment of local American expansion; the others, those of the eighteenth, denote a moment of contraction. All that I have just indicated will perhaps be clearer in the explanation of the second problem: the three American price movements.

First, the movement of prices of agriculture and livestock for local consumption: the question is complicated, but becomes clearer if we consider it in two chronological periods—for the period after 1740, and for the period that precedes that date.

For the years from 1740 to 1810, as we have seen, those prices show a clear tendency to decrease. If one sees slight signs of increase, these are only manifested after 1790–1800. How can one explain this decrease within a time in which the production of precious metals as well as issues of money increase prodigiously?[62] And within that, the population, in the same era, progresses at a rate of 0.8 percent per year?[63] The famous quantitative theory of money, I repeat, does not seem to function. The demographic element, though, does not appear to exercise its earlier influence. This change is more significant if one notes that it is not only the global population that increases, but, above all, the urban population: that is to say, the population that commonly frequents the market and thus contributes truly to the setting of prices.

There is only one last element to take into consideration: the production of agricultural goods. These, without a shadow of a doubt, greatly increase.

At the end of the eighteenth century, a Chilean document from 1798 indicates that "the lack of value and abundance at the same time is not wealth; high prices with scarcity is misery: abundance with high prices is opulence."[64] This is nothing more than plagiarism of a passage from François Quesnay, "Just as mercenary value, so is profit; abundance and not value is not wealth. Scarcity and high prices are misery. Abundance and high prices are opulence."[65]

A deliberation of the cabildo abierto of Santiago de Chile of 22 September 1753 corresponds quite well to these considerations of a theoretical nature: "The origin of the continued decadence of wheat, so prejudicial to the kingdom, originates we all know in the surplus of this fruit in the ware-houses."[66] The problem of agricultural prices in Chile, but not only in Chile, were thus those of "abundance and not value," to use Quesnay's expression again.

The explanation of the increase (or at least, of high prices in comparison with the prices of the eighteenth century) of the prices of agricultural and livestock products during the seventeenth century is more complex. We know that the quantities of precious metals produced are growing and every-thing leads us to believe that it is the same for the issue of money. Here, then, the monetarist explanation will be able to function, and it has, indeed, partially functioned. It has also, however, contributed to those movements toward price increase that began with the amelioration of the demographic situation uncompensated for by an increase in agricultural harvests, a situ-ation that suggests difficulties for urban markets. Add to that what I pre-viously indicated about that phase of expansion of the American economy of the seventeenth century and several things about that "abnormal" movement ("abnormal" in comparison with Europe) will be clear.

All that is important as much for the seventeenth as for the eighteenth, because it confirms that the inverse conjuncture of America in comparison with Europe is not only a fact relative to prices, but it begins to take on structural aspects.

Second, the prices of European products: what one can say with a certain assurance is that since the seventeenth century Spanish America, without attaining total autarky, comes to have a network of production that takes the place of European merchandise. Demand for these products diminished, at least relatively speaking, also as a result of internal production. It is in that manner, for example, that Chilean and Peruvian vineyards begin to produce wine that replaces in quality and quantity a good part at least of the wines of Spanish origin. And this without even speaking of the development of products that totally replace European products: thus, cane liquor mostly replaces brandy imported from Spain.

It is this group of circumstances that explains their fall manifested in the presence of very elevated prices. What I mean to say is that in the seventeenth century the old, Spanish commercial monopoly collapsed. Smuggling merchandise became progressively more important: Dutch, English, French, and others intervened in an ever-greater manner in the economic life of Ibero-America. Competition among them is stronger and stronger, and what all of them together present to "monopolistic" business is terrible. The high prices of European products in American markets of the sixteenth and part of the seventeenth century, which mean not only so much of the high costs of production or commercialization, but of the strong speculative benefits, are destined to be progressively reduced.[67] It is necessary to add the anticipated fall in prices of products of European origin.

Third, there remains the matter of prices for American products that were marketed interregionally. How can one explain their movement as intermediary between European and local prices? I believe that it is precisely the pressures that they receive from the other two groups of products that influence their development. It is evident that if the prices of European textiles, for example, progressively decline, textiles produced in America should in turn decline, but with a certain delay, since their purchases resisted this competition. In the same fashion, they are drawn downward by the prices of goods produced locally, chiefly by the prices of grain: that pilot price.

The considerations that I have developed are not rigid, categorical explanations. Rather more simply, they are an effort to constitute a platform for a discussion that I would hope will be profitable, even if it must achieve the complete reversal of the hypotheses I have expressed.

At the beginning of this essay, I spoke of the "harvest of works" that has accumulated about the history of prices in America. What lessons can one learn from them? I have tried to demonstrate them. I could finish my discourse here. Please allow me to make a few more observations.

The problem of prices in America puts us on guard against certain generalizations that the historiography of prices in Europe, at a certain moment, has practically forced upon us.[68] The quantitative theory of money, phase "A," phase "B," and so forth, does not explain the economic history of Europe as a whole and explains even less adequately the entire economic history of Central and South America. It is not absolutely necessary for the ambitions and illusions of the European historical school to emigrate to America at the very moment they expose all their own weaknesses.

Let us speak about those weaknesses, their limits, and their thresholds.

With regard to the history of prices in Europe, a certain convention is established henceforth upon the fact that a price of the fourteenth century does not have the same significance as a price of the eighteenth. They do not have the same meaning for the plain and simple reason that the market of the fourteenth century is rather more restrained than that of the eighteenth, and the economy of the fourteenth rather less monetarized than that of the eighteenth. In sum, the prices of the eighteenth century represent a greater reality than the prices of the fourteenth. To say that a certain amount of wheat costs five livres in 1340 in country X and six livres in 1341 must not mean that there was only a 20 percent increase, which is certainly true, but must make us reflect upon another question: what part of the wheat consumed in country X actually went to market? Because, if private, home consumption is quite strong; if another part of the wheat is used in barter; and if the part that goes to market is reduced, for example (another example that is not far from reality) to 10 percent of the total wheat consumed, then the price reflects the economic history of that 10 percent. It seems to me, however, that the heart of the problem is the other 90 percent. Under what conditions can one find it? Did someone eat it because they were hungry? Has the surplus been set aside for the future? Notions of *prosperity, difficulties,* and *crises,* in light of prices that reflect only 10 percent of reality seem very doubtful.

Also, for Ibero-America it seems to me that the problem of the market

Table 3.6
Comparative Prices (in reales)

	Buenos Aires	Asunción	Difference	Profit
linen, vara	2	6	4	8
cordovan poncho	12	16	4	120
Castillian baize	no data	20	?	96
taffeta, vara	no data	12	?	40
silk cap	16	24	8	72
silk kerchief	no data	24	?	80
knife, per unit	no data	2	?	8

is fundamental. Let us take the case of Peru at the end of the eighteenth century. What is the bulk of money in circulation? "Only from five to six million is free for use by commerce." It is, then, with regard to that sum that one must understand those famous prices. I well know that there will never be any information with which to calculate the internal market of colonial America, but it seems opportune to keep those simple calculations in mind to read price curves in a "general" manner while they reflect no more than a special situation.

This is because all of them are special in colonial America. I have previously indicated a series of doubts with regard to comparisons about interregional circulation. Allow me to explain. It is certainly possible to draw a parallel between the prices of wheat in Santiago de Chile and Lima between the end of the seventeenth and the beginning of the eighteenth century. This is very interesting. We must remember, however, that the *carga* of wheat from Santiago is 12 percent less than that of Lima.[69] And that is nothing. Let us take another example, furnished to us by J. C. Garavaglia.[70] In Table 3.6 are the differences in prices between Buenos Aires and Asunción in 1785–87.

In the table published by Garavaglia, the column "Difference" no longer exists. I have added to it to show the risks in establishing comparisons between two prices with the idea, false, that the difference represents the profit. In fact, one will be tempted to say that for one poncho whose price is twelve reales in Buenos Aires and that is sold for sixteen reales in Asunción, the profit is four reales (less the charges for transport). Now, as Garavaglia emphasizes, it is nothing. That is for the good and simple reason that structural reasons to which I alluded earlier intervene: those ponchos and linens are woven in Calamuchita by weavers paid with maté valued at the highest prices, while the peasants make their purchases from Paraguay with maté valued at the lowest prices. Thus, if the "difference" is around 60 percent, the real "profit" is more than 300 percent. What counts, then, is not the deviation existing between the current price of Buenos Aires and that of Asunción, but the structural conditions of production (in the other cases, of simple commercialization) of goods, objects of sale or purchase.

Shall we try to see things more closely?

Let us imagine having a fine series of account books for the company store of a hacienda, with indications of the prices of maté, corn, charqui, flour, and cloth. Let us put aside the fact that those prices reflect only that hacienda, not others that are a few kilometers away. There is more: we shall find that the price of the same product changes, within this system of accounting, according to the individual purchaser. One *fanega* of corn will cost more if it is for a peasant than if it is for the overseer. Macera, with his usual acuity, has elucidated the phenomenon: "Within the same hacienda, in addition, various price tables might be in force, according to the rank of the worker."[71]

Let us also, though, eliminate all that complication and suppose we have the accounts of a hacienda with uniform prices for all personnel. Before we make use of it to establish curves and calculate and show trends, let us pose a question, *the* fundamental question: what prices are we talking about? The answer will be (it can be no other) the following: those prices represent the method of reimbursement of the debt contracted by the worker against the payment of his salary. Thus, in the same fashion that his "salary" (about which all the fanatics of "free labor" go into ecstasies about as an indisputable sign of "capitalism") is not one, the indicated price is not either.

Wage and *price,* in that system of accounting, are in reality the expression of that enormous phenomenon that is indebtedness. Structurally, that is to say, in regard to economic structures in colonial America, those prices and wages are something else entirely than what we understand by those words, based on economics texts of the European and North American nineteenth and twentieth centuries. By contrast, the Jesuit fathers, in addition to being excellent administrators, knew quite well what was meant. One proof of this is the fact that in an eighteenth-century document they said clearly that, with debt, "one buys his salary." In other words, wages are nothing more than the expression of a debt measured in prices and surcharged with usury.[72] Prices and wages, however, are no longer similar, but become the measure of the value of men, as if it were a matter of slaves. A concrete example can demonstrate how well founded that apparently paradoxical disclosure is. At the time of the expulsion of the Jesuits from Peru, one Father Ojeda, who had charge of the *obraje* of Pichuichuro, plans to avenge himself before his departure by forgiving the workers their debts, a way of reducing or annulling the value of the factory.[73]

Was this a uniquely Peruvian experience? It does not displease my Mexican friends (not all, of course, but a good number) who regard Peruvian history almost with a certain disdain to say, "Those things do not happen in Mexico." Mexico also offers two good examples.[74] Certainly it is unusual, but much less than one thinks, to find wages paid entirely in kind. There is also a combination form, in silver and in kind. H. Tovar Pinzón, in a very interesting article, quite justly poses the question: "If we suppose that this money was spent away from the hacienda, who depended on this 'retail economy' or this 'economy of grain and reales'?" "What role did interurban centers play where small, retail businessmen lived in the shadow of great entrepreneurial economies as suppliers for small home markets and *show windows for all this monetary circulation*?"[75] The supposition seems somewhat too bold to me, and I find it difficult to believe that those grocers (to whom I do not, by any means, deny some role) were able to monopolize "all this circulation" (which only shows the part that has not remained in the coffers of the hacienda for the payment of debts anyway) for a most evident reason, which is that one part (a good part) of this circulation must be used to pay public and religious expenses of different types.

In addition to the prices *within* the haciendas and mines, there are certainly others, *outside*. With a little black humor, one can say that the majority aboriginal population participates in the market by means of the forced distribution of goods made by the corregidor. There is merchandise, therefore there are prices. How can we say, though, that the sum that the Indians are obliged to give for their obligatory purchases is a price? Let us set aside the fact that they must buy damaged, useless merchandise (razors, for example, for a male population that has no beards) or superfluous goods (the famous case of the Indian who finds himself with thirty-two pairs of shoes). What about the prices for which they "bought" those objects? They are four, five, or ten times greater than those of the "free market."[76] One can say that the "prices of the corregidores" represent a marginal aspect. I do not believe so. At any rate, though, what is most important is that, because of them, the following situation was created: "The Indians do not have free will to supply themselves anywhere else, not even with those necessary things that the corregidores supply them, and thus they find themselves obligated to buy them from the corregidores; because these do not permit any other stores in the solely Indian villages than their own and so they have one in each village where they have to go to make their purchases."[77] Finally, one more time, what price corresponds to what measures?

A document from 1768 shows us the problem in a much clearer fashion: the corregidores (but only the corregidores?) at the time of their purchases increased the size of their measures and decreased the prices, leaving "the provincial without supplies or seed, giving them the same produce that they took from them, *reduced in amount* (my emphasis) with a greatly increased price."[78]

It is within this context, of which I have drawn some of the contours, where the market (and thus prices) must be situated in colonial America.

Must one, faced with their complexity, give up writing the history of prices in Ibero-America? I do not believe so. I think, though, that I must try to answer, for prices, as well as wages, different questions than those that are habitually posed and to which we are accustomed from the history of prices in Europe. Arcondo, Florescano, Smith, Arcila Farías, Tandeter, Wachtel, and so many others have shown the way by clearly posing the question: inverse conjuncture (in the case of Arcondo and Tandeter and Wachtel);[79] prices and agrarian crises (Florescano);[80] prices and international trade of an American product (Arcila Farías, Smith). Posing questions clearly signifies answers equally clear, or, at least, an offer of clarity, by the posing of new questions.

NOTES

This text was finished in September 1985, and thus the reader should not be surprised if certain publications after that date are not taken into consideration. It is only as a result of giving in to friendly pressure from Enrique Tandeter and Lyman L. Johnson that I have introduced into my text, already two years "old," references to the articles reproduced in this volume.

1. For an account sheet established some fifteen years ago, see E. Florescano, "La historia de los precios en la época colonial de hispanoamérica: Tendencias, métodos de trabajos y objetivos," *Latino-América: Anuario de Estudios Latinoamericanos* (1968): 111–29.

2. I have only taken into consideration the authors who have given long series of prices. I have disregarded (but I shall use them where their contributions will serve to make my argument clearer) the works of which the statistics furnished cover

only a short period. I would also like to point out that I do not propose to offer a complete bibliography of works about the history of prices in Ibero-America here.

3. W. Borah and S. F. Cook, *Price Trends of Some Basic Commodities in Central Mexico, 1530–1570* (Berkeley and Los Angeles: University of California Press, 1958), 19.

4. Borah and Cook, *Price Trends,* 22.

5. C. L. Guthrie, "Colonial Economy: Trade, Industry and Labor in Seventeenth Century Mexico City," *Revista de Historia de América* 7 (Dec. 1939): 103–34.

6. D. A. Brading, *Haciendas and Ranchos in the Mexican Bajío: León, 1710–1860* (New York: Cambridge University Press, 1978), 183.

7. E. Florescano, *Precios del maíz y crisis agrícolas en México (1708–1810)* (Mexico City: El Colegio de México, 1969), 180–81.

8. F. de M. Hurtado López, "Estudio económico," manuscript, 79.

9. S. Galicia, "Precios y producción en San Miguel el Grande, 1661–1803," manuscript.

10. C. Gibson, *The Aztecs under Spanish Rule* (Stanford: Stanford University Press, 1964), 314, 452–59.

11. It is necessary to add to the Mexican data that of R. Garner, "Problèmes de une ville minière mexicaine à la fin de l'époque coloniale: Prix et salaires à Zacatecas (1760–1821)," *Cahiers des Amériques Latines* 6 (1972). Garner's article is very interesting, but his conclusions, favoring a tendency toward increase, are vitiated by two elements. First, the extreme insufficiency of sources, scarcely fourteen years of corn prices between 1753 and 1819; and second, the fact that he never takes into consideration that, in order to establish a tendency toward increase, it is never a question of knowing there are sharp peaks, but of seeing whether, after those peaks, there is not a vertiginous fall that takes the tendency along with it.

12. C. Rabell, *Los diezmos de San Luis de La Paz* (México City: Universidad Nacional Autonoma de México, 1986): 81.

13. A. de Ramón and J. M. Larraín, *Origenes de la vida económica chilena: 1659–1808* (Santiago de Chile: Centro de Estudios Públicos, 1982), 115. M. Carmagnani, *El salariado minero en Chile colonial: Su desarrollo en sociedad provincial: El Norte Chico, 1690–1800* (Santiago de Chile: Universidad de Chile, Centro de Historia Colonial, 1963), 78, finds the following movement for flour, charqui, and maté:

Years	
1730–39	100
1750–59	112
1770–79	117
1790–99	91

For my part, I have held (in 1962) nearly the same position; compare R. Romano, *Una economía: Chile en el siglo xviii* (Buenos Aires: EUDEBA, 1965), 40–41. Why, then, did Ramón and Larraín criticize me so violently (to the point of calumny) in the preface of their book? The answer to that question will be found in R. Romano, "Precios, historia de los precios y deshonestidad intelectual," *Allpanchis* 22 (1983): 141–43.

14. See E. Tandeter and N. Wachtel in this volume of essays.

15. P. Macera and R. Boccolini, "Precios de los colegios de la Compañía de Jesús (Arequipa 1629–1767) (n.p., n.d.; duplicated). P. Macera and R. Jiménez have also prepared a compilation of prices in Lima (duplicated) between 1607 and 1738. Unfortunately, it is a question of data too dispersed to be able to make use of it. A confirmation about the decrease in corn prices in Peru at the end of the eighteenth century comes to us from L. M. Glave and M. I. Remy, "La producción de maíz en Ollantaytambo durante el siglo xviii," *Allpanchis* 14 (1980): 116.

16. H. B. Johnson, Jr., "Money and Prices in Rio de Janeiro (1760–1820)," in *L'Histoire Quantitative du Brésil de 1899 a 1939* (Paris: Editions du Centre National de la Recherche Scientifique, 1973), 47–48. Compare in the same volume the article by K. de Queirós Mattoso, "Os Preços na Bahia de 1750–1930," 167–82, in which the author takes up again, in substance, the elements of a previous article, "Conjoncture et société au Brésil à la fin du xviiiᵉ siècle," *Cahiers des Amériques Latines* 4 (1970): 33–53.

17. F. Braudel and F. C. Spooner, "Prices in Europe from 1450–1705," in *The Cambridge Economic History of Europe* (Cambridge: Cambridge University Press, 1967), 4: 470, 475.

18. Braudel and Spooner are strongly critical in this respect: "Ruggiero Romano's claim, that everything was determined by the sharp, particular crisis of 1619–20, is surprising, but not convincing." Perhaps I have not been convincing, but I do not see that there is anything surprising about my interpretation. At the time of the publication of my article in 1962, I did not have the contribution of those authors available. If I had had it in my hands, though, I would have been happy to use their graphs expressing the prices of money in money of account and that would have proved me right about "my" dates of 1619–22. This is where the problem lies. I flatly prefer prices expressed in money of account. Braudel and Spooner hesitate between the two (even if their preference goes to grams of silver or even grams of gold), and this provides for a continual ambiguity throughout their pages. Is it in the name of that ambiguity that they find my pages "surprising"? At any rate, Braudel and Spooner seem to be unaware that even if they use prices expressed in silver, it would be necessary to introduce into this conversion the important variable of *price-silver "purchasing power,"* that is, the prices in which silver intervenes after its valuation in relation to gold. It is thus, for example, that the prices of Hungarian cattle in Vienna between the sixteenth and the eighteenth centuries evolve in three different ways according to the nominal prices, the prices in silver, and the price in silver "purchasing power."

For all this, see I. N. Kiss, "Money, Prices, Values and Purchasing Power from

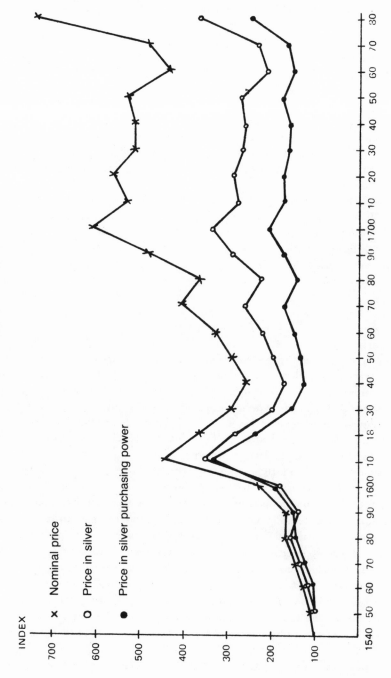

Price of Cattle in Vienna

the XVIth to the XVIIth Century," *Journal of European Economic History* 9 (1980): 459–89, from which (p. 480) I took the graph I reproduce here. In conclusion, I believe that B. A. Holderness in *Pre-Industrial England: Economy and Society, 1500–1750* (London: Totowa, Rowman, and Littlefield, 1976), 22, is completely right when he writes that "the vast analysis of Braudel and Spooner is essentially inconclusive in what is, to date, the most complete and wide-ranging survey of price and wage data for Europe after 1450. But all *modern* (my emphasis) historians are now required to consider the schedules of supply and demand for material commodities as a factor of at least equal importance to the supply of money."

This, naturally, is not to take anything away from the immense and grateful admiration that I have for Fernand Braudel (especially the Braudel of *La Mediterranée*) and from my long-time friendship with Frank C. Spooner.

19. On the other hand, believing that prices depend on the quantity of precious metals existing in the market and that *therefore* prices reveal that quantity is a very naive procedure in contrast with the one that A. von Humboldt has brought forth in "Memoire sur la production de l'or et de l'argent considerée dans se fluctuations," offprint of the *Journal des Economistes* 7:77, 78, 79 (1843), 19–20. The increase in grain prices does not express separately for a country the proportional increase of the quantity of gold and silver, any more than it gives us general information about the state of the temperature and (according to the hypothesis of a great astronomer) the number of sunspots.

20. That decrease in the population has been precisely elucidated elsewhere by W. Borah, "Population Decline and the Social and Institutional Changes of New Spain in the Middle Decades of the Sixteenth Century," *Akten des 38. Internationalen Americanisten Kongress* (Vienna, 1962), 172–78.

21. Borah and Cook, *Price Trends,* 22. This problem of the movement in prices of wheat and corn in the sixteenth century is also raised for Peru with the publication of G. Lohmann Villena, *Apuntaciones sobre el curso de los precios de los artículos de primera necesidad en Lima durante el siglo xvi* (Lima: Ediciones Solar/Hachette, 1961), which shows how the prices for a cow diminished during that same century. H. C. E. Giberti, in *Historia económica de la ganadería argentina*, gives us the prices (in pesos per unit) of cows:

	Peru	Asunción	Buenos Aires
1550	100		
1554	17		
1559	5		
1568		300(?)*	
1583		1.5	
1585			10–12
1588			8–10
1604		1.5	8.5
1660			0.5

*That price is certainly and quite probably a matter of 300 reales, that is, 37.5 pesos.

Should we speak of two movements: one (on the increase) aligned with the European movement for those grains and the other (strongly descending) for meat? I would not know how to answer. It is certain that that grand observer, B. Arzáns de Orsúa y Vela, on the great page on which he speaks to us of the fall in prices in Potosí in the middle of the 1660s, refers to llamas and cattle, lambs and hats, and knives and paper, but remains totally silent about grains. B. Arzáns de Orsúa y Vela, *Historia de la villa imperial de Potosí* (1705) (La Paz: Fundación Universitaria Patiño, 1945), 392. Nevertheless, Arzáns himself, on page 25, makes the following judgment regarding wheat: "In the space of twenty years after its [Potosí's] foundation, the fanega was worth forty pesos of nine reales and, from then on for the space of twenty years, twenty pesos." Otherwise, how can one explain that "the decade of the 40s [in the sixteenth century] situates us at the time when Spanish wheat ceases to be exportable to Mexico"? See P. Chaunu, *Seville et l'Atlantique* (Paris: S.E.V.P.E.N., 1959), 8, pt. 1: 815. The problem remains open.

22. See the fine book of M. de Carcer y Disdier, *Apuntes para la historia de la transculturación indoespañola* (Mexico City: Instituto de Historia, 1953).

23. I would like to express my reservations here about Borah and Cook's book that are also applicable to other works

a) No one has the right to mix prices that come from different sources (or places), above all when those data are scarce. The argument obviously changes if the data are *very* scarce;

b) One has even less right to apply very forced statistical treatments to those poor (in every sense) statistics;

c) One does not have the right to mix the prices of products that seem to resemble each other and that are different in reality. "Trigo" seems clear. As the *Diccionario de la Real Academia* brings to mind, though, "There are many species and among them, innumerable varieties": from "summer wheat," to "hard wheat," in addition to "common wheat." Different prices correspond to each variety. If one makes use of a price for year "A" of ten reales for "common wheat" and for the following year twelve reales for "summer wheat," one obtains an increase of 20 percent. Long live cyclic movement!

d) One has the duty to verify what measure is being spoken of in the documents with which one is working. A fanega seems to be clear as possible. That, however, is false. Here are two examples: "The fanega varied here [in Santiago de Chile] not only with regard to the fanega in Spain, *but also in neighboring areas*" (my emphasis), as M. de Sales tells us; "Representación al Ministerio de la Hacienda (1796)" in M. Cruchaga, *Estudio sobre la organización económica y la hacienda pública de Chile* (Madrid: Editorial Rens, 1929), 3: 171. Macera points out to us that the fanega is worth 160 livres in Huacho, 156 livres in the valleys along the coast, and 250 livres in Pativilca. Thus, it suffices that a friary purchases a (larger) fanega once in a "neighboring area" and a (smaller) fanega, once in the principal town and that the two prices are recorded in the latter for there to be a difference in prices;

e) Is it necessary, after all, to recall that in the same account book one can find, for one year, the prices of wheat sold, and for the following year, the prices of wheat purchased? It is not the same thing.

I know that it is not possible to respect all these conditions. At least, though, the constraints I have just indicated must be present if one does not wish to become terribly confused.

24. Florescano, *Precios*, 180.

25. F. Ouellet and J. Hamelin, *Le mouvement des prix agricoles dans la province de Quebec (1760–1851)* (N.p., n.d.; duplicated), 7. See, though, their "La crise agricole dans le Bas-Canada (1802–1837)," *Etudes Rurales* 7 (1962): 36–57.

26. Ouellet and Hamelin, "La crise," 48–49.

27. See Florescano, *Precios*, 180–81. One fact should be emphasized. From 1721 to 1792, all movements of increase were inverted by an abysmal drop in prices. And these are vertiginous falls, that absence of progression in minimum prices, those inequalities between the peaks and the depressions, the ones that establish the fundamental difference between the Mexican curve and the European curves. Only in the last twenty years of the series is the increase continuous, without extreme drops, and similar to the European movement. Florescano's consideration seems *fundamental* to me because it teaches that one must not trust in appearances. It is not sufficient for a curve to show peaks for one to be able to speak of an increase. Elsewhere, C. Morín comes to some conclusions for northwest Mexico that are similar to those of Florescano; C. Morin, *Michoacán en la Nueva España del siglo xviii* (Mexico City: Fondo de Cultura Económica, 1979).

28. A. Bezanson, R. Gray, and M. Hussey, *Wholesale Prices in Philadelphia, 1784–1861* (Philadelphia: University of Pennsylvania Press, 1935). See also W. Sachs, "Agricultural Conditions in the Northern Colonies before the Revolution," *Journal of Economic History* 13 (1953): 274–90.

29. For those cities as a whole, compare A. Cole, *Wholesale Commodity Prices in the United States, 1700–1861* (Cambridge, Mass.: Harvard University Press, 1938). See also A. Cole, "American Research in Price History," in *Studies in Economics and Industrial Relations* (Philadelphia: University of Pennsylvania Press, 1941), 97–98.

30. Cole, *Wholesale*, graph between pages 106 and 107.

31. The position of colonial America in the great "crisis" of the seventeenth century has not truly been studied. All that has been said about the subject (including what I have said) should be seriously reviewed and corrected. As for my part, I shall do so shortly.

32. I do not take the sixteenth century into consideration because the instability of the available data does not permit comparisons. In his great book, B. Slicher von Bath has established an interesting comparison between the prices of various products in 1574 and 1628, when it appears, *in general*, that there was a decrease. This was a divergence, to be sure, but prudence must be the watchword. B. Slicher von Bath, *Spaens Amerika omstreeks 1600* (Utrecht: Spectrum, 1979), 161.

33. This said, I find very interesting the attempt made by K. Brown in his study about prices in Arequipa in this volume in calculating the value of goods of basic necessity of a "hypothetical" Spanish and/or mestizo family. The totals one can see in Tables 4 and 5 greatly strengthen my ideas about a counterconjuncture of American prices in comparison with European prices. This interests me very little, however. I find that the method established by Brown merits our reflection (perhaps in combination with the one by the greatly missed W. Achilles, "Getreidepreise und Getreidehandel sbeziehungen europäisher Räume im 16. und 17. Jahrhundert," in *Zeitschift für Agrargeschicte und Agrarsoziologie,* 7 (1959), of which the lesson has, unfortunately, been lost.

34. Ramón and Larraín, *Orígenes,* 330.

35. Queirós Mattoso, "Os preços," 179.

36. A. B. Arcondo, "Los precios en una economía en transición: Córdoba durante el siglo xviii," offprint from the *Revista de Economía y Estadística de la Universidad de Córdoba* 15 (1971): 7–32. That article is from his thesis (E.P.H.E.—Section 6, Paris): "Córdoba: Une Ville Coloniale. Etudes des Prix au xviiie siècle," Paris, 1968.

37. Ramón and Larraín, *Orígenes,* 410–11.

38. See, in Slicher von Bath's *Spaens Americka,* 144, the beautiful chart that shows the regional traffic in cereals in Spanish America between the end of the sixteenth and the beginning of the seventeenth century. Naturally, all this must not make one forget that a good part, in fact, the greater part, of transactions were made by barter. Above all, one must never forget that in America, as in Europe, for the centuries in question the role of private, home consumption is predominant.

39. I realize there are exceptions: Chilean wheat exported to Peru and Paraguayan maté exported to Peru.

40. Regarding the growth in imports of those products in England during the eighteenth century, see E. Schumpeter, *English Overseas Trade Statistics, 1697–1808* (Oxford: Clarendon Press, 1960), passim.

41. See M. Wortman, *Government and Society in Central America, 1680–1840* (New York: Columbia University Press, 1982), 188. See also A. von Humboldt, *Essai Politique sur le Royaume de la Nouvelle Espagne* (Paris, F. Schell, 1811–12), 3: 55.

42. See M. Sánchez, *Historia del añil o xiquilite en Centro América* (San Salvador: 1976), 1: 319, 359–60; and R. Smith, "Indigo Production and Trade in Colonial Guatemala," *Hispanic American Historical Review* 39 (1959): 201–202. See also T. Floyd, "The Indigo Merchant: Promoter of Central America Economic Development, 1750–1808," *Business History Review* 39 (1965): 498.

43. N. Posthumus, *Neederlandsche Prijsgeschiedenis* (Leiden: E.J. Brill, 1943), 1: 415–18.

44. E. Arcila Farías, *Comercio entre Venezuela y México en los siglos xvii y xviii* (Mexico City: El Colegio de México, 1950), 135. Prices are in reales per pound. I have calculated the five-year average, taking the lowest prices into consideration.

45. Posthumus, *Neederlandsche*, 195–96. Prices are in guldens per pound.

46. The reference to the names of Beveridge, Abel, Elsas, Pribram, and Hamilton is obligatory. For a nearly complete bibliography up to 1967, see R. Romano, ed., *I Prezzi in Europa del xiii secolo a oggi* (Torino: G. Einaudi, 1967), 569–90.

47. In addition to the book cited in note 43, see E. Arcila Farías, *Economía colonial de Venezuela* (México City: Fondo de Cultura Económica, 1946).

48. R. Hussey, *The Caracas Company, 1728–1784* (Cambridge, Mass.: Harvard University Press, 1934).

49. S. Schwartz, "Free Labor in a Slave Economy: The Lavradores de Cana of Colonial Bahia," in D. Alden, ed., *Colonial Roots of Modern Brazil* (Berkeley: University of California Press, 1973), 194.

50. H. Johnson, Jr., "A Preliminary Inquiry into Money, Prices and Wages in Rio de Janeiro, 1763–1823," in Alden, ed., *Colonial Roots*, 272–73.

51. W. Pinho, *História de um Engenho do Recôncavo Matoim-Novo Caboto-Fregnezia, 1552–1944* (Rio de Janeiro: Z. Valverde, 1946), 253. I thank my friend Frederic Mauro, who pointed this book out to me.

52. I have the greater fear that I do not understand how the prices of brandy show a movement so different from those of sugar. See also the prices of "cane brandy" in Johnson, "Preliminary Inquiry," 272–73.

53. Posthumus, *Neederlandsche*, 122–23.

54. I point out here the interesting parallel between, on the one hand, the prices of sugar in St. Vincent and Tobago and, on the other, in London. S. Carrington, "'Econocide'—Myth or Reality? The Question of West Indian Decline, 1783–1806," *Boletín de Estudios Latinoamericanos y del Caribe* 36 (June 1984), 33–34.

55. A dazzling confirmation of what I have just said is found in the very fine study by H. Roessing, where the problem of tobacco in the Amsterdam market is seen in terms of its multiple geographic components. H. Roessing, "Inlandes Tabak," *Afdeling Agrarische Geschiedenis* 20 (1976): 1–594.

I take this opportunity to indicate that the book by my greatly missed friend N. Posthumus, *Neederlandische*, cited above, constitutes an exceptional source for a comparative study of the prices of products with different origins because of the attention the author has given not only to the qualities, but also to the geographic origins of the different products.

56. See N. Cushner, *Lords of the Land: Sugar, Wine and Jesuit Estates of Coastal Peru, 1600–1767* (Albany: State University of New York Press, 1980), 122. Also see S. Ramírez, *Provincial Patriarchs: Land Tenure and the Economics of Power in Colonial Peru* (Albuquerque: University of New Mexico Press, 1986), and, by the same author, "The Sugar Estates of the Lambayeque Valley," research paper, University of Wisconsin, 1979.

57. Ramón and Larraín, *Orígenes*, 160.

58. Compare Appendix 1 in E. Hamilton, *War and Prices in Spain, 1651–1800* (Cambridge, Mass.: Harvard University Press, 1947), 233–257.

59. See Tandeter and Wachtel in this volume. For the growth of the price of paper, see, for example, B. Vicuña MacKenna, *Historia de Valparaíso* (Santiago de Chile: Universidad de Chile, 1936), 2: 323.

60. Compare R. Romano, "Storia dei prezzi e storia della moneta," *Revista Storica Italiana* 75 (1963): 238–68.

61. M. Morineau, *Incroyables gazettes et fabuleux métaux* (Paris: Maison des Sciences de l'homme, 1985). The first outcry had been given by Morineau in 1969.

62. One must not forget, in fact, that during the eighteenth century, not only do the mines in America increase their production considerably, but Brazil also enters its "golden age."

63. N. Sánchez Albornoz, *La población de América desde los tiempos precolombinos al año 2000* (Madrid: Alianza Editorial, 1977), 125.

64. J. de los Iriberri, "Segunda memoria leída por el Secretario Don . . . ," published by M. Cruchaga, *Estudio* (Madrid: Editorial Reus, 1928–29), 3: 244.

65. F. Quesnay, "Maximes génerales du gouvernement economique d'un royaume agricole" (1706), in L. Salleron, *François Quesnay et la Physiocratie* (Paris, 1958).

66. Ramón and Larraín, *Orígenes, 332.*

67. Inversely, the prices of American products (cacao, sugar, dyes, and so forth) will be able to decrease in the European markets because their arrivals during the eighteenth always oblige the merchants to reduce their profit margins greatly.

68. A. Jara says in a note, "'Discovering' America, one of them [a member of the *Annales* group] arrived at our archives, with fabulous schema and European fashions. He had to follow and cultivate certain panaceas that, although they were not so new, still seemed attractive. The story goes back to 1956. It was necessary, at whatever cost, to write the history of prices. It permitted the auscultation of it all, as if Chile, Peru, or Mexico in the eighteenth century had been carrying out the British Industrial Revolution." I am the unnamed person. I had been invited to the University of Santiago de Chile by Mario Góngora to give a class there on the history of prices and about the history of money, population, and so forth in *Europe.* I spoke about this. If A. Jara misunderstood, it is not my responsibility at all. I shall not make use of any testimony (although it exists from M. Carmagnani to P. Cunill—still quite young—who kindly listened to my seminars), because during all my thirty-eight years of university teaching and in all my writings, I am always beaten, and even with fierce polemics, for "relativizing" concepts, problems, and methods according to temporal and spacial situations.

69. See M. de Salas, 1791:171. With regard to this problem of averages, apropos of Latin America I would have to reach results similar to those W. Kula reached magnificently (1970, Span. trans., 1980). But see the pioneering work of M. Mörner and F. Martínez, "Medidas como precios y como instrumentos para la explotación," *Aelpanchis* (Cuzco) No. 15 (1980): 133–50.

70. Garavaglia, *Mercado interno*, 481.

71. P. Macera, *Mapas coloniales de haciendas cuzqueñas* (Lima, 1968): lxxx–lxxxi.

72. This concept is presented by C. Hill, ed., *Saggi sulla Rivoluzione Inglese del 1640* (Milan, Feltrinelli 1957): 37.

73. Macera, *Mapas coloniales*, cxi.

74. See the beautiful pages of C. Morin, *Michoacán en la Nueva España del siglo xviii* (México: Fondo de Cultura Económica, 1979): 214ff. I would like to underscore here that in Mexico, another custom was added to the practice of the company store and the indebtedness of the worker. If the peon by chance did not go into debt, the hacienda—by being behind in the payment of wages—was in debt to the peon. See the beautiful article by H. Tovar Pinzón, "Elementos constitutivos de la empresa agraria jesuita en la segunda mitad del siglo xviii en México," in E. Florescano (ed.), *Haciendas, latifundias, y plantaciones en América latina* (México: Siglo XXI, 1975): 176–77.

75. Tovar Pinzón, "Elementos," 173.

76. For all, see J. Juan and A. de Ulloa, *Noticias secretas de América* (Buenos Aires: Mar Océano, 1953), 181–207.

77. Juan and Ulloa, *Noticias*, 190.

78. See "Representación de la Ciudad del Cuzco, en el año de 1768, sobre excesos de Corregidores y Curas," in *Colección Documental de la Independencia del Perú*, vol. 2: *La Rebelión de Tupac Amaru* (Lima: Edición de Carlos Daniel Valcarcel 1971–), 12.

79. About that problem, see also the important article of B. Slicher von Bath, "Feudalismo y capitalismo en América Latina," *Boletín de Estudios Latinoamericanos y del Caribe* 17 (1974), passim and 38–41, in particular.

80. Florescano's seems to me to be a good example, both positively and negatively. Two essential questions are posed in it. One, clearly, is about the relationship between prices and harvests, and the answer is clear. Another, somewhat unclear at the beginning, is about the fluctuations of prices and of the climate. The answer has never seemed clear to me and, with time, seems more and more confused.

4

PRICES AND WAGES IN EIGHTEENTH-CENTURY MEXICO

Richard L. Garner

INFLATION WAS ON THE MINDS OF THE RESPONDENTS TO AN ECONOMIC survey conducted by Mexico City's Consulado (Merchants' Guild) in 1805 or 1806. Although more impressionistic than statistical, it portrayed the economy of the capital as caught in the grips of prices rising more rapidly than incomes. Without knowing exactly what caused the inflation or how to remedy it, the respondents were not reluctant to express their fears that if these pressures remained, economic growth, public security, and their own personal well-being were in jeopardy.[1] Recent studies of prices and related economic topics have reached a similar conclusion that inflation had grown worse during the quarter-century before the Hidalgo Rebellion and may have contributed to the rising discontent in society at large.[2]

The Consulado's survey raises interesting questions, among the most important and most obvious being how serious the inflation was that the survey detected compared to earlier periods of eighteenth-century Mexico. The survey does not present any precise figures on how fast or long prices had been rising, but what the survey did not do can now be done. Whether Mexico City's economy or the colony-wide economy was then caught in an inflationary spiral, as the survey indicates, can be tested and analyzed through the use of several different price series for maize, wheat, and other commodities.

That the economy had a disposition toward inflation during the late colonial period has enjoyed some currency in the historical literature of the past several decades. Some scholars have put forward the thesis that because of far-reaching changes, some arising naturally from within the society and some being imposed from without, inflation was a predictable result. From within, demographic and economic growth in the range of 1 to 2 percent per year set the stage for inflation.[3] The growth in population meant more people had to be fed, clothed, housed, and employed, but an improving

73

economy meant a greater capacity to meet these most basic needs. Some price inflation could be expected simply as a result of growth in demand, but the key consideration was how effectively that demand was being satisfied. Inflation would be a greater hardship if prices rose appreciably faster than the growth in the population or the economy, and it would be less so if they moved more slowly than or at about the same rate as the other two variables. Over the long term of the eighteenth century, inflation may have been moderate and manageable in part because of increasing supplies and in part because of lagging wages. More is known about what was happening to supplies than to wages. Numerous eighteenth-century studies on mining, agriculture, and even manufacturing point up how businessmen modified their strategies and practices to increase their output in order to take advantage of a demand curve that was rising and also changing. As they plowed more and more of their profits back into their businesses, they laid the foundation for growth in the colony's productive capacity.[4] In the short run, however, including the quarter-century before the Hidalgo Revolt, the relative harmony between supply and demand could be severely tested and temporarily shattered. The relationship between what the colony needed or wanted and what it could provide proved to be fragile at best.

Mexico, although the largest and richest colony in the Spanish empire, was not the master of its own economic destiny, and that had an impact on its domestic economy. Above all, Mexico had the most productive silver mines in the New World. The steady growth in output of silver served two purposes: it added to the capital pool for the colony's internal development, but it also paid for expensive imports, imperial taxes, and other financial obligations. At the same time that the economy was expanding, the cost of defending and administering the empire was mounting, and Mexico more than any other Spanish colony could afford to underwrite these higher expenses. These complex relationships are not yet fully understood, but enough is known to suggest that Mexico's inflationary woes, however they may be described, worsened in response to the continuing and growing diversion of capital from its own internal economy toward the imperial system. Since the sixteenth century, Mexico, like other New World colonies, had served Spain's mercantilistic goals—supplier of precious metal and importer of high-tax, high-cost goods—but in the eighteenth century, it came to occupy an enhanced role in the plan to revitalize the empire. A growing, prospering economy helped, but it was not enough, and the crown turned to a more aggressive and confiscatory policy to fill its coffers. As more and more money was drawn into the imperial system, less and less was available for the domestic economy.

The interrelationship between an expanding economy (even if simply to satisfy the demand from growth in population) and a government bent on collecting more money primarily to be exported remains unexplored. It is possible, as John Coatsworth has recently argued, that by the 1780s, the colony was facing for the first time in more than a century a permanent condition of "real scarcity." He postulates that the late colonial inflation resulted from too little being produced in Mexico's domestic economy combined with a rise in world-market prices that made some of Mexico's imports more expensive. In his view, it was not an inflation that resulted from a growth in the money supply, although given the high silver output of the late eighteenth century a monetary inflation was possible. What argued against a monetary-inflation explanation was the policy of the government to appropriate more and more of the colony's wealth. Such a policy could contribute to the "real scarcity" by literally starving those industries (silver mines, commercial haciendas, and monocultural plantations) of the financing that they needed to improve or to expand their operations.[5] In modern theory, government may intervene to slow or control inflation by reducing purchasing power. In eighteenth-century Mexico that was not the rationale for intervention; rather it was a strategy to provide the government with more to spend, a policy for fanning rather than containing the flame of inflation.

Price data are far more readily available than wage data for eighteenth-century Mexico. What has interested students of prices most is the volatile and cyclical character of prices, especially grain prices. The agricultural system tended to swing between bountiful and scant harvests with one or two major famines and several minor famines in each quarter-century, although it exhibited variations in rhythm and intensity from region to region.[6] My emphasis on trends instead of cycles is not designed to discount or discredit the importance of cycles in the agricultural system, for the empirical evidence of their existence and recurrence is quite convincing. The aim herein is to examine the behavior of the secular trend that cuts through the numerous cycles during the eighteenth century and measure price inflation along the trend line. What emerges from this inquiry is that over the long term, maize prices in particular and commodity prices in general edged ever higher with each successive cycle that might contain within it a steep drop in prices before they began to climb again. This suggests that while there were times when harvests were abundant and prices were low, usually in the aftermath of famines and epidemics, the resumption of normal economic and demographic growth exerted greater pressure on supplies with attendant rises in prices. This is evident in two cases, between the famines of 1714 and 1750 and the famines of 1750 and 1786. It may also have occurred before 1714. After 1786 the experience was different. If prices declined at all, the slide was, by eighteenth-century standards, slight and brief. In this connection, I would point out that with one or two possible exceptions downward trends to match the upward trends in prices over time, say, periods of five, ten, twenty-five, or fifty years within the secular trend, do not exist. In 1806, when the Consulado survey was made, maize prices were high, but not as high as they had been twenty years earlier during the famines of the 1780s. What the respondents may not have realized is that the famines and epidemics of the 1780s brought little respite from high prices, as had occurred after earlier crises. Prices had risen sharply and steadily during the late third and early fourth quarters, and they were stuck at higher than usual levels during the late fourth quarter of the eighteenth century and the first decade of the nineteenth century.

The other side of the inflation equation is wage and salary levels. Escalating wages and salaries can be a major cause of inflation, while wages and salaries that climb slowly, remain stagnant, or perhaps even decline can act as a check on inflation. Unfortunately, no wage or salary series to match the price series has been constructed yet, and given the paucity of documentation, such a series may never be constructed. Data exist for certain occupations such as farm workers, mine employees, public officials, and urban laborers, but they are severely limited with respect to time and place. When data can be compared over time within the same region or between regions, they reinforce the general impression that wages and salaries changed very little during the eighteenth century. Wages and salaries were not absolutely static, because they could rise or fall temporarily in accord with short-term imbalances between supply and demand for labor in certain occupational categories. Over the long term, however, the demand for labor did not so exceed the supply as to cause wages and salaries to rise permanently. A possible explanation for the moderate inflation in eighteenth-century Mexico is the extent to which wages and salaries lagged behind prices.

Studies of prices and wages based on historical statistics must assume that the data reflect actual market transactions, that is, what was paid for a product or a job reflected what it was held to be worth. This is an assumption, of course, that some find hard to accept, because the system devised for determining the worth of any transaction was so primitive and unreliable in eighteenth-century Mexico. The fact is, though, that however inadequate the system may be it did exist and presumably work. Since we are working with accounts from various sources and in different formats, we cannot be sure that bookkeepers and accountants were always in agreement as to how to record a transaction. In most entries, the transactions were recorded in pesos, even though little or no money (because it was so scarce) ever exchanged hands. As of now, we can only estimate what amount of currency was in circulation during the eighteenth century. It is possible that the amount was shrinking rather than expanding to match the demographic and economic growth. In the last quarter of the eighteenth century, currency in circulation may have fallen from 36 million pesos to 31 million pesos between 1771 and 1791. This, in Claude Morin's view, represents a paradox: the higher the output of silver, the fewer the coins in circulation in the economy. The reason is that more and more money was being exported.[7] In a population that had grown from 4 million to 6 million, such a contraction meant that the currency in circulation had declined from 9 pesos per capita to 5.2 pesos. In the absence of an adequate currency other ways had to be found to transact business. Individuals bartered grains, businessmen exchanged *libranzas* (transferable vouchers), and employers paid workers in goods instead of coins. However these transactions were carried out, the accounts, if maintained at all, were kept in pesos and reales, even though few such coins ever passed between buyer and seller or employer and employee. Such a system invited fraud and abuse. Workers were the least able to protect themselves, it has been argued, because they had to accept or buy goods at prices set by their employers instead of the marketplace. The owners could realize substantial savings by setting the prices of goods (sold to workers or used in lieu of wages) higher than the actual value of the merchandise.[8] On the other hand, businessmen tried to protect themselves by discounting any paper that they had to accept (in effect asking the person who tendered the paper to pay more than the value stated on the voucher). Whatever the defects in the accounts and ledgers that have survived, the documents themselves are not fabrications. They no doubt contain errors and mistakes, but they also reflect actual transactions both in cash and in kind. In an economy in which payment-in-kind remained an important function, knowledge of costs for goods and services was essential to success in business.[9]

A colony-wide, maize price series, which I have assembled from various regional and local maize data, will be the primary source for my analysis of the movement of eighteenth-century prices.[10] Table 4.1 shows the averaged colony-wide maize prices and the averaged maize prices for the Bajío. In addition, an index number based on the average price for the colony between

Table 4.1

Colony-Wide Average Maize Prices
1700–1819
reales per fanega

Year	Colony-Wide Average	Index Number	Bajío Average	Index Number
1700	9.2	70		
1701	12.3	93		
1702	6.4	49		
1703	7.6	58		
1704	8.0	61		
1705	5.0	38		
1706	4.7	36		
1707	5.9	45		
1708	12.4	94		
1709	15.0	114		
1710	22.1	167		
1711	11.5	87		
1712	16.0	121		
1713	24.0	182		
1714	21.3	161		
1715	4.3	33		
1716	2.5	19		
1717	2.1	16		
1718	7.9	60		
1719	12.0	91		
1721	9.0	68		
1722	12.0	91		
1723	12.0	91		
1724	8.0	61		
1725	7.3	55		
1726	9.1	69		
1727	13.5	102		
1728	8.3	63		
1729	7.3	53		

Table 4.1 (continued)

Year	Colony-Wide Average	Index Number	Bajío Average	Index Number
1730	11.7	89		
1731	10.0	76		
1732	9.5	72		
1733	7.0	53		
1734	9.9	75		
1735	9.8	74		
1736	8.0	61		
1737	8.2	62		
1738	10.2	77		
1739	11.7	89		
1740	13.0	99		
1741	14.8	112		
1742	15.3	116		
1743	7.2	55	6.0	58
1744	6.3	48	5.0	49
1745	6.8	52	5.7	55
1746	11.6	88	10.5	102
1747	13.2	100	12.5	121
1748	9.4	71	6.6	64
1749	16.4	124	14.0	136
1750	31.2	237	32.9	320
1751	14.0	106	15.8	153
1752	4.0	30	4.0	39
1753	6.0	46	2.6	26
1754	4.4	33	3.6	35
1755	9.1	69	5.6	54
1756	9.5	72	7.8	76
1757	5.0	38	4.3	42
1758	7.1	54	4.9	48
1759	8.4	64	5.5	53
1760	10.4	79	8.7	85
1761	11.1	84	11.5	112

Table 4.1 (continued)

Year	Colony-Wide Average	Index Number	Bajío Average	Index Number
1762	11.0	84	11.5	112
1763	5.8	44	3.7	34
1764	8.4	64	4.7	46
1765	7.8	59	6.0	58
1766	8.4	64	7.3	71
1767	6.7	51	3.3	32
1768	6.5	49	4.3	42
1769	7.5	57	5.4	52
1770	11.3	86	1.1	98
1771	12.0	91	12.1	118
1772	17.3	131	16.1	156
1773	13.8	105	13.1	127
1774	14.0	106	13.3	129
1775	8.8	67	5.8	56
1776	12.5	95	11.5	112
1777	9.1	69	9.0	87
1778	9.0	68	9.3	90
1779	10.5	80	10.6	103
1780	13.3	101	12.3	119
1781	14.2	108	11.3	110
1782	11.8	89	6.2	60
1783	7.3	55	4.7	46
1784	10.9	83	11.0	107
1785	20.1	152	18.6	181
1786	42.0	318	44.0	427
1787	21.5	163	18.4	179
1788	15.7	119	16.1	156
1789	23.3	177	22.9	222
1790	17.8	135		
1791	15.5	118		
1792	10.2	77	6.8	66
1793	12.5	95	8.5	83

Table 4.1 (continued)

Year	Colony-Wide Average	Index Number	Bajío Average	Index Number
1794	19.9	151	11.7	114
1795	12.4	94	7.5	73
1796	12.8	97		
1797	17.9	136	10.0	97
1798	17.9	136	7.6	74
1799	16.6	126	9.0	87
1800	19.3	146		
1801	17.1	130		
1802	21.3	162		
1803	21.6	164		
1804	14.3	108		
1805	15.4	117		
1806	16.3	124		
1807	17.5	133		
1808	24.0	182		
1809	22.6	171		
1810	38.3	290		
1811	42.0	318		
1812	23.1	175		
1813	30.1	228		
1814	26.5	201		
1815	24.0	182		
1817	57.3	434		
1819	26.1	198		

Colony-wide series: 100 = average price of 13 pesos 2 reales
Bajío series: 100 = 10 pesos 3 reales

1700 and 1819 and for the Bajío between 1742 and 1799 has been calculated for each series. In Graphs 4.1 and 4.2 (prices in logarithms), I have plotted the two series with their pertinent trends. I have constructed a separate Bajío series because of the region's economic importance as well as the richness of its price data. While maize prices for the colony as a whole and for the Bajío could be volatile and irregular in their movement, they nonetheless followed a definite rising curve during the eighteenth century. It is that upward trend rather than the volatility or irregularity of maize prices that is this essay's chief focus.

For the colony-wide maize series from 1700 through 1819, the average price was 13.7 reales per fanega and during the nearly 120 years the price of maize increased by 0.9 percent each year.[11] There is a question whether the data for the independence period (1810–21) should be included in a general discussion of the eighteenth-century price trends because of the disruptive effect of the insurgency movement on the economic system and how that might influence the late colonial trends. As this is not the place to discuss the insurgency movement and its impact, I have chosen to exclude that decade from this discussion and to terminate the series at 1809. Thus, the average price between 1700 and 1809 was slightly lower at 12.2 reales per fanega and the growth was 0.7 percent per year. An annual increase of less than 1 percent may be viewed as moderate inflation. At that rate, a century would have to pass before the price of maize would double.[12] If maize prices for 1700 (9.2 reales per fanega) and 1800 (19.3 reales per fanega) are compared, we find that the cost of maize had just more than doubled. Of course, maize prices did not rise in regular steps of 0.7 percent every year for nearly 120 years. Instead they followed a much more erratic course from year to year; in some years they changed sharply, in other years less so, and in still other years not at all. In brief, the long-term rate serves as a benchmark by which to evaluate the behavior of the maize curve.

I have divided the eighteenth-century curve into four periods: 1700–14, 1715–50, 1751–86, and 1787–1809. The rationale for these divisions is that maize went from a low to a high price after which (normally because of famines and epidemics) the cost of maize tumbled. It is necessary to point out that during the period from 1700 to 1809, maize prices did not experience any sustained declines to counterbalance the sustained rises. Prices fell and often fell sharply after famines and epidemics, but never for very long before they started up again. The cumulative effect of this was that without any sustained declines maize prices tended to inch higher and higher over the course of the century.

Graph 4.1

Mexico Maize Price Trends, 1700–1809

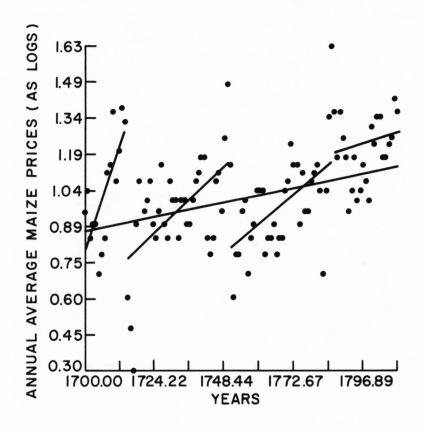

Slope of the line (regression coefficient as log):
1700–1809 = 0.003035; 1700–1714 = 0.034652; 1715–1750 = 0.011002;
1751–1786 = 0.010815; 1787–1809 = 0.003524.
Rate of growth (% per annum): 1700–1809 = 0.7; 1700–1714 = 8.3;
1715–1750 = 2.6; 1751–1786 = 2.5; 1787–1809 = 0.8.
R-squared (with four dummy variables, 1700–1714/1715–1750/
1751–1786/1787–1809) = .45.

Graph 4.2

Leon-Silao-Hidalgo-Michoacan
Maize Price Trends, 1744–1799

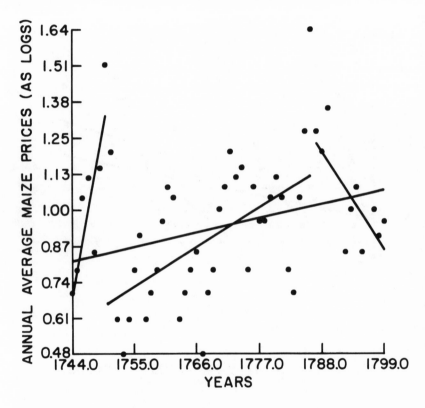

Slope of the line (regression coefficient as log):
1744–1799 = 0.004732; 1744–1750 = 0.107419; 1751–1786 = 0.012972;
1787–1799 = − 0.031462. Rate of growth (% per annum): 1744–
1799 = 1.1; 1744–1750 = 28.1;
1751–1786 = 3.0; 1787–1799 = − 6.9. R-squared (with three dummy
variables, 1744–1750/1751–1786/
1787–1799) = .33.

The first period is the least satisfactory for purposes of analysis, because the data, especially for the crucial years from 1710 to 1714 when the price of maize peaked, are so scant. We know from other sources that from 1710 to 1714 agricultural crises rocked the Valley of Mexico's economy, but we have very few actual data for there or anywhere else. If additional data are found for the valley or other regions, the trend lines and growth rates may have to be revised.[13] The final period (1787–1810) poses similar analytical problems, because some of the regional and local price data from which the colony-wide maize series has been constructed are lacking. Unlike the first period, however, maize prices appear to be reacting to a combination of factors: unpredictable weather, lack of inexpensive and suitably located land for crop cultivation, and urban growth.

The second and third periods constitute the strongest part of the colony-wide maize series. They are also of equal length, thirty-five years. The famine of 1750 (beginning with a poor maize harvest in 1749) was bad enough to drive up the price of maize to 32 reales per fanega. This famine lasted, for the most part, for a single year. In 1751, the colony-wide price dropped to 14 reales per fanega. In the previous three decades before 1750, maize prices had swung from lows of 6 to 7 to highs of 15 to 16 reales per fanega. In the 1720s and for the first half of the next decade, the price of maize remained around 9 reales per fanega. Epidemics in the late 1730s led to some shortages that caused prices to rise to 11 to 12 reales per fanega. Maize consumers benefitted from larger harvests and lower prices during the middle 1740s (the lowest in a decade), but then they had to adjust rather quickly to a near doubling of maize prices in the late 1740s. What may be missed in these maize price fluctuations is that consumers were paying more for maize on average in the 1740s than in the 1730s. This low price of the 1730s may have forced producers to cut back on plantings in order to raise prices, and that, combined with continuing population growth, eventually forced up prices as demand exceeded supply. In retrospect, the warnings of an impending crisis may be noted in the fairly wide range of maize prices in the decade before the 1750 famine. Still, the famine of 1750, which remains to be studied, provided some relief, for in the following decade maize prices fell to and remained at their lowest level in a half-century.

In the next interfamine period (1751–86) two patterns can be observed: low prices during most of the 1750s and 1760s probably led producers to cut back their production of maize, and rising prices during the 1770s into the 1780s probably resulted from worsening imbalance between supply and demand, in part the result of earlier reductions in maize plantings. When the next agricultural calamity struck, it was one of the worst in the history of the colony. Although the colony-wide maize price reached a record high of 42.0 reales per fanega in 1786, the crisis actually persisted three to four years. In Zacatecas, for example, town officials were still trying to find enough maize to feed the city as late as 1789. A caravan was dispatched to Aguas-calientes to buy maize at whatever the market price (in the midtwenties) in order to replenish the local supplies.[14] For the remainder of the colonial period, maize would be a scarcer and therefore a more highly priced grain that it had hitherto been. No doubt maize prices had fallen during the late 1780s and early 1790s as the famine's death toll had tempered demand, but they did not fall as far or remain as low as they had after earlier famines.

Like all such agricultural crises and natural disasters, the impact was uneven and selective, as some regions suffered more than others. Were the 1780 famines severe enough to invoke the Malthusian formula that the decrease in population would allow a period of recovery in agriculture? The behavior of the colony-wide maize prices suggest that while some adjustment occurred, it was not as far-reaching as some death-toll estimates might suggest that it should be.[15] What the index numbers for the colony-wide maize series indicate is a drop of more than 75 percent in the price after 1750 compared to a drop of more than 50 percent after 1786. Care must be exercised in interpreting these figures, however. Most of the data in the price series are based on transactions at Mexico City's granary, and these higher than usual prices may be a reflection of urban rather than rural developments. A steady flow of people into the viceregal capital, as the survey by the Consulado had highlighted, may have both pushed up prices more quickly after the recent crises than was the case elsewhere. In any event, the behavior of maize prices after the 1790s is different from their behavior after earlier famines.[16]

It is important to underscore again that the periods identified in the secular trend are intended to show how maize prices behaved between major agricultural crises. In general, what that behavior reveals is that despite times (some as long as a decade) of low prices, the pressures on supplies, whatever the reason, would eventually lead to higher maize prices. Those pressures may have become more frequent and intense in the second half of the eighteenth century than in the first half. The rise in the first half was less than 1 percent but in the second half was more than 2 percent.[17] In the four periods identified earlier, the growth rates were: 8.3 percent from 1700–14, 2.6 percent from 1715–50, 2.5 percent from 1751–86 and 0.8 percent (with only a 74 percent probability) from 1787–1809. These rates indicate that maize prices rose very sharply during the first period, moderately (by comparison at least) in the second and third periods, and just barely in fourth period. Of greater significance, perhaps, is the fact that prices tumbled after the agricultural crises of the first two periods so that prices began to climb from fairly low levels. This was much less the case between the third and fourth periods and may partially explain why the first half recorded slower growth than the second half. By the end of the century, the upward force on maize prices could not be entirely overcome by several minor shortages and at least one major one.

Trend lines and growth rates may be useful for describing how long- and short-term patterns evolved and changed, but they do not explain what gave rise to these patterns. Maize was raised nearly everywhere in the colony from large commercial haciendas to small individual plots. Usually as long as the weather was favorable more maize was produced than was consumed. During the eighteenth century, some producers abandoned maize because of low prices and inadequate profits, but at the same time others entered the market. Around Mexico City the number of maize-producing estates may have shrunk significantly, but in the Bajío the number may have increased just as significantly.[18] It appears, though, that maize supplies, at least in urban areas, could not keep pace with consumer needs. Guadalajara, among the half-dozen largest cities in the late eighteenth century, may not be .typical, but it is illustrative of the problem. Eric Van Young has determined that some producers close to Guadalajara dropped maize production while others at some distance (such as Altos de Jalisco) expanded output. An additional element, though, was that Indian villages, historically suppliers of maize to Guadalajara, cut back their shipments (in order to feed their own citizens) to less than 1 percent of the total delivered to the city. As a result, the city, to ensure an adequate supply of maize, had to enact measures that allowed for "interdictions against the export of grain from Nueva Galicia, the seizure of private hoards of grain, and the forced sale of privately owned maize and wheat in the city. . . ."[19] If the abundance of maize in the first half of the eighteenth century drove agriculturalists into other ventures such as wheat cultivation or land rental, then the growing scarcity during the second half attracted some new producers, but apparently not enough to ensure sufficient supplies at reasonable costs in many cities. Enrique Florescano's figures show that maize had grown more costly in and near Mexico City by the late eighteenth century because local supplies were not growing fast enough (if at all) and had to be supplemented with more expensive maize (resulting from transportation costs, among other things) from the Bajío and other regions. Abandoning maize cultivation proved to be easier than starting it up again, especially in the late eighteenth and early nineteenth centuries when credit and capital had grown expensive and tight. As the demand for maize continued to exceed the supply, prices remained high and shortages became frequent.

The question that some scholars have wrestled with is the role the maize producers themselves played in the unfolding of these events. Did they fashion their business decisions and investment strategies in such a way as to manipulate price and supply to their advantage? Did they have enough knowledge of the market, particularly the urban market, to know when to withhold maize or sell it in order to gain the highest possible price? Some of the recent hacienda literature has portrayed late colonial commercial farmers as shrewd, calculating businessmen rather than rural bumpkins with aristocratic pretensions. In John Coatsworth's opinion, they "demonstrated a primordial desire to maximize income and to minimize production costs." When times were prosperous, they "invested in their operations, experimented with new crops and new methods, and sought new markets." In times of economic slowdown "they shifted from crops to livestock, reorganized their estates into tenancies, sold out to cut losses, or abandoned their holdings altogether." Their goals and activities allow them to be compared favorably to "modern entrepreneurs."[20]

This is not to say that every agriculturalist had these skills or that even those who did always found that changes could be made as easily and smoothly as the above description might suggest. Some eighteenth-century agriculturalists certainly displayed a much greater sensitivity to the forces of the marketplace than their predecessors had or perhaps could. With respect to maize, they had probably learned some valuable lessons. They may have used past prices in part to determine current plantings so as not to flood the market and depress the price too much. They also must have understood that land, capital, and labor costs relative to maize prices could be so high as to yield only marginal profits. Finally, they may well have determined that if incomes rose or prices dropped so that consumers could afford more maize, they would not necessarily buy enough more to raise producers' revenues to levels that would justify any further investment in maize cultivation. Some preliminary findings indicate that changes in supply in reaction to changes in prices were fairly inelastic. A 10-percent change in maize prices produced only a 2.6-percent change in output. Producers could react individually to price changes by cutting or expanding supplies. It is much harder to explain how the producers in aggregate responded. Did they respond in such a way as to use supply to influence price? The extent to which the investment in and construction of storage and warehouse facilities took place may, as some have argued, represent an attempt to control the price. How much such investment and construction actually occurred remains to be documented.[21]

How agriculturalists reached these decisions is hard to detail. In his study of the Jesuit hacienda, Santa Lucía, Herman Konrad gives high marks to the local administrators because "at all times they emphasized the type of productive activities calculated to produce maximum revenues." This enormous estate encompassed a range of activities from planting crops and raising livestock to renting lands. Of relevance here is the fact that administrators constantly distinguished between internal operations and external markets. Maize played an important role in these financial considerations. It was grown primarily to cover workers' wages and rations. Any surplus would be sold in the private market, but in addition the administrators bought maize in the private market, when the price was low, to cover wages and rations or on speculation that the price would increase. The goal was to minimize costs and maximize profits as much as possible and participate in the market to the extent necessary to accomplish that.[22] Konrad's Santa Lucía study ends in the middle of the eighteenth century, though, at a time when maize supplies were abundant and prices low, and it could not address the question of what happened there as the supply of maize dwindled and prices rose in the second half of the eighteenth century. Less maize was entering the marketplace in part because Indian towns and small producers were shipping less during the second half of the century.[23] With less maize voluntarily entering the marketplace, cities through their grain-buying and -storing services were allowed to negotiate large purchases at favorable rates.[24] Administrators of large estates like Santa Lucía still may have found it more profitable during the second half of the eighteenth century to raise maize primarily for internal consumption (payment to workers as well as food for animals) than to produce it for the consumer market. Administrators now, however, had to weigh the financial merits of paying wages in maize and of earning revenues with maize, although given the currency shortage paying wages in maize instead of cash probably continued to be cheaper and easier. They may have found it too costly, however, to count on outside maize purchases to supplement internal needs. To deal with these changing circumstances, they could increase maize plantings to accommodate internal needs and exploit the external market, but in doing so they had to assume certain risks. The capital needed for the conversion could be scarce and expensive, and it might better be spent in pursuit of other agricultural projects. And of course, expanding the supply of maize would eventually cause the price to fall without necessarily creating more demand for maize or earning more profit from its sale.

Although many questions about the maize economy in the late colonial period remain to be studied, the current interpretation is that both demographic and economic developments favored large producers who could withhold their supplies from market until prices began to rise later in the harvest year or later.[25] What remains to be more fully investigated is how producers and, beyond them, brokers and merchants made those decisions that would allow them to exploit whatever advantage they might have gained because of changes in the supply and demand of maize during the late eighteenth century.

Without more complete figures on maize production, we cannot know whether a decline in production or a growth in population was the principal cause of rising maize prices or whether it was a combination of the two. We do know, of course, that some eighteenth-century agriculturalists, in particular the large commercial hacendados, substituted wheat for corn because they could expect somewhat higher returns from their wheat investments. Such shifts could reduce the total maize supply, and that, in combination with urban growth, could boost maize prices over the long term. Europeans had long preferred wheat to corn, but what may have created a larger market for wheat and flour products was the increase in bread consumption by the urban poor. In eighteenth-century Guadalajara, for example, Van Young found that some farmers switched acreage from corn to wheat to exploit this newly developing urban market.[26] To some hacienda scholars, this willingness to shift from maize to wheat or to other crops represented a more entrepreneurial spirit within the agricultural sector, for investors and producers had to be willing to risk their capital in costly projects such as irrigation ditches and storage facilities. The question that arises is whether the movement in wheat or flour prices justified these substantial investments. Data on wheat and flour prices are not as readily available as those on maize, but a wheat series covering about a half-century (from the 1740s to the 1790s) has been constructed for Dolores Hidalgo, a small town in the Bajío not far from Guanajuato. Not much of a trend can be detected for the entire period from 1741 to 1791. The growth rate is only 0.4 percent per year (51 percent confidence level). That does not present much of an incentive to shift to wheat, since in that same period maize prices rose at a rate several times faster than wheat prices. In the last two decades, 1770s to 1790s, though, wheat prices shot up at an annual rate of 12.1 percent per year, while maize also shot up but at a somewhat slower rate of 8.2 percent per year (98 percent confidence level).[27]

How producers reacted, if they reacted at all, to these price trends is hard to document. Presumably faster rising wheat prices would cause producers to increase their wheat plantings, and, if that happened as it must have with some producers, then maize plantings may have been reduced enough to cause maize prices to rise as well. Wheat producers faced many of the same risks as maize producers, though. In part the result of the depopulation after the 1780s agricultural crises, wheat and flour supplies exceeded demand, and prices tumbled during the 1790s, at least in some markets.[28]

The period of rapidly rising grain prices during the late third and early fourth quarters may have signified an economy under strain. This was the most intensive phase of the Bourbon reforms, and some of the reforms were designed, for better or worse, to stimulate the economy. Borrowings, it would appear, were on the rise, and this was a sign of expansion in business, in particular in the agricultural sector.[29] The fast-rising grain prices, however, meant that the economy's capacity to provide even basic goods was limited. This period from the late 1760s through the mid-1780s represented the strongest advance in grain prices of any comparable period in the eighteenth century. This inflationary spiral may provide a broader context in which to deal with the recurrent agricultural crises and the controversial political issues of the half-century before the 1810 uprisings.

The best available measures of the colony's economic growth in the eighteenth century are the tithe payments and the silver registrations. Other measures in connection with the published treasury accounts may be developed to shed further light on that growth.[30] Tithe accounts have been compiled for the two bishoprics of Michoacán and Oaxaca. Since the tithe was an assessment against the value of the output of the agricultural sector, it may be used as a measure of how fast that sector was growing. When the tithes for Michoacán and Oaxaca are combined from 1700 to 1800, they exhibit a strong, upward trend at 1.3 percent annually. That was more than twice the rise in the colony-wide maize prices. At these rates, over the whole century agricultural output doubled about every fifty years, but the price of maize doubled about every one hundred years. When the tithes and prices are broken down by half-centuries, they show annual increases of 1.6 percent in tithes and 0.7 percent in prices for the first half of the eighteenth century, and of 1.4 percent in tithes and 2.2 percent in prices for the second half. These trends suggest that the value of output in agriculture grew more than twice as fast as the price of maize (used in this case as a gauge for all agricultural commodities) in the first half. In the second half, though, not only did the value of agricultural output slow, but it was also overtaken by rapidly rising maize prices. What these differing growth rates point to is the possibility of a more favorable economic climate in terms of acquiring and developing land for agricultural expansion before 1750 than after. During the period from the early 1760s to the mid-1780s, when the economy was enjoying a revival, tithes grew at a rate of slightly more than 2 percent per year (compared to 1.4 percent for the second half of the eighteenth century) and prices at a rate of 3.8 percent per year (compared to 2.2 percent from 1750 to 1800). Had these rates been maintained for a century, tithes would have doubled every thirty-five years, but prices would have doubled every generation. Even during the late third and early fourth quarters, the growth in tithes was impressive by eighteenth-century standards, but the rise in prices might well have wiped out most of the gains.

In addition to tithes, we can also use the registration of silver as another measure of economic change in Mexico from 1700 to 1810. Relying primarily on data collected by Alexander von Humboldt, we can estimate that silver output grew at an annual rate of 1.4 percent. Output grew faster in the first half of the eighteenth century (to 1755) than in the second half (to 1810), although the latter period has commanded more scholarly attention than the former. The growth rates for the respective periods were 1.7 percent and 1.4 percent per year.[31] Silver registrations, like agricultural tithes, rose faster than maize prices during the whole eighteenth century and in the first half of the century, but lagged behind prices in the second half. Indeed silver registrations rose more slowly than both maize prices and agricultural tithes after 1750. The period from the late third into the early fourth quarters witnessed strong growth in silver output at an annual rate of 3.2 percent, and the surge in mining combined with the continued growth in agriculture (2.2 percent per year) may account for the sudden spurt (3.8 percent annually) in maize prices. By the end of the eighteenth century, the silver curve flattened out, although the actual registrations remained quite high even for the eighteenth century. The flattening of the curve could indicate that the cost of doing business or raising capital had risen so high that it had slowed and perhaps curtailed expansion.

Economic expansion was an important feature of the Upper Bajío during the second half of the eighteenth century. From the famine of 1750 until the early nineteenth century, all the indicators—tithes, silver registrations, and grain prices—were on the rise. Agricultural and mineral output were growing at between 1.5 and 2 percent per year, and prices were edging up at a somewhat slower rate of just more than 1 percent annually. In the twenty years before the famines of the 1780s, silver production at Guanajuato surged ahead at a rate of 3 to 4 percent a year and output at nearby districts such as Charcas and Zacatecas climbed at even higher annual rates of between 5 and 7 percent.[32] An expanding mining industry would almost certainly increase the demand for dozens of agricultural and manufactured goods. Agricultural output may have grown by about 2 percent a year from the mid-1760s until the mid-1780s, or a half to a third of the growth in mining. It would not be surprising, therefore, to find prices advancing rapidly. In figures cited earlier, both maize and wheat prices rose at rates between 6 and 12 percent each year from the 1760s to 1780s. After the famines, the picture becomes somewhat less clear, in part a result of insufficient price data. From 1787, by which time the famine had peaked, to 1810, agricultural output had slowed to between 1 and 2 percent per year, and silver production drifted, although in Guanajuato it may have actually fallen. Maize prices until 1800 (at which point the data end) plummeted by 7 percent a year. A drop in prices confirms Malthus's predictions that famines provided a correction in economies where demand had exceeded supply. That is what the 7 percent figure underscores.

While the famines of the 1780s may have been among the worst of the colonial period, they did not treat all regions equally. Some of the worst famines occurred within the borders of Michoacán (particularly the Upper Bajío), and this may account for the sharp drop in the price of maize during the 1790s. Other areas within Michoacán and beyond experienced lower death rates and, therefore, had less dramatic price adjustments. When we examine the colony-wide maize price series, we cannot detect much if any decline during the 1790s and into the 1800s.[33] Demographic changes were a major underlying cause of inflation in the eighteenth century, but economic expansion also played an important role in the acceleration of that inflation. The economy may have ceased growing by the end of the century in part because of the impact of inflation on the economy.

Zacatecas is still the only city for which we have numerous prices for commodities other than grains.[34] Data on twenty commodities in addition to maize and flour were gathered and analyzed for the period from 1760 to 1820. From the end of the agricultural crises of the mid-1780s to the outbreak of the Hidalgo Rebellion, data for the twenty commodities are almost continuous. For maize and flour, however, they are less continuous. When the data are plotted by their index numbers (1760 = 100), they show prices rising during the late third and early fourth quarters (much as the average colonial maize price did), after which they dipped in response to the mid-1780s agricultural crisis. At some point in the middle of the 1790s, they began to climb again although in an irregular fashion. When foodstuffs are separated from the other household and noncomestible items, they follow a similar pattern, even though it is somewhat more volatile.

The behavior of Zacatecan commodities, however, is more complicated than these remarks suggest. Space does not permit me to examine the trends of all the Zacatecan commodity prices, but a sample can be examined briefly. The sample includes sugar, chile, lard, soap, and wool.[35] The annual average amount of each commodity sold and recorded in the *alcabalas* records in Zacatecas was as follows: 175,000 pounds of sugar, 60,000 bushels of chiles, 5,000 pounds of lard, 210,000 pounds of soap, and 10,000 pounds of wool. The total amount of each commodity sold in a year could be higher than these figures, because some transactions escaped the alcabalas collectors. Another point to be considered is that we lack prices for half of the individual years between 1760 and 1821, and in the case of some specific commodities the lack of data is greater than that. Still, with these qualifications in mind, we can review the trends and growth rates associated with these five commodities during the last half-century before the independence movement broke out.

All these commodities increase in price between 1760 and 1815. Wool shows the smallest growth at 0.7 percent per year and sugar the greatest growth at 1.7 percent per year. In between is soap at 1.2 percent, chile at 1.3 percent, and lard at 1.4 percent per year. In the same period the colony-wide price for maize rose at 1.7 percent per year. For measuring price movements, the middle of the third quarter of the eighteenth century is a reasonable starting point because harvests were fairly ample and prices fairly low. The year 1815 is not the best point to terminate the series inasmuch as it falls in the middle of the independence period. Since, however, the prices of the five Zacatecan commodities and the colony-wide price of maize were all moving in the same direction within a range of 0.5 percent to 1.7 percent, we may infer that whatever disruptions in the form of shortages and scarcities resulted from the insurgency, they did not unduly affect one series over another. It is worth noting that the foodstuffs among the Zacatecan commodities moved higher at rates closer to the colony-wide maize series than the noncomestibles, in this case wool and soap. It has been assumed but not quantitatively shown that there was a correspondence between maize prices and other staples over the long term, and these comparisons tend to support those assumptions.

The strength of the series for the Zacatecan commodities lies in the period between the agricultural crises of the mid-1780s and Hidalgo's Rebellion in 1810 (see Table 4.2). Indeed, the results are more interesting because they are less uniform, and that raises some important issues about economic developments in the last two decades before independence.[36] The most striking result is that in four of the five commodities, trends are difficult to pinpoint or verify. Only for chile do the t-scores inspire much confidence that a trend does exist. The price of chile rose at about 2.1 percent per year (with a 98.5 percent confidence level) compared to the colony-wide maize price series that grew by 0.8 percent per year (with a 76 percent confidence level) for years 1788–1810. For sugar, lard, and soap, the growth-rate calculations were in the range of 0.2 to 0.6 percent per year (but with confidence levels in the range of 50 to 65 percent). For wool the growth was negative (−0.2 percent per year with a probability of 62 percent). For all five commodities, prices were higher in the period 1788–1810 than they had been in 1760 or during the 1760s, but except for chile they showed no strong tendency to rise or to fall from 1788 to 1810. By the late eighteenth century, prices had reached a high plateau where they more or less remained until the end of the colonial period.[37]

The lack of comparable studies in commodity-price trends makes it difficult to know how to interpret Zacatecas's trends. Over the years, I have continued to collect commodity prices for other towns and cities, but I have not yet developed a long commodity series for any other municipality or region. A few yearly comparisons are not particularly useful, because a change in prices in one place may not show in another place until the following year.[38] What we need, however, are long enough series for several cities and towns in order to neutralize the effect of local and regional conditions. Given what little data have been collected for other places, one can still detect the outline of a pattern already identified in Hidalgo, Guadalajara, and Zacatecas: prices rising rapidly during the late third and early fourth quarters followed by a decade or two of volatile prices at high levels.

The question can be asked whether Mexico's eighteenth-century inflation was a unique phenomenon, and the answer to that question is that prices were generally rising all across the Atlantic world. Similar forces were at work: rising populations, growth and diversification of urban markets, com-

Table 4.2

Zacatecan Commodity Prices, 1760–1815
(in reales and 100 = 1760)

Date	1	#	2	#	3	#	4	#	5	#	6	#
1760	21	100	160	100	15	100	16	100	148	100	10.4	100
1766	14	66	120	75	13*	87	14	88	110	74	8.4	81
1767	12	57	120	75	12	80	13	75	77	51	6.7	64
1772	22	105	92	55	33*	220	13	75	141	95	17.3	166
1786	19	90	252	151	48	320	19	119	202	136	42.0	405
1787	22	105	276	173	45	290	17	106	230	155	21.5	207
1788	21	95	120	75	27	240	18	112	224	150	15.7	151
1790	17	80	122	76	45	246	19	119	235	159	17.8	171
1791	19	90	190	118	22	146	20	125	224	150	15.5	149
1792	27	129	165	103	24	160	21	131	186	125	10.2	98
1793	27	129	133	83	37	243	23	143	165	111	12.5	120
1794	21	100	143	89	31	233	29	175	165	111	19.9	191
1795	25	120	187	117	25	166	20	125	193	131	12.4	119
1796	26	125	173	108	23*	153	20	125	188	160	12.8	123
1797	25	120	210	131	20	146	16	100	188	127	17.9	172
1799	23	110	206	128	24	160	16	110	199	135	16.6	160
1800	36	171	241	150	29	193	18	112	191	122	19.3	186
1801	26	125	241	150	35	233	17	106	202	136	17.1	164
1802	28	125	216	135	25	166	17	106	190	128	21.3	205
1804	22	105	189	118	33	220	17*	106	198	134	14.3	138
1805	22	105	184	117	26	174	16	100	195	131	15.4	148
1807	20	95	177	110	24	160	20	125	213	144	17.5	168
1808	21	100	209	131	37	246	24	150	204	136	24.9	231
1810	24	114	204	128	46	306	21	131	250	170	38.3	368
1814	79	371	234	149	37	240	18	112	215	145	26.5	255
1815	71	338	287	179	33	220	18	112	183	125		231

1—sugar in arrobas; 2—chile in *cargas;* 3—lard in arrobas; 4—wool in arrobas; 5—soap in cargas; 6—maize in fanegas.
means index number and * means estimated price.
All prices and index numbers rounded off except maize which is an average of
several series.

mercialization of agriculture, and increased business activity. Studies have tracked long-term trends in grain or commodity prices in the New World as well as in Europe. European prices (mostly wheat, but also wine, beer, meat, tallow, and so forth) had reached a plateau in the late seventeenth and early eighteenth centuries (some had actually declined) before they began an upswing that dominated much of the rest of the eighteenth century.[39] The rise in prices of European grains and other comestibles during the second half of the eighteenth century spurred production on the American side of the Atlantic economy. As prices rose in European markets after the 1750s, American producers and shippers expanded their own economic horizons beyond the West Indies to include Europe.[40] In the United States, rising wholesale prices in the eighteenth century and into the nineteenth century reflected growth in both domestic and foreign markets.[41] Mexico's agricultural exports to American or European markets, though, played only a marginal role in the eighteenth-century price inflation, although toward the end of the colonial period those exports from Veracruz reached between 2 and 3 million pesos a year.[42] What Mexico did contribute was the silver that financed a part of the Atlantic's expanding economy and in particular the growing commerce between Philadelphia and Havana.[43] That contribution, including public and private funds, may have grown several fold during the course of the century, from a low of less than 5 million pesos to a high of more than 15 million pesos per year.[44] In the part of the New World facing the Pacific rather than the Atlantic, prices over the long term of the eighteenth century may have actually declined.[45] Recently, the Chilean scholar, José Manuel Larraín, has compiled an impressive set of commodity prices for Santiago between 1749 and 1808 and for Chile during the seventeenth and eighteenth centuries.[46] Santiago's price index fell steadily from the 1690s to the 1750s after which it rose until independence, although the index never returned to the extremely high levels of the late sixteenth and early seventeenth centuries. During the second half of the eighteenth century, prices rose at a rate of less than 1 percent per year compared to a rise of nearly 1.5 percent for Mexican maize and Zacatecan commodities in approximately that same period. There are several important similarities and contrasts to be noted between late eighteenth-century prices in Chile and Mexico. Both experienced an acceleration during the period from the 1760s into the 1780s, although Chile's at scarcely less than 2 percent per year was half Mexico's. Between the famines of the 1780s and the independence movement in 1810, Chile's prices followed a much more pronounced Malthusian pattern of a sharp decline, stagnation, and a steady rise than did Mexico's.[47]

The impact of inflation can be gauged in terms of what happened to workers' and employees' purchasing power, but as valuable as that would be, it cannot be done without more comprehensive wage and salary data than now exist. Several regional and sectoral studies have compiled some such data that can be helpful in the search for and analysis of wage and salary trends. One must also recognize, however, that even if a wage and salary series could be constructed, it might only confirm what is already a widely accepted view: that wages and salaries, for the most part, were static in the eighteenth century. All would agree, though, that having a series from which growth rates could be calculated would be preferable to the current situation.

Although remuneration could take different forms, it was a common practice for employers to combine cash payments with allotments of grain such as maize. In the mining industry, a special form of payment in kind evolved because of the difficulty of maintaining a pool of workers, especially among the skilled occupations in the earliest years. It was called *partido*, and it usually allowed the worker to keep in addition to his regular wage a share of ore from a day's work. The amount of the partido could vary from camp to camp and from mine to mine within a camp, and not all workers received partidos and not all employers paid them. Others, like manual laborers in cities, may have been paid only in cash, but day workers at haciendas may have often been paid in kind. Since the sixteenth century, the compensation system had been evolving toward cash payments, but in the eighteenth century it remained a mix of payments in cash and in kind. A rising silver curve did not alleviate currency shortages, and in addition some employers found it cheaper to compensate their workers in merchandise instead of in cash. Hence, the task of constructing a wage and salary series that incorporated both payments in kind and in cash would at the very least be difficult.

From what research has been published on wage and salary levels, we know that remuneration was not absolutely fixed and that from time to time during the colonial period market forces affected the worker's total compensation. In the first century of the colonial period, depopulation made laborers scarce and opened the way not only to the introduction of a wage system, but to the payment of wages high enough (or with added incentives) to attract workers. Even after the population began to grow in the second half of the seventeenth century, miners were known to complain about labor shortages that forced them to pay high rates or to attach other premiums to attract and keep workers.[48] In the first half of the eighteenth century, hacendados were still complaining about scarce workers and high wages.[49] Labor shortages bad enough to cause officials to invoke *repartimiento,* a compulsory labor system, were reported in Oaxaca and Guadalajara during the second half of the eighteenth century even though the population was still growing.[50] These periodic complaints should not obscure the fact that as the population grew in the eighteenth century, the worker pool, especially the numbers of semiskilled and unskilled laborers, also increased. The situation in some mining camps because of the influx of vagrants and itinerants had grown so threatening that special laws to control their activities had to be imposed. It was now possible for miners to hire workers without offering them any partidos or for hacendados to hire laborers by offering them only rations.[51]

In search of eighteenth-century patterns, we can compare wage data for Santa Lucía in the middle of the century and Guanamé at the end. Both were located outside the Bajío proper, although they were close enough to have been caught up in the Bajío's economic life. The Santa Lucía data are for ranches that raised goats, cattle, and horses, while Guanamé's data cover primarily sheep ranching. Still, the occupational categories are comparable. At the very top of the occupational hierarchy were the *mayordomo,* the *sobresaliente,* and the *ayudante* in that order of importance for remuneration. For these basically managerial jobs, Santa Lucía had a range of wages: mayordomo—8 to 46 pesos per month with one fanega of maize per week; sobresaliente—7 to 15 pesos per month with one-quarter to one fanega of maize per week; and ayudante—with 6 to 14.2 pesos per month with one-quarter to one-half fanega of maize per week.[52] By way of comparison, the mayordomo at Guanamé earned 41.75 pesos per month and received one fanega of maize per week; the sobresaliente 16.75 pesos per month and three-quarters of a fanega of maize per week; and the ayudante 10 pesos per month and one-quarter of a fanega per week.[53] In the case of the mayordomo and sobresaliente, Guanamé's were paid wages at the high end of the range at Santa Lucía, and the Guanamé's ayudante (actually there were several) was paid in the upper-middle part of the range.

Below the managerial level, Santa Lucía had as many as a dozen different occupational groups, while Guanamé had a work force that consisted mainly of *vacieros* (caretakers of the animals). At Santa Lucía, vacieros were connected with goat ranches, and their standard wage was six pesos per month and nine *quartillos* of maize per week.[54] At Guanamé, the vaciero's wage was also six pesos per month, but the weekly maize allotment was only two to three quartillos. Most of the Guanamé vacieros received three quartillos per week. Two other occupations can be compared: the brander who at Santa Lucía earned three to five (the standard was four) pesos per month and rations of two to five quartillos per week and who at Guanamé earned seven pesos and rations of three quartillos per week; and the shepherd whose monthly wage at Santa Lucía was three pesos and one to two quartillos of maize per week and whose monthly wage at Guanamé was four pesos and two quartillos per week.

These figures indicate that wages and rations for these two occupations may have risen during the second half of the eighteenth century, although this is hardly enough evidence to be certain. For vacieros, however, wage rates remained static, but maize rations may have risen slightly. Raising rations (rather than wages) was not without costs to employers in the second half of the eighteenth century, because both planting and purchasing maize could entail more expense. This was partially offset, however, by the fact that employers could use a higher price in calculating how much the maize was worth in the total compensation package.

In all occupational levels, remuneration (including rations) was adjusted from time to time. These adjustments were selective rather than general, and they were probably related to temporary shifts in labor supplies at particular operations. For the largest segment of the wage earners in the ranching industry, however, the remuneration was fairly well fixed. At both Santa Lucía and Guanamé, promotions, which meant higher wages and rations, were frequently made from within the existing worker pool. For example, at Guanamé during the period of August 1801 through July 1802, the sobresaliente was named mayordomo with almost a three-fold increase, at least two vacieros became ayudantes with an increase of two-thirds in cash remuneration, and both the brander and the shepherd may have advanced, the former to ayudante with an increase in wages of one-third and the latter to vaciero with an increase of one-half. At Guanamé, where the total work force (based on the extant ledger entries for August 1801–July 1802) numbered about fifty, only about a half-dozen positions existed at the highest level. For most of the employees, the opportunity to move from the lowest level, such as shepherd, to the middle level (vaciero) or from the middle level to the highest level were few and far between. At the same time, some vacieros were demoted or transferred with a cut in wages and rations, and some moved in a lateral direction, that is, to new assignments with no change in wages or rations.

Some data for artisans and laborers in the construction trades can also be studied with respect to trends. These involved four different building projects in Zacatecas between 1749 and 1810. The craftsmen earned between twelve and twenty-eight pesos per month on three of the four projects and between twenty-four and forty-eight pesos per month on the fourth project. This fourth project (1763) was the rebuilding of the *real caja* (local treasury) in a neoclassical style with fluted columns and carved pediments and required more highly skilled craftsmen than for the other buildings. In the other three projects, artisan wages differed: those participating in the construction of an *aduana* (customs) inspection station (1749) earned between sixteen and twenty-four pesos per month and those in the construction of a *jeu de pelote* (1801) and in the repair of the Colegio de Luis de Gonzaga (1805–10) earned between twelve and twenty-four pesos per month. The range of wages for laborers on all these projects was about the same, from six pesos to twelve pesos per month. The highest paid laborers worked on the real caja and the lowest paid on the jeu de pelota and at the Colegio de Luis de Gonzaga. In 1763, the highest paid artisans at forty-eight pesos per month earned about what the highest paid mayordomos earned when their total remuneration (wages and rations converted on the basis of the average colonial maize price) is considered. Indeed, when the ranching occupations of mayordomo, sobresaliente, and ayudante are treated as a group, then this level of ranch work (again, wages and rations converted) was comparable to the earnings of the artisans, who, according to the Zacatecas documentation, were paid only in wages and not in rations. When the ranch workers' rations are converted to cash, their total compensation of about seven to nine pesos per month was comparable to the urban laborers' wages, which in Zacatecas at least did not include a ration of maize. Construction laborers, who were referred to as peones in the documents, like the vaciero and other categories, may have been faced with static wage rates and perhaps even falling rates in the second half of the eighteenth century.[55] There is certainly no unequivocal evidence that wages paid to unskilled or semiskilled workers were climbing at a rate comparable to the estimated growth in colonial maize prices. At the skilled or quasi-managerial level, employees may have had some latitude to negotiate, but even at that level the highest reported compensation was no greater around 1800 than fifty years before. Remuneration, whether in cash or in kind, for the great mass of urban and rural workers was largely fixed during the eighteenth century, and the growth in population, especially in the second half of the eighteenth century, gave the employers a distinct and potentially exploitative advantage over those working and those seeking work.

The reconstruction of late colonial Mexican, and for that matter, late colonial Spanish American, history has proceeded at a remarkable pace in the last quarter-century. As more and more studies have been published, the volume of detail and the level of complexity have grown significantly. We may now be preparing for the next stage in which synthesis and interpretation will occupy front and center. In eighteenth-century Mexico, we may offer additional insights by examining more closely the trends that characterize not only prices, but other economic activities such as agriculture, mining, and even the treasury. At times in the eighteenth century, the economy may have been on the verge of a fundamentally different pattern of growth and development. The entrepreneurial spirit was often in evidence, but it was just as often circumscribed by traditional values and obstructionist views. Most critically, perhaps, capital was always in short supply. In the end, though, what may have come to dominant its economic life, and by way of extension its political and social worlds, was a growing imbalance between what it could produce and what it needed to produce to attain and sustain that growth and development.

NOTES

I wish to thank the Liberal Arts College, the Pennsylvania State University, for providing computer funds and the American Philosophical Society and the American Council of Learned Societies for providing research funds.

1. Yale University, Latin American Collection, 12-E.

2. Examples of such studies are Enrique Florescano, *Precios del maíz y crisis agrícolas en México (1708–1860)* (Mexico City, 1971), 115–17, 124, 180–82, and Charts 7 and 9; D. A. Brading, *Haciendas and Ranchos in the Mexican Bajío, León, 1700–1860* (Cambridge, 1978), 183; Claude Morin, *Michoacán en la Nueva España del siglo xviii: Crecimiento y desigualdad en una economía colonial* (Mexico City, 1979), 189–91; John J. Tepaske, "Economic Cycles in New Spain in the Eighteenth Century: The View from the Public Sector," *Bibliotheca Americana* 1 (1983): 175–76; Richard L. Garner and William B. Taylor, eds., *Iberian Colonies and New World Societies: Essays in Memory of Charles Gibson* (published privately in State College, Pa., 1986), 125–27; John Coatsworth, "The Limits of Colonial Absolutism: The State in Eighteenth-Century Mexico," in Karen Spalding, ed., *Essays in Political, Economic and Social History of Colonial Latin America*, University of Delaware, Latin American Studies Program, Occasional Papers and Monographs, No. 3 (Newark, Del., 1982), 32–34; and Richard L. Garner, "Problèmes d'une ville minière mexicaine a la fin de l'époque coloniale: Prix et salaires à Zacatecas (1760–1821)," *Cahiers des Amériques Latines* 6 (1972): 110–11.

3. These are strictly estimates, but they are based on fairly reliable empirical data. A 1-percent growth in population may be a minimal figure and is roughly the rate for the period from the 1740s, when José Villaseñor y Sánchez's figure was published [Peter Gerhard, *Mexico in 1742* (Mexico City, 1962), 9], into the 1790s, when the Revillagigedo census was completed. Sherburne Cook and Woodrow Borah have found faster rates for shorter periods in specific regions such as "West-Central Mexico," *Essays in Population History,* 3 vols. (Berkeley and Los Angeles, 1971–79), 1:310–12, 354–55. The economic growth is based on the rates of 1 to 1.5 percent per year for agricultural tithes and mineral registrations. Richard L. Garner, "Price Trends in Eighteenth-Century Mexico," *Hispanic American Historical Review* 65 (1985): 300–301.

4. Examples of these studies would be D. A. Brading, *Miners and Merchants in Bourbon Mexico 1763–1810* (Cambridge, 1971); Eric Van Young, *Hacienda and Market in Eighteenth-Century Mexico: The Rural Economy of the Guadalajara Region, 1675–1820* (Berkeley and Los Angeles, 1981); and Richard Salvucci, "Enterprise and Economic Development in Eighteenth-Century Mexico: The Case of the Obrajes" (Ph.D. diss., Princeton University, 1982).

5. Coatsworth, "Limits of Colonial Absolutism," 34. Coatsworth is careful to note that these are ideas deserving of more research. My own work on currency exports shows that they were rising so fast that a substantial part of the value of the colony's silver production was exported and for several years more than its production was exported. Richard L. Garner, "Exportaciones de circulante en el siglo xviii (1750–1810)," *Historia Mexicana* 124 (1982): 544–98. For criticism of Coatsworth's use of treasury data, see D. A. Brading, "Facts and Figments in Bourbon Mexico," *Bulletin of Latin American Research* 4 (1985): 61–64 and my response to Brading, forthcoming in *Bulletin of Latin American Research.*

6. For an overview of how the agricultural system worked, see Enrique Florescano, "The Formation and Economic Structure of the Hacienda in New Spain," in Leslie Bethell, ed., *The Cambridge History of Latin America,* 5 vols. (Cambridge, 1984), 2:173.

7. Morin, *Michoacán en la Nueva España,* 186–87. A document in the British Library [Additions, 13978, fols. 204–206] indicates that currency exports, *excluding contraband,* from 1779 to 1791 exceeded newly minted currency by about 47 million pesos. That means that the volume of currency in circulation would have been drawn down by at least that amount and probably more if contraband is considered. The totals seem too high. The export of currency in the king's account is estimated to be 14.2 million pesos per year, when an average closer to 8 or 10 million pesos per year may be more accurate. Whatever the actual numbers may be, the shrinkage of the currency in circulation during the early fourth quarter of the eighteenth century was a reality. The document mentioned above blames the massive outflow of currency on the continuation of the commercial monopoly that favored the introduction of

high-priced flota merchandise. See John Fisher, "Imperial 'Free Trade' and the Hispanic Economy (1778–1796)," *Journal of Latin American Studies* 13 (1981): 21–56.

8. I shall discuss this later in the essay, although for now let me say that from
the several accounts that I have studied, I have had trouble proving that the owners
inflated the prices of the goods sold to workers. A major obstacle is knowing what
the market price was.

9. The impact of three devaluations in the eighteenth century should also be
considered. The devaluations allowed the treasury to cut more coins from each silver
bar. This may have added to the supply of currency, but it also required more coins
to buy the same quantity of merchandise before devaluation. Debasement involved
not only the government cutting more coins, but also keeping more (as mint fees)
of the coins cut from the bars. See Brading, *Miners and Merchants*, 143–44.

10. I discuss the sources for these series and the problems connected with constructing them in "Price Trends in Eighteenth-Century Mexico," 181–82, n. 6.
Space does not permit a discussion of maize price trends before 1700. Some general
observations about those possible trends appear in the aforementioned essay, 184–
91.

11. Trends and growth rates are based on least-square linear regressions from a
computer program, *Econopak*, developed by Dr. Milton Hallberg, professor of agricultural economics at The Pennsylvania State University.

12. The following figures indicate what happens when a rate of growth is compounded over the century:

1 percent per year = increase of 2.7 times
2 percent per year = increase of 7.2 times
3 percent per year = increase of 19 times
4 percent per year = increase of 50 times
5 percent per year = increase of 150 times

Surenda Patel, "Rates of Industrial Growth in the Last Century, 1860–1958," in
Barry Supple, ed., *The Experience of Economic Growth* (New York, 1963), 74.

13. The precise year in which the peak occurred, 1713 or 1714, cannot be
determined with any precision. Only a few maize prices exist for the decade 1710–
20, and most of them are for Leon and Silao. Charles Gibson, *The Aztecs Under
Spanish Rule: A History of the Indians of the Valley of Mexico, 1519–1810* (Stanford,
1964), 450.

14. Clements Library, University of Michigan, Zacatecas Collection, Treasury
Records and Correspondence, 1780–89, Box A: and Archivo Municipal de Zacatecas,
Actas del Cabildo, 1790, exp. 21.

15. See Van Young's discussion in *Hacienda and Market in Eighteenth-Century
Mexico*, 103.

16. That prices may have risen between 1787 and 1810 is based largely on how

high they were at Mexico City's *alhóndiga*. The distinction here is between rising prices and higher than usual prices in the postfamine period after 1787. Upon examination of Florescano's graph 15, p. 113 [*Precios del maíz*], one could propose that an upward slanting line could be fit to the alhóndiga prices from the late 1780s to 1814. If, however, a line is "sighted" for the period from the late 1780s, by which time the famines had abated and prices had fallen in the capital, to 1810, that line will have a much more flattish appearance. If one will accept trends with confidence levels of less than 99 percent, then one can endorse the interpretation of rising prices. Even that endorsement, though, must be tempered, because the rate of growth may only be about 1 percent per year, a figure that is lower than any previous period and only slightly higher than the annual average for the whole century.

17. According to the t-scores, the trend for the first half of the eighteenth century has only a 93 percent confidence level instead of the 99 percent I have generally adhered to.

18. Gibson, *Aztecs Under Spanish Rule,* 329, and Florescano, *Precios del maíz,* 183–86, for the Valley of Mexico, and Brading, *Haciendas and Ranchos,* 58–60, 69–73, and 113–14 for the Bajío.

19. Van Young, *Hacienda and Market,* 75–81, 86–94.

20. John Coatsworth, "Obstacles to Economic Growth in Nineteenth-Century Mexico," *American Historical Review* 83 (1978): 87.

21. Let me stress that this is at best a rough estimation. I have assumed that the tithe series (one for Oaxaca and another for Michoacán) that have been published represent for the most part the value of the output of maize. I recognize that tithes were paid with products other than maize. Brading (*Haciendas and Ranchos,* 68–69) believes, though, that maize constituted 75 to 80 percent of the payment. Regression analysis was used to determine the rate of change. A printout showing these calculations may be obtained from the author. I am indebted to my colleague, Dr. Spiro Stefanou, for suggesting this approach.

22. Herman W. Konrad, *A Jesuit Hacienda in Colonial Mexico: Santa Lucía, 1576–1767* (Stanford, 1980), 210–12. Konrad tends to emphasize the estate's drive for self-sufficiency, but he is not always clear on how that term is being used. Self-sufficiency can imply a policy of insulating the estate from the marketplace. That is not the case here, and self-sufficiency may not be an apt term for describing how the estate operated.

23. Florescano, "Structure of the Hacienda," 2:174–80, and Van Young, *Hacienda and Market,* 75–81.

24. Florescano, "Structure of the Hacienda," 2:174.

25. Van Young, *Hacienda and Market,* 84–86.

26. Van Young, *Hacienda and Market,* 350.

27. The data are from Flor de María López, *Dolores Hidalgo: Estudio económico, 1740–1790* (Mexico City, 1974), 41–62, but the calculations are mine.

28. I have discussed the wheat and flour markets in Guadalajara and Zacatecas after 1790 in "Price Trends in Eighteenth-Century Mexico," 311–17.

29. Linda Greenow, *Credit and Socioeconomic Change in Colonial Mexico: Loans and Mortgages in Guadalajara, 1720–1820* (Boulder, Colo., 1983), fig. 2.1, 27.

30. Herbert S. Klein, "La economía de la Nueva España, 1680–1809: Un análisis a partir de las cajas reales," *Historia Mexicana* 136 (1985): 561–609, and J. C. Garavaglia and J. C. Grosso, "La región de Puebla/Tlaxcala y la economía novohispana (1670–1821)," *Historia Mexicana* 140 (1986): 549–600.

31. The calculations are mine, but they are based on Humboldt's mint data from *Political Essay on the Kingdom of New Spain,* 4 vols. (New York, 1966), 3:292.

32. These growth rates have been calculated from treasury data found in TePaske, "Economic Cycles in New Spain," 198–203. In the case of Zacatecas, I have not only the treasury revenue from the silver taxes, but the actual silver registrations at the local treasury branch. Growth rates based on treasury receipts and silver registrations do not agree exactly, in part because eighteenth-century miners were selectively excused from paying silver taxes. For the archival sources for the silver registrations, see Richard L. Garner, "Silver Production and Entrepreneurial Structure in 18th-Century Mexico," *Jahrbuch für Geschichte von Staat, Wirtschaft und Gesellschaft Lateinamerikas* 17 (1980), 167: n. 67.

33. In the Upper Bajío, death rates reached abnormally high levels as a result of the famines and epidemics during the years from 1784 to 1786. Brading wrote of thousands dying during the series of famines and epidemics. Exact numbers will always be elusive, but Brading's investigations into parish registers on baptisms and burials suggest how much of a demographic impact the famines and epidemics had. During the previous thirty years, the ratio between baptisms allowed for a natural increase of 2.5 and 4 percent each quinquennium. During the five years after the mid-1780s agricultural crises, León's parishes recorded a negative growth of 1.1 percent. D. A. Brading and Celia Wu, "Population Growth and Crisis: León, 1720–1816," *Journal of Latin American Studies* 5 (1973): 15–22. For further comments, see Van Young, *Hacienda and Market,* 103; Greenow, *Credit and Socioeconomic Change in Colonial Mexico,* 175; and Garner, "Price Trends in Eighteenth-Century Mexico," 299–300.

34. These are analyzed in my "Problèmes d'une ville minière mexicaine," 75–111. I have reworked some of the data specifically for this essay.

35. Sugar is *azúcar* and not *pilón* or *piloncillo,* a low-grade sugar that was popular in urban centers such as Zacatecas and for which I also have a long price series.

36. I have chosen 1788 rather than 1786 or 1787 as the starting point, because shortages of maize and other grains were reported as late as the spring of 1788 in Zacatecas. Although commodity prices had fallen since the worst phase of its own agricultural crises in 1785–86, some rose again in 1787. Certainly by the second half of 1788, most of the lingering effect of the agricultural crises had passed.

37. Garner, "Price Trends in Eighteenth-Century Mexico," 299–300.

38. See, for example, *alcabala* accounts for several small towns between Cuernavaca and Zacatecas in Archivo General de la Nación, Archivo Histórico de Hacienda, legs. 154, 215, 2160, 2165, 2166, and 2171.

39. These very general remarks have been drawn from F. Braudel and F. Spooner, "Prices in Europe from 1450 to 1750," in E. E. Rich and C. H. Wilson, eds., *The Economy of Expanding Europe in the Sixteenth and Seventeenth Centuries*, vol. 4 of *The Cambridge Economic History of Europe*, 2d ed. (Cambridge, 1960–71), 391–422 and figs. 17–31, 470–81, and Jan de Vries, *Economy of Europe in the Age of Crisis, 1600–1750* (Cambridge, 1976), 84–86, 244.

40. Jacob Price, *Capital and Credit in British Overseas Trade: The View from the Chesapeake, 1700–1776* (Cambridge, Mass., 1980), 128, 136.

41. Arthur H. Cole, *Wholesale Commodity Prices in the United States, 1700–1821* (Cambridge, Mass., 1938), 102–14, and Walter Buckingham Smith and Arthur H. Cole, *Fluctuations in American Business, 1790–1860* (Cambridge, Mass., 1935), 8–21.

42. This is a rough estimate based on figures found in Miguel Lerdo de Tejada, *Comercio exterior de México* (Mexico City, 1967), num. 14. The list includes such things as wheat, sugar, chile, cochineal, cotton, and leather. Some items fell in the category of reexports. By far the biggest export was cochineal.

43. In a recent publication that explores the economic consequences of the expanding commercial ties between North America's and Spain's colonies, the importance of silver is implied, but not directly analyzed; see Chap. 1, "Silver, North American Penetration and the Spanish Imperial Economy, 1760–1800" in Jacques A. Barbier and Allan J. Kuethe, eds., *The North American Role in the Spanish Imperial Economy, 1760–1819* (Manchester, 1984). Also see Linda K. Salvucci, "Development and Decline: The Port of Philadelphia and Spanish Imperial Economy, 1760–1800" in Jacques A. Barbier and Allan J. Kuethe, eds., *The North American Role in the Spanish Imperial Economy, 1760–1819* (Manchester, 1984). Also see Linda K. Salvucci, "Development and Decline: The Port of Philadelphia and Spanish Imperial Markets" (Ph.D. diss., Princeton University, 1985).

44. In the last thirty years before rebellion erupted, silver output rose around 1 percent per year. Garner, "Exportaciones de circulante," 544–98.

45. In the 1960s, both Ruggiero Romano and Marcelo Carmagnani discussed this in articles on Chilean prices and possible trends from 1680 to 1830. Ruggiero Romano, "Une économie coloniale: le Chili au xviiie siècle," *Annales, E.S.C.* (1960): 278–279; and Marcelo Carmagnani, "La producción agropecuaria chilena. Aspectos cuantitativos, 1680–1830," *Cahiers de Amériques Latines* 3 (1969): 8–20.

46. José Manuel Larraín, "Movimiento de precios en Santiago de Chile 1749–1808: Una interpretación metodológica," *Jahrbuch für Geschichte von Staat, Wirtschaft und Gesellschaft Lateinamerikas* 17 (1980): 199–259. The essay on the longer series is included in this volume.

47. The estimated growth rates are mine, not Larraín's.

48. P. J. Bakewell, *Silver Mining and Society in Colonial Mexico, Zacatecas, 1546–1700* (Cambridge, 1971), 200, and Ignacio del Río's broader discussion of mine worker salaries in Elsa Cecilia Frost, Michael C. Meyer, and Josefina Zoraida Vázquez, comps., *El trabajo y los trabajadores en la historia de México* (Mexico City and Tucson, 1979), 92–110.

49. James D. Riley, "Landlords, Laborers and Royal Government: The Administration of Labor in Tlaxcala, 1680–1750," in Frost et al., *El trabajo y los trabajadores,* 221–29.

50. William B. Taylor, *Landlord and Peasant in Colonial Oaxaca* (Stanford, 1972), 147, and Van Young, *Hacienda and Market,* 238–41.

51. Archivo General de Indias, Guadalajara 3112, microfilm of the Bancroft Library, University of California, Berkeley; Miguel Othón de Mendizábal, "Compendio de Zacatecas," in *Obras completas,* 6 vols. (Mexico City, 1946–47), 5:191; Humboldt, *Political Essay on the Kingdom of New Spain,* 2:480; and Brading, *Miners and Merchants,* 147–49, 157, 184, 186, 193, 199, 201, 204, 277–78, 288. Brading regarded mine and refinery workers as well paid, perhaps the best paid, of all Mexico's colonial workers, and his assessment is probably accurate because of the combination of wages and partidos. They probably averaged 5 to 8 pesos per month, and some (but not all) earned ore shares of one-eighth, one-tenth, or one-twelfth of a day's digging. Owners began to reduce or eliminate the shares, but they may have left the wages alone. I have found variations in what mine and refinery workers were paid during the course of the eighteenth century, but I have not seen enough evidence to suggest that wages followed either an upward or downward trend. Compare wages paid at two different camps in the 1740s (Archivo General de Indias, Guadalajara 190) and in the 1780s (Archivo General de la Nación, Archivo de Hacienda Histórica, Minería 338, exp. 3).

52. The period covers wages for mayordomo, sobresaliente, and ayudante at goat, cattle, and horse ranches between 1739 and 1751, and those connected with goat ranching may have been slightly better paid. The range was 60 pesos per year to 552 pesos with varying amounts of maize. With these data, it is not possible to ascertain how much differential there was from ranch to ranch, within similar occupations, and from year to year. In other words, it is hard to determine if the differences represent adjustments made to reward one manager over another, to account for inflation or seniority, or to reflect more specialized work. Konrad, *A Jesuit Hacienda,* 220–21, 241.

53. Clements Library, University of Michigan, Zacatecas Collection, Treasury Records and Correspondence, 1800–1809, Box A.

54. Konrad lists a standard payment of 9 quartillos, but a range of 18 to 24 quartillos. The range is not explained; *A Jesuit Hacienda,* 220, tab. 18.

55. Clements Library, University of Michigan, Zacatecas Collection, Treasury Records and Correspondence, 1750–1821, and Miscellaneous Bound Volume.

5

GROSS NATIONAL PRODUCT AND PRICES

The Chilean Case in the Seventeenth and Eighteenth Centuries

José Larraín

INTRODUCTION

ONE OF THE GREAT PROBLEMS CONFRONTED BY ECONOMIC HISTORY IS THE effort to estimate the size of the gross national product. As is well known, most investigators have used indirect methods to estimate the aggregate measure they seek.

In the present essay, we shall refer to one of these methods, which, in our opinion, may be successfully used in this type of study. This method, which we shall describe below, is based upon the history of prices in the city of Santiago de Chile between 1659 and 1808. The early work for this essay was done in collaboration with Prof. Armando de Ramón several years ago.

This study has two objectives. The first is the description of a reliable methodology for obtaining information about the evolution of gross national product. The second, as a consequence of the earlier data, is the description and interpretation of the variation of prices and of the gross national product in the Chilean economy during the seventeenth and eighteenth centuries.

GROSS NATIONAL PRODUCT AND PRICES

Techniques and Methods

As we said earlier, the size of the gross national product is one of the great themes in economic history. Knowledge of changes in the size of the economy over time allows the researcher to interpret economic phenomena during the period analyzed, explaining the different stages of development in a country's economy. In turn, adequate information about other variables (for example, data relative to population) allows the researcher to make inferences about another of the great themes, the division of this economic product. He may illuminate, as well, the level of development achieved by one country by comparing its gross national product to that of other countries or regions.

It is, however, in the elaboration of and search for the necessary data to realize this research that it is possible to utilize the tools that economic theory provides. In one of its simplest interpretations, the gross national product is defined as one current of production. It is measured as the value resulting from the sum of all expenditures made by a society in a specific period (consumption; net private investment, both interior and exterior; and public expenditure on goods and services). This is expressed in the formula:

$$GNP = CP + NPI + PE$$

gross national product = consumption product + net private investment + public expenditure on goods[1]

Beginning with this formula we can specify those variables that we were interested in investigating and studying. In the case observed in this study, we can assume that both public expenditure and private investment represented a small portion of the total. This is so since the state made few public expenditures in Chile during the seventeenth century. It was only in the second half of the eighteenth century that the public sector's participation in the generation of the gross national product began to acquire an increased importance through, for example, the execution of a series of public works, such as of the urban renovation of the capital.[2]

We can also infer that private investment was insignificant in these years. In addition, a net exterior investment, the surplus of what is exported annually in goods and services over what is imported, transformed the country into a debtor nation that imported more than it exported during a great part of the colonial period.[3] On the other hand, we can affirm that the net interior investment was inferior in relation to total expenditure.[4] As a result of the foregoing, we shall focus our investigation on private consumption, since this represented the greatest percentage of expenditures made by Chilean society in these centuries.

It is at this moment that we should explain the method through which it is possible to obtain information about one of the most important components of the gross national product, consumption, through the study of prices. We should point out that, for this case, price series give us two types of basic information:

Table 5.1

Structure of Expenditure in Santiago de Chile

Components of Expenditure	17th century (1669–73)*		18th century (1754–58)*	
Food		68.2		79.2
Oils, dried beef, and fats	11.0		13.3	
Sugars and sweets	4.3		6.5	
Alcohol and stimulants	13.2		7.0	
Meat, poultry, and fish	17.2		27.1	
Fruits and vegetables	7.9		7.0	
Flours and starches	14.6		18.3	
Clothing		15.7		3.9
Housing		14.1		15.8
Miscellaneous		2.0		1.1

*Base years
Sources: See note 5.

a) Information about the structure of expenditure, which allows us to specify the goods and services consumed by the society being studied and to estimate the relative importance within total expenditure of each one of the goods and services. In this fashion, upon analyzing the production of these goods and services and monitoring their variations, we shall obtain information that will allow us to approach the study of the gross national product.

b) Indices of prices, which will help us in the interpretation of economic phenomena and also in the deflation of the data proceeding from those series (for example, the tithe) that are seen to be affected by the level of prices. Thus, upon eliminating this effect, we shall observe variations in these values and infer the behavior of production.

In order to realize the foregoing, we used data about prices found in the archives of the city of Santiago. The results of our research may be evaluated in the tables that follow.[5]

In Table 5.1, it can be seen that for both the seventeenth and eighteenth centuries, the greatest percentage of expenditure corresponded to the category

Foodstuffs, and, within this, to the subgroups meat, poultry, and fish, and flour and starches. The expenditure for housing was also appreciable in both centuries. For this reason, these articles will be the ones that will have priority in our analysis leading to an estimation of the gross national product.

A second step, in this sense, consisted of choosing those products that were most relevant, in accord with the amount expended on them, to construct indices of their respective prices. Twenty-four products were chosen for the seventeenth century. Expenditures for these articles rose to 78.84 percent of total average expenditure, according to the sources in the base period. For the eighteenth century, twenty-one articles were chosen, representing an expenditure of 79.76 percent of total expenditure made in the base period.

Immediately after this selection, we proceeded to determine a statistical weight for each article, as is indicated in Table 5.2. This information was then used in the construction of a general price index measured at five-year intervals during the two periods, from 1659 to 1718 and from 1749 to 1808.

We calculated the price index of agricultural and livestock products extending from the years 1659–1736 to 1749–1808 using six articles that represented an expenditure equivalent of 73.13 percent of total expenditure for agricultural and livestock products in the seventeenth century and an expenditure equivalent to 71.82 percent of expenditure in the eighteenth century.

Another index was calculated for imported products using two products: sugar and flannel and cotton cloth. The expenditure on these articles represented 35.52 percent of total expenditures on imported products for the seventeenth century and 46.30 percent for the eighteenth century. Tables 5.3 and 5.4 show the articles chosen and the assigned weights given to these indices.

It only remains for us to indicate that, for the graphs and final figures that include both centuries, we used the years 1754 to 1758 as the base period. For this, the indices made were joined in the base period 1669 to 1673 with the new period considered. The formula used for the calculation of the general price index, as well as partial indices, was Laspeyres's. We should also add in this paragraph the method used to calculate the agricultural and livestock product for the Santiago region. The procedure consisted of using the data from tithe payments deflated by the agricultural and livestock index. The result is presented in Table 5.5.[6]

Table 5.2

Selected articles, expenditures made,
and assigned weight
1669–73 (base years)

Articles	Expenditure (in reales)	Weighted Index	Article	Expenditure (in reales)	Weighted Index
Fat	15.297	8.75	Fat	24.591	11.51
Dried beef	3.979	2.27	Dried beef	3.821	1.79
Sugar	5.471	2.90	Sugar	12.228	5.30
Honey	2.592	1.37	Honey	2.767	1.20
Chile	2.718	1.61	Chile	2.247	1.86
Salt	4.744	2.80	Salt	2.880	2.38
Wine	14.912	8.81	Wine	3.335	2.76
Mutton	16.646	9.71	Mutton	48.100	20.98
Fresh fish	6.259	3.65	Fresh fish	10.506	4.58
Dried fish	4.654	2.71	Dried fish	2.682	1.17
Shellfish	1.972	1.15	Charqui	.839	0.37
Potatoes	14.225	7.87	Potatoes	9.845	6.28
Dried corn	1.369	0.76	Onions	1.133	0.72
Flour	2.372	1.30	Flour	34.889	15.47
Wheat	16.355	9.03	Rice	1.239	0.55
Dried beans	3.599	1.99	Dried beans	5.132	2.28
Lentils	2.820	1.56			
Flannel	9.383	8.64	Imported flannel	1.443	2.26
Wool	6.241	5.74	and cotton		
Cordovans	1.414	1.30	Shoes	1.044	1.64
Firewood	5.980	6.67	Firewood	11.005	11.19
Tallow	2.800	3.27	Tallow	4.532	4.61
Roof tiles	3.274	3.82			
Tobacco	.481	2.02	Snuff	1.233	
					1.10
Total	149.557	100.00		185.491	100.00

Table 5.3

Selected article and assigned weight
Price index for agricultural and livestock products

Articles	17th century (1669–73)* %	18th century (1754–58)* %
Mutton	19.92	34.06
Fat	17.95	18.68
Flour and wheat**	21.19	25.11
Potatoes	16.15	10.19
Tallow	6.71	7.48
Wine	18.08	4.48
	100.00	100.00

*Base years
**Only for the 17th century
Sources: See note 5.

Table 5.4

Selected articles and assigned weight
Price index for imported products

Articles	17th century (1669–73)* %	18th century (1754–58)* %
Sugar	25.13	70.11
Flannel and cotton	74.87	29.89
	100.00	100.00

*Base years
Sources: See note 5.

Table 5.5

Index of Agricultural and Livestock Production, 1681–1808
1754 : 1758 = 100.00

1681	21.01	1710	50.98	1752	100.79	1781	129.74
1682	20.83	1711	47.24	1753	103.25	1782	110.13
1683	20.57	1712	48.49	1754	96.85	1783	135.17
1684	28.75	1713	56.03	1755	106.46	1784	150.77
1685	28.95	1714	52.76	1756	105.00	1785	129.78
1686	29.02	1715	49.18	1757	99.26	1786	162.25
1687	31.15	1716	49.16	1758	93.49	1787	150.93
1688	34.93	1717	56.27	1759	91.11	1788	153.22
1689	37.16	1718	47.43	1760	110.28	1789	147.09
1690	33.26	1719	57.17	1761	108.68	1790	156.04
1691	31.65	1720	63.38	1762	131.11	1791	156.11
1692	33.10	1721	61.09	1763	100.95	1792	132.24
1693	31.74	1722	75.02	1764	108.33	1793	156.74
1694	19.40	1723	59.65	1765	104.10	1794	124.40
1695	17.65	1724	74.38	1766	107.09	1795	138.96
1696	22.84	1726	76.27	1767	123.17	1796	136.19
1697	24.18	1727	77.98	1768	131.38	1797	123.47
1698	22.10	1728	84.64	1769	127.14	1798	140.76
1699	24.98	1729	71.26	1770	116.68	1799	120.17
1700	24.06	1730	68.33	1771	118.82	1800	127.21
1701	27.76	1731	55.50	1772	117.34	1801	128.68
1702	26.08	1732	48.40	1773	125.71	1802	148.43
1703	35.96	1733	63.34	1774	144.99	1803	150.15
1704	39.55	1734	55.01	1775	148.84	1804	186.02
1705	45.49	1735	75.17	1776	157.16	1805	167.87
1706	46.35	1736	67.10	1777	166.03	1806	195.01
1707	37.91	1749	84.85	1778	141.16	1807	183.67
1708	48.77	1750	78.88	1779	120.74	1808	185.14
1709	46.90	1751	86.95	1780	127.29		

THE GROSS NATIONAL PRODUCT AND PRICES

Central Chile in the Seventeenth and Eighteenth Centuries

As we have indicated, our work is only concerned with what is today the central zone of the present Republic of Chile. These territories were jurisdictionally assigned to the city of Santiago during the sixteenth century. They reached in the north to the Choapa River and in the south to the Longaví River, comprising six corregimientos: Quillota, Aconcagua, Melipilla, Santiago, Colchagua, and Maule.

The city of Santiago had been founded in 1541, but because of the definitive destruction of the cities of the south at the hands of rebelling natives, it was not until 1598 that the city assumed its role as the principal urban center of the entire kingdom. From this period on, a stage of economic organization and population growth was initiated. The process of land distribution began in the central zone, and eventually agricultural property constituted the fundamental resource base both for supplying the needs of the domestic population and for sustaining commercial exchange with neighboring regions, particularly Peru.[7] This stage was not free of serious difficulties, however. The earthquake of 1647 destroyed most of the city; the great Indian uprising of 1655 laid waste to all the estancias located to the south of the Maule River; and the crisis of recoined money put the country to a severe test.

In any case, and from 1660 on, a modest, but steady and sustained, recovery was initiated that lasted throughout the following century. It is from this moment on that we shall begin our study of the gross national product and price movements in central Chile.

As is inferred from Table 5.1, the products of agricultural and livestock activity were those that constituted the bulk of consumption for the inhabitants of Santiago and its environs. Therefore, our interest was focused on the supply of these articles.

If we observe the index of agricultural and livestock production according to Table 5.5 and Graph 5.1, we can distinguish four periods with distinctive characteristics during this period of nearly 130 years. The first of these is between 1681 and 1702; the second, between 1703 and 1763, including a period between the years 1737 and 1748 with no information; the third, between 1764 and 1799; and the fourth and last from 1800 on.

The initial date of the first period, 1681, and the terminal date of the last, 1808, are arbitrary. The initial date was chosen because that was when

Graph 5.1

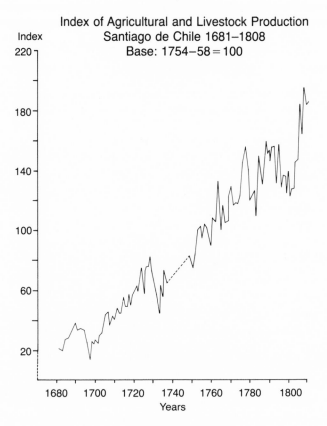

Index of Agricultural and Livestock Production
Santiago de Chile 1681–1808
Base: 1754–58 = 100

a consistent tithe record began. The concluding date was chosen because of availability of information on prices. For those periods that do not correspond to the actual initial and terminal dates of a tendency, it should be understood that they may comprise a greater number of years.

The first period, which includes the twenty-one years from 1681 to 1702, shows us a rising trend in production until 1693. It then diminishes and stagnates until the end of the century.

The abrupt increase in the external demand for wheat from the decade of 1690 on, closely following a period of poor harvests, led to a deficit in the provision of wheat, flour, and bread and to a rise in the prices of these products as well as alternative food products, such as potatoes, beans, and

Graph 5.2

General Index of Prices
Santiago de Chile 1659–1808
Base: 1754–58 = 100
(quinquenially)

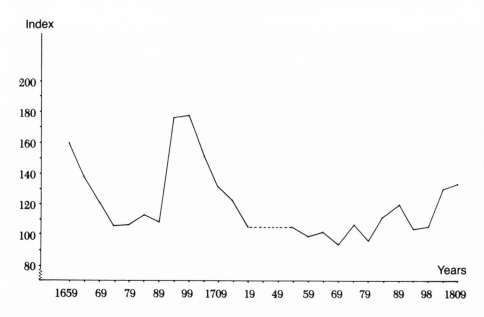

corn. This inflationary process was then generalized. The series of price increases also reached other products, with the results observed in the general price index (Graph 5.2) and in the price index for agricultural and livestock products (Graph 5.3).

For the five-year period from 1694 to 1698, the general price index reached a value of 176.50. In comparison, the previous five-year period was 109.09. The price index for agricultural and livestock products showed the following values for those years:

Year		Value	
1693		102.42	
1694		189.84	
1695		227.88	
1696		216.29[8]	

Graph 5.3

Price Index of Agricultural and Livestock Products
Santiago de Chile 1659–1808
Base: 1754–58 = 100

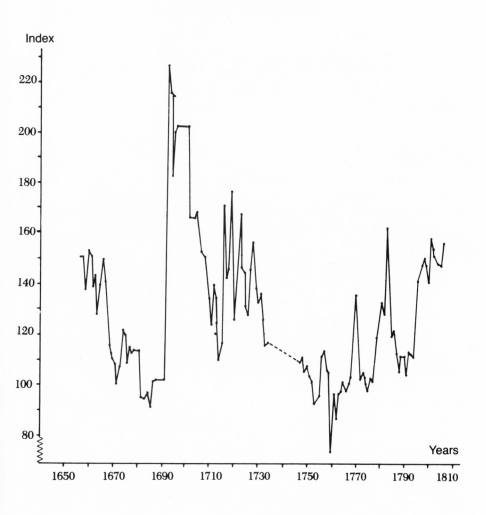

In the presence of this stimulus, farmers reacted by rededicating those lands previously planted with a diverse mix of products for local consumption to wheat cultivation.[9] The results of this change were not long awaited—a decreased production and rising prices of these neglected crops.

In a similar fashion, the contraction of external demand for tallow and cordovan coincided precisely with the increase in wheat exports, followed by the displacement of cattle toward the south in order to use additional lands for the cultivation of grain. As a result, there was a decline and then stagnation of production in these livestock byproducts until the end of the seventeenth century.[10]

The second period, which covers the sixty years from 1703 to 1763, shows us a strong growth in production until 1728. This was followed by a decline of approximately 40 percent around 1732. Production experienced a slow recovery beginning in 1733 that by 1749 reestablished the levels of 1728. There was then a modest rise around 1752 and, finally, stagnation until 1763.

The index of agricultural and livestock production, which in 1703 was 35.96, grew to 84.64 in 1728, diminishing to 48.40 in 1732, and growing to 100.79 in 1752. It then maintained itself at those levels until 1763.

This growth in production had no immediate effect on prices which remained at high levels until the middle of the decade of the 1730s, as is seen in Graph 5.3. The reason for this situation, in our opinion, was attributable to two elements. The first was an increase in exports to Peru, which neutralized the local effect of increases in production. The second was the slow process of adaptation of the Chilean economy to new conditions established by external demand. With regard to the first element, the figures below, which confirm this increase, show us the freight transported between Valparaíso and Callao in some years of the period:

Years	1692–96	9,758 tons transported
	1702–1706	18,681 tons transported
	1732–36	40,219 tons transported[11]

In the same fashion, the figures relative to the export of wheat through Valparaíso show the same tendency:

1705   65,556 fanegas exported
1715   93,458 fanegas exported
1725   122,087 fanegas exported
1735   119,605 fanegas exported[12]

With regard to the second element already mentioned, we can indicate that the incorporation of new zones of the Valley of Santiago for the cultivation of wheat, such as Colina, Lampa, Tango, and Malloco, was slow. Then, in the first decades of the eighteenth century, the continued opening of new lands extended cultivation toward Maipo, Melipilla, Aconcagua, Quillota, and the hilly, coastal area located to the south of Valparaíso.[13] This replacement of old agricultural and livestock activity by the cultivation of wheat was, however, one of the reasons for the high prices of products of customary consumption, such as potatoes, beans, wine, meat, fat, and tallow.[14]

The search for new lands for the cultivation of these agricultural products and the displacement of cattle toward the corregimientos of Colchagua and Maule[15] affected both the production of these articles and the supply of the population. The result was the high prices detected for this period. Another reason that should also be taken in account is bad harvests caused by diseases that attacked land already sown in 1732.[16]

From the following year on, however, production regained its initial force to recover its pre-1732 level, growing until 1752 and immediately afterward stagnating until 1763.

The expansion of the internal market explains to us the growth of production in those years.[17] Production, however, quickly stagnated as a consequence of the depressed situation in the export market. The consequences of this commercial crisis led to a cabildo abierto on 22 September 1753.[18]

The figures below on freight transported between Valparaíso and Callao illustrate this fact:

Five-year period   1737–41   43,540 tons transported
                    1742–46   39,959 tons transported
                    1747–51   51,066 tons transported
                    1752–56   46,596 tons transported[19]

Likewise, it was possible to observe a similar tendency in the figures relative to the export of wheat through Valparaíso that confirm what was stated earlier.[20] With regard to the behavior of prices, the price index for agricultural and livestock products showed the following values as a consequence of the expansion of production from the year 1733 on. From a value of 137.54 in 1733, the index declined to 104.32 twenty years later, reaching 73.87 in 1762, the lowest figure of the entire period studied.

This process of price decline was seen to be strengthened even more by the fall, also secular, of the prices of imported products. An index of imported products is presented in Graph 5.4 and is included in the Appendix. These index numbers fell from 175.83 in the year 1703 to 76.47 in 1753.

The third period we can distinguish in our study covers the years 1764 to 1799 and was characterized by abrupt variations in production. From a value of 118.33 in 1764, the index fell to 104.10 in 1765. It rose again to 131.38 in 1768 and then fell to 116.68 in 1770. Rising first to 144.99 in 1774 and then to 166.03 in 1777, the index fell again to 110.13 in 1782, a level similar to the one established twenty years before. From 1782 on, a new rise in the level of production culminated in 1793 with the index at 156.74. The rest of the period was characterized by important fluctuations of these values, with a tendency to fall, especially around 1799.

The situation of low prices was maintained during these years with some exceptions. If we observe the figures of the general index, we shall see that, aside from the five-year period from 1784 to 1788, where the index rose to 120.14, only small upward fluctuations stand out. In the case of the price index for agricultural and livestock products, it is possible to prove this assertion with greater detail. According to this index, the years from 1782 to 1786 and those at the end of the decade of the 1690s witnessed significant price increases.

The growth of the internal market,[21] combined with a growth of exports,[22] explains the price rises of these years. We should also bear in mind the livestock scarcity that documents from the era assert as a cause of the high prices in the years 1782 and 1785[23] and also the decline in production toward the end of the 1790s. From those years on, however, this situation began to be modified, as we shall see in the fourth period of our study.

After the abrupt fall in production around 1799, the economy began to recover rapidly in the following decade. The index for agricultural and livestock production, which in 1800 had a value of 127.21, grew rapidly to 148.43 in 1803, 186.02 in 1804, 195.01 in 1806, and 185.14 in 1808. This last index number was the highest value reached during the entire period studied, surpassing the values of previous highs recorded in 1777, 1786, and 1788.

This recovery to levels of production established twenty years before, however, only suggests to us that agricultural and livestock production in

Graph 5.4

Price Index of Imported Products
Santiago de Chile 1659–1808
Base: 1754–58 = 100

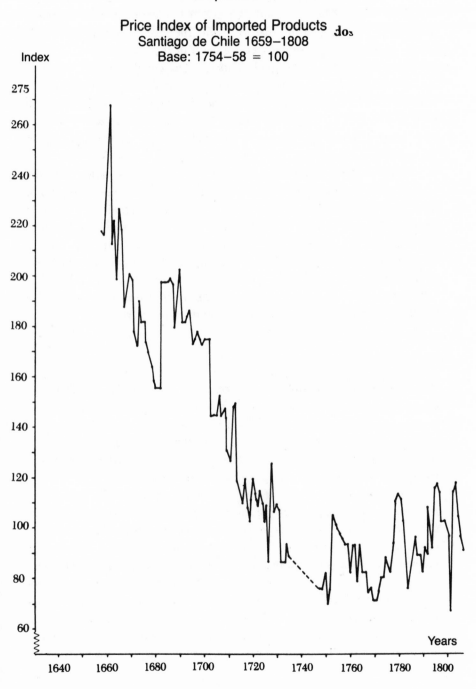

central Chile was again beginning to reach the limit of its potential. As would be seen in the nineteenth century, new techniques and additional investment were needed in order to permit the incorporation of new, cultivable lands and generate long-term growth in this sector.

On the other hand, the gradual increase in population that occurred throughout the entire eighteenth century was supplanted at the end of the same century by dramatic growth. The development of the social base, the growth of urban groups, mining groups,[24] and poor campesinos who invested their limited incomes in foodstuffs, forcefully brought pressure to bear on the internal market.[25]

This panorama foreshadowed an era of price rises, as is indicated in the general index, which went from a value of 106.93 in 1794–98 to 130.79 in 1799–1803 and then to 134.94 in the five-year period from 1804 to 1808. At the same time, the price index for agricultural and livestock products rose to a value of 128.59 in 1797 and to 151.39 in 1800. It was then maintained at similar high levels until 1808, the year in which our study ends.

Imported products also experienced slightly increased price levels as a result of the rise in sugar prices in the international market.[26]

CONCLUSIONS

At this point in our work, our concern is to offer conclusions about the objectives established upon beginning it. These refer to two aspects, the first being a methodological one, which is the description and validity of the techniques used to obtain information about the gross national product and prices in central Chile during the seventeenth and eighteenth centuries; and the second relative to the interpretation of this information.

With regard to the first objective, we should point out that everything referring to the obtaining of the information for the construction of price series and the calculation of the respective indices, together with the validity of the sources consulted and the techniques employed, is found amply explained in the works related in Note 5. We therefore consider it unnecessary to discuss it again. It only remains for us to emphasize the importance of the calculation of the structure of expenditure, as is seen in Table 5.1 and the list of products chosen to construct the general price index, according to Table 5.2, in the analysis of the consumption of Santiago's population in the seventeenth and eighteenth centuries. In these tables, one can observe the relevance that agricultural and livestock products coming from the internal market had in the consumption mix of the time.

Therefore, the study of production levels through the tithe series, deflated by the index for agricultural and livestock prices, allowed us to approach an estimation of gross domestic product. The hypothesis used in this case was to estimate the valid tendency of the resulting product index, assuming that production not included through possible omissions in collection or fraud of the contributors evolved in the same direction as our documents. Hence, the present analysis was limited only to the study of the evolution of agricultural and livestock production, excluding other conclusions about their annual value.

With regard to the general movement of prices, we can point out the existence of two strong periods of rises during the seventeenth century, followed by a price decline in the following century, with the exception of a brief lapse in the decade of 1780 and the beginning of a new period of increases from 1800 on.

The reasons for these price changes are different for each situation analyzed. The crises of production in the decade of 1650 caused the price rise detected by our index around 1659–63. This was followed by price decline tied to the recovery of production and stagnation in the export market caused by population decline in Upper and Lower Peru.[27]

The second period of price rises in the seventeenth century begins in the first years of the decade of 1690, because of an abrupt increase of high prices that was sustained for about thirty years. This indicates that the Chilean economic system had adapted itself to the new conditions posed by the external market in the first decades of the eighteenth century. With the exception of the five-year period from 1780 to 1784, the rest of the century was characterized by a situation of stable prices. The small price rises of national products were counterbalanced by a fall in prices experienced by imported products throughout nearly the entire century.[28]

We certainly need to emphasize the gradual price increase of livestock products that becomes evident from the decade of 1760 on. As we said previously, the growth in agricultural production was realized at the expense of the livestock sector, a situation similar to that observed by Professors Tandeter and Wachtel in the work already cited for Potosí in the same period.[29]

Another aspect that should be commented upon is that which refers to the different stages of growth of agricultural and livestock production. As we already pointed out, the rhythm of growth of each one of the periods analyzed was different. Between 1681 and 1702, production increased 1.2 percent annually, a rate that, after the adjustments experienced by the economic system, grew 1.5 percent annually between the years 1703 and 1763. This, then, was a period when production was consolidated and the external market stabilized. In the following years, the rhythm of growth moderated, and the rate diminished to 0.6 percent of annual growth between the years 1764 and 1799. The combination of slow growth and stable price levels indicates to us that production increases were limited by the size of both internal and external markets.

This situation changed at the end of the eighteenth century. The growth of the internal market, together with an increase in exports, promoted a rise in prices from those years on. Production regained the levels of years before, but it appears that it had nearly reached its structural limit.[30] Only in the nineteenth century would it successfully confront this new expansion of agricultural and livestock production whose solid bases were built throughout two centuries.

APPENDIX 1

Average Prices by Five-Year Periods
Santiago de Chile 1659–1718
(in reales)

Product	1659–1663	1664–1668	1669–1673	1674–1678	1679–1683	1684–1688	1689–1693	1694–1698	1699–1703	1704–1708	1709–1713	1714–1718
1. chile (fanegas)	35.57	35.42	27.61	23.42	24.66	26.68	33.00	77.69	71.81	64.00	39.98	40.48
2. sugar (pounds)	4.61	4.02	3.27	3.27	2.77	4.46	3.30	3.09	2.66	1.69	1.91	1.88
3. Imported flannel and cotton (varas)	10.25	8.69	8.52	8.23	6.98	8.07	8.08	8.03	8.26	7.26	6.73	6.01
4. meat (arrobas)	5.87	5.15	4.33	4.65	4.42	3.32	3.37	6.29	7.60	6.62	4.49	4.25
5. charqui (quintals)	20.00	21.65	19.14	16.32	16.49	13.52	12.56	20.09	18.13	19.36	22.05	19.43
6. cordovan (units)	16.38	13.93	7.68	5.14	10.57	16.00	13.00	10.50	11.48	16.00	7.15	8.48
7. dried corn (fanegas)	35.25	28.33	25.74	23.72	22.28	24.00	26.00	48.65	51.77	48.00	37.51	36.70
8. fat (botijas)	33.45	31.35	29.73	25.29	22.17	15.76	15.95	29.74	31.69	25.03	28.25	27.61
9. flour (fanegas)	17.37	18.62	16.60	15.00	20.00	15.25	22.62	45.55	41.40	32.26	23.25	18.74
10. lentils (fanegas)	31.39	33.07	25.31	23.10	20.00	23.18	24.47	46.28	44.36	45.37	28.18	29.34
11. firewood (loads)	22.37	21.73	17.54	16.18	14.28	15.27	15.71	17.67	20.00	20.00	20.00	20.00
12. shrimp (strings)	2.82	2.09	2.93	2.58	1.55	2.63	1.64	1.60	2.00	1.50	1.31	1.57
13. honey (botijas)	76.00	74.60	76.30	75.69	77.33	96.00	90.66	92.71	65.14	74.66	73.08	102.00
14. potatoes (fanegas)	23.15	23.42	20.63	14.46	13.82	24.00	18.33	27.20	24.43	24.35	21.98	21.81
15. flannel (varas)	47.61	36.57	35.01	32.43	21.33	37.33	32.85	38.02	44.41	40.00	35.87	32.96
16. dried fish (arrobas)	44.17	33.71	26.99	26.30	25.50	32.00	25.11	34.24	43.54	33.98	34.20	33.17
17. fresh fish (arrobas)	34.54	21.85	18.71	12.32	11.60	21.92	18.86	18.11	8.34	16.00	15.66	12.78
18. dried beans (fanegas)	27.06	27.63	23.08	18.62	24.00	24.00	24.00	46.79	48.83	42.71	36.88	34.13
19. salt (arrobas)	8.75	7.82	6.62	4.92	4.40	5.28	3.86	8.24	7.25	6.69	3.82	3.71
20. tallow (quintals)	52.00	33.49	26.28	31.49	32.85	13.91	13.51	28.29	47.64	24.77	24.28	27.86
21. tobacco (hands)	4.53	4.03	4.27	3.19	2.98	4.00	4.00	4.27	5.41	4.20	4.27	2.38
22. roof tiles (thousands)	158.22	155.90	164.60	159.40	168.31	183.69	199.07	206.20	246.65	224.72	190.23	198.00
23. wheat (fanegas)	17.48	12.81	11.02	8.84	15.02	12.64	14.77	36.64	33.30	23.56	18.51	11.77
24. wine (arrobas)	28.60	26.13	21.39	17.10	18.49	14.11	13.46	36.01	27.45	28.80	27.10	29.03

Sources: See note 5

APPENDIX 2

Average Prices by Five-Year Periods
Santiago de Chile 1749–1808

(in reales)

Product	1749–1753	1754–1758	1759–1763	1764–1768	1769–1773	1774–1778	1779–1783	1784–1788	1789–1793	1794–1798	1799–1803	1804–1808
1. chile (fanegas)	20.77	13.32	11.30	9.63	9.74	10.03	10.49	11.39	9.87	7.57	12.46	12.06
2. rice (pounds)	1.05	0.92	1.04	0.94	0.74	0.87	0.80	0.93	0.93	0.58	0.61	1.15
3. sugar (pounds)	1.09	1.45	1.43	1.29	1.18	1.31	1.50	1.38	1.42	1.92	1.55	1.90
4. mutton (units)	4.82	4.68	4.60	4.33	5.09	5.16	5.43	7.18	6.04	6.52	8.00	8.53
5. onions (hundreds)	2.47	2.21	1.44	1.50	1.13	1.48	1.82	1.29	0.93	1.30	1.11	1.03
6. dried beef (quintals)	20.26	15.63	19.45	23.14	22.74	20.02	23.14	35.92	28.00	23.14	23.14	23.14
7. charqui (quintals)	12.53	14.28	15.93	18.86	20.20	19.58	24.74	21.89	21.41	18.76	27.84	35.25
8. fat (botijas)	22.46	22.76	21.60	21.24	26.47	27.47	29.45	31.91	25.57	22.94	28.68	32.55
9. flour (fanegas)	16.00	11.29	14.58	12.19	15.06	9.46	13.27	12.13	10.09	13.20	18.00	18.00
10. firewood (loads)	2.74	3.21	3.28	3.33	3.28	3.22	3.22	3.22	3.25	2.60	3.36	3.15
11. honey (botijas)	44.00	64.09	71.85	57.84	65.71	58.00	71.33	68.00	65.33	85.00	60.00	73.48
12. potatoes (fanegas)	9.38	10.40	9.96	7.39	10.79	8.24	12.71	8.51	9.95	7.15	12.88	10.18
13. fresh fish (arrobas)	28.08	21.88	15.81	15.77	18.16	16.50	19.10	26.40	23.91	15.60	20.50	21.46
14. dried fish (arrobas)	30.00	23.36	22.74	21.53	29.78	33.42	38.37	36.91	25.54	19.88	34.44	41.20
15. snuff (pounds)	25.66	29.44	28.93	33.61	32.00	32.00	32.00	32.00	32.00	32.00	32.00	32.00
16. dried beans (fanegas)	19.51	19.35	14.70	22.36	18.73	15.13	18.72	18.17	15.61	13.86	18.43	16.87
17. imported flannel and cotton (varas)	3.77	4.74	4.00	3.33	2.75	3.25	5.50	3.37	3.50	3.52	3.75	3.82
18. salt (arrobas)	4.57	4.95	7.05	4.35	6.20	3.18	2.99	5.43	2.68	3.87	3.35	3.09
19. tallow (quintals)	34.00	36.63	31.98	39.81	41.87	39.33	45.96	44.00	43.01	41.73	44.06	49.22
20. wine (arrobas)	18.77	17.83	15.53	14.64	15.43	13.91	19.28	24.15	16.25	21.33	25.85	22.31
21. shoes (pairs)	10.76	12.37	12.66	10.14	7.80	8.00	8.00	8.00	8.00	7.73	10.04	8.80

Sources: See note 5

APPENDIX 3

Annual Prices of Products
Santiago de Chile 1631–1808
(in reales)

Year	mutton (un.)	fat (bot.)	flour (fan.)	potatoes (fan.)	tallow (quin.)	wine (arr.)	sugar (lbs.)	imported flannel and cotton (varas)
1631			17.14		44.10	14.00	2.29	12.00
1632		12.00	10.96		53.00	28.00	2.48	8.19
1633	6.00		16.77	16.00	56.00		2.16	
1634		21.65	14.27	16.00	38.64	21.70	2.56	9.25
1635				16.00		15.83	2.31	
1636					32.00	17.71	2.22	
1637	3.82	24.00				19.11	2.13	9.38
1638		20.00		18.00			1.85	
1639								
1640								
1641	4.10			13.64	21.87		3.36	
1642	4.00	28.00		14.75	22.01		2.50	9.78
1643	4.00	17.00		13.33	15.92	10.00	2.90	7.94
1644	4.00	14.89		8.00	26.00		2.58	8.97
1659	6.14	32.00				26.40	3.61	10.00
1660	6.00	32.00				27.71		9.06
1661	5.63	30.00	16.00		54.00	20.16	4.09	11.20
1662		33.60	17.90		50.66	30.90	6.35	10.69
1663	4.83	34.13				32.17	4.19	9.21
1664	4.74	35.00				23.95	3.89	10.00
1665	5.63	34.78				24.25	3.47	9.00
1666	4.02	31.53	16.00			23.15	5.24	9.12
1667	5.26	30.62	20.00		35.33	23.26	5.18	8.69
1668	5.83	31.34	17.62		32.76	34.01	3.55	8.21
1669	4.12	28.13	20.00		29.10	33.34	3.61	8.54
1670	4.31	31.70	21.33		28.93	23.85	3.72	8.88
1671	4.23	29.52	15.70		28.03	16.10	3.51	8.94
1672	4.42	28.07	12.91		25.55	18.53	3.11	8.00
1673	4.78	26.91	11.09		23.31	18.67	2.73	8.00
1674	4.12	24.37	12.94		24.17	17.84	3.04	8.83
1675	4.00	25.63	16.55		23.85	16.07	3.61	7.84
1676	6.00	24.57				15.88	3.43	8.00
1677						20.00	2.86	8.00
1678	5.00	23.72			32.15	19.56	3.13	7.54
1679		22.10	20.00		32.85	18.95	2.74	6.72
1680	4.42	22.32	20.00			18.05	2.80	7.20
1681								
1682								
1683								

APPENDIX 3 (continued)

Year	mutton (un.)	fat (bot.)	flour (fan.)	potatoes (fan.)	tallow (quin.)	wine (arr.)	sugar (lbs.)	imported flannel and cotton (varas)
1684								
1685								
1686								
1687	3.68	16.00			14.00	13.86	4.46	8.10
1688	2.43	15.70	15.25	24.00	13.89	14.49		8.00
1689	3.23	16.00	23.70	17.64	14.08	13.05	3.10	8.16
1690	3.50	16.00	22.06	18.94	12.86	13.97	4.26	8.00
1691	3.31	16.00					4.76	
1692								
1693								
1694	5.00				32.00	32.00	3.44	8.11
1695	6.28	20.88	53.93	40.78	36.44	41.68	3.66	8.10
1696	5.87	27.00	49.31	30.39	20.00	49.86	2.78	8.00
1697	7.04	44.70	30.48	22.04	34.04	32.77	2.91	8.00
1698								
1699	7.60	31.69		24.43	47.64	27.45	2.63	8.26
1700							2.78	8.00
1701								
1702								
1703								
1704								
1705								
1706								
1707	6.87	26.95	31.51	25.08	25.39		1.98	7.49
1708	6.13	23.16	32.81	22.32	24.46	28.80	1.92	7.07
1709	5.39	31.13	24.00	22.93	43.62	26.68	1.87	7.32
1710	5.38	39.23	20.39	24.75	40.02	23.89	1.83	7.10
1711	4.53	26.00	23.49	23.36	29.41	29.58	1.74	6.38
1712	3.68	24.26	25.15	21.68	26.12	27.71	1.68	6.19
1713	3.16	22.00	23.90	19.20	21.08	27.84	2.66	6.67
1714	3.75	28.69	22.25	23.04	27.86	32.21	2.16	7.19
1715	3.45	24.00	15.37	24.29		31.91	1.77	5.67
1716	3.60		9.79	19.61		26.89	1.61	5.54
1717	3.30	31.00	16.13	16.93		25.66	1.80	5.05
1718	7.68	35.55	24.00	28.74		27.76	2.14	5.41
1719	4.51	36.00				22.23		4.54
1720	5.08	32.00	22.00	25.47	27.71	26.48	1.98	4.54
1721	5.44	43.91	32.21	25.90		30.45	3.05	4.57
1722	5.03	44.00	23.50	24.04		29.45	2.14	5.03
1723	4.90		20.96	16.94		36.66	1.81	5.00
1724	4.01	30.12	28.63	20.71		28.75	1.93	5.27
1725	4.32	37.82	37.00	20.16		28.97	1.92	5.00
1726	4.51	28.50	24.19	24.00		28.68	1.88	
1727	4.01	24.00	17.37	22.50		32.00	2.30	

APPENDIX 3 (continued)

Year	mutton (un.)	fat (bot.)	flour (fan.)	potatoes (fan.)	tallow (quin.)	wine (arr.)	sugar (lbs.)	imported flannel and cotton (varas)
1728	4.57	23.51	20.91	19.16		24.00	1.95	3.54
1729	5.51	34.29	21.84	17.75	32.00	28.57	1.86	6.00
1730	5.60	39.04	22.27	22.40		30.64	1.70	
1731	5.13	24.00	14.00			38.40	1.92	5.00
1732	4.43	24.00	15.88	24.13		32.00		
1733	5.46	22.40	16.00	24.00		31.60	1.28	4.00
1734	4.00	20.00		20.00		32.00	1.32	
1735	4.03	27.33	15.00	16.00		24.00	1.92	4.00
1736	3.31	21.41	16.57	20.00	34.72	26.67		4.00
1737								
1738	3.00							
1739								
1740								
1741								
1742								
1743								
1744								
1745								
1746								
1747								
1748								
1749	4.00			16.38				
1750				10.58				
1751	4.50	21.02	16.00	9.00			1.24	
1752	5.00	20.00		8.08	36.00		0.96	
1753	4.00	24.16		8.73	32.00			
1754	4.37	27.97	10.38	12.71	38.58	16.30	1.56	5.00
1755	4.54	21.69	9.56	10.09	38.82	15.50	1.49	5.00
1756	4.62	20.30	11.50	9.25	33.99	16.00	1.47	
1757	5.03	22.61	10.26	8.18	30.00	16.82	1.46	4.39
1758	5.00	23.64	14.42	13.17	30.57	20.13	1.38	
1759	5.00	21.72	17.31	9.86	31.98	22.07	1.44	4.00
1760	4.00		14.62	16.88		16.00		
1761		20.38	9.14	9.91		11.14	1.21	
1762	3.50	18.52	7.90	6.64	32.00	10.32		4.00
1763	3.18	22.82	16.44	8.70		16.77		
1764	3.58	18.11	11.83	6.68		24.00	1.20	3.33
1765	4.00	24.78	11.57	6.86	34.92	21.11	1.30	5.00
1766	4.66	21.04	12.23	6.36	41.26	22.00		
1767		20.82	12.00	17.26	40.00	10.00	1.30	
1768	4.53	18.04	13.28	9.80		14.32		3.00
1769	4.93	27.43	9.29	8.41	43.28	17.90	1.16	3.00
1770	5.01	29.39	10.20	7.19	43.65	17.10	1.24	
1771	4.95	24.02	19.08	7.63	41.17	15.44	1.16	2.64

APPENDIX 3 (continued)

Year	mutton (un.)	fat (bot.)	flour (fan.)	potatoes (fan.)	tallow (quin.)	wine (arr.)	sugar (lbs.)	imported flannel and cotton (varas)
1772	5.31	24.40	23.54	14.09	39.98	14.53	1.11	3.00
1773	5.24	26.00	14.86	16.82	40.74	13.73	1.18	3.00
1774	5.35	26.37	9.01	10.41	41.87	16.31	1.29	3.00
1775	5.26	26.37	9.40	13.13	41.81	13.45	1.23	3.50
1776		23.75	12.82	8.18	32.71	12.62	1.45	3.00
1777	5.00	23.66	10.66	7.58	35.06	16.00	1.36	3.50
1778	5.00	32.03	9.26	6.80	41.70	20.00	1.30	
1779	5.00	30.15	8.54	8.16	46.22	20.00	1.23	
1780	4.64	27.93	13.49	10.18	51.30	18.84	1.59	
1781	5.24	25.88	13.93	15.94	43.72	17.18	1.66	
1782	5.82	34.17	15.99	18.84	44.21	22.67	1.61	
1783	7.37	23.40	15.51	13.18	44.20	21.84	1.42	5.50
1784		31.82		9.69				
1785	7.50	29.56	24.44	16.05			1.16	
1786	7.27	32.60	13.62	8.21		24.00	1.29	
1787	7.15	34.47	8.47	6.12		24.00	1.40	
1788	7.00	29.44	10.42	9.45		24.16	1.57	3.37
1789		30.19	10.03	8.93		20.68		3.50
1790		25.89		6.62	43.01	17.22		3.50
1791	6.30	24.47		11.62		17.19	1.28	3.36
1792	5.84	23.46	12.00	12.61		15.27	1.48	3.50
1793		19.91						3.50
1794		20.25				20.40		2.70
1795	6.00	24.20		7.02		22.06	1.49	3.45
1796	6.00	22.18				21.33	2.05	2.75
1797	6.83	21.08			41.05	24.50		4.00
1798	7.58	28.02		7.73	42.33	32.00		
1799	8.00	27.01			36.89	32.00	1.65	3.75
1800		33.44	18.00		43.98	16.33	1.64	3.80
1801		26.46						4.10
1802		26.14	18.00	6.00	45.95	24.11		3.50
1803		33.11		14.95	63.00		0.96	3.36
1804		28.06		11.31	54.48	20.00		
1805	8.50	27.67	18.00	11.85	44.02	24.05	1.98	
1806	8.42	28.02		7.34	54.30	22.17	1.69	3.74
1807	8.60	37.13		8.41	62.37	26.67	1.50	3.90
1808		32.46		10.42	64.00	20.11	1.50	3.17

Sources: See note 5.

APPENDIX 4

Price Index of Agricultural, Livestock,
and Imported Products
Santiago de Chile 1659–1808
(1754–58 = 100)

	Price Index				Price Index	
	Ag./Live. Prod.	Imp. Prod.			Ag./Live. Prod.	Imp. Prod.
1659	151.43	218.50	1697		185.35	175.13
1660	151.99	217.44	1698		200.07	178.25
1661	138.02	245.42	1699		203.39	175.39
1662	153.76	269.78	1700		203.39	173.29
1663	151.60	213.82	1701		203.39	175.83
1664	139.43	222.57	1702		203.39	175.83
1665	144.57	199.89	1703		203.39	175.83
1666	127.14	227.57	1704		166.48	145.13
1667	140.85	219.58	1705		166.48	145.13
1668	150.07	187.90	1706		166.48	145.13
1669	141.14	194.25	1707		169.03	153.17
1670	135.74	201.53	1708		161.17	145.32
1671	116.68	199.45	1709		153.57	148.74
1672	111.97	178.04	1710		151.60	144.49
1673	108.58	172.52	1711		143.14	131.22
1674	100.00	190.81	1712		135.10	127.20
1675	108.93	182.65	1713		124.77	149.42
1676	122.87	182.69	1714		140.71	150.78
1677	120.11	174.41	1715		125.76	119.88
1678	109.69	170.69	1716		110.92	115.38
1679	115.80	166.53	1717		117.78	110.02
1680	113.44	160.25	1718		171.41	120.94
1681	114.78	156.15	1719		143.86	108.01
1682	114.78	156.15	1720		146.61	104.18
1683	114.79	156.15	1721		177.83	120.20
1684	95.87	198.79	1722		126.27	114.63
1685	95.87	198.79	1723		151.48	109.37
1686	95.87	198.79	1724		148.01	115.55
1687	97.77	199.30	1725		168.14	110.94
1688	91.16	197.64	1726		145.78	103.76
1689	101.52	180.53	1727		131.02	109.87
1690	102.28	194.75	1728		127.87	87.13
1691	102.13	203.35	1729		146.58	126.65
1692	102.42	182.14	1730		157.83	107.75
1693	102.42	182.14	1731		139.46	110.94
1694	189.84	184.67	1732		133.29	107.60
1695	227.88	187.70	1733		137.54	85.03
1696	216.29	173.26	1734		126.64	85.60

APPENDIX 4 (continued)

	Price Index			Price Index	
	Ag./Live. Prod.	Imp. Prod.		Ag./Live. Prod.	Imp. Prod.
1735	116.97	94.33	1778	103.49	83.35
1736	117.58	89.96	1779	102.60	94.15
1737	110.83	76.47	1780	111.86	111.56
1738	111.12	76.47	1781	119.22	114.94
1739	106.06	83.73	1782	139.14	112.52
1740	108.37	70.19	1783	134.75	103.34
1741	104.32	76.47	1784	129.89	87.97
1742	102.28	106.96	1785	163.98	77.34
1743	93.81	103.58	1786	133.01	83.63
1744	95.88	100.97	1787	120.17	88.94
1745	96.35	98.27	1788	122.58	97.17
1746	112.06	96.61	1789	113.77	90.73
1747	114.46	94.85	1790	107.24	90.74
1748	106.45	94.36	1791	112.86	83.08
1749	89.56	83.73	1792	112.43	93.63
1750	73.87	94.36	1793	105.34	90.73
1751	97.70	94.36	1794	114.09	109.86
1752	87.93	79.02	1795	113.82	93.80
1753	97.27	94.39	1796	112.11	116.46
1754	98.78	83.38	1797	128.59	118.05
1755	102.88	83.86	1798	142.44	115.03
1756	98.65	81.30	1799	148.61	103.43
1757	100.63	75.01	1800	151.39	103.25
1758	103.52	77.30	1801	148.09	100.79
1759	117.94	72.74	1802	141.02	97.01
1760	136.64	72.59	1803	159.43	67.61
1761	120.77	75.98	1804	152.38	115.96
1762	103.45	81.30	1805	151.24	119.83
1763	105.61	81.54	1806	148.16	105.29
1764	103.41	89.03	1807	148.16	97.12
1765	98.13	87.83	1808	157.08	92.52

Sources: See note 5.

APPENDIX 5

General Price Index
Santiago de Chile 1659–1808
(1754–58 = 100)

Five-Year Period	Index	Five-Year Period	Index
1659–1663	160.87	1749–1753	105.13
1664–1668	138.42	1754–1758	100.00
1669–1673	121.00	1759–1763	101.51
1674–1678	106.93	1764–1768	94.82
1679–1683	107.87	1769–1773	107.31
1684–1688	113.00	1774–1778	96.59
1689–1693	109.09	1779–1783	112.15
1674–1698	176.50	1784–1788	120.14
1699–1703	178.28	1789–1793	104.85
1704–1708	152.68	1794–1798	106.09
1709–1713	131.66	1799–1803	130.79
1714–1718	122.37	1804–1808	134.94

Source: See note 5.

NOTES

1. Paul A. Samuelson, *Curso de economía moderna*, 12th ed. (Madrid: Aguilar de Ediciones, 1965), 224–42.

2. Armando de Ramón and José de Larraín, *Orígenes de la vida económica chilena, 1659–1808* (Santiago: C.E.P., 1982), 303–305.

3. The difference in the commercial balance would have been largely covered by exports of precious metals or, in some cases, by reducing indebtedness. Archivo Nacional de Chile, Santiago (hereinafter ANC), Capitanía General, vol. 368 and 374.

4. Marcello Carmagnani, "La producción agropecuaria chilena: Aspectos cuantitativos, 1680–1830," *Cahiers des Amériques Latines* 3 (1969): 12.

5. The sources used, their analysis, and the methods employed in Ramón and Larraín, *Orígenes*, 345–87; and José Manuel Larraín, "Movimiento de precios en Santiago de Chile, 1749–1808: Una interpretación metodológica," *Jahrbuch für Geschicte von Staat, Wirtshaft und Gesellschaft Lateinamerikas* 17 (1980): 199–259.

6. Carmagnani, in his "Producción," 3–8, uses a similar methodology for the computation of agricultural and livestock production. Nevertheless, the series of prices come from sources different than the ones used here, obtaining an unweighted, ten-year index of prices and a ten-year index of agricultural and livestock production.

7. Ramón and Larraín, *Orígenes*, 41–45.
8. See the respective Appendix.
9. Ramón and Larraín, *Orígenes*, 333.
10. Export of tallow and cordovan:

Years	*1681*	*1692*	*1699*
Tallow (quintals)	14,816	29,036	12,502
Cordovan (units)	30,260	44,010	23,820

Source: Ramón and Larraín, *Orígenes*, 267.

11. Ramón and Larraín, *Orígenes*, 252.
12. Ramón and Larraín, *Orígenes*, 286, 287.
13. Ramón and Larraín, *Orígenes*, 333.
14. Ramón and Larraín, *Orígenes*, 402, 403.
15. Ramón and Larraín, *Orígenes*, 86.
16. Ramón and Larraín, *Orígenes*, 111, 289.
17. ANC, Fondo Antiguo, vol. 34, f. 68.
18. ANC, Actas del Cabildo de Santiago, session of 22 Sept. 1753; Biblioteca Nacional de Santiago de Chile, Santiago (hereinafter BNSC), Sala Medina, Manuscritos de Medina, vol. 142, no. 2663.
19. Ramón and Larraín, *Orígenes*, 252.
20. Ramón and Larraín, *Orígenes*, 287.
21. ANC, Actas del Cabildo de Santiago, vol. 73, f. 41v.
22. Wheat exports reached 200,000 fanegas for the first time in 1788; Ramón and Larraín, *Orígenes*, 252.
23. Ramón and Larraín, *Orígenes*, 90–338.
24. It should be borne in mind that copper shipped through Valparaíso in some years represents between 15 and 20 percent of total export value; BNSC, Sala Medina, Manuscritos de Medina, vol. 257, no. 7483.
25. Ramón and Larraín, *Orígenes*, 338.
26. Ramón and Larraín, *Orígenes*, 161.
27. Ramón and Larraín, *Orígenes*, 331; Enrique Tandeter and Nathan Wachtel, "Prices and Agricultural Production: Potosí and Charcas in the Eighteenth Century," Chapter 8 in this volume.
28. Sergio Villalobos, *El comercio y la crisis colonial* (Santiago: University of Chile, 1968), 258–59, index of prices of imported products in the Appendix.
29. Tandeter and Wachtel, Id.
30. This situation is reflected as well in the case of Potosí, as is seen in Tandeter and Wachtel, Id.

6

THE PRICE HISTORY OF BUENOS AIRES
DURING THE VICEREGAL PERIOD

Lyman L. Johnson

UNFORTUNATELY FOR STUDENTS INTERESTED IN ECONOMIC HISTORY, THE surviving price record for colonial Buenos Aires is fragmentary. Unlike contemporary New Spain, where Enrique Florescano was able to use the consistent, detailed records of municipal granaries to trace the movement of corn prices over a lengthy period, and Potosí where Enrique Tandeter and Nathan Wachtel discovered a consistent and reliable record for a wide range of commodity prices in monastic account books, there is no single price record for common food staples or other essential consumer goods for colonial Buenos Aires.[1] The historian is, therefore, confronted with a difficult choice: either rely on the highly impressionistic opinions of prices found in travelers' accounts and other first-hand narratives, or attempt to create a composite price series from surviving institutional records despite their many inadequacies. I am currently working on a study of material culture in colonial Buenos Aires. Since this effort requires the precise measurement of the quality of material life experienced by working-class families, the task of creating a representative price series of basic consumer goods was undertaken, despite the many inherent difficulties and obvious problems.

Buenos Aires in the late colonial period was essentially a European city in terms of both its culture and its social forms. It is necessary, therefore, to create a price series that provides coverage of foods, beverages, and housing actually consumed in typical Porteño households. Unlike the society of late colonial New Spain Florescano studied, we cannot use a single commodity, in his case corn, to serve as proxy for the standard of living of the urban working class. For Buenos Aires in the eighteenth century, any attempt to measure changes in the cost of living requires the creation of a weighted price index that covers the diverse goods typically consumed by members of the urban working class.[2]

For colonial Buenos Aires, this ground has been covered once before.

Following up on his pioneering study of prices for late eighteenth-century Santiago, Chile, Ruggiero Romano undertook a comparison of the price histories of Santiago and Buenos Aires. The results of this comparison were published in the form of a general assertion that in both colonies prices for locally produced goods, as well as imports from other Spanish colonies and Europe, were stagnant throughout the second half of the eighteenth century, especially in the period after 1790.[3] From this summary of the price histories of these two colonial cities, Romano went on to suggest the outline of a colonial economic model that he labeled "subsistence" or "natural."[4] Although conceptually interesting, this effort was handicapped by a number of problems in both method and documentation. For the Buenos Aires case, Romano failed to stipulate the actual commodities studied and then presented his results as an unelaborated conclusion without the publication of price averages or index numbers. These rather large limitations on the usefulness of this contribution were compounded, in turn, by Romano's failure to cite his sources. Since the surviving records for this type of study are extremely limited for the city of Buenos Aires, we must assume that Romano relied on some or all of the surviving colonial-period account books of the city's monasteries and hospitals.

I decided to reexplore these sources after realizing that the wages paid to virtually all of the city's workers, from the least skilled to the most, demonstrated a strong upward trend in the late colonial period. Economic theory indicates that a sustained increase in average wages was highly unlikely if the price history presented by Romano was accurate. Wage increases on the scale of those demonstrated by my investigations could only occur in a period of stagnant prices if the economy experienced substantial and continuous increases in productivity similar in scale to those achieved in England during the early period of industrialization.[5] Because there is no evidence that Buenos Aires had substantial increases in productivity during this period, the likelihood that Romano had misread the region's price history was clear.[6] As a result, I determined to survey the surviving sources and discover the most reliable mix of compatible institutional records upon which an adequate price series could be constructed.

This decision was, in the last resort, easy to make. The account books of the monasteries of the Mercedarians and the Bethlemites and the accounts of the hospital of Santa Catalina were extant for the entire period from 1770 to 1815.[7] Although the use of a single source is the preferred method for estimating price trends, each of the extant sources for Buenos Aires was found to have missing data for one or more years during this period. The problem of missing data was further compounded by the imprecise and often unpredictable record-keeping practices that were used by the monks and lay brothers who were temporarily put in charge of the accounts of these religious institutions. Commonly, these records indicate purchases of food and drink or, less commonly, clothing in a form that permits the stipulation of a price for a standard unit (pesos per *fanega* of wheat, or reales per arroba of rice for example). In a disappointingly large number of cases, however, the sources simply note a price paid for an unspecified amount of one commodity or another, two pesos paid for chickens or five pesos for sugar, for example. In light of these problems in the documentation, price data from all three sources were pulled together to form a single series.

This decision is, fortunately, justifiable on grounds other than mere expediency. The three institutions used to compile the following series were of a similar size with similar scales of consumption throughout the period. In addition, the range, quality, and origin of goods purchased were very similar. Finally, all three institutions commonly purchased their food in the city's markets, rather than directly from rural producers. In order to avoid any consistent structural bias that might distort the resulting price series, average prices for each commodity were figured separately for each institution and then these series were compared annually to identify any serious price discrepancies. This check on the reliability of an average price calculated from disparate sources indicated broad and consistent agreement in the average price of all commodities annually and a close fit in both short- and longer-term price movements.

Because the records of these ecclesiastical establishments did not permit the creation of a price series for either fresh fish or meat, alternative sources were searched for some consistent record of prices paid for these important articles of local consumption. The only series that could be found was for salt beef purchased by the royal army for the local garrison.[8] Given an obvious preference for fresh meat and fish in the local market, salt beef is a less than ideal substitute for this consumption index. Nevertheless, there are good reasons for including it. The cabildo granted the right to supply the city with fresh beef as a monopoly to the highest bidder in a public auction. Beef prices were set annually by the cabildo in its *arancel* (list of controlled prices) and not by market factors. The profits of the concessionaires were extracted by forcing low prices on the region's stock raisers. Consumer prices, therefore, tended to remain constant during each contractual period.[9] That is, because the cabildo controlled the marketing and pricing of beef, this commodity experienced generally stable prices throughout the late colonial period. The absence in the cabildo records of any popular protest provoked by increases in the price of beef appears to confirm this assumption, since increases in the price of other articles of basic consumption, such as bread, produced immediate and often violent protest by urban consumers.[10]

Salt beef is here used as the only available proxy for the price of fresh meat, although its price was influenced by some additional elements. The two most important of these were labor, an increasingly expensive commodity in Buenos Aires, and salt, a scarce and expensive article in the local diet that was produced and sold under close municipal supervision throughout this period.[11] In addition to the labor costs associated with the provisioning of fresh meat, the production of salt beef required substantial labor inputs for salting, drying, and packing. Given the upward trend in unskilled wages, especially after 1800, the price for salt beef rose slightly faster than the price for fresh beef.

Other than the anecdotal opinion of travelers, there is no price record for fresh fish, an apparently important, but seldom discussed, part of the Porteño diet. The few citations found seem to indicate that this abundant resource was caught, cleaned, and marketed in large quantities by the population of outlying riverine villages. In Buenos Aires, the consumption of fish tended to fluctuate with the religious calendar, rather than in response to price alterations.[12] Because beef was abundant and cheap, few consumers could be won away from this preferred commodity by a decline in the price of fish, a food associated in the popular mind with religious requirements of sacrifice and self-denial.

The cost of housing was one of the most important determinants of the quality of material life experienced by the members of this society. We know from the rapid increase in urban population during the viceregal period that there must have been considerable pressure on the city's existing housing stock, especially in the decade following the creation of the viceroyalty.[13] The high cost of labor found in the building trades acted to restrain the construction of additional housing stock, despite the relatively low cost of land and common building materials. Adobe and brick were relatively inexpensive throughout the period, but wood and metal products were extremely dear.[14] There is no systematic effort in the historiography of colonial Buenos Aires to trace changes in urban real-estate values for this period. Excellent sources for such an effort are available, though. The probate inventories of the judicial archives and the records of the municipal administration of the seized properties of the Jesuit order, the Temporalidades, provide a reliable record of urban real-estate values.[15]

The utility of these rich sources is diminished for our purposes because the majority of urban residents were renters, not owners, of real estate. Although we may assume a general tendency for urban rental costs to move in the same direction and with the same periodization as real-estate values, actual rental costs for typical urban housing are the best measures of the shelter component of any cost-of-living study. Fortunately, a valuable record of rents paid for the typical housing of the popular classes has been preserved. Both the cabildo and the monastery of San Ramón owned large apartment blocks in the center city district where most of the clerks, artisans, and lesser-skilled workers lived and worked.[16] The rental records from these two sources are here combined to construct a single rental series for the period 1775–1812. It is clear that only a very small number of urban residents lived in the actual housing used here to represent the cost of housing for the entire city. Most single workers and workers with families lived in houses and apartments owned by private individuals, rather than in institutionally owned property. We cannot presume, then, that the rents paid for apartments owned by these two institutional landlords were nominally the same as rents paid to common, private-sector owners without substantial additional research. We can, however, use these institutional records as reliable indicators for the direction, scale, and periodization of changes in housing costs in the larger, private housing market. It is also reasonable to assume that the actual rents charged for this type of basic housing by these two institutions were not greatly dissimilar to the prices established in the open market.[17]

The institutional sources mentioned initially yielded sufficiently reliable data to construct price series for eight foods and beverages. These commodities were wheat, rice, garbanzos, maté, sugar, *porotos,* wine, and salt beef. In order to minimize the likelihood of misrepresenting the actual price tendencies of these commodities, every price notation for each food and beverage was recorded. Each series was then examined for price outliers, prices more than 25 percent higher or lower than the seasonal average. These transactions probably resulted from exceptional market circumstances or substantial qualitative differences that separated them from the pricing mechanism of the average purchase. This examination of the data proved reassuring, since there were very few price citations that fell outside the predictable cyclical price movements associated with seasonal changes in agricultural supplies available to the city. All prices were then averaged to provide a single annual price expressed in reales. Means were used for commodity prices rather than medians, because the mean is less susceptible to the influence of seasonal cycles in agricultural prices. Finally, no mean was calculated for a commodity in any year when fewer than five separate price citations were found.

Before discussing the movement of prices in some detail, the local importance of these comestibles must be described briefly. The wheat series is the most important series for measuring the cost of living in this colonial city. Economic historians of eighteenth-century Europe have demonstrated the central importance of bread prices for the determination of changes in the quality of life experienced by the masses of urban residents. It is commonly stated in the literature that members of the European working class consumed anywhere between 50 and 70 percent of their daily caloric intake in bread and other grain products.[18] As a result, the catastrophic effect of substantial increases in the price of bread propelled much of the violent popular protest experienced in European cities during the eighteenth century. High-ranking officials who failed to control effectively the price and availability of this essential product were the object of popular protest and mob violence.[19]

Although the diet of the Porteño working class during this period has been little studied, scattered evidence from contemporary records suggests strongly that bread was the basic staple of the urban popular-class diet in this city also. This is surprising, because most historians have assumed that the abundant supply of cheap beef would have modified European dietary patterns, producing a local diet rich in proteins and relatively low in carbohydrates. Because bread was so important, municipal authorities actively intervened in the market to prevent price increases that might trigger violent protest.[20] As was common in the Spanish colonial world of this period, the cabildo of Buenos Aires controlled the price of bread through the creation of an annual arancel that adjusted the weight of a one-peso loaf of bread to reflect changes in the market price of a fanega of wheat.[21] That is, a loaf of bread always cost one peso, but the weight of the loaf was reduced as the price of wheat rose. Because the typical working-class consumer attempted to maintain a constant level of bread consumption, we need to track the price of wheat, not the price of bread, to discover the effects of altered market conditions on the quality of life.

The price of wheat in Buenos Aires fluctuated broadly. This was a common pattern in most of the eighteenth-century societies for which we have reliable price series.[22] The volatility of grain prices was the result of both the agricultural practice of the preindustrial era and the disruptive effects of market manipulation by middlemen. Underlying these cyclical fluctuations in Buenos Aires, we can identify a strong upward tendency in price during this period. There were two periods of sustained high wheat prices that must have forced the members of the urban working class to alter their consumption patterns. The first period of high prices began in 1780 and lasted nearly to the end of the decade. This period of scarcity and high prices served as preface to a catastrophic increase in wheat prices begun during the region-wide drought of 1802–1804.[23] During this time of suffering, the previous high price of forty reales per fanega was eclipsed when the price for a fanega of wheat reached seventy and seventy-two pesos. Unfortunately, for the local population the price increases provoked by this natural disaster were sustained artificially by a succession of man-made disruptions. Two British invasions, a disruption of the Atlantic trade, and the advent of the wars of independence combined to reduce both local production and importation of wheat. As a result of these disruptions of grain supplies, wheat prices remained at historically high levels until the end of the colonial period.

Wheat prices in Buenos Aires were also affected for short periods by the often successful efforts of bakers and merchant-speculators to control the city wheat supply. By buying large quantities of unharvested wheat from financially hard-pressed farmers who needed cash to pay for expensive harvest labor and then withholding these supplies from the market, speculators were able to drive up the market price of wheat and thus increase the profitability of their bakeries.[24] In this case, the paternalistic effort of the municipal authorities to control the cost of living actually promoted the development of a price-gouging monopoly in agriculture.

The history of wheat prices in contemporary Spain was remarkably similar to that found for Buenos Aires. One recent investigator summarized the upward movement of wheat prices in Spain during the period from 1779 to 1783 as "one of the most spectacular trends registered in world economic history." He also noted numerous cyclical fluctuations of up to 100 percent in urban bread prices during the eighteenth century.[25] Obviously, the parallel behavior of Spanish prices does not substantiate the specifics of the Buenos Aires wheat series. It does, however, suggest that the volatility of wheat prices, the range of price fluctuations, and the periodization of price changes found for Buenos Aires were well within the range of actual experience in the late eighteenth-century Spanish world.

Garbanzos and porotos were common ingredients in the diets of eighteenth-century Spanish laborers and artisans. Spanish immigrants and their families continued to consume them in Buenos Aires. Both products were grown locally, but local production never completely met demand and, as a result, additional supplies were imported from Brazil.[26] Both products had similar price histories—a slight upward trend throughout the late colonial period, modified by episodes of violent cyclical price increases. There were important differences as well. Both garbanzos and porotos experienced a sharp upward movement at the beginning of the 1780s followed by a decline. For garbanzos, the more important of the two products in the local diet, the period from 1781 to 1800 saw a fluctuating downward trend in price. By 1780, an arroba of garbanzos sold for slightly more than half the 1776 price. Porotos reached forty-three reales per arroba in 1785 and then forty-eight reales in 1798. During the twenty-year period that followed the creation of the viceroyalty, however, the price for an arroba of porotos averaged slightly more than thirty-two reales. In 1802, the regional drought that had so powerfully affected the price of wheat pushed up the prices for these two staples as well. An arroba of garbanzos increased seven reales, and porotos reached a period high of sixty-four reales per arroba. From 1802 to 1811, the prices for both commodities were influenced by the diverse mix of market effects provoked by the opening of the port of Buenos Aires to foreign trade and by increased demand for local agricultural products promoted by the greatly expanded military requirements of the period. Prices for both products remained at relatively high levels after the drought, porotos ending the period 25 percent and garbanzos 21 percent above their 1775 levels.

Both rice and sugar were grown in the interior of the viceroyalty, but Porteño consumers depended primarily on imports of these products.[27] After 1790, important amounts of sugar were also imported from Cuba in exchange for locally produced dried beef and lard.[28] There is little contemporary evidence that the members of the urban working class consumed substantial amounts of rice. The monastic accounts and hospital records used to construct this price series suggest that the Spanish-born members of these religious communities ate rice regularly, both as an accompaniment to the meat, chicken, and fish eaten at their evening meals and as a sweetened pudding. Since many of the city's artisans were also Spaniards who probably sought to maintain a similar dietary regime, we may assume that rice was at least a minor component of the diet of the typical Spanish artisan's household. The place of sugar in the local diet, on the other hand, was clearly important. Virtually all urban groups in America and Europe increased their consumption of sugar during the eighteenth century.[29] Increases in sugar prices that led to a reduction in the levels of consumption were clearly perceived as a deprivation by working-class consumers.

We find that the price histories for these two products demonstrate similar characteristics—no clear trends, substantial cyclical price swings, and a roughly parallel periodization in price change. The volatile behavior of both price series is clearly illustrated by short-term cyclical price swings of 100 percent and more. For sugar we find that the period low of thirty-one reales per arroba in 1810 was followed by a year in which the average price reached, for the second time, a high of seventy-two reales. Similarly, between 1800 and 1801, the average price for an arroba of rice increased 100 percent to establish the period high of thirty-four reales. The evidence suggests that the price movements of both sugar and rice were largely determined by the external geopolitical events (wars and changing diplomatic alliances) that controlled the flow of goods to the port of Buenos Aires, rather than by changes in local or regional production.

Travelers who visited Buenos Aires and its hinterland universally noted the widespread consumption of maté among the native-born working men and women. The maté consumed in Buenos Aires was grown in Paraguay and transported to the city by a fleet of small ships. It is less clear whether this bitter local beverage was also popular in immigrant households. There is some evidence that maté was commonly served in retail stores and artisan shops that employed Spaniards and other Europeans. Migrants from the cities and villages of the interior clearly viewed maté as an essential part of their daily dietary routine, and contemporary accounts suggest that workers in the city's shops and small manufacturing plants took breaks during both the morning and afternoon to share maté.[30] Since it was also an export of some importance to the regional economy, the local price structure was profoundly affected by the commercial conditions that controlled the volume of exports from the port.[31]

Following the establishment of *Comercio Libre* in 1778, the price of an arroba of maté rose from the midteens to the low twenties. The wars that resulted from the French Revolution disrupted Atlantic trade and retarded the export of maté and other local products. As a result, local supply expanded and prices fell. Prices rose again in response to increased export opportunities created by the various commercial reforms and war-imposed expedients that opened the city to foreign ships and promoted local exports during the last fifteen years of the colonial period. Because of fundamental inelasticity in the local market (consumption increased only with population), maté prices tended to fall only when the opportunity for export sales contracted. When export demand rose, on the other hand, local consumers faced steeply rising prices. Maté was not a staple—it was a cheap stimulant, a poor man's luxury—but it was widely consumed by the urban masses. The city's popular classes must have resented the sharp price increase after 1806.

There is overwhelming evidence that the preindustrial urban working class consumed large quantities of wine, brandy, and other alcoholic beverages.[32] There is some debate among historians who have studied the European working class over the origins of this consumption pattern. Was the high level of alcoholic consumption an effort to escape the brutal deprivation of the common man's life, or was it a market-determined decision to buy the cheapest calories available?[33] It is likely that both elements influenced the increased consumption of alcoholic beverages found for much of Europe during the early modern period.

For the city of Buenos Aires, we see evidence of a similar upward trend in per capita consumption of alcohol in the late colonial period. The cabildo increasingly sought (with virtually no demonstrable success) to limit and control the widespread availability of brandy and wine in the city's *pulperías*.[34] These neighborhood shops offered drink, diversions (especially gambling), and companionship as well as dry goods for the city's consumers. Although there are no police records that would permit some estimation of the actual scale of this social problem, a systematic search of the surviving judicial records indicates that nearly every instance of violence (assaults, murders, and rapes) perpetrated during the late colonial period occurred during or after excessive drinking. Some men, then as now, believed that the regular consumption of brandy and other strong drink had a salutary effect on their health. In one case, a gunsmith stated that he took a glass of brandy four separate times during the working day for medical reasons. We can only guess what effect this habit had on his productivity. It is worth noting that this testimony about drinking habits was taken by the authorities after he had accidentally shot a customer.[35]

The actual amount of alcohol consumed on a per capita basis, however, is impossible to stipulate, although we can assume that the level of consumption in Buenos Aires did not diverge much from the levels established for Europe. If this is true, then the average adult worker in the city consumed between one and one and a half liters of wine per day.[36] Brandy produced in the interior was cheaper than imported wines and was apparently more popular among Porteño workers than among contemporary Europeans. Average consumption by volume of this much more powerful beverage was less than that for wine. Nevertheless, the documents indicate that regular brandy drinkers drank as much as a half-liter per day, a staggering amount (certainly enough to produce staggering).[37] We have no price record for brandy, but since the most common brandy in the city was distilled from wine in the interior provinces, we may assume that the price histories of these two beverages were very similar.

The monastic accounts and hospital records provide price records for both imported and domestically produced wine. Domestic wine was more commonly consumed and will be reported here. Although it took months to transport wine over the trails that linked the capital with the interior, these trade routes were free from the geopolitical disruptions that so powerfully affected the prices of other dietary staples.[38] As a result, a stable and predictable supply produced generally low prices. With the exception of the period of generalized military activity after 1806 that disrupted trade with the interior and pushed up the labor component of transportation costs, wine prices demonstrated a gradual downward tendency throughout the viceregal period. The only notable exception to this pattern was a small decline in prices in the early 1790s that reflected the effects of a greater availability of imported wines at relatively low prices. There is no evidence that working-class consumption of wine responded in significant ways to price fluctuations. Generally speaking, it appears that per capita consumption remained at a high level throughout the entire period. The increase in price at the end of the period was absorbed by the consumer's deferral of another purchase. That is, if wages remained constant, an increase in the cost of wine simply reduced the consumption of food.

This region had no more abundant food than beef. Most of the contemporary accounts by European travelers dwell on what they saw as the profligate waste of meat in the pampean region. The gauchos who annually harvested the cattle hides that were the region's dominant export commonly left carcasses to rot in the sun. It is safe to assume that the primary result of this bovine abundance was low beef prices. Cattle prices closely approximated hide prices. The cost of meat, therefore, reflected the labor and entrepreneurial costs associated with organizing the market and slaughtering the animals. As noted earlier, the city meat market was held as a monopoly privilege by various merchant speculators who provided beef at set prices authorized by the cabildo.[39] Structural control by municipal authorities effectively held down beef prices even during this period of expanding population. In addition, prices were contained by the local population's self-limiting consumption of beef, a consumption pattern that was strongly reinforced by religiously mandated abstinence on Fridays and religious feast days. Scattered evidence suggests that nearly 40 percent of the year was meatless as a result of the religious calendar.[40] The combined effect of abundant supplies, municipal price-control mechanisms, and dietary restraint produced the generally flat price series for salt beef provided in Table 6.1. The changes in the cost of salt beef, especially the dramatic price increase at the end of the colonial period, resulted, therefore, from changes in the cost of the other major components in the price of salt beef—labor and salt.

Housing obviously represented an important part of the cost of living in colonial Buenos Aires. Any effort to measure the movement of urban housing costs, however, must confront nearly insurmountable difficulties. The residents of the city—especially the working class—lived in a wide range of housing situations. A minority of married men were homeowners, or, in a small number of cases, were owners of multiple family units.[41] More commonly, married men and their families lived in rented housing, usually an apartment of one or two rooms. Working-class families living in these early tenements shared access to a rough kitchen, seldom more than an open cooking fire or adobe oven at the back of the building. Single men, on the other hand, commonly shared a room with workmates or with friends from their home towns. Immigrants from Europe and migrants from the interior of the colony tended to live with others from home regions. In some of the cases found in contemporary censuses, we find groups of as many as five to ten single men sharing a single room. Some employers offered minimal shelter to their workers as part of their compensation. This had always been an accepted part of the compensation of apprentices in artisan crafts, and in Buenos Aires, single journeymen were also occasionally housed in the homes of their employers.[42] Even in small manufacturing establishments that had little in common with the traditional artisan culture of the preindustrial city, we find housing provided for single employees. This was most common in the city's brick yards and in the largest bakeries, where slaves and free laborers shared barracklike shelters.[43]

Given this array of housing experiences, it is difficult to establish a representative unit of typical housing. Close inspection of census records suggests that the most acceptable type of housing to use as a representative standard for measuring the cost of housing for the average family was the one- or two-room apartment, a type of housing that was commonly financed and built by merchants in order to earn rental income.[44] Although the appropriateness of using this housing unit as a standard seems defensible, the investigator is presented with additional problems in creating an index, because of the broad range of rents paid in Buenos Aires as the result of locational and other considerations for units of a similar size. The averaging of widely disparate rental data from different apartments located in distinct neighborhoods and owned by both institutional and private owners would seriously restrict the reliability of any series. Fortunately, a record of rents paid for a uniform group of small apartments owned by the cabildo and the monastery of San Ramón during this period is available. Neither the apartments owned by the municipality nor the properties of the monastery are extant for the entire period. The two rent series, though, overlap for a number of years, and we find a rough uniformity in both average monthly price and in the periodization of price changes.

The average monthly rental series presented in Table 6.2 is a composite of three separate groups of one-room apartments located in the city center. In order to increase the reliability of this series, only years with a minimum of ten surviving records were included. A group of eleven apartments owned by the cabildo provided the longest single rental series (1770–1806). In thirteen of these years, the requirement of ten rent records was not fulfilled. The usefulness of these records is further compromised by changes in the composition of cabildo real-estate holdings in 1798 and again in 1805.[45] Rental data for 1798, 1801, and 1804 are from a uniform group of apartments that were similar in location, size, and price to the cabildo's units.[46] The average rental costs presented for the period 1808–12 are for forty one-room shops located in the Recova, a large, multistory, patio-style commercial structure located just south of the central plaza and owned by the cabildo.[47] A search of notarial records for these years suggests that these simple commercial locations rented for roughly the same amount as single-room apartments in the private housing market.

The resulting series of average monthly rentals indicates that the period immediately following the creation of the Viceroyalty of Río de la Plata witnessed an important increase in housing costs as a rapidly expanding urban population competed for the city's housing stock. Housing costs peaked in the mid-1780s and then slowly declined until 1810. Surviving evidence suggests that prices increased again after this date, although the average rental at the time of the cabildo abierto in May 1810 was only slightly higher than that found in 1776. This record of rental costs suggests, then, that housing construction during the 1780s and 1790s gradually caught up with the population growth caused by transatlantic and internal migrations. As a result, rental costs declined moderately in the last decade of the colonial period. The upward surge in rental costs after 1810 is probably best explained by the long military emergency that led the revolutionary government to tax or directly expropriate capital that would normally have been invested in the construction of new housing stock. The impact of these policies was compounded by disproportionate financial losses and tax increases experienced

Table 6.1

Annual average price of selected commodities expressed in reales, 1775–1811

Year	Wheat/fanega	Rice/arroba	Garbanzos/arroba	Yerba/arroba	Sugar/arroba	Porotos/arroba	Wine/botija	Salted meat
1775					44		15.5	
76	16	27	19	12	53	31	14.3	32
77	29	24		15	57		12.2	
78	27	17	18	15	68	27	14.9	28
79	28	18		16	45	36	15	
80					63	40	16	
81	40	25	27			36	15	
82		25	21	22	56		14.9	
83		16	22	22	44	28	12	24
84		24	20	20	44	28	11.8	
85	40		21	18	40	43	12.5	
86	40	21	21	23	48	32	12.7	
87		17	17	23	49		13.3	24
88	14	20	16	24	64		11.5	24
89	14.5		15	22	72		8.7	20
90			18	22	48	32	8.5	20
91	15	24	20	17			12	20

Year								
92	15	10	15	17	36	32	9.4	20
93	16	13	13	14			8.8	20
94	12	22		18	32		9	32
95	22	14	15	16	40		12.1	20
96	28	25	15	18	51	32	12.3	25
97	25	29	16	16	56	36	15.5	24
98	21	23	14	18	50	48	—	
99	21	15	15	18	52		14.8	25
1800	28	17	11	18	48		14.5	
01	34	34	18	19	29		15	25
02	26	31	25	18	36	64	—	25
03	72	23	29	19	29		13.7	
04	71	18	34	20	33	54	11.1	
05	70		31	19	33	40	14.7	
06	71	20	25	18	33	31	16	64*
07		16		23	40		18	62
08		18	28	24	40		19.5	
09	34	24		22	72		20	
1810	43	27	26	22	31	37	18.2	
11	42	26	23	40	38	44	13	
12				32			13.1	

*Based on only three citations.

Table 6.2

Average Monthly Rent Paid for Single Room Apartments
in Central Buenos Aires (1770–1812)

Year	Rent in pesos	Year	Rent in pesos
1770	5.8	1792	
1771	6	1793	
1772	7.3	1794	8.8
1773	8.5	1795	
1774		1796	
1775	7.9	1797	9
1776	9	1798	9
1777	10	1799	9
1778	10	1800	8.9
1779	10.3	1801	9
1780		1802	9
1781	11.4	1803	8.6
1782	10.4	1804	8.4
1783		1805	8.8
1784	10.8	1806	8.3
1785	10.7	1807	
1786		1808	8.4
1787		1809	8.5
1788		1810	8.7
1789		1811	11.8
1790	9.8	1812	12.2
1791	9.7		

by the merchant class, the sector that traditionally provided most investment capital for housing. In addition to these factors, rural and provincial militia units were quartered in the city after 1807, thereby intensifying the competition housing.[48]

Except for the two periods 1776–85 and 1811–12, the limited movement of average rental costs would have had small effect on the cost of living experienced by the mass of clerks, artisans, and unskilled workers who made up most renters. This assumption, however, is somewhat misleading, seeming to indicate that housing costs had little effect on the quality of material well-being. The most significant feature of this price series is the actual price paid for this type of housing, not the direction or the scale of movement in average prices. Even in the years immediately before the creation of the viceroyalty when housing costs were at their lowest level, the average price of a small apartment in Buenos Aires was well beyond the reach of nearly all urban wage earners. Particularly in times of off-season underemployment, peones, lesser-skilled bricklayers, and carpenters would have been unable to afford the modest apartments used to construct this series. Since men in this class traditionally sought independent housing when they married, the uniformly high rental costs of the colonial period must have contributed to the low marriage rate indicated for urban workers in the colonial census records. Only the accumulation of seniority and skills could produce the wage level and employment security necessary to afford independent housing, most typically a rented one- or two-room apartment. Therefore those artisans and laborers in Buenos Aires who married at all tended to be older than similarly employed men in Europe. The wages of urban workers, even skilled journeymen in the construction trades who earned ten reales per day, were clearly insufficient to afford housing suitable for a family unless their wages were supplemented by the earnings of wives and children. One important result of the high cost of housing was that young adult workers tended to prolong their residence in the homes of their parents.

Master artisans in the skilled trades needed to purchase or rent a business location as a requirement of their craft status. These men found it nearly impossible to escape the city's high real-estate costs. Although there was a handful of master artisans in colonial Buenos Aires who worked for wages, it was generally understood that a master was an independent craftsman who dealt directly with the public. Most of the city's masters, therefore, rented two-room corner apartments. They used the outside room located on the street corner, the *esquina,* as their shop, while their families lived behind a curtain in the interior room. Since the rental costs for these larger, better-located apartments were substantially higher than the average presented in Table 3.2, we may assume that many artisans in indoor trades were forced to remain journeymen, because their projected income as masters fell short of this required part of business overhead.[49]

The probate records from this period suggest that a large percentage of the working class, the city's unskilled workers and artisans, lived on the periphery of the city on unowned or unoccupied property. Their houses were called ranchos, rough adobe buildings constructed in the style commonly built by the rural population.[50] These outlying residential districts appear to have had the form and character of the *villas miserias* that provide shelter to the working poor of modern Buenos Aires. The colonial antecedent of this modern disgrace was the most accessible and affordable component of the urban housing stock available to the working class. Since, however, these squalid suburban neighborhoods were never closely surveyed in colonial censuses, we cannot discuss with confidence what part of the working class resided in the impoverished confines of these tiny houses and huts.[51]

Most of the inhabitants of these zones built their own homes, often sharing the work of making adobe bricks and constructing walls with neighbors' and family members' help. Scraps of discarded building materials and natural materials gathered in the area provided the doors and roofs for these rough buildings. The construction techniques and basic designs were drawn from the rural experience of the native-born migrants, who made up a substantial part of the work force in the slaughter yards, brick factories, bakeries, and construction projects of the city. Married members of this class, the most stable sector of this suburban population, gradually built additional rooms and outbuildings to accommodate children or, in some cases, to rent to single workers who migrated back and forth between urban and rural employment in response to changing labor demands.

For these sectors of the urban working class, we can offer no reliable estimation of housing costs. It is, however, probably safe to assume that average costs in these districts were substantially less than those presented in the urban rental series in Table 6.2. It appears that these two very different types of housing stock, the urban apartment block and the suburban rancho, were architectural manifestations of two culturally distinct urban working classes, one European and urban in origin and culture and the other indigenous and rural. Immigrant artisans, despite the punishing rental costs in the center city, shunned the suburban shanty developments that housed much of the native-born unskilled workforce. They sought instead the traditional housing of the European city. Despite the clear cost advantage of the suburban rancho, a significant portion of the city's clerks, minor bureaucrats, and skilled working men (nearly all master artisans and most European immigrants), persisted in seeking more expensive traditional housing.[52] As a result, the effect of housing costs on the average age at marriage, and therefore on family size, was differentially experienced by the city's two major ethnic groups.

Table 6.3 presents a weighted consumer price index constructed from the commodity and housing series. The weights used to create this index are presented in the note at the foot of the table. Because so little is known about the diet consumed by the urban masses of colonial Buenos Aires, the estimation of weights posed a difficult problem that has not been solved here in a completely satisfactory manner.[53] Since the foods for which reliable series could be generated were not necessarily the only foods that were important in the diet of the population, weights were constructed to establish the relative importance of each article, both in terms of actual consumption and as a proxy for other imported or domestically produced foods. It is important to remember that a number of articles of common consumption are missing from this index. Among these are fresh beef; both salted and fresh fish; cheese; and a number of commonly consumed local fruits and vegetables, including pears, peaches, onions, peppers, squash, and tomatoes. Despite the weaknesses that necessarily result from these omissions, the composite series presented here represents an unusually detailed and reliable basis for an analysis of changes in the cost of living.

Before calculating the weights used in this table, a broad array of records from the period were searched for evidence about the consumption patterns of the colonial working class. The surviving documentation is, unfortunately, very limited. Military records provided some indication of the foods consumed by soldiers in the local garrisons and sailors serving on coast-guard and naval vessels. These are special diets that obviously indicate institutional custom as well as price availability and local dietary custom.

A representative example of the diet commonly provided to seamen in the service of the king was provided by the ship's log of the *Balanda, Nuestra Señora del Rosario,* in 1806.[54] The crew received a diet that was adequate in calories and protein, but without the nutrients provided by fresh fruits and vegetables. The result was a diet that was both boring and nutritionally inadequate. It is impossible to estimate the calories and nutrients in each ration because of the form in which the ship's log was kept; we can, however, calculate the distribution of food expenditures for each of the commodities. Fifty-five percent of the total expenditure was for bread. The remainder was allocated in the following manner: meat (25 percent); maté (10 percent); and onions, salt, and other condiments (10 percent). Peones and prisoners employed by the cabildo to pave the *Calle de la Aduana* in 1805 were fed a similar diet: bread, meat, condiments, and maté.[55] Both these institutional examples provide a potentially misleading basis for any effort to generalize about the dietary regime of the city's civilian population, since these were diets determined in large part by the traditional practice of the civil and military bureaucracies, rather than by the actual preferences of independent consumers.

Fortunately, one surviving record overcomes some of these weaknesses, although it also is based on an institutional diet. The *Temporalidades* records contain a precisely detailed record for daily food expenditures incurred during the refurbishing of the Jesuit college in Buenos Aires.[56] Because the supervisor of this project, Lorenzo Cavenagoy, was accused of misappropriating funds, he provided his superiors with an unusually detailed review of all job-related expenditures, including those for food. The work force included a mixed group of bricklayers and unskilled workers, both free and slave. The project lasted 106 working days. Cavenagoy's record is particularly valuable because, unlike the surviving military records and ship's logs, it portrays the preferred diet eaten at the main midday meal by members of the working class. All the food and beverages provided to this large work party were purchased in the city's market on a daily basis and therefore reflected actual changes in consumption that resulted from price changes and availability.[57] Although we must assume that the diet of these construction workers did not replicate the complete diet of the urban masses, it does appear to be the closest approximation of that diet found in the contemporary records. Since Cavenagoy indicated that he hoped to attract and hold his workers at wages that were below the prevailing city wage rates by offering high-quality food as partial compensation, it is likely that both the range of foods and the proportions among them reflected local preferences and tastes. The most likely distortion in this diet would be the greater abundance of relatively expensive foods than was common in private purchases by individual consumers.

This document provides us with a number of surprises. The most important is, that because of religious requirements, 54 of 106 working days featured fish, rather than meat, as the main course. Although some salted fish was consumed (mostly imported cod), fresh fish caught in the nearby estuary was by far the most common main dish. Fresh beef, roasted on a spit, was the main course in the remaining 52 days. No salt or dried beef was served, since it was viewed as a slave food. In addition to these two central dietary items, workers consumed squash, onions, garlic, tomatoes, lard, salt, green peppers, and bread. The only beverage provided to workers at this construction site was maté, although we may assume wine was consumed with the evening meal. Every worker received maté after his noon meal and during morning and late-afternoon work breaks. The audit indicated that 252 pesos were spent on meat and fish, while 214 pesos (40 percent of total expenditures) were spent on bread. The proportion of food expenditure devoted to bread was remarkably similar to that spent for bread and other grains by contemporary, European urban workers.[58]

Rations, like wages, reflected differences in skills and seniority. Skilled workers on this project, both masters and journeymen, were provided with the more expensive and therefore more desirable white bread, while unskilled workers and slaves were given the more nutritious, but lower status, dark bread. The daily ration for both groups was one *quartillo,* one quarter of a one-peso loaf of bread. Using the 1783 arancel, it appears that the daily bread ration was approximately nineteen ounces. This distinction in the quality of bread provided to skilled and unskilled workers was a common feature of local custom. Although we may regard this difference in the quality of bread provided to these two groups as more symbolic than substantive, skilled workers enjoyed other significant advantages in addition to their superior wages. One of the most important of these was that they received a double food ration during the workday. During the course of this project, the average daily ration cost slightly more than one-half real. The skilled worker's double ration, then, represented an additional two and one-half reales of income per week.[59]

In addition to food and drink, the city provided twelve cartloads of wood for the cooking fires at the work site. Each cartload cost six pesos. Firewood and the most common alternative fuel, the wood derivative charcoal, were extremely expensive and scarce in Buenos Aires throughout the colonial period. The Yankee merchant David Deforest and the English officer Alexander Gillespie both noted in their journals that the city's bakeries and brick manufacturers regularly used dried bones discarded by the local abattoirs as fuel for their ovens.[60] Evidence strongly suggests that the cost of fuel was a contributing factor in the decline of home bread production and the resulting rise of large-scale commercial bakeries that used larger, more fuel-efficient ovens. Certainly, the cost of fuel would have been an important influence in determining the consumption levels of fresh beef, fish, and other foods that required cooking. This problem was compounded for the urban working poor by their limited access to cooking facilities in their small apartments and shared rooms. As a result, many single men from this class ate few cooked meals other than those provided by their employers at midday. Their evening meal was commonly a light supper, usually bread, cheese, fruits, and often brandy or wine.[61] We cannot assume, therefore, the traditional assertion that inexpensive beef promoted the consumption of abundant protein in colonial Buenos Aires. Unless consumers had access to cooking facilities and, more important, had adequate income to afford the expensive fuels that were locally available, protein consumption would be limited—regardless of beef prices.[62]

Since the expenditures for food at the Temporalidades project is the most detailed and most reliable record for food expenditures for the urban working class, it was used here as the primary basis for assigning the weights in the consumer price index. This record indicates that slightly less than 40 percent of total food expenditures were for bread. We must remember that this percentage was for the noon meal only, the meal when a member of this working group was most likely to eat meat, fish, and cooked vegetables. It is reasonable to assume that total daily expenditures for bread were actually a larger proportion of daily food costs, since bread was commonly eaten at every meal. In the morning, in fact, it was likely to be the only food eaten. In this index, bread is given a weight of 40, a conservative estimation.

Although wine was not served with the noon meal at this construction project, it was, however, an important part of the local diet, indeed of the diet throughout the Spanish world.[63] In this index, it is given a weight of 7.5, a weight suggested by the better-known pattern of consumption found for the popular classes of contemporary Spain. Rent was given a weight of 20. This is less than the proportion suggested by the rent index in Table 6.2, a type of housing affordable to only more skilled workers, and more than the proportional weight we might assign if a reliable series could be developed for ranchos on the city's periphery. These weights are very similar to those used in a broad array of studies of cost of living and real wages for preindustrial European societies. The English case is, perhaps, the most studied. The most common weights assigned to expenditures by English laborers are: between 40 and 50 percent of weekly wages for bread and other grain products; 20 percent for animal products; and 10 percent for fuel and light, beverages and condiments, and clothing. Housing costs, where estimated, are generally given a weight in the range of 17 to 20 percent.

Every serious student of cost of living readily acknowledges that any index is necessarily an imperfect instrument for representing the quality of material life, because the surviving records of consumption are so fragmentary. Nevertheless, an index of cost of living is a valuable interpretive asset, despite these inadequacies, since it is the best way to measure the impact of price changes on the lives of average people. Before turning to a brief discussion of the index for Buenos Aires, the reader is given fair warning that this index is weakest, as are all such artificial measures, as a means of precisely fixing year-to-year alterations in consumer prices. It does, however, provide us with a secure basis for indicating with some confidence the direction of changes in the cost of living and the periodization of these changes.

The movement of the cost of living index for Buenos Aires can be periodized as follows. The creation of the viceroyalty initiated a dramatic period of price inflation that peaked in 1781 with an index number of 171. The index then fell gradually, returning to the level of 1776 again in 1787. Between 1788 and 1794, we find the index at its lowest levels, with 1794 establishing the low index number for the entire viceregal period. The remaining years of the colonial period were years of sustained high prices. The five-year period beginning in 1803 was characterized by a catastrophic price rise that must have forced many of the city's poor families to the wall. This era of brutal price inflation was initiated in 1802 by a severe drought that ruined harvests throughout the pampas region, even reaching into Upper Peru. This natural disaster was followed by a political and military crisis that disrupted trade and production. Although this index ends with a decline from these unprecedented levels of high prices, the period-ending index numbers remained between 50 and 70 percent above the base year.

It is difficult, indeed, to interpret how these price changes affected the working men and women of the city and their children. As the price of wheat moved cruelly upward, especially after 1803, many of these hard-pressed individuals and families must surely have adjusted their diets and sought other, less expensive, substitutes for bread. Certainly in a city where raw protein in the form of fresh beef and fish was so abundant and cheap, there was little likelihood that actual starvation threatened many urban residents.[64] On the other hand, periods when the prices for basic necessities pushed mercilessly upward surely punished those with limited incomes and erased whatever savings the members of this class had accumulated during better years.[65]

We can extract some indication of the social costs of price inflation by creating two indices that measure the overall well-being of the population. The crude death rate, or number of deaths per 1,000 inhabitants, is one measure of the general health of the population. This statistic generally tends to reflect changes in the quality and availability of the food supply, especially in preindustrial societies. Urban populations in the eighteenth century commonly experienced rapid swings in the death rate because of epidemics and other, less spectacular, disease experiences. These epidemiological influences tend to submerge or disguise the effects of nutritional effects. As a result, two seven-year cohorts were created for Buenos Aires as a basis for measuring the impact of the cost of living on urban mortality. These large cohorts tend to reduce the distorting effect of epidemic disease. The first cohort is from 1788 to 1794, the period when we find the lowest index numbers for the consumer price index. The second period is from 1802 to 1810, the period when our price index peaks. The deaths that resulted from the two British invasions were subtracted from the total so that the resulting calculation would better reflect the effect of high food prices. During the first period, an era of generally low prices, we find an average crude death rate of 24.1 deaths per 1000 inhabitants per year. In the second period when high prices were imposed by drought, monopolistic market practices, and political instability, this rate predictably rose to 34.4.[66]

Another measure of the social costs of high prices for food and other basic consumption goods is provided by the record of admissions to the *Casa de Niños Expositos,* the city's foundling hospital.[67] In the period of low prices, the hospital averaged 85 admissions per year. During the 1802–1808 period when the cost of living index reached its high point, this average leaps to 110 admissions per year, an average annual increase of 23 percent. Perhaps the terrible impact of these large-scale economic changes is best illustrated by the famine year of 1804, when the Case de Niños Expositos admitted 120 abandoned children. This same year the cabildo was forced publicly to deplore the increasingly common practice of leaving children to die in the streets and other public places in the city.

Clothing is the most important category of common consumption good missing from the price index presented in Table 6.3. Although some records of clothing prices have survived from this period, it was not possible to construct a reliable price series that could be included in the weighted index. Three court cases involving members of the working class from the years 1781 and 1782, however, provide fragmentary, but informative, evidence of clothing costs. The first record was from a civil suit brought by a shoemaker demanding payment for shoes sold to the members of a single family. According to testimony offered to the court by master shoemakers, common shoes for an adult male cost two pesos, while ordinary women's shoes were only slightly less expensive at one peso, six reales. Children's shoes were five

Table 6.3

Consumer Price Index for the City of Buenos Aires (1776 = 100)

1776	100	1794	85.2
1777	133.2	1795	109.5
1778	128.6	1796	129.25
1779	131.1	1797	125.4
1780	153	1798	114.4
1781	171	1799	112
1782	169.4	1800	129.4
1783	163	1801	153.8
1784	164.8	1802	130.8
1785	163.7	1803	240.6
1786	165.8	1804	240.9
1787	131.4	1805	224.3
1788	100.9	1806	205.4
1789	98.6	1807	189.2
1790	97.5	1808	173
1791	97.1	1809	157
1792	88.7	1810	173.7
1793	89	1811	190.1

NOTE: The following weights were assigned to the selected commodities used in this study: wheat (40); rice (10); chickpeas (2.5); yerba (7.5); and rent (20). The series for salted meat ended in 1806. Therefore the weights were adjusted for 1807–1811 in the following manner: yerba (10) and wine (10).

reales, and shoes for an adolescent male were one peso, four reales.[68] The other two cases offer a much more complete look at the cost of a working man's wardrobe. Both inventories indicate that only a very small amount of clothing was owned by the typical members of this class, a characteristic further substantiated by the consistently low estimations of clothing value provided in the inventories of decedents in the surviving probate records.[69] A typical working-class wardrobe included: one pair of used shoes (worth twelve reales), one sombrero (sixteen reales); one poncho (thirteen reales); one pair of wool socks (thirteen reales); two shirts (sixteen and eighteen reales); one vest (twenty-seven reales); one pair of pants (twenty reales); and a cloth cap (six reales). The clothing owned by this journeyman carpenter was valued at seventeen pesos, four reales.[70] Although not an enormous amount on its face, it would take slightly more than seventeen working days for a journeyman carpenter paid the median wage to earn enough to purchase this meager wardrobe. An unskilled laborer would have to work more than a month for these same goods. Because most income was spent on food and housing, it is obvious that men and women of this class rarely purchased new clothes. Since they seldom had a second outfit, most found it difficult to wash or repair their clothing. The resulting problems of hygiene and cleanliness are obvious. Given the cost of clothing relative to a worker's potential for accumulating savings, we can see clearly why probate records from the period commonly noted that a decedent's clothing had no value— working men and women wore their clothes until they were reduced to rags.

The absence of comparable clothing prices for the remainder of this period prevents any estimation for either the direction or periodization of price changes. We may suggest, however, the likely direction for changes in clothing prices from our understanding of local commercial history. Few members of the working class purchased ready-made clothing or had clothing made professionally. Typically they purchased cloth—either the rough wool cloth manufactured in the interior or, increasingly, the wool, linen, and canvas cloth imported from Europe—and produced their own clothing. Hats, especially the broad-brimmed hats favored by both Spaniards and creoles; shoes; and ponchos were generally purchased as finished goods, or bartered for. We know that the price of domestic wool cloth and the most popular imported textiles tended to decline steadily throughout this period, although short-term trade disruptions provoked by the many wars of this era worked in a contradictory manner, pushing up cloth prices cyclically.[71] Workers benefited when international events pushed prices down as well. At the end of the colonial period—beginning with the British invasion of 1806—British and American commercial travelers and local merchants noted in their reports and correspondence a local glut of textiles that had catastrophically affected prices in both the city and the interior.[72] We must assume that the residents of Buenos Aires benefited in the short term from this price decline. Yet, regardless of the short-term effects of these politically initiated price variations, there is little evidence that there was any noticeable change in the quantity or quality of the clothing worn by the urban working class. As noted succinctly by the acute observer, Alexander Gillespie, "the poverty of the lower classes is always apparent in their garments, and their filth."[73] All the contemporary evidence seems to corroborate this harsh judgment.

In order to evaluate the effect of these price changes on colonial Buenos Aires, it is necessary to trace the movement of personal income as well. This is not a simple project. How is income to be measured? Earnings? Wages? What group or groups should stand as proxy for the society's consumers?[74] Most students of economic history prefer to use the daily wages of the working class to provide this baseline measurement, but we are forced by the documentation to recognize the incredible diversity of this class in preindustrial as well as modern society and must design some representative sample of the total wage experience. In colonial Buenos Aires, there were significant differences in the wages and earnings of artisans and unskilled workers. For the purpose of this study, I have created a weighted index of wages that includes a cross section both of skilled occupations and unskilled laborers. This wage record was extracted from the payroll records of religious establishments and various government bureaucracies.[75] In order to create the weights used here, I used contemporary census counts from 1778 and 1810 to discover the average distribution of the urban work force in manual occupations. The following occupations and weights are used here: carpenters (20), bricklayers (15), ironworkers (10), caulkers (2), ships' carpenters (1), sailmakers (1), arms makers (1), sailors (5), urban unskilled (30), and rural unskilled (15). Once constructed, this index permits us to understand more completely the social consequences of the price inflation noted in Table 6.3.

Graph 6.1 illustrates the movement of both the weighted wage index and the consumer price index. We find a strong upward trend overall in the wage index, broken only by a short moderate decline in 1799–1800. There were two lengthy periods when members of the urban wage-earning class experienced punishing increases in the prices paid for food and shelter without a compensatory increase in wages. The first of these difficult periods was the decade from 1777 to 1787. During this period, the cost of living was driven upward by a rapidly growing population and, possibly, by a growth in the money supply caused by the decision of the Spanish government to tie the silver-mining area of Upper Peru directly to the new viceregal capital. The second and more severe period of price inflation began in 1802, with a devastating drought that forced up the price of wheat and other locally produced staples. The drought-induced period of price inflation was largely overcome by improved harvests after 1804, but recovery to earlier price levels was prevented by political events—the two British invasions and the resultant militarization of the city that continued into the early national period. In fact, we can see what may have been the beginning of a new cycle of price inflation in 1810. This final increase in the consumer price index occurred without any evidence of drought or other natural disaster.

We cannot measure with precision the impact of these two difficult periods

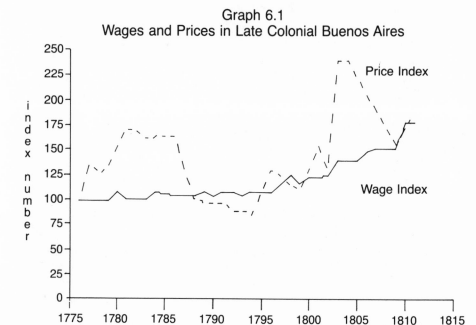

Graph 6.1
Wages and Prices in Late Colonial Buenos Aires

on the urban population of Buenos Aires, but it appears that many workers and their families must have experienced a sharp decline in basic consumption. By way of contrast, Graph 6.1 suggests that the decade from 1785 to 1795 was a period when labor demands associated with commercial expansion and an urban construction boom pushed wages upward faster than prices paid for basic consumption goods. During this decade, we may speculate, workers saved, enjoyed an improved diet, gained access to better housing, and experienced longer, healthier lives.

Although this research can offer only a preliminary assessment of the wage and price history of late colonial Buenos Aires, it is possible to suggest some conclusions that should survive future reevaluations. It is clear that the price history offered by Romano in 1963 is fundamentally flawed. His conclusion that this period was characterized by stagnant or falling commodity prices is not substantiated by this systematic analysis of institutional purchasing. The price history of this period embraced both short-term cyclical changes and a longer-term upward trend. It should be remembered that the price series offered here is compiled from the records of four distinct (but structurally similar) institutions and therefore lacks the reliability of Florescano's corn price series for New Spain. Any resulting error would likely be linked to actual price levels or, perhaps, to the periodization of price changes as represented in Table 6.1. It is important to recognize that none of the surviving price records for this period are compatible with the characterization of price movements offered by Romano.

The price summaries presented here indicate clearly the fundamental structural weakness of the colonial economy's agricultural sector. Both natural disasters and political events could, and did, provoke an immediate contraction in the supply of basic consumption goods. The drought of 1802–1803 is the preeminent example from this period, but less violent climatic events also produced shortages and high prices. This weakness could have been overcome if adequate capital had been invested in agricultural production. Investors generally shunned rural investments, however, because profit levels were historically low. During normal years, the prices paid for local agricultural production were depressed by imports from Brazil, Cuba, Paraguay, and even North America. The supply of imported goods, however, was often disrupted by the naval wars that restricted Atlantic commercial relations during this period.

It was the combined effect, then, of nature and politics that produced the cyclical character of the price series presented here. The long-term upward trend in prices, on the other hand, resulted from the rapid growth in urban and rural population after 1776. By 1810, the population of the city grew from twenty-five to approximately sixty thousand.[76] This secular trend in population naturally pulled prices upward.

Wages also ended upward during the late colonial period. The weighted index used in Graph 6.1 indicates that wages in 1810 were 70 percent higher than they were in 1776. Yet wage increases fell substantially behind prices after 1800. During the 1780s and 1790s, the city's popular classes enjoyed improved levels of material well-being. Young men entered the skilled trades in larger numbers, shops were opened, and long-term financial obligations were undertaken. Although wages continued to increase to the end of the colonial period, the effects of inflation actually diminished purchasing power of many wage earners. Perhaps here we have the origin of popular support for independence.

NOTES

1. Enrique Florescano, *Precios del maíz y crisis agrícolas en México, 1708–1810* (El Colegio de México: México, D.F., 1969); and Enrique Tandeter and Nathan Wachtel, "Prices and Agricultural Production: Potosí and Charcas in the Eighteenth Century," Chapter 8 in this volume.

2. For an effort to measure changes in the standard of living of the working class of contemporary Philadelphia see Billy G. Smith, "The Material Lives of Laboring Philadelphians, 1750–1800," *William and Mary Quarterly*, vol. xxxviii, no. 2 (April, 1981), pp. 163–202.

3. Ruggiero Romano, "Movimiento de los Precios y Desarrollo Económico: el Caso de Sudamérica en el Siglo xviii," *Desarrollo Económico*, vol. 3, no. 1–2 (April–September, 1963), pp. 31–43. See especially pp. 32–34.

4. Ruggiero Romano, *Cuestiones de historia económica latino-americana* (Caracas, 1966), pp. 24–27.

5. For the British case see Rufus S. Tucker, "Real Wages of Artisans in London, 1729–1935," *Journal of the American Statistical Association*, vol. xxxi, no. 193 (1936), pp. 73–84. See pp. 78–79 for his clothing, fuel and light, and wage series.

6. For a discussion of these relationships see James D. Gwartney and Richard Stroup, *Micro Economics: Private and Public Choice* (Academic Press: New York, 1983), pp. 247–249; and Council of Economic Advisers, "Noninflationary Wage and Price Behavior," in William G. Bowen and Orley Ashenfelter (eds.), *Labor and the National Economy* (W. W. Norton & Company: New York, 1975), pp. 163–169. This same point is discussed by Milton Friedman in the same edited volume. See his essay "What Price Guideposts?" especially pp. 177–182.

7. Archivo General de la Nación, Buenos Aires, Argentina (hereafter A.G.N.), División Colonia, Sección Contaduria, Culto de Buenos Aires, Mercedarios, hospicio de San Ramón de las Conchas, Libros I, III, and V; Culto de Buenos Aires, Bethlemitas, Convento y hospital de Santa Catalina, Culto de Buenos Aires, Mercedarios, Convento Grande de San Ramón, Libro de Gastos, 1775–1815.

8. A.G.N., División Colonia, Sección Contaduria, Caja de Buenos Aires, 1770–1815.

9. The essential materials for understanding the functioning of the city's meat market are collected in Facultad de Filosofía y Letras, *Documentos para la historia argentina* (hereafter D.H.A.), tomo IV, *Abastos* (Buenos Aires: 1914), pp. 3–206.

10. *Ibid.*, p. 240.

11. *Ibid.*, pp. 393–452.

12. The religious calendar required a large number of meatless days. Although it is difficult to fix the number of meatless days precisely, the surviving records suggest that as much as 30 percent of the year was meatless. A.G.N., División Colonia, Sección Gobierno, Temporalidades, Obra de la Universidad, 1783.

13. Lyman L. Johnson, "Estimaciones de la población de Buenos Aires en 1744,

1778 y 1810," *Desarrollo Económico,* vol. 19, no. 73 (April–June, 1979), pp. 107–119.

14. R. P. Guillermo Furlong S. J., *Las industrias en el Río de la Plata desde la colonización hasta 1778* (Academia Nacional de la Historia: Buenos Aires, 1978), pp. 112–129. For an example of how wood costs influenced housing prices see A.G.N., División Colonia, Sección Gobierno, Tribunales S10, Expediente 17.

15. Among the many properties seized by the colonial government when the Jesuits were expelled in 1767 were many single and multiple family houses in Buenos Aires. These properties were then maintained and rented by the government. These records permit an analysis of changes in rental costs and in actual real estate values. See for example, A.G.N., División Colonia, Sección Gobierno, Temporalidades, 1787.

16. A.G.N., División Colonia, Sección Gobierno, Cabildo de Buenos Aires, Propios, 1769–1815; and A.G.N., División Colonia, Sección Gobierno, Convento y iglesia de San Ramón de Buenos Aires, Inventorio de los bienes, muebles, inmuebles, 1788–1792.

17. Only scattered private sector rental agreements could be found in the notarial copybooks from this period. A direct comparison between the rents found in this source and the rents charged by institutional owners would be difficult at best, since we are unable to follow a single property over time. However, it is possible to say that there is general agreement among the sources for rents paid for single rooms. See for example A.G.N. Registro de Escribano 6, 1800, for the rental of a room to Juan González; and Registro de Escribano 3, 1785–86–87, for a rental agreement between Salvador Rubio and Mariano Rogue.

18. For estimates of food expenditures as a percentage of total expenditures in Great Britain see Rufus S. Tucker, "Real Wages of Artisans in London, 1729–1935," p. 75; Elizabeth W. Gilboy, "The Cost of Living and Real Wages in Eighteenth Century England," *The Review of Economic Statistics,* vol. xviii, no. 3 (August, 1936), pp. 135–137; and more generally in J. S. Ashton, "The Standard of Life of the Workers in England, 1790–1830," *Journal of Economic History,* Supplement ix (1949), pp. 19–38. Billy G. Smith has provided an excellent analysis of working class expenditures for contemporary Philadelphia in "The Material Lives of Laboring Philadelphians, 1750–1800," *William and Mary Quarterly,* vol. xxxviii, no. 2 (April, 1981), especially pp. 167–172. For a similar effort by economists consult Paul A. David and Peter Solar, "A Bicentenary Contribution to the History of the Cost of Living in America," in Paul Uselding (ed.), *Research in Economic History,* vol. 2 (JAI Press: Greenwich, Connecticut, 1977), pp. 15–22, for the eighteenth century material.

19. One author who has illuminated this area of popular protest is George Rudé. See his *La Multitud en la Historia* (Siglo xxi: Buenos Aires, 1971), especially chapter III, "La revuelta urbana en el siglo dieciocho," pp. 55–70.

20. When driven to impose new taxes on bread by the military emergency of

1806–1807, the government found that it was politically impossible to maintain. A.G.N., División Colonia, Sección Gobierno, Bandos, Libro 8, folio 363, for Liniers decision to revoke this tax. I have discussed efforts by the cabildo to hold down bread prices in "The Entrepreneurial Reorganization of an Artisan Trade: The Bakers of Buenos Aires," *The Americas,* vol. 32, no. 2 (October, 1980), pp. 139–160.

21. A typical arancel for bread is published in Facultad de Filosofía y Letras, *Documentos para la historia del virreinato,* 3 vols. (Buenos Aires, 1912–1913), vol. 1, pp. 72–73.

22. The work on Spanish grain prices is summarized by Juan Plaza Prieto in *Estructura económica de España en el siglo xviii* (Confederación Española de Cajas de Ahorros: Madrid, 1975), pp. 251–253. See also Earl J. Hamilton, *War and Prices in Spain, 1651–1800* (Harvard University Press: Cambridge, Mass., 1947).

23. The author thanks Enrique Tandeter for pointing out the effects of this region-wide natural disaster. Tandeter bases his opinion on the letters of Gaspar Santa Coloma, A.G.N., División Colonia, Sección Gobierno, Colección Gaspar de Santa Coloma.

24. These practices and their effects on bread prices were noted by Alexander Gillespie in his often cited *Gleanings and Remarks Collected During Many Months of Residence at Buenos Ayres and Within the Upper Country* (B. De Whirst: Leeds, 1818), p. 77 and p. 116. For complaints against monopolists forcing up wheat prices see A.G.N., Division Colonia, Sección Gobierno, Archivo del Cabildo, Ano 1803, Ano 1809, and Hacienda, Legajo 76, Expediente 2002.

25. Juan Plaza Prieto, *Estructura económica de España,* p. 933.

26. Guillermo Furlong, *Las industrias,* pp. 22–27; and Alexander Gillespie, *Gleanings and Remarks,* pp. 78–79.

27. Alexander Gillespie, *Gleanings and Remarks,* pp. 78–79.

28. Don Felix de Azara, *Viajes por la América Meridional,* 2 tomos (Calpe: Madrid, 1923), tomo II, pp. 186–187. He notes also a substantial amount of sugar imported from Lima.

29. Fernand Braudel, *Civilization and Capitalism, 15th–18th Century,* vol. I, *The Structure of Everyday Life* (Harper & Row: New York, 1979), especially pp. 224–227.

30. Archivo de la Provincia de Buenos Aires (hereafter A.P.B.A.), Criminales, 34-1-10. As part of the testimony in a criminal case it was stated that local custom required the master artisan to provide maté twice a day.

31. Azara stated that during the period 1792–1796 Buenos Aires received an average of 196,000 arrobas per year. Felix de Azara, *Viajes,* tomo II, p. 187.

32. A.P.B.A., Criminales, 34-1-12 and 34-1-11. See also Ricardo Rodríquez Molas, *Las Pulperías,* part of the series *La vida de nuestro pueldo,* no. 42 (Centro Editor de América Latina: Buenos Aires, 1982), p. 8. The cabildo and the viceregal government attempted (unsuccessfully) to control the sale of alcoholic beverages in a long series of unenforceable laws. See A.G.N., División Colonia, Sección Gobierno,

Bandos, libro 5, folios 133–139. One measure of the importance of alcohol in the local diet was the popular protest against the imposition of a new tax on aguardiente. A.G.N., *Acuerdos de Extinguido Cabildo de Buenos Aires*, Serie IV, tomo III, pp. 154–155.

33. Probably both factors played a role in determining the level of alcohol consumption. In contemporary England working men "took small beer with each main meal of the working day and ale, in no small measure, whenever he had occasion to celebrate." J. S. Ashton, "The Standard of Life of the Workers in England," p. 30.

34. A.G.N., División Colonia, Sección Gobierno, Bandos, Libro 7, folios 154–156, June 2, 1794; Bandos, Libro 8, folios 46–50, September 6, 1800; and Bandos, Libro 8, folios 365–369, April 17, 1809.

35. A.P.B.A., Criminales, Legajo 34-1-12.

36. Fernand Braudel, *Structures of Everyday Life*, pp. 236–237.

37. A.P.B.A., Criminales, Legajo 34-1-9, Legajo 34-1-19, Legajo 34-1-11, and Legajo 34-1-12.

38. Jonathan C. Brown, *A Socioeconomic History of Argentina*, pp. 33–35.

39. D.H.A., tomo iv, *abastos*, pp. 166–168.

40. A.G.N., División Colonia, Sección Gobierno, Buenos Aires, Temporalidades, 1783–1788, Obra de la Real Universidad. During a 106-day pay period, 54 days were meatless.

41. For an analysis of home ownership among artisans see Lyman L. Johnson, "The Artisans of Buenos Aires During the Viceroyalty, 1776–1810" (unpublished Ph.D. dissertation: The University of Connecticut, 1974), chapter v, pp. 244–310.

42. A.G.N., División Colonia, Sección Gobierno, Tribunales, Legajo Z4, Expediente 11.

43. A.P.B.A., Criminales, Legajo 34-1-10.

44. Susan Socolow, *The Merchants of Buenos Aires*, p. 63.

45. A.G.N., División Colonia, Sección Gobierno, Cabildo de Buenos Aires, Propios, 1770–1806.

46. A.G.N., División Colonia, Sección Contaduria, Convento y iglesia de San Ramón de Buenos Aires, Inventorio de los bienes, muebles y inmuebles, 1788–1792.

47. A.G.N., División Colonia, Sección Gobierno, Cabildo de Buenos Aires, Propios, 1808–1812.

48. A.G.N., División Colonia, Sección Gobierno, Cabildo de Buenos Aires, Propios, 1810–1811, Documentos 7–10.

49. A.G.N., División Colonia, Sección Contaduria, Convento y iglesia de San Ramón de Buenos Aires, Inventorio de los bienes y muebles, inmeubles, 1788–1792. On average *esquinas* owned by the convento rented for 10 pesos per month. This was 3 pesos more than other apartments in the same buildings.

50. A.G.N., Sucesiones 3468, Testamentaria de Victoriano Arias de Andrade, 1800; and Sucesiones 8414, Testamentaria de Agustín Sagari, 1793.

51. See Lyman L. Johnson, "Estimaciones de la población," especially pages 116–119, for a discussion of undercounting in colonial censuses.

52. Alexander Gillespie, *Gleanings and Remarks,* p. 118. He notes that, "The houses in the suburbs of Buenos Aires, in every direction, are mean, but penetrate little into the country. . . ."

53. This is a common problem, confronted by every historian who attempts to construct a cost of living index for the prestatistical past. Among the many who have confronted these problems are: Billy G. Smith, "The Material Lives of Laboring Philadelphians," pp. 167–172; Elizabeth W. Gilboy, "The Cost of Living and Real Wages in Eighteenth Century England," p. 135; and Marcello Carmagnani, *El salariado minero en Chile colonial* (Universidad de Chile: Santiago: 1963), pp. 74–78.

54. A.G.N., División Colonia, Sección Gobierno, Cabildo de Buenos Aires, Propios, 1805–1806. A nearly identical diet was provided for the men hauling rock used in constructing a new sea wall. A.G.N., División Colonia, Sección Gobierno, Cabildo de Buenos Aires, *Obras,* 1805–1806.

55. This workforce consisted of 11 prisoners, a guard, 24 peones, and a capataz. A.G.N., División Colonia, Sección Gobierno, Cabildo de Buenos Aires, *Obras,* 1805–1806. A similar diet was provided for the Spanish garrison in Havana. A.G.I., Indiferente General, 1581.

56. A.G.N., División Colonia, Sección Gobierno, Temporalidades, Obra de la Universidad, 1783.

57. This is the common shopping practice noted by Alexander Gillespie, *Gleanings and Remarks,* p. 118.

58. Elizabeth W. Gilboy, "The Cost of Living and Real Wages in Eighteenth Century England," p. 136; Billy G. Smith, "The Material Lives of Laboring Philadelphians," pp. 168–171.

59. Lyman L. Johnson, "Bakers of Buenos Aires," p. 149.

60. Alexander Gillespie, *Gleanings and Remarks,* p. 119; and David Deforest, Journal, vol. 2, p. 140, David Curtis Deforest Papers, Yale University Library.

61. A.P.B.A., Criminales, Legajo 34-1-11 and Legajo 34-1-13.

62. A.G.N., División Colonia, Sección Gobierno, Cabildo de Buenos Aires, Archivo del Cabildo, 1806, folios 767–767v. Professional bakers commonly blamed high fuel costs for their violations of the arancel.

63. Antonio Domínguez Ortiz, La sociedad española en el siglo xviii (Instituto Balmes de Sociología: Madrid, 1955), pp. 211–212; and David R. Ringrose, *Madrid and the Spanish Economy, 1560–1850* (University of California Press: Berkeley, 1983), pp. 112–114.

64. Alexander Gillespie, *Gleanings and Remarks,* p. 87, noted that the abundance of food prevented starvation, but underlined the high cost of bread, p. 77.

65. It is important to remember that dietary necessities are largely defined by culture and that, as a result, consumers will tend to remain with traditional staples

during periods of rising prices, despite the availability of lower-priced substitutes. Marx noted this tendency when he wrote, "Our wants and pleasures have their origin in society; we therefore measure them in relation to the objects which serve for their gratification. Since they are of a social nature, they are of a relative nature." Quoted in Paul A. David and Peter Solar, "A Bicentenary Contribution to the History of the Cost of Living in America," p. 10.

66. The crude death rate was calculated from burial records and population estimates provided by Alberto B. Martínez, *Historia demográfica de Buenos Aires* in Dirección General de Estadística Municipal, vol. III (Buenos Aires, 1910).

67. *Ibid.*, pp. 329–330.

68. A.G.N., División Colonia, Sección Gobierno, Tribunales, Legajo B8, Expediente 22.

69. A thorough search of all surviving probate records for this period indicated that members of this class owned approximately 30 pesos worth of clothing at the time of their deaths.

70. A.G.N., División Colonia, Sección Gobierno, Tribunales, Legajo L9, Expediente 4; Tribunales, Legajo B8, Expediente 22; A.G.N., División Colonia, Sección Gobierno, Buenos Aires 1783–1788.

71. Ricardo Levene, *Obras de Ricardo Levene* 3 tomos (Academia Nacional de la Historia: Buenos Aires, 1962), tomo II, p. 417. Levene provides average prices and index numbers for common imports—mostly textiles—during the war years 1797–1799. Most textiles reached index numbers of 200 to 300 in this three year period. He notes that in 1798 a peon would need to work for 15 days to purchase a shirt, p. 401.

72. David C. Deforest Papers, Yale University, Letter to Messers Gray and Bowen, Havana, August 9, 1807. He states that there was a glut in textiles and new imports would find no local market.

73. Alexander Gillespie, *Gleanings and Remarks*, p. 87.

74. J. Rawls, *A Theory of Justice* (Bellsnap Press: Cambridge, Mass., 1971), pp. 62, 302.

75. A.G.N., División Colonia, Sección Contaduria, Caja de Buenos Aires, 1770–1815; Archivo del Cabildo, 1770–1815; Obras Publicas, Canal de San Fernando, 1770–1808; Cabildo de Buenos Aires, obras, 1805–1806. For the ecclesiastical records see AGN, División Colonia, Sección Contaduria, Culto de Buenos Aires, Mercedarios, hospicio de San Ramón de las Conchas, Libros I, III, and V; Culto de Buenos Aires, Mercedarios-convento, gastos, libros, I, II, and III; Culto de Buenos Aires, Bethlemitas, Convento y hospital de Santa Catalina; Culto de Buenos Aires, Mercedarios, Convento Grande de San Ramón, Libro de Gastos, 1775–1815. The accounts for each year were searched and each record of wage payment was recorded. Medians were then calculated for each artisanal occupation.

76. Lyman L. Johnson, "Estimaciones de la población de Buenos Aires en 1744, 1778, y 1810," *Desarrollo Económico*, 73:09 (abril–junio, 1979), especially p. 115.

7

PRICE MOVEMENTS IN EIGHTEENTH-CENTURY PERU—AREQUIPA[1]

Kendall W. Brown

FOR SOMEONE VENTURING INTO THE NEARLY UNEXPLORED TERRITORY OF colonial Peruvian price history,[2] Lima, the viceregal capital, would seem the logical place to begin,[3] but Arequipa provides a more convenient and rewarding starting place. This is primarily because sources are available for Arequipa that cover most of the seventeenth and eighteenth centuries. First are the accounts of the local Jesuit college, which the viceregal government confiscated when it expelled the order in 1767. Currently housed in the Archivo Nacional del Perú in Lima, these records run from 1627 to 1767.[4] Missing account books interrupt the series from 1690 to 1723 and 1747 to 1755.[5] Although the Jesuit records provide nothing for the post-1767 period, the second source fills that gap: the ledgers of the Arequipan customs officials give price data on merchandise subject to the *alcabala*, running, with some gaps from 1774 to the end of the colonial period.[6] Aside from the years for which records are missing, the chief weakness of this series lies in the fact that basic foodstuffs such as wheat, corn, and potatoes were not subject to the alcabala, and thus prices for these goods are not found in the customs-house (*aduana*) records. The third source is the ecclesiastical tithe on agricultural produce, part of which belonged to the crown as the royal *novenos*. When treasury officials registered the amount collected in novenos, they usually recorded the quantity and price of the crops the novenos represented. Thus, the treasury accounts normally provide price data on basic foodstuffs, including wheat, corn, potatoes, and wine. These are not market prices, but the amount bid by the person who won the contract to buy the novenos crops from the royal treasury. Over the long term, however, they do reflect the general movement in the value of these commodities.[7] Used together, the three series make it possible to analyze price movements in colonial Arequipa.

Founded in 1540, Arequipa was the chief city in southern coastal Peru.

It early developed a remarkably diversified economy by 1600,[8] sustaining itself with its own food production and earning silver by trading wine with the mining towns of the altiplano. Although situated relatively high, at approximately eight thousand feet above sea level, Arequipa was still within the climatic zone where most food grains could be grown. For two leagues around the city, Arequipans had planted all the land in wheat, corn, potatoes, and other crops, no easy task given the extreme aridity of southern Peru.[9] In fact, crops grew only when irrigation systems provided water; otherwise, the terrain was a sterile landscape of volcanic stone and ash. Neighboring valleys were much lower in altitude, and crops such as sugarcane, cotton, olives, and grapes flourished there. Thus, while the region was extremely arid, making irrigation a prerequisite for any type of cultivation, Arequipa prospered agriculturally. In the eighteenth century, mines at Cailloma and Huantajaya pumped silver into the region, although much more came through trade with the sierra. Arequipa was also a major commercial center in its own right and served as the political and religious headquarters of the region. In the 1790s, the province of Arequipa had a population of 37,261, compared to 62,910 for Lima, 31,982 for Cuzco, and 12,032 for Trujillo.[10] In short, Arequipa was one of the principal cities of the viceroyalty, whether judged by the size of its population, the vitality of its economy, or its bureaucratic importance.[11]

TRENDS IN AREQUIPA PRICES

To begin this study of Arequipan prices, relevant information on type of merchandise, quantity, type of measure, price, and date was culled from the sources mentioned above, after which the data were manipulated by computer to make the quantities uniform for each commodity. This meant that some data had to be discarded. The Jesuits, for example, purchased sugar in *panes* (loaves) and by the arroba (approximately 25 pounds); and their olive oil in arrobas, *botijas* (jugs), and *odres* (leather flasks). The quantities represented by botija, odre, and pan are too vague[12] to be converted into a standard measure such as the arroba. Then the median[13] value for each year was selected for each item, and those values were used in the subsequent analyses. Although several hundred different commodities appeared in the sources, many appeared too infrequently to be of much use in the study of price movements. Rather than using the price series for all commodities, those for significant, frequently purchased goods were used. These fell into several categories. First, price series for goods produced in the Arequipa region included *ají* (a spicy pepper much used in the local cuisine), brandy, corn, olive oil, potatoes, sheep, sugar, wheat, wine, and *tocuyo* (a coarse cotton cloth). A second group of imported merchandise came from American sources: maté (a Paraguayan tea), baize, cloth from Quito, coca leaves, mules, salt beef, and tobacco. Third were goods imported from overseas, including pepper, Rouen cloth, iron, and paper.

At this point, a few caveats should be noted. First, the Jesuit accounts have an important gap, extending from 1690 to 1723. Thus, prices for the first two decades of the eighteenth century must be extrapolated from the preceding and following years.[14] Second, the Jesuit series stops in 1767, and the aduana data, which begin in 1774, are a totally different source. Yet the aduana data seem to fit quite well with those derived from the Jesuit accounts. Graphs for the individual commodities show that the price levels beginning in 1774 are not markedly higher or lower than those found in the final Jesuit accounts. While such evidence does not prove conclusively that the two sources are compatible, it at least offers some reassurance that they can be used together. A series built from two different sources should still be used with considerable caution, however. Table 7.1 contains the median annual prices for a selected group of commodities for the period 1627–1818.

Prices of local goods

Most of the principal local agricultural goods maintained a relatively stable price level or else declined slowly. Of the grains, wheat was extremely important because Arequipa's population was proportionately far more "Spanish" than other Peruvian cities.[15] Around 1780, on the average, Arequipa consumed approximately forty thousand fanegas (sixty thousand bushels) of wheat per year, virtually all of which was grown locally.[16] By the end of the century, wheat harvests amounted to fifty to sixty thousand fanegas; Arequipa sold a quarter of them in neighboring Moquegua.[17] Throughout the seventeenth and eighteenth centuries, the price of a fanega of wheat generally fluctuated between 4 and 6 pesos. Based on an index in which the average of the median prices for 1755–64 equals 100,[18] Arequipa suffered three crises in the price of wheat: in 1664,[19] after the great influenza epidemic of 1718–19, which reportedly killed up to two-thirds of the Indians and a sizeable segment of other inhabitants;[20] and in the early 1780s, shortly after the rebellion against the Arequipan customs house and during the Tupac Amaru revolt.[21] In each of these cases, the price surged to 10 pesos per fanega (index 205). Otherwise, prices remained quite stable (between index 60 and 120).[22]

Table 7.1

Prices of Selected Commodities in Arequipa, 1627–1818

Key to commodities:

A: wine, reales per botija
B: brandy, pesos per quintal
C: wheat, reales per fanega
D: corn, reales per fanega
E: potato, reales per costal
F: sugar, reales per arroba
G: olive oil, reales per arroba

H: sheep, reales per animal
I: ají, reales per cesto
J: *cecineta,* reales per arroba
K: Rouen cloth, reales per vara
L: baize, reales per vara
M: iron, pesos per quintal
N: paper, pesos per ream

	A	B	C	D	E	F	G	H	I	J	K	L	M	N
1627	32					72		12		3	16		20	
1628	33		32	56				12			11	10		6
1629	19			60				12			15	10	35	10
1630	28		48	56	22	72		8		4	10		32	10
1631	16							10	32	3			40	
1632	30			56						4	8			7
1633	44		48	61								8		
1634	24			64							12	10		16
1635	30	10	36	64		84	28	12		4	9	10	30	
1636	28		35	60							8			10
1637	34			62						4	14	6	50	
1638	25		32					8		4	15	7	50	12
1639	26										14	12		
1640	26					56		9		3	10	10		4
1641			32	48				9			13	10		
1642	27							9						
1643	31							7				10		8
1644	26							8						
1645			24					10			15	8		7
1646	25					58		9					50	
1647	30		24			49		8		4	11		27	11
1648						74		8						
1649	28		24	52				7		3				
1650	26			50				6	32					
1651			24					8			13			
1652	28		40	48				8				8		
1653	29		37	60				7		4	11	7		5
1654	30		45	52				6						
1655	24		36	20		68		7		4	12	6	36	
1656	27		36	64				7		3	10			6
1657	30		43	55				8		4	14			
1658	25		37	48		70		7	32	4	22	8	70	12

Table 7.1 (continued)

	A	B	C	D	E	F	G	H	I	J	K	L	M	N
1659	28			60		88								
1660	27		42	55		76		8	28	4	27	8	60	10
1661	36		48	56		72		8		4	15		50	
1662	28		45	56		76			36		11	7	26	
1663	38		48	61										
1664	32		80	72		72		7		5			50	
1665	30	13	48	68		72		8		4	9		38	8
1666	30		36							5	9	6		
1667	30		53	40		84				5	10	7	50	
1668	28		40	52				8		5	10	8		
1669	28		40	40				8	28	5	10	8	120	
1670	26	9	37	40	20	58		8		4	11	6	54	
1671	26		36	40	20			8		4		8		
1672	27		32	40	16			8		4		7		9
1673	28		32	32	14	60		8		4	14	8		
1674	20		32	56	12	56		8		4	12	8		7
1675	20		32	56	16	57	30	8		4		8		
1676	16		32	60				8	20	4	14	8	150	
1677	24		32	48	16		21	8	20	4	12	7		
1678	16		32	40		50	40	8	20	4		5		
1679	16		32	40				8	20	4		7		
1680	19		32			46		4	16	4		7	40	9
1681			32					6	16	4	9	8		
1682	24		32			42			16			6		11
1683	22									4	9	7		
1684	24					48	72	8	26	4		9		
1685	24	10	32		16	68	32	6	14	4	12	8		
1686	24		28		18	72		6		4	13	8	60	12
1687	20	10			34	80	56	6	19	4	13	8		
1688	24					72		6	24	4		9		
1723	24		80		48	56	64	4	24	4	9	4	45	8
1724	24		48		34	53	64	4	21	4	9			
1725	20	14	40		24	52	80	4	26	4	11	4	42	
1726	18			32	20	56	32	4	24	4				
1727	18	11	28		17	52	48	4	24	4		5	60	
1728	20				24	48	40	4		4		5		11
1729	20	12	32	28	32	48	40	4	24	4				12
1730	20		32		20	40	32	4	16	4		5	55	10
1731	20	12			20	36	32	4	20	4		5		10
1732	20		34		20	40	32	4	24	4		5		11
1733	20		32		20	40	32	4	16	4				8
1734	20	11	32		20	44	32	6	16	4		4		8
1735	20	11	32		20	40	40	6	16	4		4	60	7
1736	20	11	32		20	34	32	6	20			4	72	10
1737	20	11	32		20	34	40	6	19			4		9

Table 7.1 (continued)

	A	B	C	D	E	F	G	H	I	J	K	L	M	N
1738	20		32		20	34	40	6	24			4		10
1739	20		32		20	34	24	6	24			4		
1740	20	12	32		20	34	32	6	20	4				10
1741	20		36		34	44	40	6	20					
1742	20	12	40		32	52	32	6	32			3		
1743	18	10	40		34	66	48	6	36		10	4		
1744	18	9	37		20	68	48	6	36		9	4		10
1745	30	14	36		24	52	24	8	28	4	9	3		12
1746	24		44		32	52	42	8	29		9	4		14
1747	26		42		30	44	48	8	28		10			
1755	24	12	40		32	52	40	6	22	4	7	5		7
1756	24		42	40	32	52	40	6	23	4				9
1757	24	12	40	38	32	52	32	6	32	4		2		
1758	24	12		36	31	48	32	6	24	4	9			7
1759	24	13			24	45	32	8	19	4				
1760	32	17	32		28	44	36	6	20	4		2		6
1761	32	16		29	20	48	32	8	28	4				
1762	32			28	40	44	36	8	30	4				7
1763	24	12		28	23		40	8	20	4		2	40	
1764	24	11		24	24	40	64	8		4			24	7
1765	28		40			38	52	8	22				20	
1766	28	14		29			36	8					24	4
1767	32	12	40		24		48	8	16				20	5
1774						25	20		25		4		20	4
1775						25	16		20		4			
1776						25	20		14		4			4
1777														
1778														
1779						28	26		12					5
1780														
1781						28	24		12					6
1782														
1783						29	56		28	4	5	6	30	5
1784						34			16		5		30	5
1785	40	8				29	80		16	6				
1786	40	10				36	36		24	4	4	3	16	4
1787														
1788														
1789														
1790		8					24	4	20	4		2		4
1791														
1792	44	8				28	32		16	3	5	1		
1793	24	8				28	40	3	16	3	5	1		
1794	40	8				28			16		5	1		

Table 7.1 (continued)

	A	B	C	D	E	F	G	H	I	J	K	L	M	N
1795							40							
1796	32	8				24	26		16			1		
1797	48	12				28	24		16		6	2	80	7
1798		11				32	24		16		7	3		5
1799	32	8				32			16			3	29	12
1806						24			16					
1810														12
1811	32	8							12			3		
1812	40	7				26	29		10		8	3	18	12
1813														
1814	40	12				20	16				6	1	12	7
1815		10				20	16		16			1	16	6
1816														
1817	24	10				28	25		14		3	1	16	6
1818	40	12				28	24		15		3	1	17	4

Source: Prices are from the Jesuit accounts in ANP, Compañía de Jesús 28–30; and the aduana records for Arequipa, in ANP, Aduanas, legs. 1–85.

If wheat was a dietary mainstay of the Spanish population, the Indians consumed tremendous amounts of corn, much of it fermented to make *chicha*. In the early 1800s, Arequipa harvested eighty to one hundred thousand fanegas of maize each year, of which less than 5 percent might be sold elsewhere.[23] The remainder was consumed locally, especially in the numerous *chicherías* scattered throughout the city.[24] The Jesuit records contain disappointingly few corn prices after 1680, while the aduana ledgers are totally barren, since maize was not subject to the alcabala. It does seem, however, that corn was markedly more expensive during the 1600s than afterward: only once did it fall below 100, and in 1664, its index stood at 225. Scattered data from other sources indicate that after 1700, corn followed basically the same trends as wheat: fairly stable over the long term, with sharp rises immediately after the epidemic and the 1780 rebellions. The prices of the winning bids for the novenos do, however, reveal an interesting period of great stability at a lower than normal level, running from approximately 1720 to 1745. Evidently the great mortality among the Indians because of the influenza epidemic not only cut demand for corn, but depressed its value for about twenty-five years. Aside from those years, the bids fluctuated much more widely in value, with a fanega of maize being generally more expensive until about 1790, when the prices began to fall slightly. The late decline probably resulted from much greater production of corn. Tithe data show that from the beginning of the century to approximately 1740, non-Indians harvested only one to two thousand fanegas of maize per year, but then a dramatic increase in maize cultivation began. By 1770, non-Indian harvests came to approximately thirty-five thousand fanegas and reached fifty-five thousand by the end of the century.

Prices for potatoes, the third of the basic food commodities, fluctuated to a greater extent than those for either wheat or corn and grew significantly higher as the colonial period ended. Around 1680, a *costal* (bag)[25] of potatoes cost 2 pesos (index 56); after the influenza epidemic it was worth 6 pesos (index 165); and in 1800, 5 pesos (index 140). On the whole, potatoes roughly doubled in price over the eighteenth century. This was probably the result, at least in part, of the fact that potato production did not expand much. As reflected in the novenos, non-Indians in Arequipa produced about seven thousand costales of potatoes in 1700, compared with only ten thousand a hundred years later.[26] In the meantime, despite the influenza epidemic of 1718–19, the population had grown significantly by the end of the century.

Wine and aguardiente (brandy distilled from wine) ranked alongside wheat and corn as Arequipa's most important agricultural products. While wine and brandy were not essential foodstuffs, they were widely drunk in Arequipa by the non-Indian inhabitants, and more important, were the cash crops Arequipa traded to the altiplano for hard money to pay taxes and buy imported merchandise. The prices of wine and brandy were related, of course, since wine was the ingredient required to produce brandy. Changes in the popularity of the two drinks also influenced their prices. Peruvians used aguardiente primarily for medicinal purposes before the eighteenth century, when it became a popular beverage. Thereafter, Arequipan vintners began to convert their excess wine into brandy, and this helped shore up the price of wine, which had been falling since the early 1600s. By 1800, in fact, many viticulturalists distilled as much as 95 percent of their wine into brandy, the latter being the dominant product in Arequipan trade with the altiplano.[27]

Wine and brandy prices were not, however, closely correlated. Wine prices reached three relatively modest peaks: 1633 (index 167), 1663 (index 142), and 1797 (index 182). Even more impressive was the long period, from 1670 to 1759, when prices remained low, the index only moving above 100 once during that time. On the whole, wine prices declined gradually from about 1630 to about 1750, but thereafter they rose steadily until the 1790s, when they leveled off. Brandy, on the other hand, which rarely appears in the Jesuit accounts before the 1700s, achieved its peak price in 1761, when it sold for 16 pesos per quintal (index 122). Then, a gradual decline set in that saw brandy prices fall to 7 pesos per quintal (index 53) in 1812.[28] This was primarily the result of oversupply in the altiplano markets.[29] That the value of wine managed to hold up longer indicates that while the prices of the two products were related, their markets were not identical.

Sugar prices were high until 1667 (9–11 pesos per arroba), but fell to 5–6 pesos around 1680 and to 3.5 pesos by 1820.[30] The decline was quite steady, with much less fluctuation than was true of some of the other crops. In Bourbon Arequipa, sugar reached its highest price at 8.5 pesos in 1744 (index 144),[31] its lowest in 1814–15 at 2.5 pesos (index 42). Sugar undoubtedly decreased in cost as the amount of locally produced sugar increased. Over the course of the eighteenth century, a number of sugar plantations were established in the Tambo and Camaná valleys along the coast.[32] Arequipans no longer had to import sugar from Lima, Lambayeque, or the Caribbean, and the lower prices reflected that fact.[33]

The price of olive oil also showed a relatively strong downward trend, although oil prices fluctuated more than sugar prices and were strongly influenced by both the influenza epidemic and the tumults of the early 1780s. Worth approximately 5 pesos per arroba (index 104) in the late 1600s, it jumped to 8 pesos (index 167) because of the epidemic, fell back to about 4 pesos (index 83) almost immediately, and then declined very gradually for the remainder of the period except for the second, short-lived spurt in the early 1780s (index 208). As with sugar, the principal circumstance influencing the price of olive oil was probably the expansion of olive groves along the Arequipan coast.

A final example of local agricultural crops is ají, the fiery pepper featured in many of the spicy Arequipan dishes. A *cesto* (basket) of ají cost about 3 pesos from 1680 to 1740, when the price rose to 4 pesos. Thereafter, a steady decline followed until the price stood at only 2 pesos in 1820. The peak price of 3.5 pesos (index 149) occurred in 1662 and 1743–44, while it reached a low of 1.25 (index 41) in 1812.

Of cloth used in Arequipa, tocuyo was the chief type manufactured locally, aside from woolen goods woven by the Indians. A coarse cotton textile used especially by the lower classes for undergarments, a vara (about 33 inches) of tocuyo fell steadily in price from 5–8 reales around 1680 to 2–4 reales in the mid-1700s; by the end of the period, it brought only 1–2 reales.[34]

During these years, as cotton became more commonly grown in the coastal areas near Arequipa, it fell in price, and this undoubtedly contributed to the lower cost of tocuyo. Easier access to cheap European cloth, especially after 1760, also may have added to the downward pressure on tocuyo prices. In fact, by 1790, tocuyo sold for so little that it barely paid the dyers for the raw cloth they purchased from the weavers.[35]

Prices of other American goods

Of course, Arequipa was not totally self-sufficient, consuming only those articles produced locally, but conducted a brisk trade with neighboring provinces to obtain needed goods. Among this merchandise was baize, purchased from the altiplano, and as with all the other textiles commonly used in the city, its long-term trend was to decline gradually but steadily from a high of 11.7 reales per vara in 1639 (index 418). A vara cost 5–8 reales from 1650–80, and for the first half of the 1700s, it brought only 3–5 reales. By 1760, the price stood at a mere 2 reales, and although it briefly rebounded to 6 (index 214) because the Tupac Amaru revolt disturbed the producing areas, it quickly fell again, ending at 0.5 real per vara by 1818 (index 18).

Another, finer, American cloth was *paño* (woolens) from Quito. Used quite commonly in Arequipa until the late 1700s, it then appears infrequently in the documentation, perhaps because it had trouble withstanding the onslaught of European textiles that flooded into the Arequipan market under the liberalized commercial policies of Charles III and his successor. From a high of 6.5 pesos (index 144) per vara, this cloth sold at 4–5 pesos per vara in the final decades of the 1600s, but its price fell to and remained at 2.5 pesos (index 56) by the 1770s. Thereafter, the aduana records show a great influx of European cloth, but almost no paño de Quito.

Imported to Arequipa primarily from Tucumán, mules were another American product that fell in price, probably as supplies became more frequent and abundant. Whereas they had ranged as high as 90 pesos (index 486) during the preceding century, by the 1700s, a mule sold in Arequipa for as little as 10 or 20 pesos. In 1785, for example, a mule cost 10 pesos (index 54).[36] Much of the decline in price occurred in the mid-1600s, although the cost rose sharply between 1675 and 1690 to 80 and even 100 pesos per mule before it fell once again.

Teamsters who sold Arequipan wine and brandy in the altiplano often brought baize, coca leaves, meat, cheese, and other foodstuffs back to Arequipa to sell. Cecineta (salt beef) showed a modest rise in price. It sold for 3–4 reales per arroba in the seventeenth century, but then rose slightly and remained very stable after 1700 at 4 reales. Sheep rose in price during the 1700s,[37] after declining from 12 reales (index 171) per animal to 7–8 reales over the course of the preceding century. During the 1700s, however, the price rose from 4 reales (index 57) around 1730 back up to 8 reales (index 114) by 1780. Fragmentary data for the final decades of the colonial period suggest that the sheep prices might have fallen off once again, but it is difficult to prove.

The Jesuits bought few coca leaves, making it difficult to determine what the trend in their prices was. They seem to have sold for about 5 pesos per cesto around 1650, but rose to 6–8 pesos in the late 1700s. During the 1780s, a cesto went for as much as 10 pesos, but whether that was the result of the Tupac Amaru revolt is unknown.

Also purchased from the neighboring Río de la Plata, maté became extremely popular in Arequipa during the eighteenth century, except among the lower classes.[38] It generally does not appear in the Jesuit accounts, however, until 1700. During the first half of the century, it cost up to 20.5 pesos (index 167) per arroba, but then fell to about 6 pesos (index 49) after 1775.

Prices of goods from overseas

Among the goods imported to Arequipa from overseas, some of the most common were iron, cloth, paper, and pepper. Their cost in southern Peru reflected international supply and demand, developments in maritime transportation, changes in imperial commercial and tax policy, and disruptions in trade caused by the great European wars for empire. In general, most of the goods tended to fall in price as supplies to Arequipa became more frequent and regular. There were periods, though, at times quite prolonged, when Spanish maritime trade nearly ground to a standstill and prices for imported goods in Arequipa rose as a result.

Such was the case at the outset of the eighteenth century, during the War of the Spanish Succession (1701–13), when Spain still clung to the antiquated fleet system, yet lacked the vessels and men of war necessary to supply its colonies. Arequipa supplied itself from French ships, whose captains had been authorized by Philip V to visit the colonies while Spain and France remained at war with the British.[39] After the war ended and the French no longer had royal license to trade with Peru, they continued to smuggle goods into Arequipa.[40] The great fleets sailed from Cadiz to South America so irregularly that Arequipan merchants could not rely upon them for merchandise. They consequently turned to illegal channels.

The War of Jenkins's Ear, which erupted between Spain and Great Britain in 1739, disrupted imperial trade and brought an end to the old Habsburg fleet system. After the British captured Portobello in 1739, Philip V officially abolished the fleet system the following year and allowed ships to sail individually for the New World. The conflict kept the prices for European merchandise high in Arequipa for another decade. In 1750, Spain and Great Britain finally signed a new commercial treaty that paved the way for "seven years of successful and friendly relations between the commercial interests of both countries."[41]

Although the Spanish again found themselves fighting the British during the French and Indian War (1754–63), that conflict does not seem to have had much effect on the price of imported goods in Arequipa. Prices, which had dropped substantially in the 1750s, generally remained low until Spain found itself engulfed in the maelstrom of the French Revolution and the Napoleonic Wars, when prices for overseas merchandise again rose sharply in Arequipa.[42] They fell back quickly once peace returned to Europe and the Atlantic.

These trends show up most clearly in the data for paper, which appears frequently in the Jesuit and aduana accounts. Paper prices fluctuated widely (especially during the 1600s), from 16 pesos (index 222) per ream in 1634 down to 4 pesos (index 56) in 1766, 1776, 1786, and 1818. During the eighteenth century, paper prices generally remained high until the 1740s, reaching a peak at 14 pesos per ream in 1746 (index 194). Within a decade, however, a ream routinely cost only 4–6 pesos, and it remained that way until the Napoleonic era, when the price rose temporarily to 12 pesos (index 167).

Iron prices also fit the trends outlined earlier for the overseas trade. During the seventeenth century, iron prices varied a good deal, from 20 pesos per hundred pounds (index 63) in 1627 to 150 pesos (index 468) in 1676. The first half of the next century witnessed more stable, but gradually increasing prices. Iron cost 40–60 pesos per 100 pounds in the 1720s, but then rose modestly to 72 pesos (index 225) in 1736. In the 1760s, however, it fell to about 20 pesos, where it generally remained for the remainder of the colonial period, except for a sharp rise to 80 pesos (index 250) in 1797. After the Napoleonic Wars, iron prices fell to about 15 pesos (index 47).

As for pepper, its price grew higher until the mid-1700s, when it finally began to drop. Pepper evidenced a sharp increase from approximately 1730 to 1750, during the collapse of the fleet system and the wars with the British. In fact, it reached 5.5 pesos per pound (index 367) in 1747, higher than it had been during the seventeenth century. By 1760, however, pepper prices were declining steadily, reaching three reales per pound (index 25) in 1814.

One of the most common textiles imported from Europe was *ruán*, named for Rouen, the city in Normandy where it was manufactured. Ruán declined steadily in price from the 1620s, when it cost 1–2 pesos per vara (index 100–200), to the 1810s, when the price fell to 0.5 peso (index 50). Only around 1660 did a dramatic exception to this long-term trend occur: ruán briefly rose as high as 3.4 pesos per vara (index 338). During the 1700s two cycles are evident. From the second decade of the century,[43] prices rose modestly, only to decline around 1760 to about 0.5 peso per vara. It doubled in price during the Napoleonic era, but fell back to its former level once peace returned.[44]

Cost of Living

Descriptions of the series for the foregoing commodities provide a fragmentary, disjointed picture of the movement of prices in Arequipa.[45] A cost-of-living index furnishes a useful summary of the combined effects of fluctuations in the price of selected goods on the general level of Arequipan prices. The following index for the cost of living consists of the total cost of a number of goods commonly consumed in Arequipa and weighted according to the quantity two families might have used during the same amount of time. For purposes of the analysis, the families were considered to be equal in size with identical sexual and age distributions, but one was from a Hispanic background, with a relatively high standard of living, and the other from a lower-class mestizo background. Thus, their consumption differed, with the Hispanic family assumed to have used more imported cloth, a wider variety of foodstuffs, and greater quantities of nonindigenous products. The mestizo family, on the other hand, was considered to have been largely indigenous in outlook, which meant that it ate primarily Indian foodstuffs, dressed in locally produced textiles, drank chicha, chewed coca leaves, and did not use such products as tobacco, wine, and brandy. While these choices were informed by what is known about Arequipan diet and consumption patterns,[46] they still were largely arbitrary. Because the quantities of the various items remained constant over time, though, their combined cost provides an indication of how much the cost of living changed over the century.

Table 7.2 indicates the goods selected with the quantity hypothetically consumed by each family during a year's time. Each family would have obviously consumed other items in addition to those included in the table (milk, thread, and fruit are good examples). Each item in the table, however, would have been a major component of the family's consumption. Furthermore, sufficient price data are available for each of the included goods to carry out the analysis.

The next step in the analysis was to calculate the average price for each of the goods at twenty-year intervals from 1680 to 1820.[47] The price given is meant to reflect the average price of the commodity at the time listed (Table 7.3). In some instances, missing data made it necessary to extrapolate from prices for years preceding or following the date.[48] Occasionally the data are so fragmentary as to provide no indication of what the price level was at that time. These cases are marked accordingly.

Once the price per unit was established, it was then multiplied by the quantity of each item consumed by each family. The value of total consumption was then calculated for twenty-year intervals. Tables 7.4 and 7.5 show the results for the two families. In order to be able to compare the totals for each year, it was necessary to use data from other sources to supply the prices missing in Table 7.3. Prices drawn from sources other than the Jesuit or aduana accounts are shown in parentheses.

The tables reveal two striking discoveries. First, the cost of living declined. For the Hispanic family, the cost of the items decreased from 282.5 pesos in 1680 to only 211.1 pesos in 1820, a decline of 25.3 percent. The cost of living for the mestizo family fell even farther, 35.1 percent, from 199.6 pesos to 129.5. This works out to an annual decline of 0.24 percent for the Hispanic consumption pattern and 0.36 percent for the mestizo rate. The rate of decline was not particularly rapid for either, although it was 50 percent stronger for the mestizo family.

Second, the index numbers for the two tables give an excellent clue as to how eighteenth-century Arequipan prices might best be summarized. In both cases, the major decline in prices occurred before 1760; thereafter, little further decrease is evident. This seems to indicate that the two elements having the greatest influence on the long-term price trend were the influenza epidemic and the resolution of the imperial maritime and commercial crisis. The cost of living for the Hispanic family in 1720 (index 144.0) was a setback, compared to 1680 (index 124.3). Prices of wheat, potatoes, olive

Table 7.2

Hypothetical Consumption of Goods by a Hispanic Family
and a Mestizo Family in Eighteenth-Century Arequipa

Item	Hispanic family	Mestizo family
Foodstuffs:		
ají	1 cesto	1 cesto
brandy	0.5 quintal	
dried, salted meat	10 arrobas	3 arrobas
corn	3 fanegas	15 fanegas
olive oil	2 arrobas	
maté	0.5 arroba	
pepper	0.5 pound	
potatoes	3 costales	5 costales
sheep	5 animals	3 animals
sugar	2 arrobas	0.5 arroba
wheat	10 fanegas	3 fanegas
wine	10 botijas	
Cloth:		
baize	10 varas	5 varas
cloth from Quito	5 varas	
Rouen cloth	5 varas	
serge	5 varas	2 varas
tocuyo		5 varas
Miscellaneous:		
coca leaves		1 cesto
iron	50 pounds	25 pounds
mule	1 animal	1 animal
paper	1 ream	
tobacco	5 pounds	

Table 7.3

Value of Basic Items at Twenty-Year Intervals in Arequipa, 1680–1820, in pesos de ocho*

Item	1680	1720	1740	1760	1780	1800	1820
Foodstuffs:							
ají (cesto)	2.5	3.0	2.8	2.5	2.0	2.0	1.8
brandy (quintal)	10.0	14.0	12.0	16.0	9.0	9.0	11.0
corn (fanega)	5.0	4.0	?	3.8	5.0	3.5	?
cecineta (arroba)	0.5	0.5	0.5	0.5	0.5	0.5	0.4
olive oil (arroba)	5.0	8.0	4.0	4.5	3.0	3.0	3.0
maté (arroba)	?	12.0	16.0	9.0	6.0	6.0	?
pepper (lb.)	14.0	16.0	28.0	12.0	9.0	6.0	3.0
potatoes (costal)	2.0	8.0	2.5	3.5	?	5.0	?
sheep	0.8	0.5	0.8	0.8	0.5	0.4	?
sugar (arroba)	5.7	7.0	6.5	5.5	3.5	4.0	3.5
wheat (fanega)	4.0	10.0	4.0	4.0	7.0	5.5	?
wine (botija)	2.3	3.0	2.5	4.0	5.0	4.0	3.5
Cloth (all in varas):							
baize	0.8	0.5	0.4	0.3	0.8	0.3	0.1
cloth from Quito	4.0	3.0	3.3	2.5	2.5	?	?
Rouen cloth	1.3	1.3	1.3	0.5	0.6	0.9	0.4
serge	0.4	?	0.3	0.3	1.0	0.1	1.1
tocuyo	0.7	0.4	0.3	0.3	0.4	0.3	0.3
Miscellaneous:							
iron (quintal)	40.0	45.0	72.0	30.0	25.0	29.0	17.0
mule	70.0	25.0	?	18.5	10.0	10.0	?
paper (ream)	10.0	8.0	10.0	6.0	5.5	12.0	4.0
tobacco (pound)							
coca leaves (cesto)	5.0	2.5	7.0	?	6.0	7.0	6.0

*For the quantities of each item, refer to Table 1.

Table 7.4

Value of Items Consumed by a Hypothetical Hispanic Family
in Eighteenth-Century Arequipa, in pesos de ocho*

Item	1680	1720	1740	1760	1780	1800	1820
Foodstuffs:							
ají	2.5	3.0	2.8	2.5	2.0	2.0	1.8
brandy	5.0	7.0	6.0	8.0	4.5	4.5	5.5
cecineta	5.0	5.0	5.0	5.0	5.0	5.0	4.0
corn	10.0	8.0	7.8	7.6	10.0	7.0	(8.0)
olive oil	10.0	16.0	8.0	9.0	6.0	6.0	6.0
maté	5.5	6.0	8.0	4.5	3.0	3.0	(6.0)
pepper	0.9	1.0	1.8	0.8	0.5	0.4	0.2
potatoes	6.0	24.0	7.5	10.5	(18.0)	15.0	(13.5)
sheep	4.0	2.5	4.0	4.0	2.5	2.0	(2.0)
sugar	11.4	14.0	13.0	11.0	7.0	8.0	7.0
wheat	40.0	100.0	40.0	40.0	70.0	55.5	(55.0)
wine	23.0	30.0	25.0	40.0	50.0	40.0	35.0
Cloth:							
baize	8.0	5.0	4.0	3.0	8.0	3.0	1.0
cloth from Quito	20.0	15.0	16.5	12.5	12.5	(25.0)	(15.0)
Rouen cloth	6.5	6.5	6.5	2.5	3.0	4.5	2.0
serge	2.0	(1.8)	1.5	1.5	5.0	.5	5.5
Miscellaneous:							
iron	20.0	22.5	36.0	15.0	12.5	14.5	8.5
mule	70.0	25.0	(22.0)	18.5	10.0	10.0	(10.0)
paper	10.0	8.0	10.0	6.0	5.5	12.0	4.0
tobacco	22.7	21.1	18.8	21.0	20.0	20.0	20.9
Total	282.5	327.4	244.2	227.3	258.5	240.1	211.1
Index (1760 = 100)	124.3	144.0	107.4	100.0	113.7	105.6	92.9

*For the quantities of each item, refer to Table 2.

Table 7.5

Value of Items Consumed by a Hypothetical Mestizo Family
in Eighteenth-Century Arequipa, in pesos de ocho*

Item	1680	1720	1740	1760	1780	1800	1820
Foodstuffs:							
ají	2.5	3.0	2.8	2.5	2.0	2.0	1.8
cecineta	1.5	1.5	1.5	1.5	1.5	1.5	1.2
corn	75.0	60.0	58.5	57.0	75.0	52.5	(60.0)
potatoes	10.0	40.0	12.5	17.5	(30.0)	25.0	(22.5)
sheep	2.4	1.5	2.4	2.4	1.5	1.2	(1.2)
sugar	2.9	3.5	3.3	2.8	1.8	2.0	1.8
wheat	12.0	30.0	12.0	12.0	21.0	16.5	(16.5)
Cloth:							
baize	4.0	2.5	2.0	1.5	4.0	1.5	0.5
serge	0.8	(.7)	0.6	0.6	2.0	0.2	2.2
tocuyo	3.5	2.0	1.5	1.5	2.0	1.5	1.5
Miscellaneous:							
coca leaves	5.0	2.5	7.0	(6.5)	6.0	7.0	6.0
iron	10.0	11.3	18.0	7.5	6.3	7.3	4.3
mule	70.0	25.0	(22.0)	18.5	10.0	10.0	(10.0)
Total	199.6	183.5	144.1	131.8	163.1	128.2	129.5
Index (1760 = 100)	151.4	139.2	109.3	100.0	123.7	97.3	98.3

*For the quantities of each item, refer to Table 2.

oil, and wine were all significantly higher because of the epidemic, while only the price for mules was markedly lower. By 1740 (index 107.4), however, the food shortages had ended. Probably because of the smaller population, only the best land had to be farmed, and crop yields possibly improved. Goods from overseas remained relatively high in 1740, though, because of the disruption of the fleet system and war with the British. Ruán, paper, iron, and pepper were all considerably higher in 1740 than in 1760, by which time the transatlantic commercial system had finally begun to provide regular, frequent supplies of merchandise. On the other hand, food costs remained relatively low and stable. As a result, the cost of living for the Hispanic family dropped a little more (index 100). In 1780, the Indian revolt forced upward both agricultural prices and commodities from the altiplano and was the primary cause of the upturn at that time. Its effects were short-lived, though, since it did not alter any basic economic relationships. Around the turn of the century, population growth brought basic food prices to a modestly higher level than they had been in 1760. The principal difference between 1800 (index 105.6) and 1820 (index 92.9) was the cost of imported merchandise, which generally dropped in price once the Napoleonic period ended.

The index for the mestizo family followed a roughly similar pattern, with two noteworthy exceptions. First, it declined in 1720 (index 139.2), compared to 1680 (index 151.4), largely because corn and mules were less expensive and more than offset the general rise in food prices. Whereas wheat cost 10 pesos per fanega as late as 1723, corn was valued at only 4 pesos in 1722.[49] This means that the demand for maize fell much more than that for wheat, because of the higher mortality among the Indians. Second, the index for 1800 (97.3) was roughly the same as for 1820 (98.3), whereas for the Hispanic family, the 1800 index was nearly thirteen points higher. The lower-class family obviously consumed fewer imported goods and thus did not feel the increase caused by the Napoleonic wars as strongly.

CONCLUSION

A number of circumstances undoubtedly contributed to the decline and subsequent stagnation of prices in Arequipa during the Bourbon century. Probably most important was the sustained expansion of regional agriculture until late in the 1700s. Arequipan viticulture boomed, in particular because brandy, which only became popular at the beginning of the century, emerged as the major cash crop. Wine continued to find a strong demand in the altiplano. Yet by 1780, output of the regional vineyards had finally matched and even exceeded demand. This prevented prices for brandy and wine from rising and eventually led to a significant decline in the value of aguardiente.[50]

Unlike some parts of Peru, Arequipa remained self-sufficient in basic foodstuffs, generally growing abundant crops of wheat, corn, and potatoes. While occasional disruptions in the normal food supply occurred, as during the indigenous rebellion touched off by Tupac Amaru in 1780, Arequipa was, on the whole, able to feed itself with little difficulty. Its balance between agricultural output and population was certainly healthier than that of Lima, where agricultural problems combined with the larger population to provoke crises in the food supply and dependence upon Chilean cultivators for wheat.[51]

Because of the relatively healthy condition of Arequipan farms, the prices of basic foodstuffs remained comparatively stable at the end of the period, even though the population had grown significantly since the catastrophic influenza epidemic of 1718–19. While prices for some goods jumped because of the epidemic (wheat, for example, was still 10 pesos per fanega as late as 1723, and olive oil and potatoes doubled in price),[52] the longer-term effect of the high mortality was probably to dissipate inflationary pressure on such foodstuffs for several decades. Only when the population had recovered its pre-1717 level and begun to rise above it late in the century did the price of foodstuffs show any serious, prolonged rise.

Of course, occasional droughts and floods also influenced agricultural production and thus the price of local crops. The Moquegua valley, largest wine and brandy producer in the region, suffered floods in 1747 and 1750, which reportedly inflicted more than 1 million pesos of damage on the vineyards.[53] Floods were also a problem for the farms around the city of Arequipa in 1754, forcing the city council on 6 April to prohibit the export of any more wheat and flour to other provinces out of fear that Arequipa would experience shortages.[54] In 1792, a drought hit the Moquegua valley, and wine production in 1793 seems to have fallen by about 25 percent compared to previous years.[55] In the main, however, the region remained remarkably free of natural disasters during the eighteenth century, with the exception of the aforementioned epidemics. Even the earthquake of 1784 proved relatively minor by Arequipan standards.[56]

As already noted, the massive Indian uprising in the early 1780s also influenced prices. While the rebellion failed to ignite the Arequipa region, with the exception of the province of Cailloma, it did interfere with the local economy. Markets for Arequipa viticulture lay in the territories where the influence of the rebellion was felt most directly, and items such as baize, which Arequipa normally purchased from the altiplano, temporarily rose in price. As far as Arequipan prices were concerned, the result of the rebellion was a short-lived upsurge; within a few years, though, prices had returned to normal.

Furthermore, royal fiscal policy also played a role in the story of Arequipan prices. After 1760, the crown imposed new and higher taxes on the region and improved collection procedures. The result was dramatically higher fiscal revenues.[57] Higher taxes undoubtedly added to the cost of many goods. At the same time, though, the mounting financial pressure of the fiscal reforms on the lower classes probably caused them to step up agricultural production in the hope that they could pay their tribute and other taxes with any surplus they might produce beyond what they needed for self-sustenance. Until 1784, when it was abolished, Indians also had to produce crops and other goods to raise money to pay the *reparto forzoso,* the quota of merchandise forcibly distributed among them by the local corregidor (provincial governor). This further stimulated production, which tended to keep prices down.

The nature of the market also worked against inflationary pressure. Although the region produced increasingly greater quantities of merchandise, be they foodstuffs or textiles, there was little chance of exporting these goods to any new markets. Thus, southern Peru and the altiplano had to absorb them, but demand there by the late eighteenth century appears to have become relatively inelastic.[58] As production mounted and demand for Arequipan goods, especially brandy, flagged, prices fell.

Diversification of the regional economy also meant lower prices in some cases. Over the course of the century, for example, the price of sugar and olive oil dropped substantially, primarily because of the expansion of sugar and olive plantations along the Arequipan coast. Local production removed the need to carry in such goods from the north, and the price fell as a result.

In a similar vein, easier availability of imported European goods also contributed to the fall in prices. Abolition of the fleet system permitted single vessels to sail independently to Peru, thereby providing more frequent supplies. Proclamation of Comercio Libre in 1778 removed the Lima monopoly on transatlantic trade, and Arequipa began receiving merchandise from Buenos Aires, via Potosí and Arica, as well as Lima. Then, around 1790 the Cinco Gremios Mayores de Madrid (Five Major Guilds of Madrid) established a factor in Arequipa, and local merchants began to complain that the market in imported goods was flooded. While such a situation obviously worked against the Arequipan merchants, the competition certainly favored the consumer by keeping prices down.[59] Smuggling along the isolated Arequipan coast, especially at the beginning of the eighteenth century and after 1790, also had a significant effect on price levels for imported goods.

Thus, for a variety of reasons, Arequipans were probably better off in terms of prices at the end of the Bourbon century than they were when Philip V came to power. Judging from the cost-of-living indexes, however, the real decline in prices came before 1760; afterward, most prices remained relatively stagnant.[60] Perhaps those earlier years, when prices fell for wealthy and poor alike and the growing popularity of brandy gave the region a second, extremely valuable export product, were the period of real prosperity. After 1760, brandy prices began to fall, and the Bourbon monarchs began to tighten their grip on Arequipa, centralizing political power through institution of the intendancy system and draining silver from the region through much higher taxation.[61] In 1760, though, these problems lay in the future.

NOTES

1. The author is grateful for the financial support received from the American Philosophical Society and Hillsdale College summer research funds, which made possible the archival research in Peru.

2. Relatively little work has been done on the colonial price history of viceregal Peru. Three important exceptions are R. Romano, "Movimiento de los precios y desarrollo económico: El caso de Sudamérica en el siglo xviii," *Desarrollo Económico* 3 (Buenos Aires, 1963): 31–43; E. Tandeter and N. Wachtel, "Prices and Agricultural Production: Potosí and Charcas in the Eighteenth Century," Chapter 8 in this volume; and P. Macera and R. Boccolini, *Precios en Arequipa, 1627–1767* (Lima, 1972). I have seen a reference to the last work, but have been unable to locate a copy of it. It is apparently a small, mimeographed edition put out by Macera's Seminar on Andean History. To these might be added the data in M. Haitin, "Late Colonial Lima: Economy and Society in an Era of Reform and Revolution" (Ph.D. diss., University of California at Berkeley, 1983), 349–77, running in some cases from 1790 to 1840.

3. Tandeter and Wachtel also cite another price study by P. Macera, in collaboration with R. Jiménez, *Precios en Lima, 1667–1738* (Lima, 1972). As with Macera's work on Arequipa, this is undoubtedly drawn from the account books of the Jesuit colleges. I have likewise been unable to locate a copy of this work.

4. The Jesuit accounts are found in the Archivo Nacional del Perú (hereinafter ANP), Compañía de Jesus. Legajo 28 contains Obligaciones deste Colegio de Arequipa, 1627–79; Libro de Gastos del Colegio de Arequipa, 1627–52; and Libro de Recibo del Colegio de Arequipa, 1627–79. Legajo 29 holds Libro de Gastos del Colegio de Arequipa, 1679–90; and Libro de Gastos del Colegio de Arequipa, 1653–79. Legajo 30 has three *libros de gasto,* for the years 1723–35, 1735–47, and 1755–67. On a monthly basis, the accounts give the quantity purchased and price paid for the various items consumed by the college.

5. In comparison, relatively few account books have survived from the Jesuit colleges of Lima. The Compañía de Jesús section of ANP has only two ledgers from the Cercado college, for 1667–90 and 1718–38. For San Pablo, the data are even more fragmentary.

6. See ANP, Aduana de Arequipa, legs. 1–85. This is a newly opened section of the archive, containing some material previously located with the documentation

from the *caja* of Arequipa and a massive amount of data not previously available to the public.

7. The tithe data for Arequipa, as reflected in the royal novenos, are listed in K. Brown, *Bourbons and Brandy: Imperial Reform in Eighteenth-Century Arequipa* (Albuquerque, 1985), 224–29.

8. See, for example, S. Van Bath, "Economic Diversificaiton in Spanish America around 1600: Centres, Intermediate Zones and Peripheries," *Jahrbuch für Geschichte von Staat, Wirtschaft und Gesellschaft Lateinamerikas* 16 (1979), 53–95.

9. J. de Zamácola y Jáuregui, *Apuntes para la historia de Arequipa {1804}* (Arequipa, 1888), 9.

10. See J. Fisher, *Government and Society in Colonial Peru: The Intendant System 1784–1814* (London, 1970), 251–53; and Haitin, "Late Colonial Lima," 11–12.

11. A much fuller analysis of the economy, society, and political structure of Arequipa can be found in Brown, *Bourbons and Brandy.* For the 1600s, see K. Davies, *Landowners in Colonial Peru* (Austin, Texas, 1984).

12. Arequipan municipal officials did, however, order producers to use a standard fifty-five-*libra* measure for the botija of wine. See J. Valdivia, *Fragmentos para la historia de Arequipa* (Arequipa, 1847), 114. When shipping it to the altiplano, a small amount of additional wine was added in case of spillage. At La Paz, for instance, the botija seems to have measured fifty-seven libras. Refer to Libro Manual de Alcabalas de La Paz, 1791, fol. 138, Archivo General de la Nación (Buenos Aires), Sala XIII, 3-4-4.

13. A comparison of the mean and median values showed very few differences between the two.

14. The extrapolation was made by calculating the trend line for the missing period based on the data from the years immediately preceding and following.

15. According to G. Vollmer, *Bevölkerungspolitik und Bevölkerungsktrukur im Vizekönigreich Peru zu Ende der Kolonialzeit, 1741–1821* (Bad Hamburg vor der Höhe, 1967), 328, late eighteenth-century Arequipa was 30 percent Spanish, compared to 17 percent for Lima, 15 percent for Cuzco, and even small percentages for the remaining cities.

16. In 1780, for example, the Arequipa city council reported that the ten flour mills ground an average of 3,116 fanegas per month. Archivo Municipal de Arequipa (hereinafter AMA), LAR .01, fol. 12. Additional quantities, of course, were retained as seed or sold to other cities. See, for instance, AMA, LAC 22, fol. 279; and AMA, LAC 26, fol. 19; and B. de Salamanca, *Arequipa, 1796–1811; La relación del gobierno del Intendente Salamanca,* ed. by J. Fisher (Lima, 1968), 41.

17. P. Macera and F. Márquez Abanto, "Informaciones geográficas del Perú colonial," *Revista del Archivo Nacional del Perú* 28 (1964): 221.

18. So that the series of the various goods could be compared, similar indices

were compiled for each commodity, with the average of the annual medians for the years 1755–64 equal to 100. References to these indices are found throughout the following paragraphs.

19. Apparently Arequipa suffered an agricultural crisis in the early 1660s, judging from the price levels of its crops. The study of Arequipa landholding in Davies, *Landowners,* does not, however, extend much beyond the midseventeenth century and does not mention what this crisis was.

20. Colonial references to the epidemic include Valdivia, *Fragmentos,* 174; Zamácola, *Apuntes,* 44 (which claims that more than half of the population of Arequipa died and many villages were deserted); and F. Echevería y Morales, "Memoria de la Santa Iglesia de Arequipa, 1804," in V. Barriga, ed., *Memorias para la historia de Arequipa,* 4 vols. (Arequipa, 1940–52), 4:47. It is also mentioned in H. Dobyns, "An Outline of Andean Epidemic History to 1720," *Bulletin of the History of Medicine* 37 (1963): 512.

21. Autos seguidos contra Da. Cathalina Espinosa, Archivo Histórico Departamental de Arequipa (hereinafter AHDA), Corregimiento 1780-I; and AHDA, Intendencia 1791-III. Wheat prices were still 8–10 pesos as late as 1783 (AMA, LAC 25, fol. 61). In Arequipa, the upheaval began in January 1780, with a revolt against the establishment of an aduana in the city, approximately ten months before Tupac Amaru launched his rebellion. See G. Galdós Rodríguez, *La rebelión de los pasquines* (Arequipa, 1967); and Brown, *Bourbons and Brandy,* 197–219. The revolt against the customs house disrupted agriculture to some extent in Arequipa, and then the more serious outbreak in the altiplano made the situation worse. Not only did Arequipans expend considerable energy and money in helping to put down the rebellion, but the hostilities interfered with Arequipan-altiplano trade.

22. Municipal leaders strove to maintain a stable wheat price in particular. They regulated Indian production to prevent prices from falling too low for the Spanish growers (see V. Travada y Córdova, *Historia general de Arequipa* [Arequipa, 1923], 133, but at the same time prohibited farmers from exporting wheat and flour to other cities if a shortage threatened to make bread too expensive for consumers. See AMA, LAC 22, fol. 279; AMA, LAC 26, fol. 19; and Salamanca, *Arequipa,* 41.

23. Macera and Márquez Abanto, "Informaciones geográficas," 221–22.

24. An author writing during the mid-1700s estimated that there were three thousand chicherías in Arequipa, doubtless an exaggeration, but still an interesting illustration of the indigenous taste for the traditional Andean beverage. See Travada, *Historia,* 127.

25. Judging from the prices, a costal of potatoes equaled a fanega. Also see Macera and Márquez Abanto, "Informaciones geográficas," 225, which says that in 1804 potatoes cost "4 a 6 pesos costal fanaguero."

26. These are calculated from the novenos data in Brown, *Bourbons and Brandy*, 224–29.

27. Macera and Márquez Abanto, "Informaciones geográficas," 222.

28. Brandy also declined substantially in price in Lima around the end of the eighteenth century. See Haitin, "Late Colonial Lima," 152.

29. Changes in the markets for Arequipan wine and brandy are discussed in Brown, *Bourbons and Brandy*, 40–44, 76–88.

30. N. Cushner, *Lords of the Land: Sugar, Wine, and Jesuit Estates of Coastal Peru, 1600–1767* (Albany, 1980), 122, asserts that sugar supplies had outstripped demand in Peru as early as 1700.

31. This brief upturn in sugar prices may have resulted from the *nuevo impuesto*, a temporary tax on brandy, wine, sugar, and honey instituted in 1742. See, for example, AMA, LAC 21, fol. 634–635; and AMA, LAC 22, fol. 57, 78. It seems to have had little impact on viticultural prices.

32. By this time, Tambo plantations produced twelve thousand arrobas of sugar annually. Macera and Márquez Abanto, "Informaciones geográficas," 222.

33. The province of Abancay near Cuzco was also a major sugar producer in the eighteenth century. See Haitin, "Late Colonial Lima," 21. Much of the sugar consumed in Arequipa may have come from there, perhaps in exchange for wine and brandy, since Cuzco was one of Arequipa's principal trading partners.

34. Its peak price was 12.7 reales (index 577) in 1660; the lowest, 1.2 reales (index 55), in 1796.

35. See the description of the Arequipan textile industry in the report of Intendant Alvarez y Jiménez's *visita*, in Barriga, *Memorias*, I, 53–56.

36. A mule sold to an Indian under the infamous repartimiento de comercio was officially priced at 35 pesos by the royal decree of 1756. See the decree in Archivo General de Indios (hereinafter AGI), Lima 1098.

37. Of the sixteen different commodities Romano studied for the period from 1765 to 1810, sheep prices were the only one to increase. See Romano, "Movimiento de los precios," 32.

38. Travada, *Historia*, 127.

39. AGI, Indiferente General 2720, is an entire bundle of papers dealing with the French ships appeared along the southern coast during the war. They called at Arica in particular, because through that port they gained access to the silver of Potosí, but their cargoes also helped replenish the shelves of Arequipan merchants.

40. In 1717, for example, the Prince of Santo Buono sent the Conde de Bena to Arequipa to stop the contraband trade with the French. The viceroy had received reports that the Arequipan merchant guild and even the convents and monasteries were trafficking with the smugglers. AMA, LAC 20, fol. 490. Santo Buono's envoy had little success. As late as 1724–25, more French ships were trading along the

coast, and viceregal authorities were trying futilely to prevent the local residents from buying from the smugglers. (See AMA, LAC 21, fol. 180; and AMA, LCED .07, fol. 26–27, 36, 54.)

41. G. Walker, *Spanish Politics and Imperial Trade, 1700–1789* (Bloomington, Ind., 1979), 210. Walker provides a good discussion of the abolition of the fleet system. The title of the book is misleading, however, since it contains relatively little information on imperial trade after 1740.

42. This was another peak period for contraband, primarily from the United States and Great Britain. Refer to Macera and Márquez Abanto, "Informaciones geográficas," 231–33; "Informe anónimo sobre los desembarcos clandestinos de mercaderías entre Mollendo y Arica, 1800," ANP, Superior Gobierno 27, cuad. 855; Salamanca, *Arequipa*, 57–59.

43. For a good description of the considerations influencing ruán prices in Potosí, which were also relevant to Arequipa, see Tandeter and Wachtel, "Prices and Agricultural Production."

44. These data contradict T. Anna's contention that prices remained very high even after Napoleon's fall. See *The Fall of the Royal Government in Peru* (Lincoln, Neb., 1979), 122–23.

45. The question might also be raised of how prices in Arequipa compared with those in other Peruvian cities. A very cursory examination of the Jesuit accounts for Lima and Cuzco (see the expense books in ANP, Compañía de Jesús 30a, 31, 41, 42, 42a) gives the impression that food was probably more expensive in Lima than Arequipa and cheapest in Cuzco during the first half of the eighteenth century. Imported goods cost less in the capital, whereas their prices were roughly equal in the two provincial cities.

46. On indigenous food consumption, see S. Antúnez de Mayolo R., *La nutrición en el antiguo Perú* (Lima, 1981). J. Descola, *Daily Life in Colonial Peru 1710–1820* (London, 1968), especially 127–46, deals with diet and clothing, but his treatment is superficial and impressionistic and says little about indigenous consumption. Neither of these works is geographically specific to Arequipa.

47. Because of the missing Jesuit accounts, no value is available for 1700; instead one is presented for 1680 to show the price levels in the late seventeenth century. Furthermore, since the Jesuit data only start again in 1723, the values for 1720 are really for three years later. Likewise the prices for 1820 reflect the data for 1818, the last year for which ANP has Arequipan aduana accounts.

48. The extrapolation assumed that prices had moved in a linear trend during the period. The extrapolated prices used in the tables are consequently the trend values.

49. "Testamento otorgado por Melchora Gonsales, Arequipa," 2 Dec. 1722, fol. 18, AHDA, Corregimiento 1721-V.

50. Brown, *Bourbons and Brandy*, 85–89.

51. The gloomy picture of Lima agriculture is drawn primarily from D. Ramos, *Trigo chileno, navieros del Callao y hacendados limeños entre la crisis agrícola del siglo xvii y la comercial de la primera mitad del siglo xviii* (Madrid, 1967); and O. Febres Villaroel, "La crisis agrícola en el Perú en el último tercio del siglo xviii," *Revista Histórica* 27 (Lima, 1964), 102–99. A recent study of late eighteenth-century Lima is Haitin, "Late Colonial Lima."

52. Unfortunately, the lack of corn data in the Jesuit accounts makes it impossible to evaluate the effect of the epidemic on this indigenous staple. Equally unfortunate, because the Jesuit accounts are missing for years immediately before and after the influenza outbreak, it is impossible to know exactly what the total effects of the epidemic were on the production and price of basic foodstuffs.

53. F. Domínguez, *El Colegio franciscano de propaganda fide de Moquegua (1775–1825)* (Madrid, 1935), 34.

54. AMA, LAC 22, fol. 279.

55. Refer to the 1790 and 1793 novenos data for Moquegua in Brown, *Bourbons and Brandy*, 229.

56. Arequipans claimed that the 1784 earthquake caused anywhere from 6 to 30 million pesos in damages, ruining almost all the buildings and houses in the city. Such claims seem to have been exaggerations, however, designed to persuade the king to take mercy on the city and not reestablish the royal customs house. See AMA, LAC 25, fol. 73; AMA, LCA .01, fol. 291–92, 298–301; and AGI, Lima 1098, Escobedo to Gálvez, Lima, 20 Aug. 1784. Powerful tremors had also devastated the region in 1600 and 1604 and, coupled with a volcanic eruption, had left the vineyards covered with ashes. See V. Barriga, ed., *Los terremotos de Arequipa, 1528–1868* (Arequipa, 1951).

57. From an annual income of less than sixty-seven thousand pesos at the beginning of the eighteenth century, revenues of the Arequipa and Cailloma treasuries shot up to nearly half a million pesos by 1800, an increase of 750 percent. Data for the Arequipa and Cailloma treasuries are located in AGI, Contaduría 1790, 1823, 1868; AGI, Lima 1281–89, 1303–1304, 1790; AGI, Charcas 231; Archivo General de la Nación (Lima) (hereinafter AGN), Real Hacienda, Caja de Arequipa 2, 3, 5, 16–19, 23, 25; and AGN, Real Hacienda, Caja de Cailloma 170–76. Also see the accounts for Arequipa and Cailloma in J. TePaske and H. Klein, *The Royal Treasuries of the Spanish Empire in America*, 3 vols. (Durham, 1982), vol. 1.

58. See K. Brown, "A Evolução da Vinicultura em Arequipa, 1550–1800; Um Aspecto da Agricultura Colonial," *Estudos Ibero-Americanos* 6 (1980): 47–49, for a description and analysis of the problems encountered by Arequipan wine and brandy producers at the end of the century.

59. For a general work on the *gremios*, see M. Capella and A. Matilla Tascón, *Los*

Cinco Gremios Mayores de Madrid (Madrid, 1957). Regarding the disputes arising out of their entry into the Arequipan market, refer to Autos seguidos ante el Real Tribunal del Consulado por los comerciantes de Arequipa, solicitando que se deje sin lugar la creación de la Factoría que los comisionados de los Cinco Gremios Mayores de Madrid, han establecido en la ciudad de Arequipa, 1791, ANP, Real Tribunal del Consulado, Gremios Mayores de Madrid 249, Cuaderno 185; Testimonio del informe que el cabildo y consulado de la ciudad de Lima, dieron el expediente seguido sobre la implantación de Casa-Factorías en Arequipa, Cuzco y demás lugares interiors del Reyno, considerando perjudicial al comercio del Perú, 1792, ANP, Real Tribunal del Consulado 151; and Expediente sobre el establecimiento de fábricas en el Perú por los Gremios de Madrid, 1796, AGI, Indiferente General 1623.

60. These results are generally similar to those of Tandeter and Wachtel, "Prices and Agricultural Production"; and Romano, "Movimiento."

61. By dramatically increasing the tax burden on Arequipa, Charles III undoubtedly offset to a considerable extent the effect of lower prices.

8

PRICES AND AGRICULTURAL PRODUCTION
Potosí and Charcas in the Eighteenth Century*

Enrique Tandeter and Nathan Wachtel

AT THE BEGINNING OF THE DECADE OF 1960, R. ROMANO PUBLISHED HIS pioneering articles on prices in eighteenth-century Chile, and more generally on South America. The moment of applying a method properly belonging to French historiography after 1930 to a new territory seemed to have arrived. Would it open, then, a Labroussian era in research on colonial America? E. Florescano's thesis about Mexico and A. Arcondo's about Córdoba seemed to suggest this.[1] Nevertheless, this tendency was frustrated, and those early works were not continued. Twenty years later, they appear as a brief episode, rather than the beginning of a new era.

That frustration may be explained by two circumstances. On the one hand, in the 1960s, it began to be realized in Europe that price history had reached a dead end. The methodological difficulties inherent in the elaboration and reading of the series stirred up lively polemics, as well as a certain skepticism. On the other, it was seen in Latin America that prices were not a sufficient indicator for societies in which broad sectors, especially the indigenous ones, were outside the radius of market influence. The debate was not truly confronted; nevertheless, a small number of researchers were disposed to continue the initial movement. Paradoxically, historians of Latin America lamented that situation, and complaints about the lack of good price curves for the regions or periods they studied became common. Nevertheless, rare are the authors who, like D. A. Brading, confront the concrete working up of the needed series.[2] In that way, a vast field that has scarcely been explored has remained practically abandoned.

For our part, conscious of the limits of price history, we think that that variable cannot be dispensed with, be it to confirm or to rectify our hypotheses about the socioeconomic evolution of colonial Peru. It is a question of one guiding thread, among others, in a territory still unknown. It is not necessary to insist on the exceptional character of Potosí as an observation point. For more than three hundred years, the famous Cerro Rico represented, thanks to its silver production, the principal development pole of the Viceroyalty of Peru (and, after 1776, of the new Viceroyalty of Río de la Plata). It was a complex market, intercrossed by at least four economic levels and as many differentiated conjunctures:

1) the European economy, both with regard to products of its manufactures and to merchandise of Asian origin redistributed in America; a conjuncture we would call "oceanic";
2) the currents of interregional interchanges of Peru in the broad sense— the American conjuncture;
3) the traffic in what were essentially food products from the hinterland, which defined the regional conjuncture;
4) the merchandise and services of Potosí itself, or of a zone very nearby, which sketched the local conjuncture.

The source we used is of exceptional richness, the books recording expenditures of the Friary of San Antonio de Padua of the Franciscan Order in Potosí, which comprised nearly a century and a half, from 1676 to 1842. We have recorded all the data about merchandise bought and salaries paid by the friary. Of among more than two hundred products and services, we preserved forty series for their homogeneity and continuity. Lamentably, the quality of the source declines as the nineteenth century advances, so we have arbitrarily stopped the study in 1816.[3] Therefore, our research chronologically covers an extended eighteenth century, a period that shows, as a salient feature, the new flowering of indigenous revolts.

THE OCEANIC CONJUNCTURE

In our series, three products imported from outside America are conspicuous: Rouen linen, paper, and cinnamon. They constitute a significant aggregate for the study of the behavior of European merchandise in Potosí during the eighteenth century.

First-quality Rouen linen (ruan florete)

Rouen linen, made in Normandy, was a fabric particularly valued in the Indies, figuring "in the first line of stock of the trade fairs of Portobelo, Puebla, Los Angelos [sic], and Mexico City"[4] (Table 8.1 and Graph 8.1).

Table 8.1

Oceanic Conjuncture: Prices of Rouen Linen, Paper,
and Cinnamon in Potosí

	Imported Products		
Year	Rouen Linen[1]	Paper[2]	Cinnamon[3]
1676	—	132	—
1677	—	132	100
1678	—	118	150
1679	138	125	200
1680	132	145	—
1681	117	178	—
1682	115	227	125
1683	101	178	—
1684	176	184	150
1685	154	239	75
1686	151	—	—
1687	239	316	—
1688	252	263	—
1689	252	224	—
1690	403	172	—
1691	252	158	—
1692	167	132	350
1693	151	145	287
1694	151	158	219
1695	167	132	225
1696	189	148	—
1697	201	211	—
1698	214	—	—
1699	—	211	—
1700	164	197	125
1701	184	184	—
1702	170	184	—
1703	151	211	—
1704	138	526	—
1705	201	487	—
1706	201	461	—
1707	119	447	—
1708	98	211	—
1709	113	158	125
1710	142	—	—

Table 8.1 (continued)

Year	Imported Products		
	Rouen Linen[1]	Paper[2]	Cinnamon[3]
1711	107	158	—
1712	94	79	—
1713	89	99	—
1714	88	99	—
1715	69	66	—
1716	60	92	—
1717	—	184	—
1718	101	—	94
1719	135	184	—
1720	113	164	—
1721	151	211	—
1722	126	—	—
1723	126	250	—
1724	164	—	—
1725	176	—	—
1726	176	—	187
1727	164	171	187
1728	157	184	225
1729	157	—	—
1730	146	—	—
1731	—	184	225
1732	151	158	—
1733	—	—	—
1734	113	158	—
1735	119	158	—
1736	132	184	—
1737	—	92	150
1738	110	184	112
1739	119	263	175
1740	151	263	—
1741	—	263	—
1742	—	289	—
1743	—	329	—
1744	—	—	—
1745	113	—	—
1746	—	211	—
1747	101	211	450

Table 8.1 (continued)

Year	Imported Products		
	Rouen Linen[1]	Paper[2]	Cinnamon[3]
1748	98	172	—
1749	—	—	225
1750	113	105	—
1751	—	132	—
1752	138	95	—
1753	—	—	87
1754	—	—	94
1755	—	—	—
1756	126	—	112
1757	—	118	—
1758	126	138	—
1759	116	132	—
1760	—	92	150
1761	101	118	300
1762	—	132	250
1763	—	138	275
1764	126	—	275
1765	—	105	250
1766	—	—	275
1767	147	—	275
1768	113	—	—
1769	101	105	—
1770	101	105	—
1771	—	105	—
1772	85	105	—
1773	—	—	—
1774	—	—	—
1775	113	92	—
1776	—	79	—
1777	101	—	—
1778	—	105	—
1779	—	105	100
1780	70	79	—
1781	—	122	—
1782	—	132	—
1783	—	—	—
1784	—	—	—

Table 8.1 (continued)

Year	Imported Products		
	Rouen Linen[1]	Paper[2]	Cinnamon[3]
1785	—	79	—
1786	—	66	300
1787	—	—	—
1788	—	72	—
1789	—	66	—
1790	—	86	—
1791	—	79	—
1792	—	79	—
1793	—	70	—
1794	—	86	187
1795	—	66	—
1796	—	76	—
1797	—	99	—
1798	—	178	—
1799	—	184	350
1800	—	—	—
1801	—	283	300
1802	—	—	300
1803	—	132	150
1804	—	—	—
1805	—	181	—
1806	—	164	—
1807	—	122	—
1808	—	—	—
1809	—	132	—
1810	—	211	—
1811	—	—	—
1812	—	184	—
1813	—	—	—
1814	—	211	—
1815	—	—	—

[1]1770–1779 = 100 = 7.95 reales/vara
[2]1770–1779 = 100 = 60.8 reales/resma
[3]1770–1779 = 100 = 64 reales/libra

Its price can be considered, then, as representative of textiles as a whole, the largest category of European manufactured products that were imported into America.[5]

The curve for Rouen linen from 1677 to 1780 allows us to distinguish two movements of long-term duration: from 1684 to 1716 and from 1718 to 1780. Their average indices, with a base of 1770–79, are 166 and 126, that is to say, a fall of 24.1 percent between the two periods.

The first period can be split into a phase of price rise, 1684–90, and another of price decline, 1691–1716, this last particularly brutal, since it falls from 403 in the index for 1690 to 60 in 1716. The fall can certainly be attributed to an increase in supply; legal, Spanish traffic, however, is not responsible whatsoever for this process. The trade fair at Portobelo, where, in principle, the entire Viceroyalty of Peru was supposed to supply itself, was held irregularly during this era: in 1696, then in 1708, 1722, and 1731.[6] Isolated ships, either *avisos* or *de registro,* did not compensate for the crisis of the system of flotas and galleons. According to the data published by A. García-Baquero, the total traffic from Cadiz to America suffered a continual decline from 1681, the initial year of his series, reaching its lowest point in 1709, and falling again in 1714 to a nearly nonexistent level.[7]

How, then, is the increase in supply explained? The cause should be sought outside the legal traffic, principally in French smuggling, organized by the merchants of Saint-Malo and Marseille, to whom the War of the Spanish Succession offered propitious circumstances for infiltration into Spanish possessions in the Pacific. As G. Walker recently showed, that offensive contributed directly to the crisis of the legal system.[8] The appearance of French ships permitted the holding of informal trade fairs in those ports, during which merchandise, especially textiles, was sold at prices much lower than Portobelo's. At the same time, around 1713–15 difficulties in the supply of mercury and a drop in silver production in Potosí, which could have accentuated the drop in prices, were recorded. In 1716, a year in which Rouen linen reaches its lowest level, its poor relation, "ordinary" Rouen linen, merits a mention in the *Historia de la Villa Imperial de Potosí* by Arzáns de Orsúa y Vela:

In these two months of June and July [of 1716], the amount of textiles that entered, both from China and from France, was so great that it came to be valued more cheaply than in Spain, since ordinary Rouen linen was sold in Arica for one real and at most for one and one-half reales, and in this Villa for three reales; in statements from the French, they paid more than they earned, and for

Graph 8.1

Oceanic Conjuncture

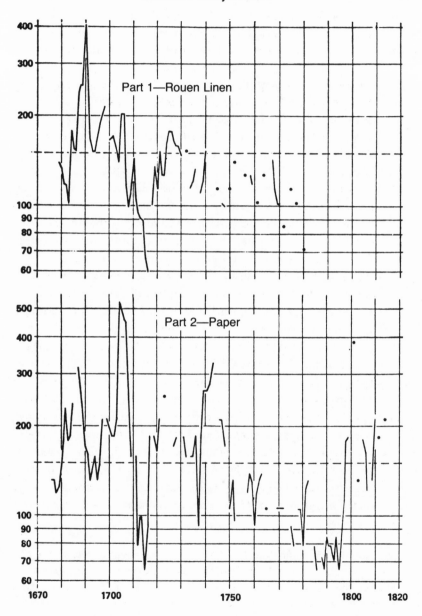

Part 1—Rouen Linen

Part 2—Paper

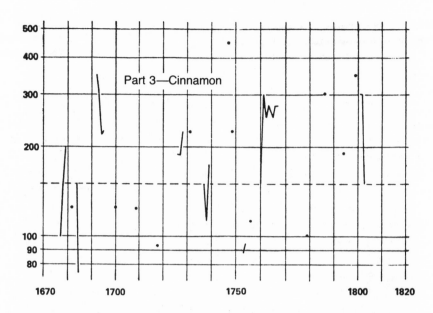

Part 3—Cinnamon

some goods they lost 50 percent because in Europe, some considerable shipments of Rouen linen cost them two and one-half reales a vara, and the same happened with other goods, too. In this kingdom, the cheapness was for fear of the greater loss with which they were threatened by the death of the most Christian Louis XIV of France, and also because one could no longer carry silver in *piña* to the ships in safety. . . .[9]

The arrival of merchandise was such that, ironically, the competition among the smugglers turned out to be ruinous for many of them. Certain political circumstances also interfered with this change in conjuncture. On the one hand, repression of contraband by the colonial authorities, who until then were tolerant or even accomplices of the French, was made effective by the viceroy, the Príncipe de Santo Buono. On the other, a change in attitude on the part of France with regard to the smugglers was feared; in fact, the expedition of Martinet, a French official in the service of the Spanish crown with the support of the authorities of his country, was able to destroy traffic interloping into the Pacific in 1717.[10] In Potosí, says the chronicler, "Now piñas did not flow to foreigners like rivers, but as brooks."[11] As a result of this, prices began to rise in 1718:

Textiles . . . arrived . . . through Buenos Aires and so high in price . . . that it was very scandalous, since people were already accustomed to buying those of

France very cheaply. In truth, Spanish greed is ordinarily insufferable, and much more so in these kingdoms, where monstrosities are seen in this particular. . . . The French sell their merchandise better and with great profit and not for having thrown them out of this kingdom was this Villa alleviated. . . .[12]

The war between 1719 and 1724, in which Spain opposed France, England, and Holland, provided the opportunity for the return of French smugglers to the Pacific. Their track may be found in the drop in price of Rouen linen in Potosí in 1722–23. The legal traffic between Lima and Portobelo was profoundly affected by contraband. In January 1722, when it was announced to merchants in Potosí that the galleons had arrived in Cartagena, "no one went there, because they knew with certainty that various shippers brought them textiles from the French more conveniently. . . ."[13] As a result of the severe repression, the interloping traffic could not again reach the extent of the first decade of the century and, after 1724, disappeared almost entirely.

After the relatively high level of the price of Rouen linen around 1718–26, from 1727 on a downward movement begins that, beyond minor fluctuations, is prolonged until the end of our series in 1780. This tendency matches the sustained increase in activity in the port of Cadiz in the direction of the Indies between 1726 and 1778, measured both in the number of ships and in tonnage, according to the statistics compiled by A. García-Baquero.[14] The disappearance of French smuggling, however, just as it had developed during the first quarter of the century, did not mean that in the future the Potosí market would depend entirely on legal traffic, be it that passing through Lima or that proceeding from Buenos Aires. On the contrary, English contraband, both in Cartagena and in the Río de la Plata area, and the interloping commerce of the Portuguese in this last region, contributed to supplying Potosí in a significant manner.

Paper

The price series for Rouen linen is interrupted at the precise moment when we would measure the effect of Comercio Libre on Potosí (compare Table 8.1 and Graph 8.1). Prices for paper will permit us to bridge this gap. This merchandise occupied an outstanding place among European exports to America: 6.4 percent of the total, by weight, of the cargo of the fleets leaving Cadiz between 1717 and 1735 and 11.9 percent between 1757 and 1766. With 5.4 percent of the total exported between 1720 and 1751, it is in third place among the groups of manufactures, greatly below textiles, but almost with the same weight as the sum total of metallurgical products.[15] Paper imported to America is not usually a product of Spain itself, but of Genoa or France, although the Catalan industry may have contributed to the supply around the end of the century.

The price curve for paper coincides in a notable fashion with the one for first-quality Rouen linen until 1780. Also, in this case, the years around the middle of the second decade of the century mark a very clear inflection, with the minimum in 1715, one year before the minimum for Rouen linen. The fall in price is even more abrupt here. Paper suffered various years of scarcity from 1704 to 1707, with indices between 526 and 446 that then fall to 66 in 1715.[16] The first two great phases of the curve, 1679–1715 and 1716–80, mark average indices of 209 and 157 respectively, with a fall in price of 24.9 percent, almost identical to the fall of 24.1 percent observed for Rouen linen between 1684–1716 and 1718–80. Let us emphasize that the price rise of 1739–43, which coincides with the years of colonial war among the European powers, constitutes an exception in the tendency, although it does not fundamentally affect the long-term movement.[17]

In 1780, the series for paper, as the one for Rouen linen, shows a fall in price that very probably should be interpreted as a first result of Comercio Libre. Then, a rise is seen in 1781–82, connected with the Anglo-Spanish war. The income from *alcabalas*, a tax on trade, registers a fall of 23 percent in Potosí between 1779–80 and 1781–82, while imports into the port of Buenos Aires fall 30 percent.[18] The series for paper shows a lacuna for 1783–84 to then offer, between 1785 and 1796, data of great interest that permit a global evaluation of the impact of Comercio Libre on the Potosí market. According to J. Fisher, the annual average of exports from all Spanish ports to America between 1782 to 1796 is 400 percent higher than the amount exported in 1778.[19] That notable increase in the traffic is reflected very clearly in the price of paper in Potosí, where the fall in price is accelerated. The average index of 1785–96, equal to 75, is 64.1 percent lower than that registered in 1679–1715. This is 52.2 percent less than that of 1716–80, and, obviously, was 25 percent below the base years 1770–79. It should be emphasized even more that on three occasions, in 1786, 1789, and 1795, the annual index falls to the level of the secular minimum of 1715.

From 1797 to 1814, the wars disrupting the traffic between Europe and America can be seen again.[20] The price of paper rises to an average index of 182, an intermediate, equidistant level with regard to that of 1679–1715 (= 209) and 1716–80 (= 157).

The downward movement in prices for Rouen linen and paper in Potosí contrasts in a surprising fashion with the upward trend that the historiography registers for the eighteenth century in Europe, which is where those products come from. On confirming a similar discordance in Santiago de Chile, Romano proposed three types of explanation: 1) These are manufactured products that, in Europe itself, suffer a price rise to a lesser degree; 2) The tendency toward decline in America can result from an increase in traffic and strong competition between different producers; and 3) An elevated price level during all the seventeenth century, and at the beginning of the eighteenth, might have permitted absorption of the European price rise of the eighteenth century. All these circumstances are confirmed with regard to the cases of first-quality Rouen linen and paper in Potosí:

1) Linen and hemp fabrics in France show, between the base period 1726–41 and 1771–88, a price rise of 36 percent, much lower than that of cereals, whose prices are generally used to evaluate the secular trend.[21] Paper exhibits stable prices in Holland from the end of the seventeenth century, and in England certain qualities of paper experienced a downward movement of 25 to 30 percent in the second half of the eighteenth century, relative to the beginning of the century.[22]

2) Although competition among different producers (Italian, French, or Catalan paper; French or Silesian linen) does not clearly appear, the relationships between the increase in supply and the fall of prices is evident.

3) Despite the fact that our source does not go back farther than 1676, the third hypothesis may be confirmed, thanks to the series published by P. Macera for Lima and Arequipa.[23] These show notable analogies, between approximately 1670 and 1760, for the cases of linen and paper, with respect to the Potosí curves. We assume, then, that the Arequipa series for the period from 1620 to 1680 may give some idea of the movement of the entirety of the southern Peruvian area that includes Potosí. Prices of linen and paper, for the base years 1627–50 = 100, reach average indices in Arequipa in 1627–88 of 126.5 and 127.8, respectively. Put another way, by the seventeenth century, prices of some merchandise imported to Peru already diverge from European trends in such a way that the high level reached around the decade of 1680 could well absorb the European increase of the eighteenth century and permit a profitable trade even with prices falling throughout the entire century.

Cinnamon

The series for cinnamon in Potosí, more fragmentary than the two preceding cases, allows us to verify, by contrast, some of the mechanisms that we have analyzed for European manufactures (compare Table 8.1 and Graph 8.1). This spice represented, by weight, 2.3 percent of the exports from Cadiz to America between 1720 and 1751, with a percentage, naturally, much higher in value.[24] The curve of Potosí prices for cinnamon coincides in general with those for linen and paper until around 1740. It diverges, on the other hand, during the two following decades and after 1760 presents a wholly divergent movement. On average, it increases 22.2 percent between 1677–1718 and 1726–79, approximately the same dates for which linen and paper showed declines of 24.1 percent and 24.9 percent. The price of cinnamon even reaches an average index for 1786–1803 of 264, greater by 54 percent than the indices of 1677–1718. The series for Arequipa, on the other hand, tells us that cinnamon also suffered a rise in price during the seventeenth century, since with respect to an index of 1627–1650 = 100, it rose to an average of 184 for 1679–88.[25] Why, in this case, was the price rise prolonged during the eighteenth century? One of the explanatory elements refers, without a doubt, to its origin in the Asian colony of a European nation. Unlike paper, whose price in Europe remained relatively stable, and textiles, which show a moderate rise, the price of cinnamon in Amsterdam rises 141 percent in the second half of the eighteenth century, with respect to the period 1683–1750.[26] It is worthwhile noting as well that the commercialization of that spice was monopolized in Europe by the Dutch East India Company.[27] The combination of the two circumstances worked, then, in such a fashion that in that case, the higher price level at the end of the seventeenth century was insufficient to absorb the rise in the eighteenth century.

THE AMERICAN CONJUNCTURE

We shall only present some examples of American products: manufactured products, such as textiles; or agricultural ones that are processed, such as sugar; or those of minor processing, such as maté. We shall add other articles, such as oil, soap, wine, fish, and salt, whose prices seem to follow similar tendencies.

Textiles

Our series include three types of textiles produced in Peru: coarse *sayal* and light *sayalete,* wool cloths manufactured in the Cuzco region, and coarse *tocuyo,* cotton cloth coming, in general, from Cochabamba.

The three curves show a clear contrast between two periods: an elevated level during the last decades of the seventeenth century and the first three or four of the eighteenth century; much lower prices during the second half of the eighteenth century and the first decades of the nineteenth (compare Table 8.2 and Graph 8.2). Sayal presents an average index of 130 for the years 1676–1741 and another of 91 for 1743–1814; sayalete, 177 for 1683–1743 and 91.6 for 1747–1813; finally, tocuyo, 145.2 for 1690–1730 and 99.8 for 1742–1812. For American textiles, the decrease between the first period and the second is, respectively, 29.7 percent, 48.2 percent, and 31.3 percent.

The contraction of 1730–40 can be found in the only study we have at our disposal for the textile industry in Peru. In fact, according to F. Silva Santisteban, "the era of greatest rise for the obrajes corresponds to the last decades of the seventeenth century and the first decades of the eighteenth."[28] He does not clearly explain the rise, but he enumerates some hypotheses about the decline: the "vanity" of the high-born and plebeians, which led them to buy imported textiles; the competition of French and English fabrics, cheaper and of higher quality; also, the competition from the centers of production in Upper Peru and the Río de la Plata region. The two primary circumstances coincide with the observations made earlier with respect to the curve for first-quality Rouen linen. As C. Sempat Assadourian points out, *obraje* production during the sixteenth and seventeenth centuries was in a complementary, rather than a competitive, relationship with European textiles, while in the eighteenth century, imported fabrics invade precisely the cheaper market, until then reserved for the obrajes.[29]

Under those conditions, the spectacular fall in the prices of imported textiles that the series for first-quality Rouen linen shows between 1690 and 1715 must have had repercussions in American production. For sayalete and tocuyo, the observed decrease, 1685 and 1690, coincides with that for linen, and its size is of the same order (79.3 percent and 75 percent, on the one hand, and 85.1 percent, on the other). A difference exists, however. While the fall in prices for linen lasts twenty-six years (1690–1716), those for sayalete and tocuyo last for fifty-eight and fifty-three years (1685–1743 and 1690–1753). In the case of sayal, the decline is not shown except from 1706

Table 8.2

American Conjuncture: Prices of American Textiles in Potosí

	American Textiles		
Year	Coarse Cotton Cloth[1]	Coarse Woolen Cloth[2]	Light Woolen Cloth[3]
1676	—	80	—
1677	—	—	—
1678	—	80	—
1679	—	103	—
1680	—	114	—
1681	—	111	—
1682	—	114	—
1683	—	103	290
1684	—	132	—
1685	—	91	348
1686	—	137	203
1687	—	—	—
1688	—	100	—
1689	—	—	—
1690	348	129	—
1691	—	106	—
1692	232	103	—
1693	—	137	—
1694	203	126	—
1695	174	149	—
1696	116	171	—
1697	—	—	238
1698	174	—	—
1699	—	137	130
1700	174	—	—
1701	—	109	290
1702	—	—	217
1703	174	183	203
1704	—	—	232
1705	145	—	—
1706	145	229	232
1707	—	206	—
1708	130	—	211
1709	—	—	232
1710	130	—	232

Table 8.2 (continued)

| | American Textiles | | |
| | Coarse Cotton Cloth[1] | Coarse Woolen Cloth[2] | Light Woolen Cloth[3] |
Year			
1711	87	—	174
1712	—	—	232
1713	116	194	232
1714	—	—	203
1715	101	137	—
1716	101	160	145
1717	—	—	—
1718	—	—	116
1719	—	—	198
1720	116	160	159
1721	145	—	—
1722	116	—	116
1723	116	—	116
1724	116	—	—
1725	109	137	232
1726	—	—	—
1727	—	120	159
1728	130	137	145
1729	—	—	174
1730	87	—	—
1731	—	—	—
1732	—	—	—
1733	—	—	—
1734	—	137	116
1735	—	—	—
1736	—	137	116
1737	—	—	87
1738	—	—	87
1739	—	—	87
1740	—	114	87
1741	—	69	—
1742	101	—	80
1743	116	97	72
1744	—	—	—
1745	—	—	—
1746	—	—	—

Table 8.2 (continued)

| Year | American Textiles | | |
	Coarse Cotton Cloth[1]	Coarse Woolen Cloth[2]	Light Woolen Cloth[3]
1747	116	91	87
1748	109	—	72
1749	101	—	87
1750	116	114	87
1751	116	149	—
1752	—	—	116
1753	—	—	—
1754	101	—	—
1755	—	—	—
1756	101	—	—
1757	—	91	116
1758	—	—	87
1759	116	86	72
1760	109	—	83
1761	—	—	72
1762	—	—	—
1763	—	69	58
1764	—	91	—
1765	116	91	—
1766	—	—	—
1767	—	114	72
1768	—	—	—
1769	116	98	145
1770	—	—	116
1771	116	91	—
1772	116	114	—
1773	—	91	—
1774	—	—	—
1775	101	103	116
1776	—	—	—
1777	—	—	87
1778	87	—	—
1779	80	—	83
1780	—	—	—
1781	101	—	—
1782	—	114	87

Table 8.2 (continued)

| Year | American Textiles | | |
	Coarse Cotton Cloth[1]	Coarse Woolen Cloth[2]	Light Woolen Cloth[3]
1783	94	74	—
1784	—	82	—
1785	—	69	101
1786	72	63	72
1787	65	—	58
1788	77	—	58
1789	—	—	58
1790	—	—	—
1791	—	—	58
1792	—	—	64
1793	—	—	58
1794	65	97	—
1795	—	—	—
1796	72	77	87
1797	116	—	—
1798	—	—	87
1799	116	91	72
1800	—	91	—
1801	—	—	—
1802	—	91	—
1803	—	—	—
1804	—	75	—
1805	—	—	72
1806	87	—	—
1807	—	—	72
1808	116	—	—
1809	—	—	119
1810	—	—	—
1811	—	91	—
1812	80	—	—
1813	—	—	232
1814	—	57	203
1815	—	—	—
1816	—	—	—

[1]1770–1779 = 100 = 3.45 reales/vara
[2]1770–1779 = 100 = 8.75 reales/vara
[3]1770–1779 = 100 = 3.45 reales/vara

on, with a fall of 70 percent in thirty-five years (1706–1741). It is thus confirmed that the increase in supply of imported textiles and the consequent fall in prices at the beginning of the eighteenth century genuinely affected the American textile market, although with a certain chronological lag.

In his study on the obrajes of the Cuzco region that supplied woolen textiles to Potosí, M. Moscoso Sánchez suggests three elements that explain the decline: smuggling from Buenos Aires that fed Upper Peru, the "great, consuming market," and even reached the producing center of the Cuzco region; the destruction of the obrajes after 1780 as a result of the Tupac Amaru rebellion; and the negligence of absentee owners, who rented out their obrajes. He proposes, therefore, a periodization different from Silva Santisteban's: "Cuzco's textile industry reached its apogee in the course of the seventeenth century and two-thirds of the eighteenth. . . ."[30] Curiously, our three curves also show this new inflection. A relatively stable phase is seen, in fact, between approximately 1740 and 1770, which appears more genuinely in the case of tocuyo, followed by a downward accentuation from 1769–1772 that is prolonged during the two following decades.

After 1796, during the years of war that end with the Peace of Amiens, the prices of American textiles show a certain recovery. B. Larson shows the development of the textile industry in Cochabamba for that period.[31] It is not a matter of an isolated phenomenon. What our series indicate is that the new producers, who took advantage of the opportunity of unsatisfied demand after twenty years of continuous decline in textile prices, could scarcely put their production at the "normal" level of prices in 1740–70.

Sugar

The curve for sugar prices between 1676 and 1816 is characterized by its secular trend toward stagnation, although fluctuations and differentiated phases may be distinguished in it (compare Table 8.3 and Graph 8.3). Its three long-term movements, 1681–1739, 1740–75, and 1776–1810, have average indices of 107.7, 113.9, and 109.7, respectively. The three movements differ markedly among themselves; the first presents a rise between 1681 and 1699, followed by a decline from 1700 to 1739; the second, a rise from 1740 to 1743, and a decline between 1744 and 1775; the third, a rise from 1776 to 178(2), and a decline from 178(3) to 1810. Stated in another way, while in the first case the period or rise continues for eighteen years and that of decline for forty years, in the two following, the rises are

Graph 8.2

American Conjuncture: Textiles

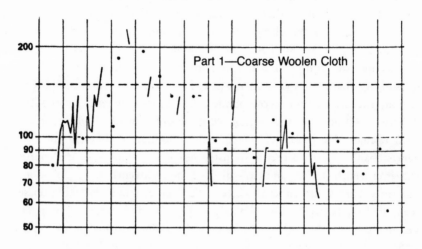

Part 1—Coarse Woolen Cloth

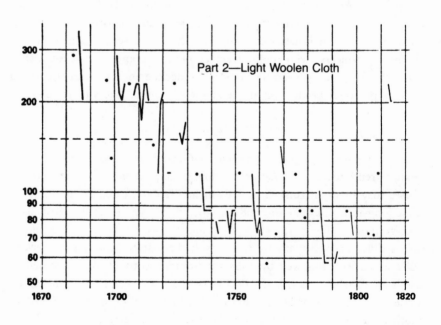

Part 2—Light Woolen Cloth

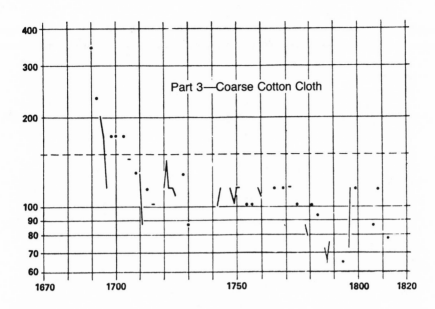

reduced to four and seven (?) years, with declines of thirty-two and twenty-eight (?) years.

In her study on the sugar haciendas of Lambayeque, S. Ramírez-Horton also shows a phase of price decline between 1693 and 1743, followed by stagnation at the inferior level until 1793.[32] The author attributes the decline to a dual process of growth of regional production and loss of markets. While in Lambayeque the number of sugar haciendas grew, their traditional markets, Panama and Portobelo, came to be supplied by sugar from the Antilles. The same thing happened in southern Peru, at the end of the eighteenth century when the Arequipa region increased its sugar production at the same time that the Buenos Aires market was invaded by sugar from Cuba and Brazil.[33] It seems, then, that the phenomenon of overproduction, and the consequent decline of prices, affects all the producing regions of Peru throughout the course of the century in an analogous way.[34] In Lambayeque, the decline reaches 65 percent between 1693 and 1742; in Lima, from 1695 to 1734–35, it is 42 percent. In Arequipa, which serves us as an indicator for the entire southern Peruvian area, for want of a Cuzco series that would correspond to Potosí's supplying region, prices fall 53 percent between 1687 and 1738–40; in Potosí, from 1699 to 1739 the decline is 45 percent; in Córdoba, between 1720 and 1742, it is 40 percent; in Santiago de Chile, between

Table 8.3

American Conjuncture: Prices of Honey, Soap, Oil, Sugar, and Maté in Potosí

	American Products				
Year	Honey[1]	Soap[2]	Oil[3]	Sugar[4]	Maté[5]
1676	—	1	87	135	—
1677	—	—	69	126	—
1678	—	—	—	126	—
1679	—	98	—	113	—
1680	—	91	—	88	—
1681	120	76	—	76	—
1682	111	72	95	679	—
1683	109	63	—	88	—
1684	120	87	—	107	—
1685	—	109	—	126	—
1686	120	153	—	126	—
1687	130	153	—	126	93
1688	139	120	—	129	78
1689	120	98	—	120	78
1690	—	76	—	126	93
1691	—	—	—	101	148
1692	—	65	—	101	125
1693	—	81	—	101	187
1694	111	99	—	120	187
1695	111	131	—	120	187
1696	111	153	—	126	140
1697	—	98	—	126	101
1698	—	87	134	132	101
1699	—	87	52	139	125
1700	—	109	82	126	114
1701	113	109	121	126	101
1702	111	109	78	120	125
1703	114	111	60	112	117
1704	146	109	48	113	125
1705	114	109	—	101	125
1706	100	109	56	94	109
1707	102	163	56	98	93
1708	130	153	65	113	97
1709	130	109	65	120	109
1710	130	98	—	116	101
1711	111	90	—	107	101

Table 8.3 (continued)

| Year | American Products | | | | |
	Honey[1]	Soap[2]	Oil[3]	Sugar[4]	Maté[5]
1712	111	76	—	104	101
1713	102	98	—	—	93
1714	—	—	74	—	—
1715	124	98	60	135	86
1716	106	119	69	107	70
1717	98	98	—	88	62
1718	106	—	—	—	64
1719	111	94	101	118	66
1720	111	90	103	93	54
1721	111	109	121	151	62
1722	120	113	87	113	62
1723	150	98	78	113	54
1724	131	87	87	107	70
1725	111	87	107	113	125
1726	93	87	56	107	101
1727	83	87	69	107	107
1728	93	82	82	107	132
1729	93	109	—	113	132
1730	95	131	74	88	117
1731	83	120	52	82	109
1732	65	—	—	—	195
1733	111	—	—	—	—
1734	102	65	52	76	171
1735	102	65	78	76	140
1736	111	76	56	76	140
1737	130	—	95	76	125
1738	93	—	87	76	125
1739	93	120	66	76	171
1740	88	—	80	79	156
1741	93	120	117	85	140
1742	102	109	113	139	109
1743	120	109	113	170	125
1744	111	104	113	126	117
1745	102	109	69	126	117
1746	102	—	87	120	117
1747	111	109	80	113	—
1748	130	109	95	94	93

Table 8.3 (continued)

	American Products				
Year	Honey[1]	Soap[2]	Oil[3]	Sugar[4]	Maté[5]
1749	130	98	69	88	109
1750	130	105	87	94	130
1751	130	98	156	139	117
1752	111	109	126	145	117
1753	111	—	121	126	100
1754	95	—	104	126	117
1755	120	98	109	126	109
1756	139	109	102	120	93
1757	167	120	99	132	93
1758	130	98	113	132	93
1759	111	114	87	126	93
1760	130	—	82	113	93
1761	102	98	74	107	125
1762	102	104	195	113	117
1763	93	—	101	132	
1764	78	109	216	113	125
1765	111	98	130	113	125
1766	79	—	69	101	—
1767	93	94	113	132	132
1768	111	98	104	113	128
1769	111	97	81	101	125
1770	93	98	87	120	125
1771	99	87	92	101	125
1772	83	81	78	101	93
1773	107	129	88	98	125
1774	111	109	104	90	93
1775	116	99	95	76	97
1776	97	98	106	115	78
1777	93	98	152	118	93
1778	93	98	106	82	78
1779	109	101	92	101	93
1780	83	65	76	113	84
1781	106	68	104	145	101
1782	134	76	137	145	101
1783	134	87	130	—	140
1784	130	136	199	113	144
1785	120	—	216	113	125

Table 8.3 (continued)

	American Products				
Year	Honey[1]	Soap[2]	Oil[3]	Sugar[4]	Maté[5]
1786	—	123	134	132	95
1787	79	114	87	126	95
1788	93	109	78	123	109
1789	106	—	61	116	103
1790	102	87	87	113	103
1791	106	76	52	129	104
1792	125	98	87	101	93
1793	93	106	121	94	117
1794	106	75	95	113	106
1795	85	87	69	101	93
1796	111	99	121	101	93
1797	138	93	87	101	93
1798	86	98	77	101	97
1799	102	153	78	101	103
1800	—	101	52	94	101
1801	102	87	56	113	104
1802	—	109	—	113	89
1803	—	—	113	123	130
1804	—	120	181	113	—
1805	56	—	—	98	—
1806	74	—	139	98	146
1807	83	—	63	94	140
1808	77	—	96	101	—
1809	—	—	78	101	—
1810	65	—	69	94	—
1811	—	—	—	157	—
1812	—	—	—	176	140
1813	—	—	—	138	—
1814	—	—	—	138	—
1815	—	—	—	—	—
1816	—	—	—	195	—

[1] 1770–1779 = 100 = 86.5 reales/odre
[2] 1770–1779 = 100 = 146.8 reales/quintal
[3] 1770–1779 = 100 = 122.3 reales/arroba
[4] 1770–1779 = 100 = 63.6 reales/arroba
[5] 1770–1779 = 100 = 51.2 reales/arroba

Graph 8.3

American Conjuncture: Other Products

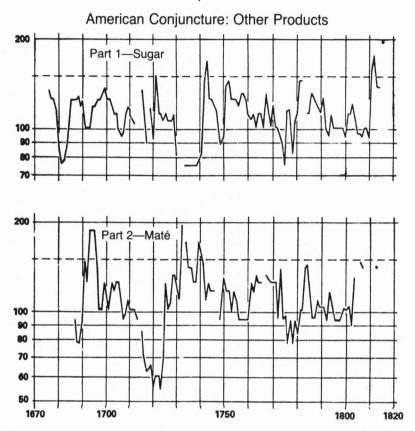

1695 and 1733, prices decline 64 percent, a percentage practically equal to Lambayeque's.[35]

Lamentably, the data available for the second half of the eighteenth century do not permit comparison of sugar prices in the different markets. Fragmentary data for Córdoba, Buenos Aires, and especially Santiago de Chile suggest that in the regions that sugar from the Antilles or Brazil reached, prices declined with respect to the preceding decades.[36] We have seen that, for different reasons, that was also the case in Lambayeque. On the other hand, the two long-term movements that occur in Potosí between 1740 and 1810 show average indices at a level similar to that of the period 1681–1739. This divergence between Lambayeque and Potosí confirms that the producing regions met with different fates throughout the course of the century. While the crisis in northern Peru, from 1720 on, is such that few production units will survive it, in the Cuzco region, in accord with the works of M. Mörner and J. Polo y La Borda, the picture seems less somber.[37] Nevertheless, the Potosí series, with its abrupt rises of 1740–43 and 1776–8(2), followed by prolonged declines, explains the why of the complaints about a "crisis" in the Cuzco region during the second half of the century, and in particular after 1780.

Maté

The price curve for maté presents a profile all its own: strong rises in 1690–95 and 1724–3(2), followed by very accentuated falls in 1696–1723 and 173(4)–60 (compare Table 8.3 and Graph 8.3). From the decade of 1760 on, a more stable phase begins, with minor oscillations until 1802, with a new, pronounced rise during the first decade of the nineteenth century.

It is lamentable that our series for maté only begins in 1687, since we do not know of the fluctuations of the decades 1660 and 1670, a period during which, as J. C. Garavaglia has shown, Paraguayan production grows considerably. It is in that moment that its commercialization reaches the Upper Peru markets.[38] Would the decline registered in Potosí in 1687–89 prolong an earlier movement? We know that the strong rise of 1690–95, from an index of 78 to 187, corresponds to the first interruptions in this traffic, decisive precisely in Paraguay to stop the tendency toward price decline. These attempts were in vain, and the curve falls turbulently to the level of 1717–23, with a secular minimum of 54 in 1720. During the first two decades of the century, the amounts of maté sent from Asunción show a marked increase. The growth in production is indicated by the statistics of the tithes, whose annual averages show a rising tendency opposed to that of prices:

1686–95: 175 arrobas
1696–1705: 323 arrobas
1706–23: 281 arrobas[39]

The price rise in 1724–32, until reaching the secular maximum with an index of 195, is the result of local circumstances, disturbances, and rebellions that interrupted the trade in maté almost totally. Subsequently, prices decline anew until 1760, when the curve enters a relatively stable phase, with a tendency toward stagnation until the end of the century, despite the apex of 1781–84, the result of a new interruption in the traffic.

Other American Products

We cannot analyze in detail all the other series of American—Peruvian, in its broadest meaning—products. We shall, nevertheless, pause for a moment with some examples that present specific similarities. Almost all are characterized, despite features original to each case, by a general tendency toward stagnation, even decline, in particular during the second half of the eighteenth century (compare Tables 8.3 and 8.4 and Graphs 8.3 and 8.4). It is for this category of products that Romano's interpretations seem to be most pertinent.

The price of food oil suffers strong oscillations, but two long-term movements may be read in the curve: a rise in the first half of the century, until the peak in 1754, followed by a tendency toward decline until the end of the series.

The curve for soap seems to present, also through strong oscillations, an upward orientation until 1708, with prices of the decades 1710 and 1720 at a relatively low level. The rise of 1739–40 follows, then a slow fall to the minimum of 1780, after which they again begin strong oscillations (see Figure 8.3).

Stability is most evident in the price curve for wine, a product of the Cinti region (see Graph 8.4). The price of sixty-four reales per *botija* [fifty-seven-libra jug] reappears frequently throughout all the period, with very weak oscillations at that level. A more accentuated minimum is also seen, nevertheless, in 1780 and a slight tendency toward decline after 1786.

The curve for honey oscillates, in a similar fashion, with regard to an almost constant level, at eighty to ninety-six reales per wineskin, with a tendency toward decline shown at the end of the series.

The series for Pacific Ocean fish, conger, and dogfish show features that may seem divergent. Conger oscillates around a base level, forty to forty-eight reales per arroba, with the minimums rising during the second half of the eighteenth century (see Graph 8.4). On the other hand, dogfish remains stable until the decade of 1720, to then fall until the end of the century.[40] Can the price curve of *charquecillo* (dried fish) be considered as a result of different types of fish? It shows more clearly than the earlier cases two long-term movements: a rise from the beginning of the eighteenth century until the maximum of 1755, then a disruption of the trend and decline until the end of the period. Curiously, charquecillo shows an evolution parallel to that corresponding to charqui (dried meat), as we shall see later. In some fashion,

Table 8.4

American Conjuncture: Prices of Salt, Wine, Dried Fish, Conger, and Dogfish in Potosí

| Year | American Products | | | | |
	Salt[1]	Wine[2]	Dried Fish[3]	Conger[4]	Dogfish[5]
1676	—	89	—	75	—
1677	—	107	—	67	—
1678	—	83	—	67	151
1679	—	101	—	83	166
1680	—	101	—	83	181
1681	—	83	—	91	151
1682	—	83	—	91	—
1683	—	95	—	83	121
1684	—	—	—	111	151
1685	—	95	—	91	151
1686	—	95	—	99	155
1687	—	107	—	116	151
1688	—	107	—	125	181
1689	—	—	—	95	151
1690	—	107	—	91	151
1691	—	95	—	116	166
1692	—	95	—	99	181
1693	—	95	—	106	151
1694	—	95	—	106	159
1695	—	95	—	99	159
1696	—	95	—	99	—
1697	—	89	—	91	—
1698	—	95	105	83	151
1699	—	95	—	82	155
1700	—	101	—	58	181
1701	—	101	—	62	151
1702	—	95	—	62	129
1703	—	95	—	81	110
1704	—	107	—	83	136
1705	—	101	—	83	114
1706	—	95	—	83	121
1707	—	95	—	77	121
1708	—	95	—	75	114
1709	—	95	66	83	118
1710	—	112	84	91	—

Table 8.4 (continued)

		American Products			
Year	Salt[1]	Wine[2]	Dried Fish[3]	Conger[4]	Dogfish[5]
1711	—	118	—	83	—
1712	—	95	—	83	135
1713	—	95	—	83	135
1714	—	—	—	—	—
1715	—	89	—	83	—
1716	—	95	—	99	181
1717	—	95	—	99	159
1718	—	95	—	104	—
1719	—	95	—	116	181
1720	—	95	63	116	181
1721	—	107	—	102	151
1722	—	107	84	83	181
1723	131	83	126	83	181
1724	190	95	—	87	151
1725	—	118	—	99	136
1726	95	107	126	79	—
1727	—	107	—	75	181
1728	—	95	68	67	—
1729	95	107	74	58	106
1730	95	95	—	71	91
1731	—	101	—	—	—
1732	—	89	—	—	—
1733	—	83	—	58	—
1734	—	107	—	83	—
1735	—	107	84	99	151
1736	—	107	105	99	151
1737	—	107	105	108	121
1738	—	95	105	133	—
1739	95	95	105	133	—
1740	95	107	105	104	—
1741	—	107	—	75	—
1742	119	83	89	83	136
1743	119	83	97	—	136
1744	119	95	84	—	151
1745	—	95	63	99	121
1746	—	95	—	99	121
1747	95	101	—	83	79

Table 8.4 (continued)

| | | American Products | | |
Year	Salt[1]	Wine[2]	Dried Fish[3]	Conger[4]	Dogfish[5]
1748	—	95	105	83	94
1749	—	95	—	71	94
1750	95	89	95	99	—
1751	—	107	100	99	114
1752	95	107	105	—	—
1753	95	118	105	99	151
1754	—	107	105	—	—
1755	—	107	147	133	151
1756	95	107	108	99	144
1757	—	107	—	99	106
1758	—	107	100	99	106
1759	—	95	105	99	106
1760	—	95	100	75	76
1761	—	95	121	—	—
1762	—	95	126	—	100
1763	—	95	126	—	106
1764	—	95	126	125	83
1765	286	95	116	99	95
1766	—	95	126	—	—
1767	95	95	116	91	—
1768	95	95	116	91	91
1769	190	95	84	83	
1770	95	95	95	99	76
1771	95	95	105	99	112
1772	—	95	95	108	83
1773	95	95	111	125	136
1774	119	95	105	116	76
1775	—	95	108	102	127
1776	—	118	95	83	—
1777	—	118	103	91	91
1778	—	118	—	91	—
1779	79	77	89	83	—
1780	95	68	89	91	—
1781	143	83	100	99	—
1782	—	118	126	116	106
1783	—	95	130	99	91
1784	—	112	126	99	83

Table 8.4 (continued)

Year	Salt[1]	Wine[2]	Dried Fish[3]	Conger[4]	Dogfish[5]
			American Products		
1785	—	107	116	99	76
1786	—	95	116	99	—
1787	—	95	116	—	—
1788	—	71	95	99	—
1789	—	95	—	—	—
1790	—	83	84	—	—
1791	—	92	—	—	—
1792	95	89	89	—	—
1793	—	95	105	150	—
1794	—	—	97	108	—
1795	95	—	105	116	—
1796	119	95	105	116	—
1797	95	95	92	108	—
1798	100	89	86	121	—
1799	95	99	95	—	—
1800	—	89	74	—	—
1801	—	—	103	99	—
1802	—	—	95	—	—
1803	95	83	95	91	—
1804	95	92	84	—	—
1805	119	89	74	83	—
1806	119	—83	—68	67	—
1807	95	—	66	50	—
1808	95	—	74	91	—
1809	95	118	65	—	—
1810	—	—	47	—	—
1811	—	—	—	—	—
1812	95	—	74	—	—
1813	95	—	95	—	—
1814	—	—	58	—	—
1815	—	—	—	—	—
1816	—	—	—	—	—

[1]1770–1779 = 100 = 2.1 reales/pan
[2]1770–1779 = 100 = 67.6 reales/botija
[3]1770–1779 = 100 = 76 reales/arroba
[4]1770–1779 = 100 = 48.1 reales/arroba
[5]1770–1779 = 100 = 52.5 reales/arroba

Graph 8.4

American Conjuncture: Other Products

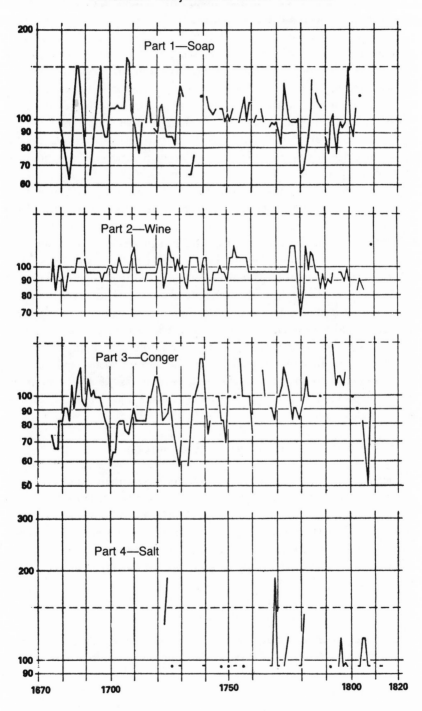

Part 1—Soap

Part 2—Wine

Part 3—Conger

Part 4—Salt

this merchandise marks a transition toward the movement that characterizes those coming from the Potosí region.

The same occurs with salt, a product that arrived in the Villa Imperial from the mines at Yocalla or from the salt pits at Coipasa and Uyuni (see Graph 8.4). The prices registered in the Franciscan friary evidently refer to the salt used for food, but we ought not forget that it is a question of an indispensable input for the Potosí mining industry, which uses it in the process of amalgamation of silver with mercury. Is that double use reflected, perhaps, in our curve? We note in the latter two peculiarities. On the one hand, the price of sixteen reales per loaf of salt is repeated throughout the whole century; on the other, strong rises are observed, twenty-four, thirty-two, and even forty-eight reales per loaf of salt, at regular intervals (1724, 1742–44, 1765, 1769, 1774, 1789, 1796, 1805–1806). Nevertheless, the price of salt never falls below the level of sixteen reales. Everything passes as if the movement alone saw itself affected by sudden rises without declines relative to the base level. The apexes of 1724, 1742–44, and 1805–1806 may suggest that the rises may have been the indirect result of meteorological irregularities, during which the agricultural crises would have drawn the Indians away from the production and commercialization of salt.[41] How, though, would we explain the base level? Perhaps it might be convenient to introduce a new circumstance here. Salt forms part of the circuits of exchange of the Indians, generally under the form of barter, and for it, it would present certain characteristic features that, as we shall see in the following paragraph, are typical of more "Indian" food products, such as quinoa and chuño.

THE REGIONAL CONJUNCTURE

The regional exchanges converging on Potosí essentially consist of food products, be they agricultural or livestock. It may be considered that this area included the regions of Oruro to the north, Cochabamba and La Plata to the east, Chichas to the south, and Carangas to the west, that is to say, approximately the vast zone called Charcas, which corresponds to the Archbishopric of La Plata, a territory for which we have a notable series of tithe incomes at hand.

Grains and tubers

For grains (quinoa, wheat, three types of corn: Indian corn, white corn, and chochoca) and tubers (potatoes, chuño), our sources are fragmentary until around 1720. From that date on, we can trace more or less complete curves, depending on the case, until the beginning of the nineteenth century.

Inasmuch as those crops are cultivated in different ecological zones, located at different altitudes, it might be supposed that their prices do not present the same fluctuations, which would lead to doubting the legitimacy of grouping them in one single category. Nevertheless, it suffices to observe the respective curves to confirm that, on general lines, they present analogous pictures, with approximately coincident maximums and minimums (compare Table 8.5 and Graph 8.5).

As we shall see below, the native agricultural system is inspired by an ideal of complementarity, in a way that grains and tubers can be mutually substituted in case of a bad harvest. When the production of corn, for example, is insufficient, the demand for potatoes increases, and the prices of both products tend to rise.

We shall consider the most spectacular apexes and their coincidence among the different curves:

—1722–23: chochoca, Indian corn, chuño, potatoes.
—1734: chochoca, white corn, chuño, quinoa.
—1741–42: chochoca, Indian corn, white corn, quinoa.
—1750–51–52: chochoca, Indian corn, quinoa, wheat, chuño.
—1755–56: chochoca, Indian corn, quinoa, wheat, chuño, potatoes.
—1783–84: chochoca, Indian corn, white corn, quinoa, chuño, potatoes.
—1804–1805: chochoca, Indian corn, white corn, quinoa, potatoes.

Are we in the presence of cyclical oscillations? Observation of the curves permits situating those maximum points in the apogee of movements whose periodicity varies between eight and fifteen years, and, in this last case, at times, minor periods of six or seven years may be distinguished. Their reading is not easy because of the lacunae in the series and an element of arbitrariness inherent in such exercises, but nevertheless, for the less fragmentary curves, it is possible to propose the following chronologies:

chochoca	Indian corn	quinoa	chuño
172(0)–25	171(6)–26	(lacunae)	171(9)–27
1726–3(9)	1727–40	1727–41	1728–39
1741–46	1741–47	1742–49	1740–47
1747–60	1748–59	1750–59	1748–62

1761–72	1760–71	1760–73	1763–73
1773–80	177(3)–80	1774–81	1774–78
(lacunae)	1781–8(7)	1782–89	1781–91
179(1)–96	(lacunae)	1790–1800	1792–1800
(lacunae)	1796–1810	180(1)–180(9)	1801–11

A certain coherence among the different series appears that justifies the calculation of a general agricultural price index uniting grains and tubers (compare Graph 8.6). We adopted the decade 1770–79 as a base period equal to 100, as we have done for individual products, both for reasons of documentation, being the most complete data, and because the oscillations are much less violent during those years. It would no doubt be convenient to weight the index, since corn represents the most important product of those reaching the market. While the actual state of our knowledge does not permit us to go on to precise calculations, though, we are content with an approximate instrument. We shall limit ourselves, then, to including the three types of corn separately, that will then constitute almost half the component elements of the general index. The curve thus obtained presents a synthesis, imperfect but convenient, that permits a clearer determination for all grains and tubers, the succession of movements more or less in ten-year periods throughout the duration of the eighteenth century, which we shall call "cycles":

I	1716–26 (11 years)
II	1727–39 (13 years)
III	1740–49 (10 years)
IV	1750–64 (15 years)
V	1765–80 (16 years)
VI	1781–89 (9 years)
VII	1790–1800 (11 years)
VIII	1801–1810 (10 years)

These cycles have a mean duration of 11.9 years, analogous to that observed in other regions of America or Europe. According to the classic, though disputed, interpretation, they would be linked to variations in meteorological conditions. Although these last do not, by themselves, determine regular cycles, certain correspondences appear evident to us. We have tried to collect, year by year, information of a qualitative type about the climatological history of the southern Andes.[42] The picture thus obtained permits confirmation of

Table 8.5

Regional Conjuncture: Prices of Grains and Tubers in Potosí

| | Regional Agricultural Products | | | | | | | |
Year	Wheat[1]	Quinoa[2]	Indian Corn[3]	White Corn[4]	Chochoca[5]	Potatoes[6]	Chuño[7]	General Index
1676	—	—	—	—	—	—	—	—
1677	92	—	—	—	—	—	—	—
1678	—	—	—	—	—	—	—	—
1679	23	—	—	—	—	—	—	—
1680	—	—	—	—	—	—	—	—
1681	31	—	—	—	—	—	—	—
1682	—	—	—	—	—	123	—	—
1683	—	—	147	—	—	114	119	—
1684	—	—	—	—	—	—	—	—
1685	—	—	—	—	—	—	—	—
1686	—	195	147	—	—	86	119	—
1687	—	—	—	—	—	—	—	—
1688	—	—	—	—	—	—	—	—
1689	—	—	—	—	—	—	—	—
1690	—	—	147	—	—	—	—	—
1691	—	—	—	—	—	—	—	—
1692	—	—	—	—	—	—	—	—
1693	—	—	—	—	—	—	—	—
1694	—	—	—	—	—	—	—	—
1695	—	—	—	—	—	—	—	—
1696	—	—	—	—	—	—	—	—
1697	—	—	—	—	—	—	—	—
1698	—	—	—	—	—	—	—	—
1699	—	—	—	—	—	—	—	—
1700	—	—	—	—	—	—	—	—
1701	—	—	—	—	—	—	—	—
1702	—	—	—	—	—	—	—	—
1703	—	—	—	—	—	136	—	—
1704	—	—	—	—	—	—	—	—
1705	—	—	—	—	—	—	—	—
1706	—	—	—	—	—	—	—	—
1707	—	—	—	—	—	—	—	—
1708	—	—	—	—	—	—	—	—
1709	—	—	101	—	—	148	—	—
1710	—	—	—	—	—	—	—	—
1711	—	—	—	—	—	—	—	—
1712	—	—	—	—	—	—	—	—
1713	—	—	—	—	—	—	—	—
1714	—	—	111	—	—	108	—	109.50
1715	—	49	—	—	—	—	104	76.50
1716	—	—	101	—	—	74	—	87.50
1717	—	114	111	—	—	56	90	92.75

Table 8.5 (continued)

Year	Wheat[1]	Quinoa[2]	Indian Corn[3]	White Corn[4]	Chochoca[5]	Potatoes[6]	Chuño[7]	General Index
					Regional Agricultural Products			
1718	—	—	—	—	—	—	—	—
1719	—	—	111	—	—	49	60	73.33
1720	60	163	—	—	110	83	—	104.00
1721	—	—	—	—	156	99	—	127.50
1722	—	—	184	—	—	173	164	173.66
1723	—	—	184	—	208	99	164	163.75
1724	—	146	111	—	117	49	119	108.40
1725	—	81	83	—	78	49	75	73.20
1726	62	49	83	—	91	62	75	70.33
1727	62	81	92	—	91	62	75	77.16
1728	—	—	111	—	—	74	82	89.00
1729	—	107	101	—	182	99	97	117.20
1730	—	—	111	—	—	99	97	102.33
1731	85	195	92	—	117	49	75	102.16
1732	—	—	92	—	110	—	—	101.00
1733	—	163	—	—	117	—	75	118.33
1734	—	211	120	207	164	—	149	170.20
1735	—	143	111	124	156	—	90	124.80
1736	—	146	115	—	156	—	97	128.50
1737	65	195	115	—	143	—	82	120.00
1738	—	98	111	124	130	—	104	113.40
1739	—	98	—	124	78	—	90	97.50
1740	—	98	92	124	—	111	134	111.80
1741	—	81	166	—	182	—	164	148.25
1742	—	114	157	331	159	—	209	194.00
1743	92	107	138	—	104	—	119	112.00
1744	—	98	92	103	78	—	90	92.20
1745	92	98	92	—	104	54	90	88.33
1746	85	90	92	—	78	—	75	84.00
1747	47	130	83	98	91	66	71	83.71
1748	56	98	120	—	96	—	82	90.40
1749	49	85	92	—	97	—	97	84.00
1750	42	98	111	—	156	—	119	105.20
1751	131	138	166	—	117	56	209	136.16
1752	54	155	129	98	125	62	119	106.00
1753	115	114	—	88	104	74	149	107.33
1754	154	140	203	145	130	74	149	142.14
1755	142	195	239	—	—	123	209	181.60
1756	123	163	184	—	166	74	104	135.66
1757	102	118	129	120	143	87	119	116.71
1758	—	130	—	186	156	—	164	159.00
1759	71	81	92	124	130	—	149	107.83
1760	83	124	111	114	117	—	104	108.83
1761	54	98	129	114	130	116	97	105.42

Table 8.5 (continued)

Year	Wheat[1]	Quinoa[2]	Indian Corn[3]	White Corn[4]	Chochoca[5]	Potatoes[6]	Chuño[7]	General Index
				Regional Agricultural Products				
1762	58	98	120	124	130	99	90	102.71
1763	71	98	—	124	130	—	104	105.40
1764	46	—	—	83	130	—	90	87.25
1765	46	110	—	124	130	—	90	100.00
1766	—	—	—	—	—	—	90	90.00
1767	—	90	—	124	91	—	97	100.50
1768	—	98	—	124	78	—	90	97.50
1769	92	114	—	—	130	—	104	110.00
1770	77	98	111	—	78	—	90	90.80
1771	133	98	92	—	78	123	90	102.33
1772	—	98	—	—	78	111	90	97.25
1773	90	98	101	—	130	148	90	109.50
1774	—	107	—	103	109	93	104	103.20
1775	85	98	—	93	121	83	112	98.66
1776	131	117	111	—	121	86	119	114.16
1777	—	106	101	—	110	82	119	103.60
1778	123	—	92	—	110	99	112	107.20
1779	77	81	92	103	65	74	75	81.00
1780	77	81	83	—	78	62	75	76.00
1781	69	78	111	—	—	99	134	92.20
1782	92	98	115	166	143	74	—	114.66
1783	77	130	129	186	—	123	209	142.33
1784	69	98	111	124	—	99	209	118.33
1785	61	98	111	103	91	74	104	91.71
1786	77	81	74	93	—	74	75	77.16
1787	77	65	74	83	104	86	60	78.42
1788	77	65	—	—	—	72	75	69.75
1789	52	65	—	—	78	62	75	66.40
1790	46	98	—	—	—	74	60	69.50
1791	38	98	—	—	104	62	60	72.40
1792	31	107	—	—	—	74	90	75.50
1793	123	98	—	—	143	74	90	105.60
1794	54	114	92	—	130	74	75	89.83
1795	46	98	74	93	84	74	75	77.71
1796	78	98	92	135	78	68	90	91.28
1797	86	122	—	143	119	68	75	102.16
1798	77	98	—	114	104	72	90	90.83
1799	92	106	—	124	—	62	82	93.20
1800	84	81	101	—	—	62	75	80.60
1801	—	—	101	—	—	62	82	81.66
1802	—	—	111	—	—	86	—	98.50
1803	—	90	111	—	—	74	104	94.75
1804	—	—	129	—	130	74	—	111.00
1805	—	155	138	207	—	99	—	149.75

Table 8.5 (continued)

Year	Wheat[1]	Quinoa[2]	Indian Corn[3]	White Corn[4]	Chochoca[5]	Potatoes[6]	Chuño[7]	General Index
1806	74	98	129	155	—	62	—	103.60
1807	112	90	111	124	—	62	119	103.00
1808	102	98	120	135	104	56	104	102.71
1809	—	90	74	93	—	62	60	75.80
1810	37	—	74	—	—	49	60	55.00
1811	—	—	—	—	104	99	60	87.66
1812	92	114	111	145	—	99	112	112.16
1813	—	—	—	145	—	99	134	126.00
1814	—	—	—	—	—	105	—	105.00
1815	—	—	—	—	—	—	—	—
1816	—	—	—	—	—	—	—	—

Regional Agricultural Products

[1] 1770–1779 = 100 = 26 reales/carga
[2] 1770–1779 = 100 = 24.6 reales/carga
[3] 1770–1779 = 100 = 21.7 reales/carga
[4] 1770–1779 = 100 = 19.3 reales/carga
[5] 1770–1779 = 100 = 30.8 reales/carga
[6] 1770–1779 = 100 = 16.2 reales/carga
[7] 1770–1779 = 100 = 26.8 reales/carga
[8] 1770–1779 = 100

the fact that the great scarcity crises in Potosí coincide, in almost all cases, with meteorological irregularities. It is generally a matter of drought years; more exactly, in conformity with a well-known schema, the crises result from a succession of bad years, when various catastrophic harvests exhaust all reserves and prices are runaway. Let us repeat the principal maximums of our curves:

—1723: drought in 1721, 1722, 1723, preceded by the great plague epidemic of 1719–20;
—1734: drought in 1732, 1733, 1734, accompanied by a smallpox epidemic in 1732;
—1741: drought in 1741, 1742;
—1755: drought in 1755, preceded by excessive rain in 1753;
—1783–84: drought years;
—1805: droughts in 1804–1805.

The violence of the price rises of those years seems to be an American characteristic. Their amplitude and intensity greatly exceed, both in Potosí and Mexico City, those seen in Europe.[43] In order to facilitate comparisons, we shall show the data for wheat and Indian corn:

	Indian Corn			Wheat	
	Amplitude (%)	Intensity (%)		Amplitude (%)	Intensity (%)
1716–23	82.2	36.8			
1726–34	44.6	20.8			
1740–41	80.4	40.2			
1747–55	188.0	72.1	1750–54	266.7	136.2
1759–61	40.2	20.3	1765–71	189.1	89.1
1771–76	20.6	10.1			
1780–83	55.4	31.9			
(1787–94)	24.3	12.1	1792–93	296.8	148.4
1795–1805	86.5	44.8	1795–99	100.0	64.8

It is known that, in Mexico and France, the years of great scarcity were accompanied by great famines, disturbances, and spectacular increases in mortality, as well as in criminal activity. According to Florescano, and more recently, Brading, the price rise of 1785–86 represents the greatest catastrophe of the century for Mexico.[44] In view of the even stronger extent of the Andean fluctuations, it would be appropriate to expect analogous crises in our region. Nevertheless, this does not appear to have been the case. Although the documentation at times mentions great famines in the Andes, these are not comparable to those of France in 1709 or of Mexico in 1785. We lack good demographic studies for our region; in particular, we do not have at our disposal mortality curves elaborated on the basis of parish registers. Notwithstanding, it is admitted that after the great plague epidemic of 1719–20 and that of smallpox at the beginning of the decade of 1730, the Andean population does not show peaks in the mortality statistics for the rest of the eighteenth century. The example of 1719–20 is significant in itself, since it corresponds to relatively low agricultural price indices, 73.3 and 104, the rise only being registered three years later in 1722–23, with indices of 173.6 and 163.7. Another social and political crisis, that of 1781, with the revolts of Tupac Amaru and Tupac Catari, also presents itself as a paradox. It is situated, in fact, after a very accentuated fall in agricultural prices, which did not rise to a maximum point until two or three years later, in 1783–84, when they reacted to a wave of droughts.

Why, then, are the "classic" mechanisms of the Old Regime not seen in

Graph 8.5

Regional Conjuncture: Grains and Tubers

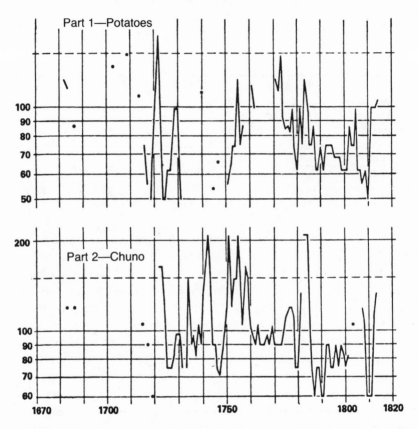

the Andean world? Let us remember that we are in the presence of a society for which prices are an insufficient indicator of general material wellbeing, as they are not in Europe. The Andean world, in fact, shows the joining of two different economic spheres: on the one hand, the market, supplied not only by the haciendas, but by small, Indian or mestizo producers; on the other, the sphere of barter and private consumption, to which one part of mestizo or Indian production is dedicated. It is true that, in the Europe of the seventeenth and eighteenth centuries, the practice of barter represented a sector whose importance J. Meuvret showed in his notable article.[45] Nevertheless, it can be assumed that barter has an even greater weight in the Andes, where the two spheres, that of nonmonetary exchange and that of

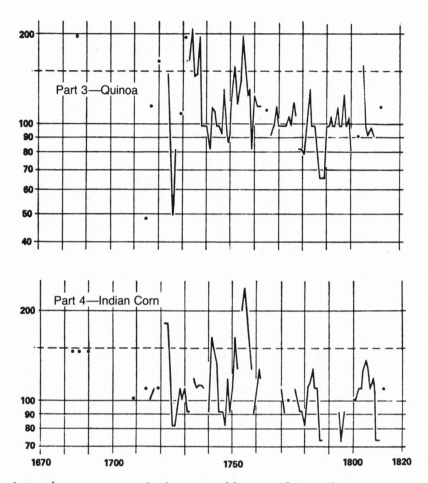

the market, seem more clearly separated because of the traditional character and ritual of reciprocity bonds among indigenous groups.

We are confronted with different problems with regard to all these points. It is difficult to evaluate the measure of domination that production of the haciendas exercised in the Upper Peruvian agricultural market. We cannot calculate the percentages of mestizo or indigenous production that was channeled into the market, of that which was dedicated to barter, or of that which served private consumption.

The ideal of self-sufficiency represents, in fact, one of the continuities of Andean societies. The ruggedness of the terrain determines very varied ecological zones arranged at regular intervals, which leads to a vertical economy that tends to associate complementary products commonly produced across

Graph 8.6

Regional Conjuncture: General Index

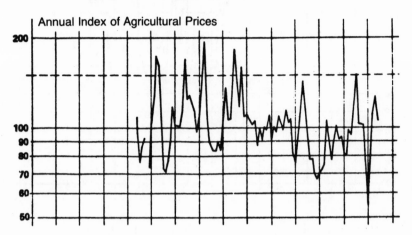

Annual Index of Agricultural Prices

distinct zones, in accord with the "vertical archipelago" model.[46] This complementarity also permits the division of risk and compensation for the eventual meteorological irregularities. Our maximum prices correspond to exceptional years during which the price rise affects both the producers of the puna and those of the temperate zones, but nevertheless, even in those moments of acute crisis, compensation strategies can be effective. In fact, despite the fact that ethnic solidarities have suffered a slow process of erosion and fragmentation under colonial domination, these same survive, though in a partial manner. Although the ancient ethnic groups may have lost their distant "colonies" a long time ago, the traditional scheme is prolonged in the networks of exchange, precisely under the form of barter.

We attempt an approach, arbitrary but suggestive, to these problems, starting from actual ethnographic data. At the beginning of the decade of 1970, C. Fonseca made an effort to evaluate, in a region of the central Andes, the varieties of utilization of indigenous production.[47] He was thus able to reconstruct, at the level of the village, the division of an entire year's harvests: 50 percent for private, home consumption, 10 percent for seeds; 10 percent for barter, 10 percent for payments in kind, and 20 percent for sale in the market. It is not a matter of projecting those orders of magnitude retrospectively from a distance of two centuries, but of being able to assume that the present mechanisms were similar, from which two observations would be deduced:

1) Vertical complementarity, the practice of barter, and the continual displacements of the population from above to below constitute one of the original features of the Andean world and permit attenuation of the severity of famines during bad years.

2) The distribution of indigenous production implies various forms of inflexibility. In fact, the part dedicated to the market is taken away from the same resources that should assure private, home consumption, for which reason it cannot exceed strict limits. At the same time, the Indians of the eighteenth century had the obligation to acquire money in order to satisfy their tribute, as well as to pay for the products that were imposed upon them by way of the forced distribution of merchandise. Both demands are unavoidable, and their satisfaction appears compelling.

The natives had at hand but two ways to obtain that money: the sale of their labor or the sale in the market of one part, inevitably depending on chance, of their production. Under those conditions, in function of the conjuncture, they confront two different types of difficulties:

1) In the event of a violent rise in prices, during the years of bad harvest, the percentage of production dedicated to private subsistence increases, with the consequent reduction, or even disappearance, of the surplus dedicated to the market. At the same time, because of the high prices, it seems even more indispensable to reserve part of the production so as to obtain other articles to consume through barter.

2) Inversely, in the event of low prices, in a market flooded by supply, and taking into account the rigidities shown in the division of production, the gains obtained by sale in the market are few, and the mechanisms of colonial exploitation may also be blocked.

It may be concluded, then, that although the spheres of barter and the market are found to be differentiated, in the Andes they are also related, since, according to the years, the indigenous producers grant to one and the other one part, more or less important, of their harvests. Could, then, the barter sector indirectly influence the market? What characterizes barter is a system of equivalences very different from prices, which are generally characterized by great stability. We observed that in the cases of the most "indigenous" products, chuño and quinoa, for example, a notable feature appears. In both series, despite fluctuation, there is a recurrent price, twenty-four reales for both chuño and quinoa. These prices appear to oscillate both above and below that price that would then fulfill a role of base level. Said in another way, it may be assumed that the barter sector acts, in certain circumstances, as a regulator of the market. Further, it can be seen that the recurrence of the base price is more frequent in the period between approximately 1760 and 1800. We shall specify the significance of this phenomenon later on.

The general agricultural price index presents oscillations simultaneously more frequent and extensive during the first half of the eighteenth century (see Graph 8.6). It is seen as well that the maximums of 1722, 1734, 1742, and 1755 (indices: 173, 170, 194, and 182) are at higher levels than those of 1783 and 1805 (indices: 142 and 149). Detailed analysis of the curve allows distinguishing, beyond the more or less ten-year cycles already indicated, long-term movements corresponding to three contrasting phases.

The first phase, whose beginning, because of the lacunae, only appears in 1716, extends throughout more than forty years until 1758, or 1764 if the final date of the ten-year cycle is adopted. A high price level characterizes it. Is it a matter, perhaps, of a long, upward movement? The tendency of the maximums is not clear, while that of the minimums seems, as a whole, positive (1726:70, 1739:97, 1749:84). This last reading is confirmed by the average index of the four cycles included in the phase, the last of which marks a clear increase with respect to the first three:

I	1716–26 : 107.5
II	1727–39 : 112.5
III	1740–49 : 108.5
IV	1750–64 : 120.5

The second phase, from 1759 to 1789, corresponds without a doubt to a downward movement. For nearly thirty years, maximum peaks are not registered, save in 1783 when the index, 142, reaches a level very much lower than those of the preceding phase. The cyclical minimums decline regularly (1764:87, 1780:76, 1789:66, the secular minimum). The downward tendency is confirmed by the average indices of the phase's two cycles:

| V | 1765–80 : 98.8 |
| VI | 1781–89 : 94.5 |

The tendency then shows an inflection. From 1790 until at least 1805 a third phase persists that was characterized by an upward movement. A growth of the maximums is, in fact, seen (1793:105, 1805:149), as well as of the minimums (1789:66, 1795:77, 1800:80). The average indices of the cycles of the phase confirm the tendency:

VII   1790–1800 : 86.2
VIII   1801–10 : 97.6

In short, we may propose the following periodization for the movement of agricultural prices during the eighteenth century in Potosí:

1. 171(6)–58 : rise (?)
2. 1759–89 : decline
3. 1790–180(5) : rise

If we compare this chronology with the three phases Florescano distinguishes in Mexico for corn prices, the analogy seems evident. Let us remember the Mexican movements:[48]

1. 1721–54 : "slight" rise
2. 1755–78 : decline
3. 1779–1814 : rise

Nevertheless, beyond the formal analogy, the two conjunctures, the Andean one and the Mexican one, show a fundamental difference. In Mexico, the averages of the two downward cycles, 1754–65 and 1765–78, are at the same level as the first two upward cycles, 1720–27 and 1727–36, and the movement that begins in 1779 reaches a much higher level. Average prices from 1720 to 1778 oscillate between 11.65 and 15.54 reales, while from 1779 on, their fluctuations are between 15.33 and 25.95 reales. On the contrary, in Potosí average indices of 113.2 are seen for the period 1716–64 and of 97.3 for that of 1765–89, that is to say, a decrease of 14 percent, and an average index of 91.6 for 1790–1810, that is to say, an even more accentuated decrease of 19 percent. Thus we again encounter the greatest inflection we recorded above for the years around 1760, when the fluctuations of agricultural prices in Potosí became narrower. Said in another way, the whole of the period can be broken down into two secular movements: the first, between 1716 and 1760, is characterized by strong and frequent oscillations with a high price level; the second, from 1760 to 1810, at least, characterized by much weaker oscillations and a lower price level.[49]

What does the inflection in Potosí's agricultural conjuncture around 1760 mean? It is necessary to examine a whole complex of circumstances, which will only be mentioned briefly here. They are climatic evolution, demographic history, production movements, and general economic context. The influence of climate should doubtlessly not be exaggerated. Nevertheless, in the picture we have elaborated, the first four decades of the century appear catastrophic. From 1705 to 1742, there are no fewer than twenty-four bad years, generally droughts, at times, excessive rains or freezes, that is to say, two of every three years were bad. It is tempting to establish a correlation between those unfavorable conditions and the phase of high prices. In contrast, after 1742, observations about meteorological irregularities become rare, to the point that for some decades, in particular those of 1760 and 1770, we totally lack them. Does this reflect a lack of sources? The hypothesis of a more favorable climate, given that the good years correspond precisely to the phase of low prices, as to the low level of 1744–49, should not be discarded. It is not surprising, then, to again encounter new successions of droughts at the end of the eighteenth century.

Lamentably, in the present state of Andean studies we know almost nothing about the movements of agricultural production. We shall try, then, to approach the problem through the examination of tithe revenue from the Archbishopric of La Plata, a jurisdiction that included the city of Potosí (see Table 8.6). The Archive of the Cathedral of Sucre retains series of exceptional richness from the end of the seventeenth century until the end of the eighteenth century, which, for the beginning of the nineteenth century, may be completed with the summaries found in the Archivo General de Indias.[50] We shall not linger here over any but the essential data directly relative to the interpretation of prices.

The Archbishopric of La Plata corresponded to the area supplying Potosí, especially with grains and tubers. It included twenty-one provinces, subdivided simultaneously into minor jurisdictions for the collection of the tithes, which were rented out, generally annually, at times for two to four years.[51]

A first curve (a), almost complete between 1674 and 1817, indicates the global revenues expressed in their nominal value (compare Graph 8.7). Its reading allows distinguishing the following fluctuations:

1. From 1674 to approximately 1705, the oscillations are weak, with revenues more or less stable;
2. After 1705, the curve has a downward inflection. Revenues diminish,

Table 8.6

Regional Conjuncture: Tithes of the Archbishopric of La Plata

Year	Tithes of the Archbishopric of La Plata					
	1	2	3	4	5	6
1676	92.200	82	—	—	—	—
1677	94.408	89	—	—	—	—
1678	81.103	72	—	—	—	—
1679	—	—	—	—	—	—
1680	—	—	—	—	—	—
1681	—	—	—	—	—	—
1682	85.399	76	—	—	—	—
1683	86.599	77	—	—	—	—
1684	90.209	80.3	—	—	—	—
1685	91.445	81.4	—	—	—	—
1686	90.373	80.4	—	—	—	—
1687	86.342	76.8	—	—	—	—
1688	—	—	—	—	—	—
1689	86.634	77	—	—	—	—
1690	88.208	78.5	—	—	—	—
1691	—	—	—	—	—	—
1692	100.168	89	—	—	—	—
1693	103.615	92.2	—	—	—	—
1694	102.193	91	—	—	—	—
1695	80.723	71.8	—	—	—	—
1696	94.408	84.9	—	—	—	—
1697	—	—	—	—	—	—
1698	91.680	81.6	—	—	—	—
1699	88.639	78.9	—	—	—	—
1700	—	—	—	—	—	—
1701	83.621	74.4	—	—	—	—
1702	87.162	77.6	—	—	—	—
1703	89.885	80	—	—	—	—
1704	—	—	—	—	—	—
1705	96.771	86	—	—	—	—
1706	—	—	—	—	—	—
1707	84.679	75.4	—	—	—	—
1708	83.040	73.9	—	—	—	—
1709	—	—	—	—	—	—
1710	—	—	—	—	—	—
1711	78.406	69.8	—	—	—	—
1712	83.020	73.9	—	—	—	—
1713	—	—	—	—	—	—
1714	95.247	84.8	109.50	77.4	—	—
1715	84.654	75.3	76.50	89.4	—	—
1716	72.264	64.3	87.50	73.5	—	—
1717	—	—	92.75	—	89.5	—
1718	77.470	68.9	—	—	92.1	74.8

Table 8.6 (continued)

	Tithes of the Archbishopric of La Plata					
Year	1	2	3	4	5	6
1719	67.587	60	73.33	81.8	106	56.6
1720	54.005	48	104.00	46.2	116.9	41
1721	51.129	45.5	127.50	35.7	119.1	38.2
1722	63.269	56.3	173.66	32.4	117.7	47.8
1723	88.526	78.8	163.75	48.1	117.3	67.2
1724	78.661	70	108.40	64.6	113.4	61.7
1725	60.317	53.7	73.20	73.4	107.9	49.8
1726	57.592	51.3	70.33	72.9	99.9	51.3
1727	61.270	54.5	77.16	70.6	91.1	59.8
1728	58.037	51.6	89.00	58	90.2	57.2
1729	63.156	56.2	117.20	48	94.2	59.7
1730	59.112	52.6	102.33	51.4	101	52.1
1731	54.350	48.4	102.16	47.4	114.3	42.3
1732	57.127	50.8	101.00	50.3	119.4	42.5
1733	55.513	49.4	118.33	41.7	121	40.8
1734	64.929	57.8	170.20	34	123.6	46.6
1735	65.681	58.4	124.80	46.8	125.2	46.6
1736	60.246	53.6	128.50	41.7	124.7	43
1737	64.198	57.1	120.00	47.6	123.7	46.2
1738	70.191	62.5	113.40	55.1	120.6	51.8
1739	72.670	64.6	97.50	66.3	130.5	49.5
1740	76.091	67.7	111.80	60.6	128.1	52.8
1741	87.250	77.7	148.25	52.4	124.2	62.6
1742	109.613	97.5	194.00	50.3	120.6	80.8
1743	87.317	77.7	112.00	69.4	118.7	65.4
1744	83.400	74.2	92.20	80.5	114.6	64.7
1745	—	—	88.33	—	106.4	—
1746	—	—	84.00	—	90.7	—
1747	85.079	75.7	83.71	90.4	89.7	84.4
1748	—	—	90.40	—	96	—
1749	82.662	73.5	84.00	87.5	98.5	74.6
1750	89.324	79.4	105.20	75.5	101.8	78
1751	91.889	81.8	136.16	60.1	110.2	74.2
1752	97.316	86.6	106.00	81.7	123.2	76.3
1753	100.890	89.8	107.33	83.7	130.6	68.3
1754	104.576	93	142.14	65.4	132.2	70.3
1755	125.538	111.7	181.60	61.5	135.5	82.4
1756	119.044	106	135.66	78.1	135.8	78
1757	102.255	91	116.71	78	136	66.9
1758	109.428	97.4	159.00	61.3	130.7	74.5
1759	102.912	91.6	107.83	84.9	119.5	76.6
1760	102.011	90.8	108.83	83.4	115.1	78.9
1761	98.601	87.7	105.42	83.2	110.9	79.1
1762	101.499	90.3	102.71	87.9	102.5	88.1
1763	106.689	94.9	105.40	90	99.9	95

Table 8.6 (continued)

Year	Tithes of the Archbishopric of La Plata					
	1	2	3	4	5	6
1764	101.043	89.9	87.25	103	98.8	91
1765	101.356	90.2	100.00	90.2	97.6	92.4
1766	97.363	86.6	90.00	96.2	98.7	87.7
1767	105.317	93.7	100.50	93.2	96.6	97
1768	114.450	101.8	97.50	104.4	98.7	103.1
1769	—	—	110.00	—	98.3	—
1770	105.786	94.1	90.80	103.6	101.1	93.1
1771	91.578	81.5	102.33	79.6	101.5	80.3
1772	101.979	90.7	97.25	93.3	101.7	89.2
1773	120.101	106.9	109.50	97.6	102.3	104.5
1774	121.179	107.8	103.20	105.5	104.1	103.5
1775	117.270	104.3	98.66	105.7	104.8	99.5
1776	109.848	97.7	114.16	85.6	102.5	95.3
1777	119.093	106	103.60	102.3	97.7	108.5
1778	120.410	107	107.20	99.8	96.1	111.3
1779	116.308	103.5	81.00	127.8	98.4	105.2
1780	116.680	103.5	76.00	136.2	102.4	101.1
1781	83.578	74.4	92.20	80.7	104.5	71.2
1782	147.938	131.6	114.66	114.8	102.3	128.6
1783	175.375	156	142.33	109.6	101.8	153.2
1784	209.775	186.7	118.33	157.8	102.1	182.8
1785	146.800	130.6	91.71	142.4	98.9	132
1786	122.775	109	77.16	141.3	92	118.5
1787	135.499	120.6	78.42	153.8	81.6	147.8
1788	138.126	123	69.75	176.3	75	164
1789	129.630	115.4	66.40	173.8	72.7	158.7
1790	123.503	116	69.50	158.3	76.8	143.2
1791	121.711	108.9	72.40	149.7	78.4	138.3
1792	121.399	108	75.50	143	79.6	135.7
1793	134.138	119.4	105.60	113.1	83.1	143.7
1794	130.599	116.2	89.83	129.4	87.8	132.3
1795	133.082	118.4	77.71	152.4	90.4	130.9
1796	121.612	108.2	91.28	118.5	92.9	116.5
1797	121.500	108.1	102.16	105.8	89.4	120.9
1798	132.757	118	90.83	129.9	88.2	133.8
1799	149.906	133.4	93.20	143.1	91.2	146.3
1800	149.884	133.4	80.60	165.5	91.7	145.5
1801	157.717	140.4	81.66	171.9	92.9	151.1
1802	178.492	158.8	98.50	161.2	101.3	157
1803	193.276	172	94.75	181.5	102.8	167.3
1804	180.231	160.4	111.00	144.5	106	151
1805	232.035	206.5	149.75	137.9	109	189.4
1806	180.978	161	103.60	155.4	105.8	152.2
1807	—	—	103.00	—	100.1	—
1808	—	—	107.71	—	96.8	—

Table 8.6 (continued)

	Tithes of the Archbishopric of La Plata					
Year	1	2	3	4	5	6
1809	146.389	130.3	75.80	171.9	91.4	142.6
1810	125.503	111.7	55.00	203	94.6	118
1811	—	—	87.66	—	95	—
1812	—	—	112.16	—	—	—
1813	—	—	126.00	—		
1814	182.986	—	105.00	—		
1815	170.853	—	—	—	—	—
1816	140.566	—	—	—	—	—
1817	166.20	—	—	—	—	—
1818	—	—	—	—	—	—
1819	—	—	—	—	—	—
1820	—	—	—	—	—	—

Column Titles:
1. Tithes (Pesos)
2. Tithes (1770–1779 = 100)
3. Index of Agricultural Prices in Potosí (1770–1779 = 100)
4. Tithes Deflated by Index of Agricultural Prices in Potosí
5. Index of Agricultural Prices in Potosí in Moving Averages (seven years centered on the fourth year)
6. Tithes Deflated by Index of Agricultural Prices in Moving Averages

Graph 8.7

Regional Conjuncture: Index of Tithes

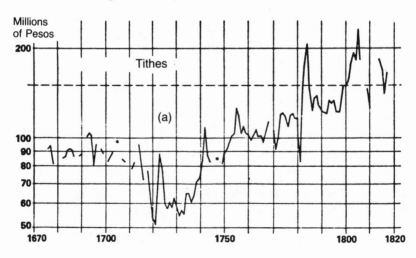

first slowly, until 1715, then precipitously, until reaching their minimum in 1720–21. The movement is interrupted with the maximums of 1723–24, but the decline is prolonged until approximately 1731–33;

3. From 1734 on, revenues rise very rapidly to the maximum peak of 1742. This is followed by what, despite some lacunae, can be read as a lower level between 1743 and 1749. Then the upward movement again takes hold, more slowly than before, until around 1788. Significant irregularities are also seen, such as the maximum peaks of 1755 and 1783–84, and the fall of 1781;

4. After 1788, revenues again tend downward until 1797, to rise to the absolute maximum of 1805. The oscillations are now stronger, with a tendency that, as a result of the lacunae, seems to be oriented toward a standstill.

Do these diverse phases correspond to parallel production movements? It is known that the revenues for tithes expressed in money do not directly reflect production and that it is also necessary at times to read them "backward." The maximum peaks of the curve (a) correspond very exactly to the highest peaks of prices: 1723, 1742, 1755, 1783–84, 1805, with the sole absence of the peak of 1734, which here is minor. We know that those years correspond to catastrophic harvests that provoke the brutal price rise. Although the quantities harvested might be small, the large landowners then obtain considerable profits. They are the ones who, in fact, cause the monies paid at auction for tithes to rise so as to be able to speculate with the amounts of agricultural products collected as tithes. The movements in money of the tithes follow, then, an inverse movement with regard to that of the harvests.[52]

The declines in curve (a) in 1720–21 and 1781 are more simply explained. The first is related to the plague epidemic that devastated the central and southern Andes. With regard to the second, evidently it corresponds to the Tupac Amaru and Tupac Catari revolts, whose negative effect on the collection of the tithes is easy to imagine. Let us underscore that, because of droughts, the maximum peaks of agricultural prices are only reached in 1783–84, coinciding with a maximum in tithe revenues.

It is necessary, then, in order to be able to interpret curve (a), to proceed not to its correction, but to its "deflation," by means of a price index. While the tithes correspond to the Archbishopric of Charcas as a whole, we should use an average, weighted index that might take into account regional and even local differences. While we know almost nothing about the history of prices in Upper Peru, be it a matter of La Plata or Cochabamba, we shall be content with using the index we elaborated earlier for Potosí. Among the possible methods of calculation, all arbitrary, we have chosen two that seem to us to correspond to the characteristics both of prices and their violent oscillations and of the tithes, the first being subject to speculation in a time of bad harvest. Thus we sketch two corrected curves in a different fashion. One, (b), has been deflated, as is usual, by the moving average of the price index for periods of seven years, centered in the fourth year. The other, (c), was directly deflated by the annual values of the price index (compare Graph 8.8).

Curve (b), corrected by moving averages, keeps the maximum peaks of 1723, 1742, 1784, and 1805, with even the peak corresponding to 1755 present, though attenuated. On the contrary, curve (c), deflated with the annual index, deletes the maximum peaks corresponding to scarcity and transforms them into minimum points. If this last curve is compared with the one corresponding to the agricultural price index, it is confirmed that, logically, they show inverted cycles, since the depressions of one coincide very exactly with the culminating peaks of the other (compare Graphs 8.6 and 8.8).

With regard to long-term movements, despite the differences shown, curves (b) and (c) indicate approximately the same tendencies, which serve to specify, from 1714–17 on, the beginning of our price indices, those the nominal curve (a) suggested:

1. During the first third of the century, the decline is confirmed. Even more, it is a matter of a dizzy fall that reaches, in 1722, the absolute minimum of the period, indices of 48 and 32. Despite the rise of 1725–26, the depressed movement is prolonged until the secondary minimum of 1734, indices of 47 and 34;

2. From 1735 to 1788, on the contrary, the rising global tendency is affirmed, with an irregular pitch: a rapid rise until about 1747, where a lacuna makes interpretation difficult, then stagnation, including a fall during one decade; an abrupt rise in 1759–64, followed by a slow rise, which in curve (c) is accelerated in 1779–80; finally, after the interruption of 1781, a strong rise, with the maximum for the whole period in 1788, with an index of 176 in curve (c).

3. During the last decade of the eighteenth century, at least until 1797, the stagnation of income in money corresponds in curves (b) and (c)

Graph 8.8

Regional Conjuncture: Index of Tithes

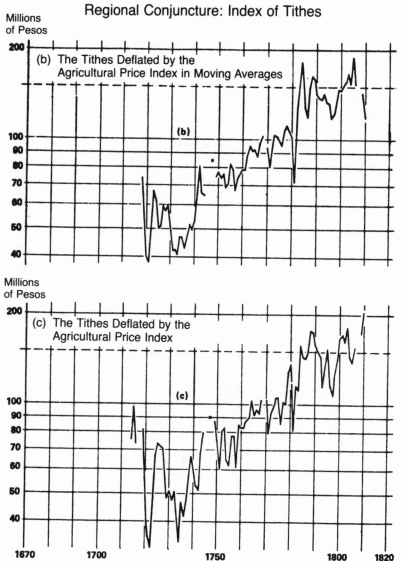

Millions
of Pesos

(b) The Tithes Deflated by the
Agricultural Price Index in Moving Averages

(b)

Millions
of Pesos

(c) The Tithes Deflated by the
Agricultural Price Index

(c)

1670   1700   1750   1800   1820

to a net retrocession. The first years of the nineteenth century attend a new rise, interrupted in curve (c) by the fall of 1805.

If it is admitted that the deflated curves, and most especially curve (c), reflect, at least in an approximate manner, the real movements of production, the chronology of their inflections leads to two observations:

1. If the decline in the first three decades of the century coincides with a succession of meteorological irregularities, similar to that produced after 1790, the inflection on the rise in production after 1734 is shown even while the unfavorable climatic phase, which will be prolonged until 1742 or even 1755, lasts. Let us underscore, then, that the climate in and of itself would not be the determining element.

2. It is seen that the long-term movement of prices does not undergo its downward inflection until after 1758, when production has already been growing for more than two decades. How can we interpret these discordances?

Let us again take up the tithe curves. The increase of income in money after 1734 allows the tithes to recoup their level of the end of the seventeenth century, that is to say, ninety to one hundred thousand pesos, around 1750–54. The corrected curves suggest that that level is already reached in the decade of 1740, but we have seen that in the decade 1750 there is stagnation, if not retrocession. Agricultural production seems, then, to hit its ceiling. Put another way, the growth of production between 1734 and approximately 1747 would correspond to a simple phase of recovery. It would not be until after 1760 that production, on regaining its growth, overtakes the level of the seventeenth century. In curve (c), the years 1714–19 are situated in index 80 around the decade 1760 between 84 and 104, while the years 1788–89 culminate in more than 175. The phase that is extended, approximately, between 1760 and 1790 would correspond, then, to true growth. This would coincide, logically, with the long-term, downward movement in agricultural prices.

Could the three phases of agricultural production during the eighteenth century in turn be explained: fall, recovery, growth? It would be necessary to examine the demographic evidence, insofar as the actual state of our knowledge, although very fragmentary, permits it. If the population of the city of Potosí seems to diminish throughout the century, the central and southern Andes have a different evolution.[53] There is agreement on situating the demographic nadir for the whole colonial era in the period from 1690 to 1730, recording the lowest level after the plague epidemic of 1719–20, which is correlated with the minimum in tithes and, surely, in production. Then, after two centuries of decrease, the demographic conjuncture is inverted. Recovery is shown with variable dates according to regions, but the growth of the population seems general halfway through the eighteenth century and is prolonged until the beginning of the nineteenth century.[54]

Let us recapitulate the hypotheses or questions that we have reached:

1. The fall, and low levels of production, coincide during the first third of the century with a demographic minimum, but prices are at a high level, doubtless in correlation with an unfavorable meteorological phase.

2. The rise in production after 1734 is probably related to the demographic recovery, while prices continue high for at least two reasons: on the one hand, the period continues climatically unfavorable; on the other, the growth in production is limited to a recovery to its level at the end of the seventeenth century.

3. After 1759, agricultural prices enter a long, downward phase lasting thirty years, at the same time that a movement of growth in production is produced, probably favored, besides, by good climactic conditions. Would it be a matter, then, of a period of relative abundance in which the increase in production would have been greater than that of population? We lack adequate data to answer, and it should be taken into account besides that the effects of growth are different according to the social stratum being considered. Let us only remember that during this phase, the prices of quinoa and chuño, the most "indigenous" products of our series, tend to stabilize at the base level.

4. Without a doubt, the rise in prices after 1790 was not solely the result of the reappearance of the drought years. It could be surmised, taking into consideration the observed precedent in the middle of the century, that agricultural production has encountered a new ceiling.

Livestock products

Beef, charqui (dried llama meat), tallow, and cheese, like grains and tubers, were part of the regional market that converges on Potosí. The curves obtained for these products present, nevertheless, less violent oscillations. The distinction of more or less regular cycles does not seem pertinent for this category, for which reason we shall stay with the long-term movements.

Beef prices follow phases analogous to those of agricultural prices, but the levels of the curve, as in comparison with Mexican corn, suggest a different interpretation (compare Table 8.7 and Graph 8.9). The following fluctuations can be distinguished:

1. from 169(8) to 172(1) rapid fall;
2. from 1728 to 1752 more or less regular rise;
3. from 175(4) to 1790 first a brutal rise with respect to the preceding phase, with a lacuna in 1753 that makes a reading difficult; after 1755, stagnation with some depressions, in particular in 1772 and 1780;
4. from 1791 to 1804 a pronounced fall;
5. a clear rise from 1805 on.

As a whole, as for grains and tubers, there is a thirty-year rise from the decade of 1720 on; a greater inflection in 1755, a date close to that of agricultural prices; then stagnation that is prolonged with a fall until 1804. As much as the tracing of the curve, the levels of prices are interesting. Paradoxically, in the case of beef, these last are in disagreement with the long-term movements. From 1721 to 1752, prices are situated, despite the trend, at a relatively low level, average index: 55.6, while from 1754 to 1790, they are maintained at a high level, average index: 103.6. We have seen that during the same chronological phases, despite apparently similar movements, agricultural prices have, in reality, an inverse evolution, first a high level, then a very low level. From this contrast, a question could be raised regarding agricultural growth in the years from 1760 to 1790: might this not have been effected at the expense of livestock? Such a process, classic in European countries, is problematic in the Andean world. Because of the vertical arrangement of agricultural zones at regular intervals, lands for tending animals could serve for the cultivation of corn or wheat only with difficulty. Will there have been less open fallow lands for the herds? More detailed research on this point is also necessary.

Charqui constitutes the product of animal origin whose consumption is most widespread in the indigenous world (compare Table 8.7 and Graph 8.9). Despite the lacunae in the series, an upward phase in the first half of the century, until 1758, can be distinguished, then a decline in the second half. It presents, then, always the same point of inflection, which, logically, for charqui means the same as what the movement from a lower level of prices to another that is higher does for beef. The same movements are present in the cases of tallow and cheese, but with a chronological difference

Table 8.7

Regional Cattle Products

Year	Cheese[1]	Tallow[2]	Charqui[3]	Beef[4]
1676	—	—	—	—
1677	—	—	—	—
1678	—	—	—	—
1679	—	—	—	—
1680	—	—	—	—
1681	—	—	—	—
1682	115	—	—	—
1683	—	—	—	—
1684	—	—	—	—
1685	101	—	—	—
1686	—	—	—	—
1687	—	—	—	—
1688	—	—	—	—
1689	—	—	—	—
1690	—	—	—	—
1691	—	—	—	—
1692	—	—	—	—
1693	—	—	—	—
1694	—	—	—	—
1695	—	—	—	70
1696	—	—	—	76
1697	—	—	—	70
1698	—	—	54	106
1699	—	—	—	—
1700	—	—	—	—
1701	—	—	—	—
1702	—	—	—	—
1703	—	—	—	47
1704	—	—	—	47
1705	—	—	—	47
1706	—	—	—	41
1707	—	—	—	35
1708	—	—	—	—
1709	—	—	—	41
1710	—	—	—	47
1711	—	—	—	—
1712	—	—	—	—

Table 8.7 (continued)

Year	Cheese[1]	Tallow[2]	Charqui[3]	Beef[4]
1713	—	—	—	—
1714	—	—	—	—
1715	—	—	—	—
1716	—	—	—	—
1717	—	—	—	—
1718	—	30	94	—
1719	—	—	—	—
1720	115	—	67	—
1721	—	—	—	—
1722	94	—	—	35
1723	87	—	—	—
1724	—	30	—	—
1725	58	13	—	—
1726	58	—	—	—
1727	58	—	—	—
1728	65	—	—	47
1729	—	—	—	47
1730	—	—	—	59
1731	—	—	—	59
1732	—	—	—	—
1733	—	—	—	—
1734	—	—	—	53
1735	58	—	—	53
1736	—	—	—	61
1737	58	—	—	—
1738	—	60	101	—
1739	58	—	—	—
1740	63	—	88	59
1741	79	60	94	47
1742	72	—	—	59
1743	87	37	—	62
1744	72	—	67	—
1745	58	—	67	—
1746	58	—	—	—
1747	72	47	84	59
1748	51	—	67	—
1749	—	43	—	53
1750	87	38	88	53
1751	72	—	94	62

Table 8.7 (continued)

Year	Cheese[1]	Tallow[2]	Charqui[3]	Beef[4]
1752	58	47	94	59
1753	58	60	—	—
1754	—	—	121	106
1755	89	60	—	117
1756	72	—	108	102
1757	72	—	104	117
1758	—	47	131	115
1759	72	49	108	117
1760	87	47	98	—
1761	—	—	108	—
1762	115	30	108	—
1763	115	—	104	117
1764	58	—	—	—
1765	115	—	108	—
1766	61	—	—	—
1767	72	—	—	—
1768	58	—	—	—
1769	84	—	—	82
1770	72	—	84	94
1771	87	—	175	89
1772	79	—	—	70
1773	87	154	91	117
1774	173	79	94	117
1775	144	96	99	117
1776	—	109	94	108
1777	—	—	81	—
1778	—	85	85	106
1779	58	76	—	76
1780	44	62	—	70
1781	43	81	108	106
1782	87	66	—	82
1783	106	66	101	—
1784	87	98	—	—
1785	87	83	111	—
1786	115	90	—	106
1787	—	88	—	88
1788	108	88	101	127
1789	87	76	94	117
1790	87	65	—	117

Table 8.7 (continued)

Year	Cheese[1]	Tallow[2]	Charqui[3]	Beef[4]
1791	—	85	103	106
1792	87	68	94	111
1793	115	68	162	—
1794	87	60	—	58
1795	87	64	—	82
1796	87	77	88	82
1797	101	79	94	88
1798	87	62	81	82
1799	87	76	—	82
1800	58	77	—	76
1801	101	77	—	78
1802	—	77	—	70
1803	79	68	—	72
1804	76	64	—	68
1805	—	68	—	117
1806	87	51	—	117
1807	36	64	67	117
1808	58	68	—	117
1809	—	79	—	140
1810	—	92	—	140
1811	101	77	—	123
1812	101	105	—	152
1813	101	82	—	155
1814	—	154	—	—
1815	—	128	—	—
1816	—	79	—	—

[1]1770–1779 = 100 = 110.9 reales/unit
[2]1770–1779 = 100 = 187.2 reales/hundredweight
[3]1770–1779 = 100 = 59.4 reales/hundredweight
[4]1770–1779 = 100 = 17 reales/quarter

Graph 8.9

Regional Conjuncture: Beef Products

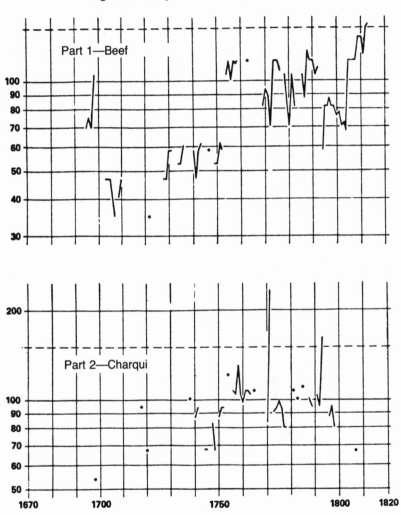

(compare Table 8.7). The downward inflection is produced more belatedly in 1773 and 1774. A rise in the price of tallow is recorded, as in the case of beef, after 1806 and perhaps for cheese after 1807.

THE LOCAL CONJUNCTURE

Finally, a market for local production exists in Potosí, as well as one for services and labor. The prices of such products as bricks, roof tiles, tableware, and even chickens, all show the same characteristic, a single, long, downward movement, more than secular and of very accentuated pitch. Let us simply indicate some statistics (compare Table 8.8):

—bricks: average index for 1676–87: 313.8; for 1770–1814: 97.8; that is to say, a decline of 65 percent;

—tableware: average index for 1677–90: 222; for 1782–1810: 96.3; a decline of 56.6 percent;

—chickens: average index for 1677–86: 160.6; for 1782–1813: 83.9; a decline of 47.7 percent.

We know that the population of Potosí diminishes perceptibly after the middle of the seventeenth century, with more than 150,000 inhabitants around 1650, 70,000 at the beginning of the eighteenth century, and 20,000 in 1779. It then increases to about 40,000 in 1790–1800.[55] The local conjuncture's downward trend results, without a doubt, from the limits imposed by a shrinking market. These also can explain the notably rectilinear character of the curve of wages for unskilled labor, which were maintained without fluctuations at four reales a day, without food, during the whole period. Would stable wages in a conjuncture of depressed prices, at least in the second half of the eighteenth century, have resulted in an improvement in the condition of the workers? Doubt remains, of course, about how the annual total of wages, collected by an individual and, even more, by his family, evolved, while demand for labor was weakened.

CONCLUDING REMARKS

Global evidence is impressive, beyond the analyses or the hypotheses we have been able to propose for a determined category of products: the movement of prices in Potosí during the eighteenth century clearly differs from the general conjuncture in Europe. Ruggiero Romano had insisted, in his articles, on the originality of the South American conjuncture: a fall of 40 to 50 percent from the beginning until the end of the century, stability from

Table 8.8

Local Conjuncture: Prices of Bricks, Tiles, Tableware, Chickens, and
Unskilled Labor in Potosí

	Local Products and Salaries				
Year	Bricks[1]	Tiles[2]	Table-ware[3]	Chickens[4]	Unskilled Wages[5]
1676	277	281	—	—	—
1677	277	—	209	157	150
1678	338	312	254	229	—
1679	—	—	—	114	—
1680	—	312	239	—	—
1681	300	312	179	—	—
1682	—	312	179	143	—
1683	277	281	239	171	—
1684	—	250	239	171	125
1685	246	250	254	157	—
1686	304	344	254	143	—
1687	492	—	187	—	—
1688	—	219	224	—	—
1689	—	—	179	—	—
1690	—	—	251	114	—
1691	—	—	179	114	—
1692	—	—	179	143	—
1693	215	203	179	143	—
1694	—	—	172	143	—
1695	—	—	149	114	—
1696	—	219	149	143	—
1697	—	312	—	—	—
1698	—	312	164	—	—
1699	—	250	149	114	—
1700	—	156	149	114	112
1701	—	180	149	—	112
1702	185	—	149	—	100
1703	—	187	149	120	—
1704	231	—	298	171	—
1705	—	187	119	—	—
1706	—	—	119	143	—
1707	—	—	134	—	100
1708	—	—	164	—	100
1709	—	—	134	—	—
1710	—	—	142	—	—

Table 8.8 (continued)

	Local Products and Salaries				
Year	Bricks[1]	Tiles[2]	Table-ware[3]	Chickens[4]	Unskilled Wages[5]
1711	—	—	134	—	—
1712	—	—	142	—	—
1713	—	—	—	—	—
1714	—	—	119	—	—
1715	—	—	—	—	—
1716	—	—	—	—	100
1717	—	—	119	—	100
1718	—	—	—	—	—
1719	—	—	—	—	—
1720	—	—	149	—	—
1721	—	281	179	—	—
1722	—	—	—	—	—
1723	—	—	134	—	—
1724	—	187	149	—	—
1725	—	—	142	—	—
1726	—	—	134	—	—
1727	—	—	134	—	—
1728	385	—	134	114	100
1729	—	—	—	114	—
1730	—	—	119	—	100
1731	—	—	—	—	—
1732	—	—	—	—	—
1733	—	—	—	—	—
1734	—	156	—	—	—
1735	—	156	—	—	—
1736	—	—	—	114	—
1737	—	—	—	—	—
1738	108	112	119	—	100
1739	108	—	—	—	—
1740	—	125	119	—	—
1741	—	125	82	—	—
1742	—	125	92	—	—
1743	—	102	119	—	—
1744	—	—	—	—	100
1745	—	—	—	86	—
1746	—	—	—	—	—
1747	108	109	119	—	—

Table 8.8 (continued)

	Local Products and Salaries				
Year	Bricks[1]	Tiles[2]	Table-ware[3]	Chickens[4]	Unskilled Wages[5]
1748	—	109	119	—	—
1749	—	—	119	—	—
1750	185	—	119	—	—
1751	—	—	104	—	—
1752	—	—	119	—	—
1753	—	—	119	—	—
1754	—	—	134	—	—
1755	—	—	119	—	—
1756	—	—	100	114	—
1757	138	—	134	114	100
1758	—	—	149	86	100
1759	154	156	—	—	100
1760	138	—	119	—	—
1761	154	156	97	100	100
1762	—	—	119	—	100
1763	—	—	119	—	—
1764	—	—	—	—	—
1765	—	—	179	—	—
1766	—	—	119	—	—
1767	—	—	—	—	—
1768	—	—	—	—	—
1769	—	—	75	—	100
1770	108	125	—	—	—
1771	—	—	—	—	—
1772	92	94	—	—	—
1773	—	—	119	—	—
1774	—	—	90	—	—
1775	—	—	104	—	—
1776	—	94	—	—	100
1777	—	94	119	—	100
1778	—	—	—	—	100
1779	—	94	65	—	—
1780	—	—	83	—	100
1781	—	—	—	—	100
1782	—	—	75	131	—
1783	92	94	—	—	100
1784	—	—	—	86	—

Table 8.8 (continued)

			Local Products and Salaries		
Year	Bricks[1]	Tiles[2]	Table-ware[3]	Chickens[4]	Unskilled Wages[5]
1785	—	—	—	—	—
1786	—	78	—	—	—
1787	—	102	—	86	100
1788	—	—	90	—	100
1789	—	—	90	—	—
1790	123	—	144	—	—
1791	—	—	—	—	100
1792	—	—	90	—	—
1793	92	94	82	—	100
1794	—	94	97	—	100
1795	92	—	90	—	—
1796	—	94	75	86	100
1797	—	94	—	86	—
1798	—	—	90	71	—
1799	—	—	—	86	100
1800	—	—	—	—	—
1801	—	—	—	—	—
1802	—	—	—	—	—
1803	—	—	—	57	—
1804	—	—	—	—	—
1805	—	78	60	—	—
1806	—	94	—	—	100
1807	—	—	—	86	—
1808	—	109	179	69	100
1809	—	109	—	46	—
1810	—	—	90	57	—
1811	—	—	—	—	—
1812	—	94	—	114	131
1813	—	—	—	114	100
1814	—	125	—	—	—
1815	—	—	—	—	—
1816	—	—	—	—	—

[1] 1770–1779 = 100 = 13 reales/hundred
[2] 1770–1779 = 100 = 12.8 reales/hundred
[3] 1770–1779 = 100 = 6.7 reales/dozen
[4] 1770–1779 = 100 = 3.5 reales/whole
[5] 1770–1779 = 100 = 4 reales/day

1765. Our study confirms that interpretation on general lines, although we may suggest nuances or corrections to focus the problem from the strategic point of view that constitutes Potosí. We are confronted, in fact, with various conjunctures, superimposed or even interwoven, which correspond to the different economies whose flows converge on the Upper Peruvian market.

The first level is that characteristic of the oceanic conjuncture: for products imported from Europe, the decline throughout the century is even more accentuated than what Romano suggested. It is precisely after 1765 that the fall is accelerated, particularly during the period of peace in the decades 1780–90, under the effects of Comercio Libre, which multiplies commercial traffic. Nevertheless, our curves curiously show that the price decline provoked by French trade around 1715 is of the same order as the one resulting from Comercio Libre seventy years later.

The second level, characterizing the American conjuncture, presents, in turn, two types of behavior. On the one hand, the textile sector suffers from European competition, with a resulting decline of 30 to 50 percent, with a downward inflection around 1730–40 and, once more in disagreement with Romano, another inflection after 1770. The crisis of the obrajes in their two stages is thus confirmed, as well as the limits of income-yielding capacity that faced the import-substitution projects during the war years at the end of the century. On the other, certain American products suffer because of the relative narrowness of their markets, from which results a tendency toward stagnation of their prices during the whole period. Maté, food oil, wine, and salt belong to that type. With regard to sugar, it had reached relatively remote markets, as, for example, Panama, but competition from Antillean and Brazilian production in those markets reduced it to the level of commercialization of the products we have just mentioned.

The third level is characteristic of the regional conjuncture and is defined by the agricultural and pastoral economy of Charcas. It includes two contrasting periods, separated by an inflection around 1760. Previously, there were high prices and fluctuations, at once widespread and violent; then, prices were much lower and stability greater. The study of the tithes of the Archbishopric of La Plata, or Charcas, permits the establishment of a correlation between the movement of three decades of price decline, 1760–90, and the hypothesis of agricultural growth.

The last level, the local conjuncture, is characterized by opposition between the strong decline of products such as roof tiles or bricks, and the long stagnation of wages.

Do any of these conjunctures perhaps play a preponderant role with respect to the others? It would be hoped that agricultural prices were the ones that, as in other places, fulfilled a central role. Although a generalization of the downward movement after 1760 is seen, it would appear that the diverse economic levels have autonomous features and that other elements enter into play. At least the tone of the whole leaves no room for doubts. The conjunctures that cross in Potosí show a clear downward trend that, particularly during the second half of the eighteenth century, contrast vividly with the European conjuncture. Why these disagreements? The reservations with which we today confront schema of a general type, as that of F. Simiand (Phase A: "progress"; Phase B: "depression") lead to a certain prudence before formulating rigidly comparative conclusions. The quantitative theory that E. Hamilton proposed in his admirable works gives no account of the peculiarities of Potosí. In fact, the Cerro Rico's silver production shows, at least from the decade of 1730, a clear upward trend. The yearly output doubles from 1740 to 1800, thanks to the growing exploitation of the mitayo labor force.[56] Prices then decline during a period of increases in the production of silver. Nevertheless, perhaps the beginning of an answer could be found if the question is posed in a different fashion. Would there perhaps exist a relationship between the conditions of production of the precious metal and the general conjuncture of prices?

Potosí presents itself to us, in fact, as a great mining center in which silver appears as one type of merchandise among so many, with its own price masked behind the official price uniformly fixed by the Spanish crown for all its American possessions. The costs of production of the metal, however, increase in Potosí throughout the century, at the same time as the pure silver content of exploitable mineral diminishes.[57] Those structural difficulties in the mining economy constitute without a doubt a determining element that orients the other products sold in the Potosí market downward. It is informative now to make a comparison with Mexican mining centers, where an inverse process is seen: the production of silver increases during the eighteenth century, with an acceleration in the decade of 1770. Correlatively, the production costs of the metal diminish, while the prices of other types of merchandise show an upward trend.[58] Thus, one feels the temptation to see one of the keys of the problem in the variable characteristics of mining economies. The whole process set a situation of colonial dependence that gives place, in Europe and Andean America, to inverse conjunctures, united by mechanisms that assure the functioning of the system and whose detailed model remains to be constructed.

From that point of view, and by way of conclusion, we propose two hypotheses relative to the problem of indigenous revolts:

1. With respect to the Labroussian interpretation of what happened in 1789 in France, the Andean world shows an analogous situation, which is at the same time paradoxical. The revolts of Tupac Amaru and Tupac Catari exploded after a long period of agricultural growth: in 1781, this had already lasted more than twenty years and would be prolonged for even ten years after the revolts, which, save for local exceptions, do not appear to influence the thirty-year agricultural movement. Will one be able to speak of revolt in the midst of abundance? Not exactly. Let us remember that the curves for the tithes that we have examined above reflect in overwhelming proportion the production of the haciendas, since the Indians escaped payment of the tithe in principle and should not have paid but one-twentieth on products of European origin. In those conditions, growth in hacienda production cannot result, in the absence of better techniques, except from of an extension of surface. This was not necessarily realized in detriment to the indigenous communities, since *tierras baldías* were available then. All in all, it should be noted that in the face of the haciendas' advance, the communities have but limited possibilities of, in turn, extending the areas they have available. One can ask if the part of the Indians in agricultural growth coincides, proportionally, with the rhythm of demographic increase; the movement of thirty years that show the curves of the diezmos, could it correspond, in reality, to a slow restriction of indigenous resources?[59]

2. The curve for agricultural prices shows that the rebellion exploded at the end of a long period of low prices. Upon examining the fluctuations in more detail, it is confirmed that the years 1779–80 correspond very exactly to one of the most profound falls of the century. The general index shows, in fact, a brutal decline at the end of the decade: in 1776, 114; 1777, 104; 1778, 107; 1780, 81; 1790, 76. It is necessary to go back more than sixty years to encounter a level so low in the years 1725–27. We have seen that the indigenous world is confronted with difficulties in two types of situation, both during excessive rises and during the phases of low prices. The years 1759–80 are an example of this last possibility. The Indians encounter an oversupplied market and have difficulties obtaining the money indispensable for paying tribute or payment for forced distributions of goods. One more coincidence? We know that the system of forced distribution of merchandise reaches its apogee in the period extending from 1750 to 1780.[60] Then, will it not be by chance that the rebellion explodes in the moment in which the

crisis reaches, for the Indian world, its sharpest degree? The rebellion would then have a fiscal origin, independently of its other dimensions, ideological or messianic, but with a schema once more paradoxical with respect to the Labroussian interpretation. Since if 1789 corresponded in France to the culmination of prices, 1780 indicates, in the Andes, the second minimum of the century. We find two conjunctures not only different, but also opposed: the Andean world, also in this, shows in some manner the reverse of the European world.

NOTES

This research was partially funded by a grant from the Joint Committee on Latin American Studies of the American Council of Learned Societies and the Social Science Research Council, New York. We thank Father Lorenzo Calzavarini and Professor Mario Chacón for having facilitated our access to the source used and Eduardo Míguez for his help in gathering the data. We should also thank Maurice Aymard, Adolfo Canitrot, Olivia Harris, Herbert Klein, Michel Morineau, and Ruggiero Romano for their comments on earlier versions of this work. One of these was presented in December 1980 during a conference held at the Institute of Latin American Studies of the University of London. Responsibility for the analysis and hypothesis offered rests solely with the authors. A French version of the work was published in *Annales E-S-C* (Paris), 3 (1983), with the title "Conjonctures inverses. Le mouvement des prix a Potosí pendant le xviiie siècle," while a Spanish version was published by Centro de Estudios de Estado y Sociedad (CEDES) (Buenos Aires, 1983).

1. R. Romano, *Una economía colonial: Chile en el siglo xviii (Buenos Aires, 1965)*; R. Romano, "Movimiento de los precios y desarrollo económico: El caso de Sudamérica en el siglo xviii," *Desarrollo Económico* (Buenos Aires), 3 (1963): 31–43; E. Florescano, *Precios del maíz y crisis agrícolas en México (1708–1810)* (Mexico City, 1969); A. Arcondo, "Córdoba. Une ville coloniale. Etude des prix au xviiie siècle" (Ph.D. diss., Paris, 1968).

2. D. A. Brading, *Haciendas and Ranchos in the Mexican Bajío: León, 1700–1860* (Cambridge, 1978). Compare also P. Macera and R. Boccolini, *Precios en Arequipa, 1627–1767* (Lima, 1975); P. Macera and R. Jiménez, *Precios en Lima, 1667–1738* (Lima, 1975); B. Larson, "Rural Rhythms of Class Conflict in Eighteenth-Century Cochabamba," contained herein.

3. All data from the source are expressed in pesos and reales (1 peso = 8 reales), coins that actually circulated in the Spanish possessions in America. Their content in pure silver and weight varied very little throughout the eighteenth century, which

allows us to use nominal prices without any manipulation. All the indices are calculated on the base 1770–79 = 100.

4. J. Savary des Bruslons, *Dictionnaire universel de commerce* . . . , 6th ed. (Geneva-Copenhagen, 1750–65), 3: col. 1162.

5. A. García-Baquero González, *Cádiz y el Atlántico (1717–1778)* (Seville, 1976), 2: graph 14.

6. G. Walker, *Spanish Politics and Imperial Trade, 1700–1789* (London, 1979), passim.

7. García-Baquero, *Cádiz,* 2: graph 13.

8. Walker, *Spanish Politics,* passim.

9. Piña is unminted silver upon which tax owed to the crown has not been paid. B. Arzáns de Orsúa y Vela, *Historia de la Villa Imperial de Potosí,* ed. L. Hanke and G. Mendoza (Providence, Rhode Is., 1965), 3: 55.

10. D. Dahlgren, "L'expedition de Martinet et la fin du commerce français dans la mer du Sud," *Revue de l'Histoire des Colonies Françaises* (Paris), 1 (1913): 315–18.

11. Arzáns de Orsúa y Vela, *Historia,* 3: 71.

12. Arzáns de Orsúa y Vela, *Historia,* 3: 74.

13. Arzáns de Orsúa y Vela, *Historia,* 3: 137.

14. García-Baquero, *Cádiz,* 2: graph 13.

15. García-Baquero, *Cádiz,* 2: graph 14.

16. Arzáns de Orsúa y Vela, *Historia,* 2: 421.

17. García-Baquero, *Cádiz,* 1: 369.

18. Archivo General de Indias, Seville (hereinafter AGI), Charcas 699, Certification of the Administrator of Royal Customs of Potosí, Potosí, 22 Apr. 1802; J. C. Garavaglia, "Comercio colonial: Expansión y crisis," *Historia integral argentina* (Buenos Aires, 1970), 1: table 3, 329.

19. J. Fisher, "Imperial 'Free Trade' and the Hispanic Economy, 1778–1796," *Journal of Latin American Studies* 1 (1981): 21–56.

20. A. García-Baquero González, *Comercio colonial y guerras revolucionarias* (Seville, 1972).

21. C. Labrousse, *Esquisse du mouvement des prix et des revenus en France au xviii͏ͤ siècle* (Paris, 1933), 2: 329.

22. N. Posthumus, *Nederlandsche Prijsgeschiedenis* (Leiden, 1943), 2: 305–307, 761, 763, 765; W. Beveridge, *Prices and Wages in England from the Twelfth to the Nineteenth Century* (London, 1939), 458.

23. Mancera and Jiménez, *Precios en Lima;* Mancera and Boccolini, *Precios en Arequipa.*

24. García-Baquero, *Cádiz,* 1: 312.

25. Macera and Boccolini, *Precios en Arequipa,* 50.

26. Posthumus, *Nederlandsche,* 1: 148–50.

27. Savary des Bruslons, *Dictionnaire,* 1: col. 697.

28. F. Silva Santisteban, *Los obrajes en el Virreinato del Perú* (Lima, 1964), 162.

29. The author cites the French traveler Frézier, who noted in 1713 with regard to Peruvian textile production: "The manufactures of flannel [and] cotton cloth were something of a problem for European commerce"; C. S. Assadourian, "Sobre un elemento de la economía colonial: Producción y circulación de mercancías en el interior de un conjunto regional," *EURE* (Santiago de Chile), 3 (1973): 158.

30. M. Moscoso Sánchez, "Apuntes para la historia de la industria textil en el Cuzco colonial," *Revista Universitaria* (Cuzco), 51-2, 122-5 (1962–63): 84.

31. B. Larson, "Economic Decline and Social Change in an Agrarian Hinterland: Cochabamba (Bolivia) in the Late Colonial Period" (Ph.D. diss., Columbia University, 1978), 222–74.

32. S. Ramírez-Horton, *The Sugar Estates of the Lambayeque Valley, 1670–1800: A Contribution to Peruvian Agrarian History* (Madison, 1974), 28–29.

33. Ramírez-Horton, *Sugar Estates*, 30; J. Polo y La Borda, "La hacienda Pachachaca (segunda mitad del s. xviii)," *Histórica* (Lima), 1 (1977): 240–41; P. Macera, *Las plantaciones azucareras en el Perú, 1821–1875* (Lima, 1974), xvi; G. Tjarks, "Panorama del comercio interno del virreinato del Río de la Plata en sus postrimerías," *Humanidades* (La Plata), 36 (1960): 29–30.

34. Compare the example of the Jesuit haciendas that responded to the decline in the price of sugar with an increase in production throughout the eighteenth century; N. Cushner, *Lords of the Land: Sugar, Wine, and Jesuit Estates of Coastal Peru, 1600–1767* (New York, 1980), 122–23.

35. Ramírez-Horton, *Sugar Estates*, 28–29; Macera and Boccolini, *Precios en Arequipa*, 45; Arcondo, "Córdoba"; Romano, personal communication.

36. Arcondo, "Córdoba"; Romano, personal communication.

37. M. Mörner, *Perfil de la sociedad rural del Cuzco a fines de la colonia* (Lima, 1978); Polo y La Borda, "Hacienda Pachachaca."

38. J. C. Garavaglia, "La production et la commercialisation de la 'yerba maté,' dans l'espace péruvien (xviᵉ–xviiᵉ siècles)" (Thesis, Ecole des Hautes Estudes en Sciences Sociales, Paris, 1979), 278–79.

39. We are grateful for J. C. Garavaglia's personal communication.

40. We have at our disposal more fragmentary data for other varieties of fish, such as corina and other edible, fresh fish, that suggest an analogous evolution, on the one hand, between the prices for corina and conger and, on the other, between those of the spotted dogfish and other edible, fresh fish.

41. Código Carolino, Lib. 3, Tít. 1, Ord, 52 in E. Martiré, *El Código Carolino de Ordenanzas Reales de minas de Potosí y demás provincias del Río de la Plata (1794) de Pedro Vicente Cañete* (Buenos Aires, 1974), 2: 234; also compare with British Library, Add. Mss. 13983, Areche, Potosí, 29 Apr. 1780, f. 95: "[Salt] is apt to be scarce when the Indians dedicate themselves to tasks in the countryside, and for this reason, and the lack of pasture for their mules and sheep, they do not come with it."

42. The following were of particular utility for the working up of that chart. Arzáns de Orsúa y Vela, *Historia;* Biblioteca Nacional de Bolivia (Sucre), Mss. Rück,

"Anales de la Villa Imperial de Potosí, años 1722–1834," 26; J. Lastres, *Historia de la medicina peruana*, vol. 2; *La medicina en el virreinato* (Lima, 1951).

43. Florescano, *Precios del maíz*, 135–39.

44. Florescano, *Precios del maíz*, 174–77; Brading, *Haciendas and Ranchos*, 189ff.

45. J. Meuvret, "Circulation monétaire et utilisation économique de la monnaie dans la France du xviᵉ et du xviiᵉ siècle," in *Etudes d'Histoire moderne et contemporaine* (Paris, 1947), 25–28.

46. J. Murra, *Formaciones económicas y políticas del mundo andino* (Lima, 1975).

47. C. Fonseca Martel, "Sistemas económicos en las comunidades campesinas del Perú" (Ph.D. diss., University of San Marcos, Lima, 1972).

48. Florescano, *Precios del maíz*, 180–82.

49. Observation of the agricultural price index in moving averages of seven years, centered on the fourth year, allows adjustments of that reading: three great, cyclical movements succeed one another from 1716 to 1760–65; then a stable phase extending from 1765 to 1785; followed by a strong fall in price from 1785 to 1789; and finally, a clear rise after 1790.

50. Archivo de la Catedral de Sucre, Sucre, Libros del Cabildo; AGI, Charcas 725.

51. Let us remember that the rate of one-tenth was only applied, in principle, to nonindigenous producers. The Indians, in turn, owed only one-twentieth on products of European origin. The application of those rates was cause for complaints and lawsuits, but it can be conceded that their characteristics did not vary, in practice, during the period studied. The characteristics of its rental justify, as we shall see later, the use of the annual agricultural price index in order to deflate the curve of the tithes.

52. Larson, "Economic Decline," 169–221.

53. Compare N. Sánchez-Albornoz, *La población de América Latina desde los tiempos precolombianos al año 2000* (Madrid, 1973), 125ff.

54. Sánchez-Albornoz, *Población*.

55. D. Santamaría, "Potosí entre la plata y el estaño," *Revista del Instituto Panamericano de Geografía e Historia* (Mexico City, 1973), 99.

56. E. Tandeter, "Forced and Free Labour in Late Colonial Potosí," *Past & Present* 93 (1981): 98–136.

57. E. Tandeter, "La rente comme rapport de production et comme rapport de distribution: Les cas de l'industrie miniere de Potosí, 1750–1826" (Thesis, Ecole des Hautes Etudes en Sciences Sociales, Paris, 1980), 22–24, 257, 359–62.

58. D. A. Brading, *Miners and Merchants in Bourbon Mexico, 1763–1810* (Cambridge, 1971), 157–58; Florescano, *Precios del maíz*, 193–95; R. Garner, "Problemes d'une ville miniere mexicaine a la fin de l'epoque coloniale: Prix et salaires a Zacatecas (1760–1821)," *Cahiers des Amériques latines* 6 (1972): 75–111.

59. It could also be supposed that the increase of revenues for the tithes arose

from abusive collections from the Indians. Despite the fact that these abuses existed, as a certain number of lawsuits proved, they appear to have been limited and do not call into question the hypothesis of agricultural growth.

60. Compare J. Golte, *Repartos y rebeliones: Tupac Amaru y las contradicciones de la economía colonial* (Lima, 1980).

9

RURAL RHYTHMS OF CLASS CONFLICT
IN EIGHTEENTH-CENTURY COCHABAMBA

Brooke Larson

A DECADE AGO, IN THE MIDST OF THE HEATED DEBATE OVER ANDRÉ FRANK'S contribution and his shortcomings in not giving sufficient attention to the internal dynamics of societies,[1] Enrique Florescano quietly published his monograph on maize prices and agricultural crises in eighteenth-century Mexico and discovered the pulse of agrarian life in central Mexico.[2] He drew his inspiration and much of his methodology from the rich, French historiographical tradition in agricultural price history.[3] Perhaps Florescano's most significant contribution, like that of Labroussian history, was to show the social significance of the agricultural cycles and trends that he plotted. As Krzysztof Pomian wrote recently, Ernest Labrousse's study of economic fluctuations was really social history in the best sense of the term.[4] Labrousse used his price and revenue statistics to study the impact of prices and income on people in eighteenth-century France, particularly the peasants and wage workers. Florescano's substantive contribution was of the same order: he studied how the fluctuations of grain prices affected different social groups in Mexico during the eighteenth century. For example, he showed that in regions where transportation was poor, markets extremely narrow, and seasonal price fluctuations relatively sharp, the commercial interests of peasants and landlords were diametrically opposed. Without access to urban markets, hacendados had a vested interest in the extreme vulnerability of the local peasantry and laboring poor to seasonal shortages and high staple prices. Whenever the opportunity arose, landlords used their economic power to inflate local grain prices.[5]

Florescano also studied the social repercussions of cyclical crises in grain production. Analyzing the ways in which subsistence crises ruined livestock; slowed or halted textile production; and resulted in massive starvation, epidemics, banditry, and migration, he uncovered the fragile links between grain production and industry, between wages and maize prices. He verified

Gibson's earlier observation that maize was always "a key statistic in the colonial period—an index to the cost of a whole range of articles" and, we might add, a yardstick against which to measure short-term changes in the relative economic position of the landowning elite and the peasantry.[6]

More recently, D. A. Brading plotted secular movements of grain prices and production in the León region of the Mexican Bajío during most of the eighteenth century. As had Florescano, he drew the conclusion that many landlords managed to prosper at the direct cost of peasant livelihood in years of poor harvest. Brading devoted more attention to the subterranean relations of agricultural production, however, and emphasized the importance of rent income for landlords in the intervals between scarcity, high cereal prices, and high commercial profits.[7] Where mercantile accumulation occurred intermittently, tenancy played an important role in subsidizing hacienda enterprises from one year to the next.

The rural world of eighteenth-century Mexico Florescano and Brading studied was one whose temporal rhythm was marked more by recurrent phenomena than by irreversible events. Unlike Frank and other "dependency theorists,"[8] these historians locate the rhythm of material life in colonial Mexico not so much in the global booms and busts of the world market as in the ebb and flow of agricultural production, in the structural antagonism between small- and large-scale producers, and in the slow deterioration of the economic position of Mexico's peasantry.

Except for Marcello Carmagnani's work on colonial Chile,[9] Florescano's study has no counterpart in Andean historiography. As a step in that direction, I want to offer a microanalysis of the rhythm of grain production and marketing, and its role in defining class relationships, in the Cochabamba region of Upper Peru in the late colonial period. By most contemporary accounts, Cochabamba was one of the most important maize- and wheat-producing regions in the Andes, and like the Bajío for Mexico, Cochabamba was often called the granary of Upper Peru.[10] The province was situated in the broad, mountainous zone, running on a north-south axis, that straddled to the west the altiplano (the mining zone and trade corridor) and to the east the tropical lowlands of the Upper Amazon Basin (Figure 9.1). Although Cochabamba's territory was vast and its terrain as varied as any Andean zone along the eastern slopes of the cordillera, the province was famous for its temperate climate and the warm, moist valleys of Cochabamba, Cliza, and Sacaba, where three-quarters of the population lived and worked in the late eighteenth century.[11] Like most Andean people, Cochabambinos took advantage of extreme ecological diversity to cultivate a wide variety of Andean

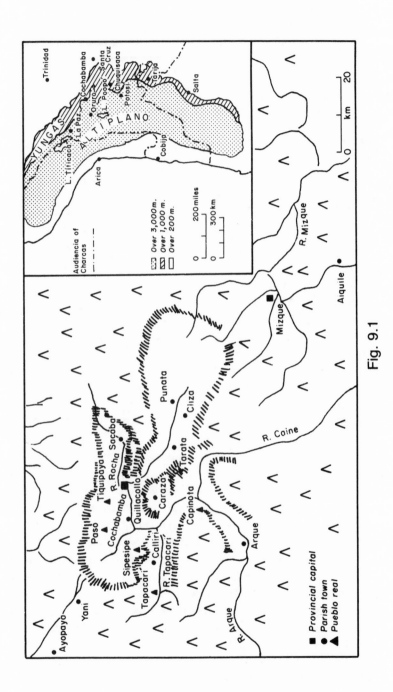

Fig. 9.1

and European crops. Cochabamba's fertile valleys were particularly suitable for planting grains, though, and maize was the region's staple crop under the Incas as well as the Europeans. In the first republican census of 1846, José María Dalence estimated that Cochabambinos cultivated about twice as much maize as wheat.[12] Wheat was the more marketable crop in larger towns, but maize was the principal item of peasant consumption and local exchange. In fact, on many valley haciendas landlords allocated the richest irrigated fields, called *maicas,* for maize seed. Wheat often flourished on patches of dry hillside or bottomland.

In contrast to the western highland provinces of Upper Peru, Cochabamba was a region of many haciendas and a large mestizo population in the late eighteenth century.[13] Five independent peasant villages (*pueblos reales*) still controlled some territory in the Cochabamba and Capinota valleys, but most fertile land in the valleys and river gorges of the province was privately owned. In 1786, about 73 percent of the population classified by colonial authorities as "Indian" lived on haciendas or estancias.[14] While the seigniorial regime was well entrenched in Cochabamba, though, tenants and laborers on estates were fairly mobile geographically. Peasants moved frequently across estate boundaries and between country and town. Not surprisingly, racial and ethnic distinctions had long become blurred. In this respect as in others, agrarian society in Cochabamba resembled more closely the Mexican Bajío than rural life on the nearby altiplano.[15]

Peasant and Landlord competition in the Marketplace

Throughout Cochabamba's central valleys, peasant participation in the staple market was widespread in the eighteenth century.[16] At weekly fairs, peasants congregated before dawn and haggled until well past midday over prices of grains, potatoes, coca, *tocuyo,* and *bayeta* cloths, livestock, tallow, salt, *ají,* and other items. The central market of the region was held on Saturdays on the outskirts of Cochabamba, a town of about 22,300 persons in the late 1780s.[17] Two satellite fairs were held on Sundays in the towns of Quillacollo, a few miles west of Cochabamba, and Cliza, en route to the jungle town of Santa Cruz. To the west of the central valleys, situated in two river valleys that cut and twisted their ways through the mountains to the altiplano, were two other market towns: Arque and Tapacarí. Like the open-air markets in the central valleys, they were held once a week, but as we shall see, these markets took their special character from their proximity to the highlands. All these markets had one trait in common, however. They were basically subsistence markets where many if not most sellers were small-scale producers who turned into petty traders on the appointed market day of the week.

How much of the region's surplus grain did peasant producers actually market after a good or mediocre harvest? Without notarized records of retail transactions that occurred at these fairs, the historian must find circuitous routes to assess the significance of peasant participation in market exchange. From the simple fact that the weekly fairs at Cliza, Quillacollo, and Cochabamba were situated in areas of dense peasant population, we might well assume that these markets were focal points of exchange for this social stratum. Of course, it is also possible that peasants participated in these markets on behalf of their landlords, as porters, servants, and middlemen. If we consider for a moment the pattern of land tenure and labor relations on valley estates, it will be easier to grasp social patterns of local exchange.

Like the Bajío in the same period, Cochabamba had a complex, variegated system of land tenure. Many valley estates were parceled out to small-scale cultivators who paid rent. This is not to say that demesne agriculture was unimportant. The persistence of service tenure (*obligación*) and the onerous requirements of domestic servitude (*pongueaje*) were testimony to the continued importance of production on the demesne for direct appropriation by the landlord.[18] More remarkable, though, at least in comparison to many highland haciendas in neighboring provinces, was the predominance of Indian and mestizo tenants, called *arrenderos* in Cochabamba.[19]

Trial records reveal the importance of tenancy by the amount of rent tenants complained they paid in cash, kind, and/or labor services. Although it was common for peasants to pay only a few pesos a year for access to pastures and the right to collect firewood in the river valleys, there were many other peasants whose tenure required them to provision their landlords with four, five, or more teams of oxen, as well as with laborers, whom they themselves hired.[20] On some estates, service tenure mandated labor recruitment outside the tenant's own household. How many tenants in Cochabamba hired outside laborers (*peones* or *jornaleros*) to provision the demesne is difficult to say precisely. Scattered pieces of evidence, however, leave the impression that many haciendas in the central valleys were populated by customary tenants as well as subletters and squatters who worked for those tenants in one capacity or another. What is more, many tenants also worked separate patches of land under sharecrop arrangements with the landlord. Could it be that in the late eighteenth century some landowners were disposing of pieces of the demesne to peasants already living on their estates? On the one hand, in doing so, they freed themselves of some administrative costs and concerns while still appropriating a share of the harvest each year. On the other, it is conceivable that landlords allowed tenants (who were increasing in number throughout this period) to extend the arable land up scrubby hillsides. Whether sharecropping marked the advance of crop land into scrub or the demise of demesne agriculture, the distinctive feature of land tenure was the proliferation of tenants, sharecroppers, and subtenants who extended their direct control over the region's productive resources. It would follow, then, that in years of good and average harvests, most peasants who engaged in market transactions often did so as independent agents, not merely or exclusively in the service of their landlords.

We might expect that commercial competition from peasant producers would stimulate considerable commentary and complaint by contemporary landowners. This indeed was the case in the late eighteenth century. The cabildo of Cochabamba had never succeeded in establishing municipal controls over the grain market. There was no central grain market (*alhóndiga*) where the state could regulate prices and standardize the weights and measures used in grain transactions. Producers often sold flour directly to bakers. In 1817, the cabildo compiled a list of 450 bread shops that annually purchased between forty and fifty thousand *fanegas* of corn flour.[21] By licensing bakers, the municipal government tried to restrict the number of people selling bread and regulate prices and quality. The minutes of various town-council meetings in the last years of colonial rule are replete with complaints by cabildo members about the anarchic bread market.[22] In particular, they worried about the proliferation of bread sellers who did not belong to the bakers' guild. After harvesting their wheat and maize and turning it into flour, many peasants then procured the necessary firewood and aniseed, baked the dough in their own earthen ovens, and peddled the bread from baskets on the streets of Cochabamba and other towns. According to council members, Cochabamba and other valley towns were ringed with earthen ovens. In 1824, the intendant, Martín Ruiz de Somocurcio, expressed his dissatisfaction with the situation.

Nowhere else in the world are the essentials of life sold without being properly weighed. Only in Cochabamba are the people disposed to accept whatever an old, usurious haggler is willing to give them for their money. The infinite expansion of the guild [of breadmakers] and the fact that most are mestizas and of the most miserable station in life are insuperable obstacles to regulating the sale of this vital necessity.[23]

If the intendant sounded excessively frustrated, he probably expressed the feeling of most government officials who looked back over some forty years of abortive attempts to establish an effective municipal grain market. At least since the arrival of the intendant, Francisco de Viedma, in 1784, intendants had tried to assert government control over retail grain sales and levy a tax of one peso on every fanega of flour purchased by members of the bakers' guide.[24] In the last years of colonial rule, Intendant Ruiz de Somocurcio proposed one final scheme to centralize the local sale of grain, a plan that was clearly in the interests of Cochabamba's largest landowners—some of whom served on the town council.

In 1824, the intendant called for the formation of a joint stock company, a Sociedad de la Panadería Pública, which would monopolize the sale of bread in the city. Ruiz de Somocurcio argued that this course of action would allow the state to raise the needed revenue through levies on the wholesale purchase of flour, while conceding a monopoly on retailing bread to a few of the city's wealthiest vecinos—those who purchased company shares at five hundred pesos each.[25] Although the plan was never implemented (and indeed independence from Spain was soon to come), the proposal itself is interesting. Here was the intendant, a Spaniard eager to raise 50,000 pesos annually from the local population to supply funds to the royal army, who realized that one of the greatest concessions he could make to the wealthier hacendados of Cochabamba was to sanction and protect their monopoly over the local grain trade and wipe out the competition they faced from the petty merchants and producers by dismantling the numerous ovens that ringed the city.[26] By concentrating the bread trade in the hands of wealthy landowners—the shareholders of the company—the intendant was quite willing to squeeze the small-scale grain producers who sold bread directly to the consumer. Indeed, this was the interpretation of several more humanitarian (and antiroyalist?) members of the council. In May 1824, the municipal procurator, who represented the needs and grievances of the community before the cabildo, criticized the Spanish intendant's proposal. Such a monopoly over the bread trade, he argued, would hurt the region's poor farmers—those who were already destitute from the burdens of more than a decade of intermittent warfare. The procurator advocated that "absolute, free trade" be allowed to prevail in the region.[27]

The minutes of the last council meetings in the colonial era, particularly the remarks by Ruiz de Somocurcio, reveal how some council members perceived the decentralized grain market as almost barbaric, one that served the interests of no one, no one, that is, except the "poor farmer." Even those landlords and authorities who were not willing to take such direct action on behalf of their own class interests voiced concern about the limited opportunities for commercial profit, the narrow grain market, and the shortage of specie.

No one articulated these concerns better than the prolific intendant, Francisco de Viedma. Among the new breed of professional administrators sent by the crown to rule the vast Intendancy of Santa Cruz de la Sierra (of which the Cochabamba valleys were the center), Viedma was one of the most energetic, competent, and respected men of his day. Like many other Europeans who arrived in the Andes to take up their new posts, Viedma was struck by the contrast between magnificent, exotic landscape and abundant natural resources and the poverty he saw all around him.[28] His immediate concern, therefore, was not the landlord who felt edged out of the local grain market by peasants. He framed the problem instead in terms of a glutted market; what we would perhaps refer to as a "crisis of overproduction." The symptoms were the same as those in some regional economies in eighteenth-century France: narrow and saturated markets; lack of investment capital and entrepreneurial activity; and above all, a lethargic peasantry.[29] Invoking the image of the habitually idle peasant, entrapped by his own "archaic" forms of behavior, Viedma wrote in 1788:

We must be aware of this overabundance [of grain] in order to be able to find a solution to the problem, for this is the fundamental cause of people's sloth and laziness. As people acquire the means of subsistence so as not to be forced to gaze at the ancient face of hunger, they are content with [the traditional crops like] maize, potatoes and ají . . . as they pass through a languid and licentious life. It would not be so were these fruits scarce. . . .[30]

Thus, the formidable task before him was to stimulate the regional economy. His diagnosis of Cochabamba's economic ills was essentially mercantilist, with a strong physiocratic emphasis on the need to improve agriculture. Specifically, Viedma believed that the prosperity of the region depended on the steady export of cash crops to distant markets where produce could be exchanged for cash. Where else, but the mining towns of the altiplano? With characteristic embellishment, he wrote:

[Cochabamba] is a natural provider for the puna provinces where Nature has been so miserly with her blessings; where a sterile and arid land of bald hills and cold winds hides glittering riches in its veins. If those riches could but be discovered and pulled from the depths of that bleak earth, we would see a renaissance of

prosperity, and Cochabamba would need no other industry than the cultivation
and export of wheat and maize.[31]

His prognosis for the region's growth reflected a pervasive feeling of
nostalgia among the local landed elite for a bygone era of prosperity and
monopoly; for the classic age of silver, when Potosí was the largest and most
thriving silver town in all America. The modest recovery of Potosí since the
middle decades of the eighteenth century apparently had not redounded to
the benefit of Cochabamba's large grain producers. In Viedma's view, the
fundamental cause of the region's sluggish grain trade could be attributed
to the long-term decline of distant mining towns as centers of consumption.
Their atrophy had resulted in a chronic overabundance of traditional foodcrops, depressed grain prices, and worse, and turned a potential yeomanry
into lazy peasants who wasted their time drinking *chicha*.

As we will see shortly, though, for most peasants, prices could hardly
ever be considered depressed. Furthermore, prices oscillated considerably
from year to year. When we analyze Viedma's reports on agricultural conditions, it is important, therefore, to bear in mind his position in local
society and his philosophical point of view. While he and his successors
proposed short-term solutions to the glutted market by trying to regulate
and concentrate exchange, they set their sights on the western horizon of
the altiplano where potential markets might be conquered and, in the opposite direction, on the verdant horizon to the east where new tropical cash
crops might be developed. As individual landlords, though—including Viedma
himself, who settled in the region between 1784 and his death in 1809—
they had to make ends meet each year. In many cases that meant waiting
it out until poor weather forced grain prices up to a level where they could
make substantial profits in the local market and, better yet, in the export
markets of Arque and Tapacarí.

CYCLICAL AND SEASONAL RHYTHMS OF EXCHANGE

Viedma's genuine concern for Cochabamba's "decayed" state of agriculture
and sluggish grain trade led him to undertake a close study of harvest and
market conditions in the province. During his administration, he wrote a
series of reports on weather conditions, harvest yields, and crop prices.[32] On
first reading, these trimester and semiannual reports that span more than
two decades (from 1784 to 1808) reveal that the region suffered prolonged
drought and acute shortages in 1783–84 and 1803–1804. Both crises oc-

curred after two or more years of little rainfall. The earlier subsistence crisis followed closely on the heels of the Tupac Amaru rebellions, and curiously enough, this cyclical downturn coincided with one of Mexico's worst famine crises of the colonial period.[33]

In Cochabamba, however, times were even harder two decades later. The disastrous harvest of 1804 was the nadir of four consecutive years of drought or frost. By 1804, wheat and maize prices had rocketed to unprecedented height, and Viedma's 1805 report reveals the full horror he felt as a witness of the human misery all around him.[34] For the moment, though, our concern is not so much with these unfortunate years that punctuated so dramatically the beginning and the end of the intendant's series of reports. Let us first examine the interim period of relatively mild seasonal fluctuations.

In 1785, the first year for which there exists a complete set of reports, the region's economy was just recovering from four years of poor harvests (the result of insurgency followed by a dry spell). To help matters along, the valley fields were blessed with an early and heavy rainfall, and they nourished rich, abundant crops harvested by peasants in June and July. After the 1785 harvest, foodcrops and seed were abundant, and planting conditions for the following agricultural year looked good (Table 9.1). In the second set of reports, Viedma described the 1786 harvest as mediocre; interestingly, he also reported that after two successive harvests (1785 and 1786) of average to good yields, the local grain market was saturated. Peasants in neighboring highland provinces also enjoyed favorable conditions in those years, and Viedma reported that the Cochabamba valleys exported little grain. Under these circumstances, the region was apparently inundated with grain supplies. Viedma reported that "even Cochabamba's inflated and numerous population would be incapable of consuming all local [foodcrops] over the next two years."[35] The price of grain fell sharply in two years: from fifty-eight reales a fanega of wheat at the end of the crisis year 1784 to a mean unit price of eighteen reales for wheat and maize in 1786.

Did eighteen reales (two and one-quarter pesos) actually represent a "deflated price" for a peasant or day laborer whose daily wage was fixed at two reales? At the going wage, the purchase of one fanega of maize required nine days of labor. If Charles Gibson's estimate of the average yearly consumption of an Indian family in central Mexico may be applied here, then a peasant household consumed between ten and twenty fanegas of maize annually.[36] Assuming eighteen reales a fanega represented an average price in Cochabamba, peasants' staple food (and livestock feed) cost them between twenty-two and one-half and forty-five pesos each year. In total labor time (at the

Table 9.1. Harvest Conditions and Grain Prices, 1784–1808

Year (a)	Months (b)	Wheat (reales per fanega) (c)	Maize (reales per fanega) (d)	Harvest Conditions (Cochabamba Valley) (e)
1784	Sept.–Dec.	58	—	poor harvest; flooding
1785	Jan.–Apr.	32	20	abundant rain followed by dry planting season; rich harvest; abundant wheat from previous harvest, good yield foreseen
1785	May–Aug.	32 29.7	16–20 18	
1785	Sept.–Dec.	25	16	
1786	Jan.–Apr.	14–17	16	beginning of harvest: sufficient grain to supply growing local population for two years; little grain exported; planting late, poor harvest foreseen
1786	May–Aug.	19–20 18.1	16–20 18	
1786	Sept.–Dec.	19–20	20	
1787	Jan.–Apr.	16	20	lack of rain; but previous year's harvest kept most agricultural prices from rising drastically; planting under favorable conditions; good harvest expected for next year
1787	May–Aug.	25 22.3	22 22	
1787	Sept.–Dec.	26	24	
1788	Jan.–Apr.	20	22	too much rain; much maize seed rotted in moist soil
1790	Jan.–Apr.	16	20	little rain; good harvest expected only for irrigated crops; grain supply sufficient for local population because of the abundant grain supplies from past years
1792	Jan.–Apr.	20	24	
1793	July–Dec.	—	—	poor harvest; price level is maintained because of abundant grain stored from past harvests
1794	Jan.–Apr.	12	16	heavy rains; rich harvest
1794	June–Sept.	12	16	
1795	Jan.–Apr.	12	16	abundant harvest
1795	June–Dec.	12	16	
1796	Jan.–June	12	14	good harvest
1797	July–Dec.		28	poor maize harvest; no scarcity because of abundant grain in municipal granary
1798	Jan.–June	12	22	abundant rainfall; rich yields
1799	July–Dec.	28	24	poor harvest, but little scarcity; prices slightly higher than usual
1800	July–Dec.	32	24	serious shortage of water; drought destroyed much of wheat crop
1804	July–Dec.	132	112	two successive years of worst drought in history of Cochabamba; almost all planting lost; severe famine crisis
1806	Jan.–June	40–48	32	poor weather, but prices have declined; good harvest foreseen
1806	July–Dec.	40	32	
1807	July–Dec.	60	28	poor rainfall; planting delayed; poor harvest expected; prices slightly higher
1808	July–Dec.	32	24	hot and dry; planting delayed; poor harvest foreseen

Source: AGN, Sala IX, Intendencia, 5,8,3; 5,8,4; 5,8,5; 5,8,6; 5,8,7; 5,9,1; 5,9,2.

fixed market value) that represented between 90 and 180 days a year. Of course, many peasant families spent much of that time cultivating their own fields for home consumption. Still, the point is that the labor requirement for satisfying subsistence needs in eighteenth-century Cochabamba was formidable—even in times of apparent abundance and deflated prices. Grain prices quoted by Viedma in 1786 were high even compared to average maize prices in the Bajío in the same period. In an "ordinary" year of fairly high prices, Brading writes, maize usually cost about fourteen reales a fanega.[37]

If maize prices were relatively high in 1786, a year of plenty, what happened when the weather turned very bad? In fact, Viedma's last trimester report in 1786 forecast trouble. The rainy season was late and by early 1787, the new crop was already stunted. What is remarkable, however, is that the intendant predicted no serious food shortage in the region. He believed that sufficient grain had been stored from previous harvests to feed the local population adequately, remained confident through the poor harvest of 1787. On 1 September, he reported that much of the crop had died for lack of rainfall, but he considered grain prices (twenty-two reales a fanega of maize) to be relatively unresponsive to the low volume of production that year. The reason, he explained, was the existence of grain reserves people could draw on from previous years.[38] Was he assessing the significance of price oscillations from the peasant and wage laborer's point of view, or from that of landlords finally able to dispose of some of their surpluses?

This seasonal pattern of one or two successive years of ordinary to cornucopian harvests followed by a year of poor weather (extensive flooding, as in 1788 and 1797, or drought, as in 1792 and 1807) occurred with an almost uncanny consistency between 1785 and 1800. Despite the considerable seasonal variation in harvest yields, Viedma never reported serious shortages of wheat and maize. When frost and drought ruined crops (especially in the highlands) in 1792, Viedma assured the Consulado of Buenos Aires that maize was still readily available (at a price of twenty-four reales a fanega). So it was again in 1797, 1799, and 1800. He apparently did not consider prices in those years to be particularly unstable. Furthermore, as we have seen, under favorable harvest conditions, landlords felt themselves to be competing with small-scale producers who provisioned their own households and much of the urban population with foodstuffs. Under these local market conditions, some landlords sought their commercial profits in the export markets of Arque and Tapacarí. In the region's two western ports, grain prices were generally higher and tended to fluctuate more sharply from year to year.

Viedma himself realized that large-scale grain producers depended on the export market for their greatest returns in years of poor harvests. In late 1786, when officials began to fear a poor season was ahead, Viedma commented that the great compensation for drought and frost throughout the highlands was the anticipated return from the export trade.[39] In 1792, he again reported that the deterioration of weather conditions had affected the highlands more seriously than the central valleys, where cultivators could draw on water from reservoirs to irrigate their fields—at least in the early phase of a dry spell.[40] Of course, many highland peasants also had access to irrigated land, especially around Lakes Poopó and Titicaca. Extensive cropland throughout the western zone of the Cochabamba province and in the neighboring provinces of Paria and Sicasica, however, was unirrigated (*temporal*) land, dependent on rainfall alone. Partly as a result of this, food prices in the western markets of Arque and Tapacarí were often several reales higher than in the town of Cochabamba after a poor growing season. It is true that the cost of transporting cereal from the central valleys to those markets accounted for some price inflation. Even so, most landlords who owned mule trains preferred to sell their surpluses at Arque because market conditions were more favorable there than in the central valley towns. It was not only a matter of the vulnerability of highland cultivators to the level of rainfall each year. More important, a few wealthy landlords managed to exercise considerable power over the grain trade at Arque.

In 1787, Viedma remarked upon the ability of large grain sellers to manipulate prices almost at will.[41] Several elements may explain why supply controls were more concentrated in the two western port towns. In the first place, we know from various Consulado reports between 1780 and 1801 that ownership of mule teams was increasingly concentrated during that period.[42] Cochabamba no longer regularly imported mules from Tucumán, Salta, or Córdoba, and the price of pack animals rose steeply in those decades. Most small-scale producers in the central valleys were unable to transport much grain to the western towns. Second, the landlords of the Cliza valley gradually developed a system of grain storage in and around the town of Arque (and probably Tapacarí). The landlords commissioned Indians to store the grain in safe, dry places and to leak supplies to the market at propitious moments.[43] Finally, as we shall see, landlords who farmed the tithe often sold much of the cereal they collected at Arque and Tapacarí, which further concentrated sources of supply.

In years when the grain grade flourished at Arque, this town came alive with highland and valley traders, but Arque never assumed the characteristics of a major market town. With a population of about 5,929 persons in 1788, the town was just a way station along a mountainous trade route,[44] a quiet bend in the river valley where pack drivers carrying European cloth, textiles, and coca from Cuzco, and wines and cottons from coastal Peru might rest and replenish their supplies on their journey to the provincial capital of Cochabamba and points east and south. Only in the months after harvest, particularly in those years of scarce rainfall, did the town swell with people buying, selling, and milling grain.

Who exactly were these people? We might well ask. Viedma himself offers a clue. In 1787 he wrote that "the scarcity of water usually drives many people down from nearby provinces and compels them to purchase provisions necessary for their own subsistence."[45] After the dry spell of 1792, he wrote again that Cochabamba's grain surpluses would supply Indians from Paria and Sicasica provinces.[46] Viedma's statements are corroborated by two independent observations of hacendados. Questioned by a royal mill inspector about their business, both men mentioned the trade they conducted with Indians who came down from the puna to the town of Tapacarí to purchase grain, grind it in the hacendados' mills, and transport it out on the backs of their own llamas.[47] Some of these Indians may have been serving as pack drivers for Spanish merchants or enterprising caciques who provisioned Oruro, Potosí, and other towns with valley produce when highland crops were scarce. Viedma, however, seemed to think that many purchasers were highland cultivators, otherwise fairly self-sufficient, trying to make it through a bad year.

This glimpse of the demand side of the grain market in Arque and Tapacarí in the late eighteenth century raises a series of fascinating questions about land tenure and agricultural rhythms in the highland provinces of central Upper Peru that future ethnohistorical research may help to answer.[48] At this point, we know that the rapidly growing Indian population in Upper Peru in the late eighteenth century and the redoubled efforts of royal administrators to raise tribute income undoubtedly spelled heavier pressure on the productive capacity of most native comunidades.[49] Did the grain trade at Arque and Tapacarí—the points of contact and unequal exchange between the Andean highland *comunidad* and the Spanish valley estate—flourish more than ever before, as those pressures intensified in the last years of colonial rule?

TIMES OF CRISIS, TITHES FOR PROFIT

Landlords in late colonial Cochabamba were quite aware of the seasonal instability of the export market. On the one hand, they knew that frost in

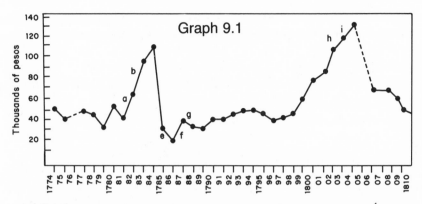

Graph 9.1

*Parishes include those in the districts of Cochabamba proper, Sacaba,Tapacari, Arque, Ayopaya, and Cliza.

the highlands in February or March, for example, would probably ruin some of that year's potato and barley crops and thus stimulate the export trade. On the other, hacendados also knew that two successive years of plentiful rainfall without extensive flooding would result in considerable competition from the peasantry. While weather conditions during planting might indicate much about the coming harvest, however, there was a constellation of forces that determined the actual size and quality of the grain harvests in any given year. It was precisely the export market's vulnerability to weather and harvest conditions and the landowner's inability to always accurately predict the actual harvest yield and market demand that made tithes a speculative venture. Landlords were willing to take the risk, though, and bid against each other for the chance to collect the tithe, because it offered a rare opportunity for potential mercantile accumulation.

Every year, about twenty tithe farmers bid for the right to collect roughly one-tenth of a parish's grain harvest (except in the parishes of the Indian comunidades where they collected somewhat less than a tenth). The movement of tithe revenue over time (which was the fluctuating income the church received) depended on the final auction price of the tithe. The revenue from Cochabamba's parishes that belonged to the Archbishopric of La Plata ranged between twenty-five and forty thousand pesos between the early 1770s and 1809[50] (see Graph 9.1 and the Appendix). In addition, the parishes in the Cliza valley (which belonged to the Bishopric of Santa Cruz) usually produced between ten and twenty-five thousand pesos more. The amount a prospective tithe farmer was willing to bid depended on his expectations of financial gain, and those expectations were influenced to some degree by forecasts of the upcoming harvest. Let us compare the agricultural reports on planting conditions and the seasonal fluctuation of tithe revenue for specific years.

Recall, for a moment, Viedma's earliest and most complete reports of crop conditions in the years 1785–87 (see Table 9.1). In the first agricultural year (1785–86), planting conditions were excellent, following several years of poor harvest. Tithe revenue for 1786 amounted to about twenty-three thousand pesos. Compared to other years, the church fared poorly in 1786. Very little revenue came in from parishes in the Cliza valley. The following agricultural year (1786–87), planting was late because of drought. Viedma predicted a poor harvest in two trimester reports in late 1786 and early 1787. As weather deteriorated, tithes went up. They climbed to some forty-two thousand pesos. The next year (1787–88), cultivators enjoyed good rainfall, and everyone expected an abundant harvest. In 1788, tithe income dipped slightly. Was there, in fact, an inverse correlation between the anticipated volume of grain production and tithe revenue? A cursory look at the tithe curve itself corroborates this hypothesis.

Between 1774 and 1809, tithe revenue peaked sharply twice: around 1783–84 and in 1803–1804. Tithe farmers paid record prices of 114,000 pesos in 1784 and a staggering 122,735 pesos in 1804—precisely at moments of extreme food scarcity and deprivation. At the end of 1804, Viedma wrote vividly and poignantly about the calamity that forced thousands of peasants off their lands in search of food. The other side of the picture, though, one that often eludes the historian, was one in which considerable profits accrued to a few speculators. For them, times were not so bad when they could sell the grain they had stored and/or collected in tithes for as much as 168 reales a fanega of maize (in 1804). Florescano's conclusion that Mexican landlords gained at the direct expense—indeed survival—of peasants during times of crop failure is borne out by the Cochabamba example with horrifying clarity.[51]

It is difficult to imagine at first that in the midst of starvation and misery, tithe farmers still managed to expropriate one-tenth of the meager harvest of peasant households. As always, peasants must have found ways to resist the tithe collector's demands. Many of the beggars who flocked to the soup kitchens opened by Cochabamba's two nunneries in 1804 were undoubtedly peasants who had abandoned their fields to avoid tithe, rent, and tribute exactions, as well as to feed themselves. And surely tithe collectors themselves were not a little nervous about their own safety as they made their rounds, forcing peasants to open their near-empty storage huts and surrender part of the crop. The records left to us belie the notion that tithe collectors faced financial loss during subsistence crises, though. Except for one case, I found no evidence in the notarial and trial records I consulted to suggest that they incurred heavy losses during times of famine.[52] Tithe collectors were known to seize anything of value, though they preferred livestock if they could not find sufficient grain. It is telling, for instance, that members of the cabildo inspected the granaries of many of the region's largest haciendas during the 1784 famine crisis only to discover many landlords hoarding maize and wheat, which they were slowly releasing to the market and exporting to the highlands.[53] Some of that grain was produced on their own demesnes, but part of the surplus was probably tithed grain that some landlords had contracted the right to collect.

What rate of return could tithe speculators expect under such conditions? This leading question needs more investigation before we can answer with certainty or plot the seasonal variation of tithe profits. One unlikely source offers an important clue, however. In 1774, a royal treasury official argued that many tithe farmers managed to avoid paying the 4 percent *alcabala* (later raised to 6 percent) on the value of the tithe. Furthermore, the treasury official proposed that tithe farmers be taxed on the value of the sale of tithed cereal, rather than on the value of the auction price. In the course of his argument, he mentioned the considerable difference between the two amounts.

If the tax were levied on the sale of tithed grain, royal revenue would increase, for the tithe farmer who bids ten thousand pesos for the right to collect the tithe in a parish will often sell the grain he collects for fifteen to sixteen thousand pesos.[54]

A 50 or 60 percent return on tithes was apparently normal in the early 1770s. The significance of the profit rate is all the more striking when we recall that the return on most usurious investment was fixed at 5 percent and that the return on the capital value of most agricultural enterprises in Cochabamba was rarely more than 4 or 5 percent. In fact, this kind of profit was more than an investor could reasonably hope to realize in any other activity in the region, including the long-distance trade in *tocuyo* cloth, which actually flourished only briefly in the late 1790s.

On the basis of my analysis of the structure and rhythm of the grain market in Cochabamba, it is indeed reasonable to suppose that tithe speculators profited most in years of scarcity and a flourishing export trade. Tithe collectors who owned mule trains and granaries in Arque probably captured much of the export market there and managed to manipulate prices to their own advantage. In times of scarcity, Arque was not only a symbol of highland Indians meeting Spanish hacendados in an unequal exchange relationship, it was the point of connection between valley peasants forced to surrender their crops to tithe farmers and highland consumers forced to purchase their subsistence at monopoly prices.

This specter of grasping landlords waiting in the wings for disaster to strike so they could squeeze the peasantry dry must be placed in the context of conjunctural trends and contemporary market mentality. It is important to recall that Viedma and other members of his class perceived themselves to be competing in most years with peasant producers who provisioned their own households and many town dwellers with much of their food. It was not the cyclical crises of 1784 and 1804 as much as the perpetual "crisis of overproduction" that disturbed the landowning class from one year to the next. Their economic behavior in years of natural disaster may be explained simply in terms of their own consciousness of their individual and class interests at a specific historical moment. The structural evolution of local land tenure and marketing relations had produced a large peasant class that undermined the monopoly power of landowners in most years. Furthermore, the reinforcement of colonial constraints on manufacturing and long-distance trade after around 1780 established certain boundaries within which landlords could maneuver on behalf of their own material interests. Nor were Cochabamba's speculating landlords willing to wait until Viedma's dreams of a second age of silver and insatiable consumers at Potosí were realized. As they well knew, their better bet was to mobilize collateral, bid shrewdly, and then bide their time until the towns and markets of Cochabamba swarmed with hungry highland peasants and pack drivers looking for grain to buy. Under these specific circumstances, tithe speculation—perhaps the ultimate form of economic parasitism—represented the most "rational" form of economic behavior on the part of the landed elite.

CONCLUSION

In this discussion, I have taken the viewpoint of the landowners to try to understand why they felt compelled to exploit the tithe, sometimes brutally, for their own commercial advantage. Through their words and actions, many landlords saw tithe speculation as the only alternative to stagnation and the growing competition from market-oriented peasants in the region. Unlike many regions in central Mexico, that competition did not pit indigenous units against a seigniorial regime. In Cochabamba, commercial competition assumed more of a class than a cultural character: small-scale producers confronted their own landlords in the marketplace. Landlord lamentations about a lost age of apparent commercial monopoly, long-distance trade to mining towns, unlimited supplies of specie, and luxury consumption should not, however, be construed as evidence that the balance of class forces had tipped in favor of the peasantry. While the peasantry, as a class, competed effectively with landowners, individual peasant households were subject to the pressures of rapid demographic growth in the central valleys in the late eighteenth century. Peasants found themselves competing with one another more and more for space to plant and space to sell. Furthermore, colonial authorities worried about the floating population that swelled in the last decade of the century. Moreover, renewed royal efforts to impose civil taxes (most especially, tribute) increased the burdens that weighed on most small-scale cultivators. For many peasants, the conjuncture of these trends spelled their gradual pauperization. Consequently, few peasants were able to accumulate enough cash to make the great leap from leaser to independent smallholder. In short, peasant participation in the local market in staple foodstuffs did not signal widespread peasant proprietorship in this region. That was to come a century or so later.[55]

On the other hand, the gulf between peasants and landlords widened in years of poor harvests and narrowed in seasons of abundance. While the decisive commercial advantage might have eluded landowners after mediocre and bountiful harvests, though, the windfall profits accumulated by speculators after extremely poor harvests obviously did not dissipate in good years and "sluggish" trade.[56] The tithe farm was ultimately a mechanism of accumulation of rentier income for the church and mercantile capital for individual speculators. As the key source of accumulation in this regional economy, the tithe served to keep most peasants subordinate—if not always in local exchange relations, then in relation to property ownership. The very activity of tithe investment, however, stimulated some distinct realignments within the landowning class.

Those members of the propertied class who wanted to participate and succeed in the tithe venture had to close ranks and unite. Each year they bid, speculators had to draw on considerable equity in real estate to post the mandatory bond. Like many other landowners in the eighteenth century, Cochabambinos had extensive properties encumbered with accumulated debt. Prospective landlords usually turned to other landowners for help in posting bond. To whom precisely did they turn? To their kinfolk, fictive kin, and in-laws who possessed unencumbered land. The surnames and kinship ties of frequent tithe speculators in the late eighteenth and early nineteenth centuries strongly suggest that members of the wealthiest landed families tended to trade places from year to year as speculators and bondsmen.[57] Those who played the tithe game (generally at least forty individuals each year) belonged to a fairly exclusive club. The entry requirements were the usual ones: property assets and good connections. If the nature of this enterprise had a discernable effect on the social hierarchy, it was to sharpen the differences within the landowning class between the small, interlocking elite of speculators and the pensioners—downwardly mobile landowners who lived almost exclusively off rent.

As historians engage in systematic comparative analysis in the future, we shall probably discover that competition and struggle between peasant producers and landowners was the driving motif of many regional economies in eighteenth century Spanish America. In Cochabamba and the Mexican Bajío, for example, the proliferation of small-scale agricultural producers with surplus staples to sell motivated landlords to undercut peasant commercial competition in various ways. Florescano argued that in some areas of central Mexico, hacendados retrenched by cutting back production and selling off parcels of land. In the short run, those landlords circumvented peasant competition simply by storing grain and artificially inflating prices.[58] As we have seen, Cochabamba's landlords also tried to turn economic fluctuations to their own advantage. Hoarding their own yields, however, was ineffective, since landlords already leased most their estate land and eviction of their tenants would not have helped them capture much more of the local market. Tithes, on the other hand, at once allowed them to expropriate grain directly from their competitors and capture some of the export trade. As did many landlords in the Bajío, Cochabamba's landlords depended on rent to tide them over in years when grain prices were relatively low. Whether landlords tried to manipulate the market by hoarding their own grain or by farming the tithe, they responded to peasant competition essentially in the distributive realm.

These were by no means universal or logical responses, however. In the León region of the Bajío, many landlords met the challenge of small-scale producers by "rationalizing" their productive enterprises. In many cases, landlords invested in the construction of irrigation works and converted dry maize land into irrigated wheat fields. Some of these landowners recruited sharecroppers to work seasonally on the wheat lands by allowing them to farm parcels of marginal land on the haciendas. In turning from the production of maize to wheat (primarily a European item of consumption), León's hacendados avoided direct competition with small-scale maize cultivators and at the same time opened up possibilities for long-distance trade with towns and cities.

It was this possibility of reaching new urban markets in the Bajío that may explain why León landlords confronted peasant competition by altering the basic structure of production, while Cochabamba's landowners responded retrogressively to peasant production and exchange. The León elite ultimately did not have to depend on the vicissitudes of the harvest cycle to generate demand for their surpluses. The rapidly growing urban markets in food crops throughout the Bajío area beckoned. The focal point of that demand was Guanajuato, which had long outpaced Potosí as the leading mineral producer in the Americas. Of course, many large landowners in León did not seize the opportunities for commercial gain in those markets. Instead, they became simple rentiers, abandoning all production to small-scale tenant cultivators. Brading's study, however, illuminates a small stratum of "energetic entrepreneurs" who struck out to capture part of the urban market in foodstuffs by transforming their estates "through extensive capital investment."[59]

In Cochabamba, the elite had no such option. As Viedma pointed out, no landlord could reasonably hope to recover investments in agricultural improvements or even cover transport costs by regularly exporting grains to Potosí. Without the commercial opportunities that León's landlords enjoyed—stifled in their few attempts to introduce cash crops in eastern Cochabamba—the landed elite looked upon land not so much as a factor of production in a dynamic enterprise as a source of rent, collateral, and essentially free (that is, unremunerated) labor. They had little incentive to improve their properties, increase productivity, or alter land tenure and labor relations. Furthermore, the elite was beginning to appreciate the possibility of exploiting the highland market in years of dearth. The very existence of that market demand from highland peasants was the legacy of more than two centuries of colonial exploitation in the form of mita, tribute, and the enforced distribution of merchandise. In the late colonial period, Cochabamba's largest landlords, beset by local peasant competition, turned the destructuration of Andean highland villages to their own commercial advantage.

Appendix

Church Tithe Income From Cochabamba's Parishes, 1765–1810[a]

	1765	1774	1776	1778	1779	1780	1781	1782	1783	1784	
Archbishopric of Charcas											
Cochabamba	2,500	2,350	2,400	3,300	2,575	2,630	3,200	3,050	5,525	5,500	7,500
Sacaba	2,800	5,090	4,240	4,070	3,970		4,200	4,200	5,300	8,175	10,525
Choquecamata				80	130	92	185	200	150	450	
SUBTOTAL				4,150	4,100	92	4,385	4,400	5,450	8,625	10,525
Tapacarí	1,000	1,600	1,320	2,290	2,125	2,355	3,000	800	2,000	3,750	4,125
Calliri					3,608	3,130	4,043	3,310	4,600		8,588
Sipesipe	700	2,250	1,337	2,000	1,400	1,600	1,950	1,200	3,800	4,650	4,550
Quillacollo	1,550	3,700	1,925	3,150	3,075	2,210	3,125	3,000	5,200	7,350	
Paso	600	1,200		80		900	785	550	2,250	1,300	1,750
Tiquipaya	1,000	1,000	1,000		1,674	1,300	2,000	1,100	782	4,300	4,500
SUBTOTAL		9,750	5,582	7,520	11,882	11,495	14,903	9,960	18,632	21,350	23,513
Arque	3,400	5,100	4,400	5,040	4,900	4,705	5,262	3,985	6,620	8,225	12,250
Colcha	1,575	2,000	1,350	1,970	1,600	1,425	1,767	450		2,260	3,000
Capinota	850	1,409	1,600	1,125	1,674	1,617	1,664	1,350	2,660		3,500
Carasa	3,700	7,350	6,600	2,875	2,500	3,800	3,150	5,120	5,750	8,900	
SUBTOTAL		15,959	13,702	14,735	11,049	10,247	12,493	8,935	14,400	16,235	27,650
Ayopaya											
Yani		1,300	2,000		900	379	400	530	850	2,880	4,500
Palca							625				
Machacamarca							740				
Charapaya		1,100		1,225	950	1,270	649		111	100	1,172
SUBTOTAL		2,400	2,000	1,225	1,850	1,649	2,414	530	961	2,980	5,672
SUBTOTAL	19,675	35,449	27,924	30,930	31,456	26,113	37,395	26,875	44,968	54,690	74,860

Bishopric of Santa Cruz											
Mizque		1,350	1,400	1,892	1,750	1,300	525	1,750	2,400	1,500	3,630
Totora											
Pocona											
Tintin		2,200	500	1,800	2,500	2,300	2,370	2,050	4,300	3,950	6,300
Ayquile		340	2,205	3,200	2,310	2,757	2,700		3,465	5,670	125
Chalguani, Pasorapa			150		675	400	719		100	970	15,725
SUBTOTAL		3,890	2,050	5,897	8,125	6,310	6,371	6,500	6,800	9,885	15,725
Cliza											
Tarata		9,500	7,500	10,860	7,800		9,500	8,720	11,550	16,600	17,500
Paredón											
Punata		7,200	6,678	7,800	7,074	6,820	7,550	7,334	12,550	16,500	14,412
Arani		2,500	2,250	2,403	2,700	2,835	3,300	2,550	782	6,500	6,982
Veintena of Tarata and Paredón										5,900	
SUBTOTAL		19,200	16,428	21,063	17,574	9,655	20,350	18,604	24,882	45,500	38,894
Valle Grande		2,760	2,000	2,485	2,050	1,950	3,150	3,300	4,600	4,000	4,420
Chilon											
Samaipata											
SUBTOTAL		2,760	2,000	2,485	2,050	1,950	3,150	3,300	4,600	4,000	4,420
Yuracarees	—	—	—	—	—	—	—	—	—	—	—
SUBTOTAL	26,968	25,850	20,478	29,445	27,749	17,915	29,871	28,404	36,282	59,385	59,039
TOTAL	46,643	61,299	48,402	60,375	59,205	44,028	67,266	55,279	81,250	114,075	133,899

[a]Figure 3 illustrating the movement of church tithe income from Cochabamba between 1774 and 1810 was compiled from the tithes generated by the *partidos* of Cochabamba or the Cercado, Sacaba, Tapacari, Arque, Ayopaya, and Cliza. The latter was part of the Bishopric of Santa Cruz. I excluded tithe income generated by the partidos of Mizque, Valle Grande, and Santa Cruz, which are outside the region of study.

	1785	1786	1787	1788	1789	1790	1791	1792	1793	1794	1795
Archbishopric of Charcas											
Cochabamba	—	1,900	3,300	3,500	4,375	4,600	3,000	3,705	2,900	3,040	3,315
Sacaba	4,550	2,550	3,825	3,715	3,715	4,300	4,200	4,485	5,310	5,200	3,880
Choquecamata		200	—		40		100	150	85	150	90
SUBTOTAL	4,550	2,750	3,825	3,715	3,755	4,300	4,300	4,635	5,395	5,350	3,970
Tapacari	4,000	500	662		1,425	1,600	1,200	1,904	5,500	2,000	1,800
Calliri	1,710	1,500	2,750	2,500		2,300	2,100	2,299	2,875	2,705	2,135
Sipesipe	487	1,200	1,700	1,700	1,500	1,200	1,300	2,000	2,100	2,155	1,655
Quillacollo	500	1,900	3,925		2,500	3,200	2,555	3,225	2,100	2,270	1,905
Paso		400	400	400		350	450	600	505	650	455
Tiquipaya	1,416	1,000	1,000	1,281	1,200	1,500		1,500	1,100	1,500	1,450
SUBTOTAL	8,113	6,500	10,437	5,881	6,725	10,150	7,605	11,528	14,180	11,280	9,400
Arque	4,100	2,500	3,950	5,187	3,850	3,630	3,000	3,105	2,810	3,727	3,731
Colcha	2,250	1,575	1,400	2,700		2,043	1,500	1,400	1,800	2,250	2,310
Capinota	1,610	1,365		1,550	1,100	950	850	825	1,100	1,120	1,000
Carasa	3,000	2,500	2,200	2,000		2,700	2,446	2,000		3,100	2,900
SUBTOTAL	10,960	7,940	7,550	11,437	4,950	9,323	7,796	7,330	5,710	10,197	9,41
Ayopaya											
Yani	1,610	1,150	688				1,150			1,100	1,000
Palca	1,025		700		850		1,005	1,000	2,825	950	924
Machacamarca	360		200	250	250		500	1,805		670	924
Charapaya			400	565	300		410			775	885
SUBTOTAL	2,995	1,150	1,988	815	1,400		3,065	2,805	2,825	3,495	3,733
SUBTOTAL	26,618	20,240	27,100	25,348	21,205	28,373	25,766	30,003	31,010	33,362	30,359

Bishopric of Santa Cruz											
Mizque	950		1,819	1,900	1,205	1,450	1,600	2,250	1,250	1,120	800
Totora	2,575		1,700	2,055		1,550	1,650	2,000	1,495	1,400	1,660
Pocona	1,450		1,315	1,320	1,190	1,650	3,200	1,300	1,620	1,325	1,380
Tintin			2,470	2,915	3,310	3,190	1,600	2,100	2,771	2,200	1,897
Ayquile	2,800	2,730	2,060		1,785	1,925	1,400	1,850	1,400	1,700	2,225
Chalguani, Pasorapa			2,050			2,125		480	2,030	1,925	1,830
SUBTOTAL	7,750	2,730	11,414	8,190	7,490	11,890	9,450	9,980	10,566	9,670	9,792
Cliza											
Tarata	6,510		12,775	3,150	6,195	8,360	10,120	7,100	7,700	6,525	6,615
Paredón	4,550			2,050		1,750	2,350	2,600	2,400	1,500	2,530
Punata				4,360	4,340	3,500	4,000	4,500	4,620	3,450	4,350
Arani			3,370	4,155	3,690	4,000	3,350	3,730	4,175	4,700	3,370
Veintena of Tarata and Paredón					2,860			2,900	2,750	2,775	3,300
SUBTOTAL	11,060	7,125	16,145	13,715	17,085	17,610	19,820	20,830	21,645	18,950	20,165
Valle Grande	5,200	2,940	2,630	1,900	2,930	1,640	2,400	1,700	1,600	2,035	2,539
Chilon		1,650	1,850		1,800	690	1,100	700	1,200	900	1,315
Samaipata		1,150	920		850		510	800	517	690	924
SUBTOTAL	5,200	5,740	5,400	1,900	5,580	2,330	4,010	3,200	3,317	3,625	4,778
Yuracarees	—	—	—	—	—	—	—	—	—	—	—
SUBTOTAL	24,010	15,595	32,959	23,805	30,155	31,830	33,280	34,010	35,528	32,245	34,735
TOTAL	50,628	35,835	60,059	49,153	51,360	60,203	59,046	64,013	66,538	35,607	65,094

	1796	1797	1798	1799ᵇ	1800	1801	1802	1803	1804	1806	1807	1808	1809	1810
Archbishopric of Charcas														
Cochabamba	3,150	3,350	3,800							4,200	4,550	4,605	3,380	2,600
Sacaba	4,966	4,025	4,620							5,540	7,418	7,100	5,560	4,883
Choquecamata	200	130	200							504	710	200	180	205
SUBTOTAL	5,166	4,155	4,820							5,945	8,128	7,300	5,740	5,088
Tapacari	2,020	1,400	1,550						2,100	4,160	2,100	3,800	3,000	2,000
Calliri	1,550	1,400	2,350							2,300	1,700	2,100	1,550	
Sipesipe	1,750	1,761	1,900						3,005	2,120	2,000	2,000	1,240	
Quillacollo	2,000	2,580	2,750						4,200	3,200	2,200	2,100	1,810	
Paso	400	430	435						705	605	810	550	470	
Tiquipaya	1,200	1,000	1,075						2,100	2,030	1,600	1,513	900	
SUBTOTAL	8,920	8,571	10,060						16,270	12,355	12,110	11,263	7,970	
Arque	3,100	3,050	3,355						5,150	5,030	5,300	3,800	2,805	
Colcha	2,500	1,790	1,825						2,820	2,040	1,700	2,861	2,760	
Capinota	800	1,000	1,050						—	1,500	1,100	965	866	
Carasa	2,800	2,887	3,550						3,705	3,100	2,555	2,550	2,200	
SUBTOTAL	9,200	8,727	9,780						11,675	11,670	10,655	10,176	8,631	
Ayopaya														
Yani	1,100	800	825						2,160	2,350	2,225	1,600	1,000	
Palca	655	750	650						2,100	2,875	3,200	1,900	775	
Machacamarca	600	650	625						1,160	1,000	1,520	1,000	250	
Charapaya	700	600	465						2,200	1,500	1,725	1,150	400	
SUBTOTAL	3,055	2,800	2,565						8,070	7,725	8,670	5,650	2,425	
SUBTOTAL	29,491	27,607	31,025	36,422	42,335	46,057	71,177	80,455	84,685	46,160	44,428	43,340	36,209	26,714

Bishopric of Santa Cruz

	1	2	3	4	5	6	7	8	9	10	11	12	13	14
Mizque	1,440	1,400	1,470	605	1,250	935	975	650						
Totora	1,250	1,760	1,525	2,840	2,200	2,725	2,200	1,900						
Pocona	1,417	1,115	1,390	805	1,035	1,510	1,340	700						
Tintin	2,600	2,300	2,700	4,000	3,730	4,500	2,900	2,750						
Ayquile	1,700	1,155	2,194	2,410	2,340	2,600	1,900	1,785						
Chalguani, Pasorapa	1,610	1,190	1,005	2,125	3,000	2,700	1,710	2,310						
SUBTOTAL	10,017	8,920	10,284	12,785	13,555	14,970	11,025	10,905						
Cliza														
Tarata	6,500	7,455	8,400	7,500	11,960	8,000	9,175	6,075						
Paredón	1,850	2,500	1,700	5,260	4,000	2,900	3,200	2,225						
Punata	2,940	3,075	3,800	5,800	3,800	4,500	3,995	2,149						
Arani	2,602	2,650	2,700	3,800	4,100	4,510	3,300	2,425						
Veintena of Tarata and Paredón	2,900	3,900	3,200	1,862	2,620	3,240	3,100	3,825						
SUBTOTAL	16,792	19,580	19,800	24,222	26,480	23,150	22,770	16,699						
Valle Grande														
Valle Grande	2,250	2,500	2,650	4,000	3,200	2,500	3,110							
Chilon	1,250	1,100	1,400	2,310	2,050	1,300	1,390							
Samaipata	905	900	1,075	1,685	1,675	1,760	2,223							
SUBTOTAL	4,405	4,500	5,125	7,995	6,925	5,560	6,723							
Yuracarees	—	—	—		50	25	120	183	355					
SUBTOTAL	31,214	33,000	35,209	40,965	48,215	51,122	65,593	72,516	74,710	45,052	47,680	45,165	39,538	33,872
TOTAL	60,705	60,607	66,234	77,387	90,550	97,179	136,770	152,971	159,395	92,108	88,505	75,747	60,586	

[b] For the years 1799–1804, I found only sums of tithe revenue remitted from Cochabamba's parishes in the Archbishopric of Charcas and the Bishopric of Santa Cruz. Fortunately, two years of that series (1797 and 1798) overlapped with data from other records that gave a parish-by-parish account of tithe returns. The sums of both records were fairly consistent for those years. Royal treasury books recorded tithe income of 60,607 pesos and 66,234 pesos for 1797 and 1798, respectively. The church documents' estimates of total tithe income in 1797 and 1798 were 61,598 pesos and 66,884 pesos, respectively. This two-year cross-check suggests strongly that the gross estimates of tithe income for the years 1799–1804 (for which there are no extant royal account records of tithes) recorded in the church documents are reasonably accurate. To estimate the total tithe income from the Province of Cochabamba between 1799 and 1804, I calculated the percentage of gross tithe revenue that Mizque, Valle Grande, and Santa Cruz proper generally contributed and subtracted that percentage (about 23 percent) from the total tithe income.

Sources: 1774–75: AHMC, leg. 1392, ff. 636–681; 1777–78: AGN, Sala XIII, 5, 2, 6, leg. 2; 1779–80: 5, 3, 1, leg. 3; 1781: 5, 3, 2, leg. 4; 1782: 5, 3, 3, leg. 218; 1784: 5, 3, 3, leg. 5; 1785: 5, 3, 4, leg. 6; 1786–87: 27, 2, 3, leg. 225; 1787–89: 27, 2, 4, leg. 226; 1790: 5, 4, 4, leg. 12; 1791: 27, 3, 2, leg. 229; 1792: 5, 4, 6, leg. 14; 1793: 27, 3, 3, leg. 230; 1794: 5, 5, 1, leg. 16; 1795: 5, 5, 2, leg. 17; 1796: 5, 5, 3, leg. 18; 1797: 5, 5, 4, leg. 20; 1799–1804: RAH, MI, ML, 9/1725, 1807; 1806–10: ANB, MI, Tomo, 2, 6 Apr. 1825.

NOTES

1. See A. Frank, *Capitalism and Underdevelopment in Latin America* (New York, 1967).

2. E. Florescano, *Precios del maíz y crisis agrícolas en Mexico, 1708–1810* (Mexico City, 1969).

3. Some classics well known to many colonial Latin Americanists include: E. Labrousse, *Esquisse du mouvement des prix et des revenues en France au xviii^e siecle* (Paris, 1932); a condensation of this work and another volume by Labrousse has been published in Spanish: *Fluctuaciones económicas e historia social* (Madrid, 1962); J. Meuvret, *Etudes d'histoire economique* (Paris, 1971); F. Braudel and F. Spooner, "Prices in Europe from 1450 to 1750," in *Cambridge Economic History of Europe* (Cambridge, 1967), vol. 4. See also, W. Kula, *An Economic Theory of the Feudal System* (London, 1976).

As had Labrousse before him, Florescano conceptualized historical time as multiple periodicities. He emphasized two levels of recurrent movement, one seasonal and the other cyclical. The first represented year-to-year fluctuations in agricultural prices and production, while the second, cyclical movement marked severe agricultural crises that occurred at intervals of between ten and twenty years. Florescano also distinguished the secular trend that intersected cyclical oscillations and seasonal variations. On this level, he was concerned not only with long-term price and demographic trends, but also with the slow, conjunctural motion of institutions and structures.

4. K. Pomian, "The Secular Evolution of the Concept of Cycles," *Review* 2 (1979): 563–646.

5. Florescano, *Precios de maíz,* 88 and 184 and *passim.*

6. C. Gibson, *The Aztecs Under Spanish Rule* (Sanford, 1964), 311; Florescano, *Precios de maíz,* 141ff.

7. D. Brading, *Haciendas and Ranchos in the Mexican Bajío, León 1700–1860* (Cambridge, 1978), 11 and 103. An early study of price movements in colonial Mexico is W. Borah and S. Cook, "Price Trends of Some Basic Commodities in Central Mexico, 1531–1570," *Ibero-Americana* 40 (Berkeley 1958).

8. See A. Frank's recent book, *Mexican Agriculture, 1521–1630* (Cambridge, 1979).

9. M. Carmagnani, *Les Mecanismes de la Vie Economique dans une Societé Coloniale. Le Chilé 1680–1830* (Paris, 1973).

10. See, for example, A. Vázquez de Espinosa, "Compendio y descripción de las Indias Occidentales," in *Biblioteca de Autores Españoles* (Madrid, 1969), 231: 410.

11. In 1788, the region's population was about 125,245, about half of whom were registered as Indians. The manuscript of Francisco de Viedma's 1788 census is in the Archivo General de la Nación (hereinafter AGN), Buenos Aires, Sala IX, Intendencia, leg. 5.8.5. The census was published (with several errors) in F. de

Viedma, *Descripción geográfica y estadística de la Intendencia de Santa Cruz de la Sierra* (Cochabamba, 1969).

12. J. Dalence, *Bosquejo estadístico de Bolivia* (Chuquisaca, 1851), 269.

13. E. Grieshaber compares hacienda-village relations in the highlands and valleys of Upper Peru in his unpublished study, "The Survival of Indian Communities in Nineteenth Century Bolivia" (Ph.D. diss., University of North Carolina, 1977).

14. AGN, Sala XIII, Padrones, 18.2.1, leg. 46 and 18.2.2, leg. 47.

15. In 1788, mestizos and cholos numbered 42,054, more than one-third the total population in the province. AGN, Sala IX, Intendencia, leg. 5.8.5. The Bajío's predominantly mestizo population is discussed by D. Brading, *Miners and Merchants in Bourbon Mexico 1763–1810* (Cambridge, 1971), 227ff.

16. For a fascinating account of commercial competition between peasants and landowners in Cochabamba around 1914, see A. Pearse, "Peasants and Revolution: The Case of Bolivia," *Economy and Society* 1 (1972): 403–404.

17. Viedma, *Descripción geográfica*, 46.

18. For more discussion of social productive relations, see my unpublished study, "Economic Decline and Social Change in an Agrarian Hinterland: Cochabamba in the Late Colonial Period" (Ph.D. diss., Columbia University, 1978), chap. 2.

19. Inventories of haciendas sometimes reveal what part of an estate's lands was allocated to a tenantry. The 1784 inventory of one hacienda in the river valley of Calliri, for example, showed that tenants leased more than 40 percent of the estate's land. Other inventories indicate that this hacienda was not atypical. Tasación de la haz.[da] Aramasi, Calliri, 1784. Archivo Histórico Municipal de Cochabamba (here-inafter AHMC), leg. 1066 (uncatalogued and without foliation).

20. Exp. del Yndígena Esteban Pablo contra su patrón . . . , 1795, AHMC, leg. 1273 (uncatalogued and without foliation).

21. "Informe . . . sobre la contribución de harinas . . . ," 1 Dec. 1817 in *Digesto de Ordenanzas, Reglamentos, Acuerdos, Decretos de la Municipalidad de Cochabamba* (Cochabamba 1900), 3: 242–47. A fanega was equivalent to about 1.6 bushels.

22. As far as I know, most of the cabildo records are missing. Some of the minutes of the council meetings fortunately have been published in the *Digesto* cited above. Although spotty, these records span the years between 1617 and 1899.

23. *Digesto*, 272.

24. *Digesto*, 197ff., and Viedma, *Descripción geográfica*, pp. 47–48.

25. *Digesto*, 272–80.

26. *Digesto*, 272.

27. *Digesto*, 283.

28. Viedma, *Descripción geográfica*, 159ff.

29. Viedma, *Descripción geográfica*, 137; T. Haenke, "Memoria sobre el cultivo de algodón . . . ," *Telégrafo mercantil*, Buenos Aires, 2 (1801), 289–95.

30. Viedma, *Descripción geográfica*, 160.

31. Viedma, *Descripción geográfica*, 164–65.

32. These reports on the "scarcity or abundance of fruits" were written in accord with the instructions to intendants as stated in Article 67 of the *Real Ordenanza para el establecimiento e instrucción de intendentes . . . en el virreinato de Buenos Aires,* 28 Jan. 1782. The reports are summarized very schematically in Table 1.

33. Brading, *Haciendas and Ranchos,* 189–92; Florescano, *Precios de maíz,* 174ff.

34. Viedma to Consulado, Buenos Aires, AGN, Sala XIII, Cajas reales, leg. 5.8.7, 13 Jan. 1805.

35. Viedma to Consulado, 6 Sept. 1786, AGN, Sala IX, Intendencia, leg. 5.8.3.

36. Gibson, *The Aztecs, 311; see also* Brading, *Haciendas and Ranchos,* 184.

37. Brading, *ibid.*

38. Viedma to Consulado, 1 Sept. 1787 and 31 Dec. 1787, AGN, Sala IX, Intendencia, leg. 5.8.4.

39. Viedma to Consulado, 3 Jan. 1787, AGN, Sala IX, Intendencia, leg. 5.8.3.

40. Viedma to Consulado, 30 Apr. 1792, AGN, Sala IX, Intendencia, leg. 5.8.5.

41. Viedma to Consulado, 1 May, 1 Sept., and 1 Dec. 1787, AGN, Sala IX, Intendencia, leg. 5.8.4.

42. Various reports on the problem of mule transportation are found in the AGN, Sala IX, Consulado, leg. 4.6.4, XIV. See also N. Sánchez Albornoz, "La saca de mulas de Salta al Perú, 1778–1808." *Anuario del Instituto de Investigaciones históricas* (Rosario), 8 (1965): 261–312.

43. The testimony of an Indian accused of stealing grain offers information about native middlemen in Arque who managed the storage and retailing of grain for large landlords from the Cliza valley. Apelación del López Roque, 1759, Archivo Nacional de Bolivia, Sucre, exp. 24.

44. Viedma, *Descripción geografica,* 71.

45. Viedma to Consulado, 3 Jan. 1787, AGN, Sala IX, Intendencia, leg. 5.8.3.

46. Viedma to Consulado, 30 Apr. 1792, AGN, Sala IX, Intendencia, leg. 5.8.5.

47. Real visita a los molinas de grano, 1799, AHMC, leg. 1213 (uncatalogued and without foliation).

48. An obvious question this analysis raises is the extent to which peasant participation in these staple markets reflected the disintegration of "vertical" landholding patterns of highland comunidades that once had direct access to valley lands. See J. Murra, "El control vertical de un máximo de pisos ecológicos en la economía de las sociedades andinas," in Murra, *Formaciones económicas y políticas del mundo andino* (Lima, 1975).

On the "destructuration" of Andean social organization, see N. Wachtel, "Hommes d'eau: le probleme uru (xvie–xviie siècle)," *Annales E.S.C.* 33 (1978): 1127–59; T. Saignes, "De la filiation à la résidence: les ethnies dans les vallées de Larecaja," *Annales E.S.C.* 33 (1978): 1160–81; K. Spalding, "The Shrinking Web: The Transformation of Local Andean Society Under Spanish Rule" (1979), ms.; and B. Larson, "Caciques, Class Structure and the Colonial State in Bolivia," *Nova Americana* (Turin), 2 (1979).

49. N. Sánchez Albornoz, *Indios y Tributos en el Alto Perú* (Lima, 1978).

50. Royal treasury accounts were kept (usually in a haphazard way in the local, unbound Relaciones juradas) of the tithe revenue which tax farmers from every parish in the province owed the church every year and of the alcabala they paid the royal treasury. A compilation of that information in the extant account books allows us to follow the rough movement of tithes for each parish and for the region as a whole between 1774 and 1810.

51. I should emphasize that the auction price of tithes reflected anticipations of the market value of grain (not the actual volume or value of cereal after harvest) and is therefore but a crude and indirect index of fluctuating grain production and prices. On tithe revenue and agriculture, see M. Carmagnani, "La producción agropecuaria chilena. Aspectos cuantitativos, 1680–1830," *Cahiers des Amerique Latines* 3 (1969): 3–21; A. Bauer, "The Church and Spanish American Agrarian Structure: 1765–1865," *Americas* 28 (July 1971); 78–98; and Brading, *Haciendas and Ranchos,* 68–73 and 180–89.

52. See my study, "Economic Decline," 209–11.

53. Libro de Cabildo, 10 Feb. 1784, *Digesto,* 3: 128.

54. Autos . . . contra el Alferez real . . . sobre los diezmos, 1774, AHMC, leg. 1213 (uncatalogued and without foliation).

55. See Pearce, "Peasants and Revolution" and L. Olen, *Canton Chullpas: A Socioeconomic Study of the Cochabamba Valley* (Washington, D.C., 1948).

56. Kula, *An Economic Theory,* 182–83.

57. See my study, "Economic Decline," 214–18.

58. Florescano, *Precios de maíz,* 187–88.

59. Brading, *Haciendas and Ranchos,* 37. Although I have emphasized the role that mercantile incentive played in stimulating agricultural production in León, there were other differences between the two regions that help explain León's dynamism and Cochabamba's relative stagnation. One that deserves mention here was that many landed families in León originally accumulated capital outside the region, in mining and overseas commerce, which they eventually invested in agricultural improvements under the stimulus of market demand for wheat. In Cochabamba, on the other hand, few landowners (except monasteries) had capital funds to invest in cash-crop agriculture. Contemporaries interested in stimulating new agricultural enterprises often commented on the difficulty most landlords had in raising the capital they would need to initiate such projects.

The Price of Cacao, Its Export, and Rebellion in Eighteenth-Century Caracas

Boom, Bust, and the Basque Monopoly

Robert J. Ferry

Protest and León's Rebellion

The decade of the 1740s was a time of troubles in Caracas. The policies of the Real Compañía Guipuzcoana, Spain's first monopoly company, chartered to do business in Venezuela in 1728, provoked bitter controversy and occasional violence from the residents of the Caracas province. In January 1741, the Council of the Indies received a petition protesting the Guipuzcoana Company signed by "eleven widows, vecinas of Caracas and *cosecheras de cacao,*" in which the women claimed that, taken collectively, more than four thousand *fanegas* of cacao were harvested annually on their haciendas. The harvests were abundant ("thanks to God"), but they had little else besides cacao to sell, and because of the low prices offered by the Basque monopoly company, they had become "indebted and subjugated" to it. The widows informed the council that the previous years had been ones of growth, that these haciendas had been expanded and new ones planted, and that much of the development had been financed with credit from the Caracas ecclesiastical establishment. They warned, however, that now there was danger of foreclosure, because the price paid for cacao was not enough to pay what was owed. If prices did not rise, the church stood to suffer in a more fundamental way, for the tithes were falling and people had nothing with which to make gifts (*limosna*) to the divine cult. Further, the importation of African slaves, so essential to the steady expansion of cacao agriculture, had become part of the Basque monopoly as a result of the removal of the English *asiento* in 1739, but the widows protested that the monopolists offered only a very few slaves for sale. The company charged "twenty, twenty-five, and more" fanegas of cacao for each one, while twenty years earlier, the same quantity of cacao would have purchased three slaves from the English sellers. What especially galled the widows was the very contrary image of itself that the company projected: "They would make you believe that the company is the cause of progress in the province, because the people of this city can take advantage of the fact that the company will buy at a reasonable price all the cacao that we can grow, but it is certain that for the most part they do not pay even ten pesos." At this price, the widows' haciendas, despite their bountiful harvests, had become nearly "useless," which was "a great misfortune."[1]

Other protest memorials followed, including one written in November 1744, by ninety-four "interested citizens, both merchants and planters" of Caracas, members of most of the elite families of the town who represented the ownership of more than 1 million cacao trees, about 20 percent of all the cacao trees in the province in that year. They pointed out to the crown that while the price paid for cacao in Caracas by the Guipuzcoana Company then stood at nine pesos the fanega, it was common knowledge that the same cacao would bring fifty-two pesos in Veracruz. Therefore, the protestors argued, the Guipuzcoana Company was keeping the purchase price for cacao at prices far below what they would have been in a free market, denying planters reasonable profits and denying the crown its fair tax share of those profits.[2] So that its complaints against the company might be heard by the king's court, the Caracas cabildo kept two of the town's more influential citizens resident in Spain for several years, but neither the personal advocacy of these men (the Marqués de Toro and the Conde de San Javier) nor the series of protest memorials written by the collective elite made any discernible impression on the crown. With the active support of the Caracas governors, especially the Basques, Martín de Lardizábal (1732–37) and Gabriel José de Zuloaga (1737–47), the company continued to set the price paid for cacao in Caracas and influence the economic and political life of the colony in numerous ways. The attitude of the populace smoldered in resentment and intrigue, and as early as 1745, Governor Zuloaga knew that rebellion was near at hand:

I was told secretly by several different ecclesiastics, both seculars and regulars, that a plot has been formed here by the Conde [de San Javier] and Don Alejandro [Blanco Uribe] and their partisans, and as a part of it, they have made an alliance with the majority of the many Isleños from the Canary Islands who live in this city and in the different areas adjacent to it. Although the conde and d. Francisco de Ponte, his cousin, plan to travel to court to present their case, they and many others intend to begin something here; to be better able to do it, they have elected alcaldes and a procurador general favorable to the thoughts of the conde and d. Alejandro Blanco, and they have gone so far as to propose violence. If I do not agree with them or defer to them, they will rise in rebellion against me, arrest me if necessary, and arrest the agents of the Guipuzcoana Company so that they can do away with it altogether.[3]

The uprising did not, however, take place for another five years. Juan Francisco de León was a native of the Canary Islands who had lived in the Caracas province for several decades by 1749. He was a man of considerable influence among the Isleño population and among the many immigrants whose cacao haciendas dotted the fertile Tuy valley east and south of Caracas. In the late 1740s, with cacao prices at eight pesos the fanega, many of these planters floated cacao beans down the Tuy in canoes and sold them to Dutch merchants who waited at the river's mouth. Suspicious that León was a participant in this illegal trade and had not exercised the obligations of his office as *teniente de justicia* to stop it, the governor replaced León as *teniente* in the Tuy valley of Panaquire with a Basque employee of the Guipuzcoana Company. This was the last straw for León and those who followed him, and in April 1749, some two thousand men, most of them Isleños, but also many mixed-race pardos, Indians, and free blacks, marched on Caracas to call for the expulsion of the company. Their intention was to protest, and they brandished their weapons to show the seriousness of their discontent. When the governor, frightened by León's mob in the central plaza, fled the city disguised as a priest, and took refuge on the coast in the fortress at La Guaira, many were surprised and angered to find that their protest had been suddenly transformed into rebellion, for in fact they had driven the foremost representative of the king from his position of authority. In frustration, León and his men first cut off traffic on the La Guaira–Caracas road and then proposed to force the governor to return to Caracas even if it were necessary to attack the contingent of royal and Guipuzcoana Company troops stationed at the La Guaira fortress. A concerned elite, enthusiastic in their support of León while the issue was merely a protest, but now afraid that they would be accused of fomenting and abetting rebellion, advised the Isleño caudillo that an armed confrontation with soldiers of the crown could lead to a general civil war. "Then in such case they will kill all of us," León responded, "for there is no reason why I alone should die in defense of this province."[4]

What had taken place was understood by the lieutenant governor, Domingo Aguirre y Castillos, a frequent friend of the elite and occasional opponent of Luis Francisco de Castellanos, the governor who had abandoned his post and taken refuge in La Guaira. In a letter to the king, Aguirre showed his understanding of the pressure that had been brought to bear on the province by the policies of the Basque governors and the Guipuzcoana Company and, although his fears of what the eventual outcome of the uprising might be clouded his view of León's objectives, he knew very well that the Isleño chief had broad popular support.

Juan Francisco de León, until now your majesty's faithful vassal, has been made over by the government into a renegade of justice addicted to disobedience; . . . he will be a rebel powerful enough to establish a principality here, a principality whose main strength will consist in the liberty of black slaves and Indians, who will come here from the surrounding provinces and from the nearby islands, and even religion and the Catholic faith will be shaken. . . .[5]

Perhaps the best sense of the intense antagonism León and those who followed him, however inadvertently, into rebellion felt can be understood from a statement León made in response to the warning that he and his men were about to commit a serious crime of lese majesty by attacking La Guaira. As Aguirre recalled in his letter to the king, León had said:

All that was lacking was for us to be accused of treason and rebellion, for his majesty is ruining the settlers of this province by giving it over to the Vizcayans [i.e., the Basque Guipuzcoana Company, the Basque governors, and their subalterns] as if they were its conquistadors, although in truth there is nothing left to give them but our very wives, for everything else is already theirs, the settlers of the province work and cultivate the provincial lands for them, lands that we had cleared at our own expense and with our own sweat.[6]

As it happened, the worst was avoided as León called off the attack on La Guaira in exchange for a promise from Governor Castellanos, which he did not keep, to return to Caracas. No one was killed in the brief siege of the port. From this point forward, León's Rebellion became first a stalemate, but then, with the arrival in 1751 of veteran royalist troops under the command of a determined military governor, Brig. Felipe Ricardos, all threat and even thought of rebellion were brought to an end. León's support dissolved as several of his elite allies were arrested and deported, and object lessons were made of a few of his compatriots at the other end of the social scale. Among those singled out by Ricardos for exemplary punishment were three who had marched to Caracas with León in 1749: Juan "Muchingo," free mulatto; Raimundo Romero, zambo; and Andrés Rodríguez Betancourt, Isleño. The Canary Islander met a relatively privileged death before a firing squad and was given an immediate burial, but the two men of color were hanged and their severed heads, "as an example and for the embarrassment of the population," were placed on public view, one nailed to the door of the fugitive León's house in the Candelaria barrio of Caracas, and the other placed on a post alongside the camino real leading from Caracas to the Tuy.[7]

With these acts, Governor Ricardos brought the will of the king before the province's residents with unmistakable clarity. The executions and arrests stopped the rebellion, and when León surrendered in January 1752, all that remained to be done was to make certain that a similar affront to royal authority would not take place again. León was sent to Spain and was dead before the end of the year; his sons served long terms in African presidios. The León house in Candelaria was pulled down, its ruins spread with salt, and a copper placard bearing the following inscription was erected where the house had stood.

This is the justice of the king our señor, ordered to be done by the excellent señor d. Phelipe Ricardos, lieutenant general of the armies of his majesty, his governor and captain general in this province of Caracas, with Francisco León, owner of this house, for obstinacy, a rebel and traitor to the royal crown, and therefore a criminal. May the destruction and spreading of salt stand to the perpetual memory of his infamy.[8]

The rest of Caracas received more moderate treatment. By early 1753, all those elites who had been held in Caracas or Spanish jails were released, to a large extent because there was little concrete evidence linking any of them directly to León. Ricardos's method of punishing these citizens was to order an increase in the *alcabala* tax paid by the city as a whole. The sum of 150,000 pesos would be collected annually for twelve years, a substantial increase over the customary 35,000 to 40,000 pesos usually paid. Of the total amount, 100,000 pesos were to pay for the yearly cost of quartering the large contingent of troops that was to be permanently stationed in the city, and 50,000 pesos would repay, in the course of twelve years, the amount already spent by the king to pacify the province. Angered by the continued charges of their collective guilt, the cabildo insisted on the city's innocence and argued that the province could not afford to make such payments, but Ricardos's decree was put into effect nevertheless.[9] To facilitate the return to business as usual of the Guipuzcoana Company, it was resolved as early as 1751 that the price to be paid for cacao in Caracas would be determined by the company factor together with a regidor appointed by the cabildo.[10] There were other reforms applied to the company by royal order, but perhaps none was more significant than the decision the company's directors agreed to in 1752, permitting a new issue of company stock, doubling it in quantity, and offering this stock to the Caracas elite.[11]

This combination of force and reform ended the threat of rebellion, which did not appear again in Caracas until the nineteenth century. The memory of León's rebellion remained alive during the second half of the eighteenth century, however, and reemerged in revolutionary Caracas. Independence was declared on 5 July 1811, and in the 20 September edition of *La Gazeta de Caracas* an executive order was published, issued by one Rodulfo Vasallo, director of public works in the revolutionary town

to demolish with all solemnity the post of ignominy that the system of tyranny and oppression raised a half century ago on the plot where the magnanimous Juan Francisco de León had his house, and that has unjustly stained the memory of this caudillo of those valiant men who at that time tried to shake off the hard mercantile yoke the avaricious and despotic kings of Spain had used to constrain the commerce of these provinces, using for the purpose the swindling Guipuzcoana Company, whose exclusive privileges made Venezuelans groan for more than forty years.[12]

PRICES

The events of a difficult decade, the protests of the early 1740s, the León revolt, and the repression directed against Caracas by Governor Ricardos in the early 1750s were not rooted in any single cause. At the upper reaches of colonial society, there was a tradition of conflict. From the beginning of the century, in reaction to what were among the Bourbon monarchs' first efforts at centralization of authority, the Caracas cabildo had resisted what it considered the usurpation of its authority by royal governors and the New Granadian viceregal regime. This tradition of political opposition carried over to colonial attitudes toward the Guipuzcoana Company, and many of the elite resented the Basque monopoly primarily because of the close collaboration, viewed as collusion, between the company and Basque governors.[13] At a different level of society, Juan Francisco de León and the other Canary Islanders who settled near the Tuy River had received permission to do so only after a prolonged struggle with both royal governors and Caracas elites,[14] and they were particularly sensitive to any challenge to their authority in the Tuy valleys where they had planted their cacao. The assignment of a Vizcayan as teniente de justicia in the valley of Panaguire to replace León, who was one of its principal founders and one of the first to grow cacao

Graph 10.1

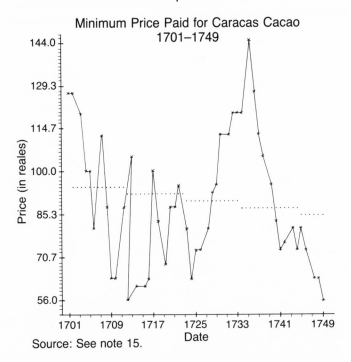

Minimum Price Paid for Caracas Cacao 1701–1749

Source: See note 15.

there, was therefore a provocation of the most serious sort. The most immediate precipitating cause of the 1740s unrest, however, was the declining price paid for cacao exported from Caracas (Graph 10.1).

Falling prices threatened different groups of planters in somewhat different ways. After generations of planting, by the middle of the eighteenth century the elite had substantial holdings in cacao haciendas, but, with their families expanding at a rate greater than the productive capacity of their agricultural wealth, declining prices meant declining per capita wealth, which in turn challenged their accustomed social status and prestige.[15] Declining prices represented unmitigated disaster for many of the more recent immigrants, especially those such as Juan Francisco de León, whose successes during the prosperous 1720s and 1730s had brought them to the threshold of gentry status by the 1740s. Governors concerned about smuggling had denied them transport of their cacao by sea to La Guaira, obliging them to depend on expensive overland carriers. For these planters, the extremely low prices of the 1740s brought their profit from cacao sales to a point below the cost of legal mule transport from the Tuy. To a large extent from necessity, many planters then began to float their harvests in canoes to the mouth of the river, where high-paying Dutch smugglers waited to buy them.

Without reservation, both elite planters resident in Caracas and their more modest Isleño counterparts in the Tuy blamed the Guipuzcoana Company for arbitrarily forcing down the price paid for cacao after 1735. A second view, however, had it that prices fluctuated in accordance with the rules of supply and demand. This latter point of view was expressed by a friend of the company, Sebastián de Eslava, former viceroy of New Granada, advisor to the Council of the Indies, and author of the instructions carried to Caracas by the military governor, Felipe Ricardos. Eslava believed that prices in Caracas fell during the decade before the León uprising because so much cacao was sent to New Spain that the Mexican market had been glutted. While prices paid in Veracruz were at forty and forty-three pesos, they remained strong at thirteen and fourteen pesos in Caracas. Oversupply brought the Mexican price down to twenty-three and twenty-four pesos, and as a result, in Caracas only seven and eight pesos could be offered for a *fanega* of cacao.[16] Without a satisfactory price series for cacao sales in New Spain, it is impossible to determine with any precision the long-term influence of the Mexican market on Caracas prices, but a comparison of the correlation between prices and exports to Mexico for different sets of consecutive years—for several successive years of abundant exports, on the one hand, and scant exports, on the other—provides a preliminary test of Eslava's opinion that an abundance of cacao available in Mexico was responsible for the low prices paid in Caracas.

At first glance, it appears that Eslava was correct, and prices in Caracas did respond sensitively to oversupply in Mexico. He was wrong, however, to suppose that substantial quantities of cacao were shipped to New Spain for many years before 1749. Exports did not increase significantly until after 1744, but from 1745 to 1748, Caraqueños did ship more cacao to Mexico than had ever been sent during any previous four-year period. These 97,737 fanegas represented an annual mean of 24,434 fanegas, almost 50 percent more than the annual mean for the half-century 1701–49 (16,398 fanegas). True to his supply-and-demand argument, during these four years the minimum Caracas price did fall from eleven pesos to eight. A test of the general responsiveness of prices to supply can be made by comparing this observation to other periods of high and low cacao exports to Mexico. During the first half of the eighteenth century, there was only one other four-year period in which a quantity similar to that of 1745–48 was sent to New Spain; from

1721 to 1724, a total of 96,118 fanegas was loaded for Veracruz, and on this occasion, too, the Caracas price dropped, from twelve pesos to eight pesos the fanega. By contrast, however, consecutive low-export years did not result in higher prices. From 1739 to 1742, the amount of cacao shipped to Mexico was only 52,284 fanegas (an annual average of 13,071 fanegas, 20 percent less than the fifty-year annual average), but instead of rising, the minimum price declined from twelve pesos in 1739 to nine pesos in 1742. A final comparison, also for a four-year period of scant exports to Mexico, similarly shows no increase in the Caracas price for cacao. In 1712, the lowest minimum price in the eighteenth century, seven pesos (to be reached again only in 1749), was paid, while a somewhat less than average amount of cacao was exported for Mexico, 13,526 fanegas. The following year, a respectable quantity of beans, 16,942 fanegas, was carried across the Caribbean to Veracruz, but in that year of increased exports the Caracas price also rose to more than thirteen pesos, a high point that would not be reached again until the 1730s. In the next two years exports then fell, first to a subaverage 13,088 fanegas in 1714, and then to a century-low 4,300 fanegas in 1715. Prices, rather than rising in response to a declining supply as the Eslava argument would have it, fell back to eight and then seven and a half pesos per fanega.

These data are inconclusive on the matter of the overall effect of the quantity of Caracas exports on the price paid for cacao in Caracas. Many other circumstances could have influenced the Mexican market, not the least of which would have been the cacao arriving there from other sources, especially Guayaquil. Furthermore, Eslava's observation about the impact of 1740s exports on prices may have been true for those years even if there is no clear correlation between Caracas exports and prices for the rest of the half century. The Mexican market was, after all, only one destination for Caracas cacao. The Guipuzcoana Company had been carrying an ever-greater share of cacao to Spain during the 1730s and early 1740s, but Eslava made no mention of the possible impact of the European market on Caracas prices. With one exception, before 1725 New Spain always received at least 60 percent of the Caracas cacao exported, and in many years 90 percent of Caracas beans went to Veracruz. Thereafter, with the creation of the Guipuzcoana Company, it was rare for more than 40 percent to go to Mexico, with exports there averaging only about one-third of the total until 1745, when the New Spain share rose again to 50 percent and more (Graph 10.2). What may have struck Eslava, or rather his informants, was less the greater absolute quantity and more the greater proportion of cacao sent to Mexico

Graph 10.2

Exports to Mexico as Percentage
of all Cacao Exports
1701–1749

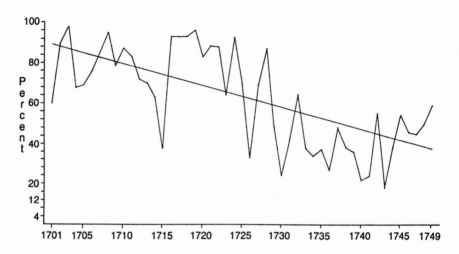

Source: Eduardo Arcila Farias, *Economia colonial de Venezuela*
(Caracas, 2d. ed., 1973), 2 vols.,
I:153–57.

after 1745, for this was cacao not carried for profit by the Guipuzcoana enterprise and was therefore a source of some controversy. In any event, the role of the market in determining Caracas cacao prices will be determined only when price information is available for Mexico and Spain. What is more important for the present study is the fact that Caraqueños perceived the company as largely responsible for their economic woes, and it is this perception that deserves further consideration.

Traditionally the business of shipping Caracas cacao to Mexico was a simple affair. By a custom known as *tercio buque* ("one-third of the hold"), hacienda owners, *cosecheros* as they are referred to in eighteenth-century documents pertaining to commerce, were allotted one-third of the cargo capacity of every ship for their beans. They paid freight charges on the cacao and assumed responsibility for any loss that might occur in transit. Within twenty-four hours of the ship's arrival in Veracruz, the captain of the vessel was obliged to transfer the cacao to agents named by the cosecheros in that port. This was the preferred method of shipment for the larger-scale hacienda owners who could forego immediate cash payments for their cacao in Caracas. By sending cacao on consignment to an associate in Mexico, they incurred transportation costs and ran the risk of losing the cargo at sea, they depended on the reliability of their associate in Veracruz or Mexico City, and they had to wait for extended periods before receiving the profits from the sale of their beans. Frequently such profits returned not as cash, but as credits to be drawn on merchants in Mexico or Spain, which meant that many of the Caracas cosecheros who shipped cacao in the tercio buque functioned much like merchants in that their assets were not always liquid and they were often located outside Caracas. The great advantage of doing business in this fashion was, of course, that the Caracas seller could profit from the much higher prices usually paid for cacao in New Spain.

Once the third part of the hold was filled with cosechero cacao, both those hacienda owners who had more cacao to ship than there had been space for in the cosecheros' tercio buque and those who needed to exchange their beans for cash or credit in the Caracas market could sell their beans at current market prices to either local merchants, who also were given an allotment of one-third the ship's capacity, or to the ship's captain, who reserved the final third for himself in the name of the owners of the vessel.[17]

Until 1721, those who had cacao for export or sale could do business with the captain or supercargo of any ship that happened to be taking on cargo at La Guaira. In that tumultuous year, a political struggle over contraband commerce resulted in the temporary replacement of the governor of Caracas by Antonio José Álvarez de Abreu, who, to the great disgust of the Caracas citizenry, was named to the position by the viceroy of New Granada.[18] The cabildo, which had traditionally exercised the privilege of assuming gubernatorial power in the absence of the king's appointed official, resented this assertion of authority from the newly created viceroyalty. To make matters worse, during his short tenure Álvarez de Abreu introduced the *alternativa* to La Guaira shipping, a system requiring that the first ship entering port had to be loaded to capacity before any subsequent vessel could open its hold for cargo. It is not entirely clear what was regarded as troublesome about the policy when it was introduced in 1721. Its ostensible purpose was to expedite commerce, to attract shipping by giving every vessel that might arrive at La Guaira looking for cargo an equal chance to take on cacao, but influential Caraqueños resisted the alternativa, presumably because cosecheros wanted to select the ship, captain, and crew that were to take their cacao to New Spain, and probably they favored Caracas-owned vessels. Andrés de Urbina, owner of more than fifty thousand cacao trees and recognized as the *mayor cosechero* in Caracas at that time, went to Spain to obtain the repeal of the plan. He won his case, and the royal cédula issued in favor of his appeal, dated 25 May 1722, would be known to a generation of Caraqueños as the "cédula de Urbina."[19]

The alternativa was inoperative from 1722 until 1731, but in that year the cédula de Urbina was overturned, and the alternativa was again instituted as rule. This was done at the request of the powerful Guipuzcoana Company, which was then striving to gain control of the colony's cacao trade. By condition of its charter, the Basque monopoly was allowed to participate in the traditional trade with New Spain only in exceptional circumstances, and Caracas cosecheros, merchants and shipowners continued to ship their own cacao on the basis of tercio buque in noncompany ships to Veracruz. The alternativa, however, made it possible for every second ship to load at La Guaira to be a company ship. The company did not offer the tercio buque privilege and was unable to do business in New Spain. Therefore, hacienda owners with beans for market had to either sell their cacao to the monopoly at current prices, or, if they wanted to trade in the Mexican market, wait until others had sold their harvests to the Basques and the company ship had loaded and departed. To wait for the company to load its ships angered the elite Caracas cosecheros, who were unwilling to sell to the monopoly and thereby forfeit the considerable commercial profit they stood to make if they sold their beans on their own account in Mexico. While they waited and watched the quantity of cacao exported to Spain in company ships steadily increase, in New Spain shortages drove up prices there, or so the Caraqueños believed, which in turn heightened the discontent and frustration of many of them.[20]

The elite of Caracas did not make formal objection to the creation of the Guipuzcoana Company, most likely because its monopoly did not extend to the trans-Caribbean cacao trade and they were not denied the profit from the sale of cacao in Veracruz. They did complain, however, about low prices and especially about the alternativa policy. The Caracas cabildo wrote to the crown in 1745 that the system had so slowed the trade that it had become common for a year and a half to pass before a ship departing for Veracruz to return, take a cargo, and be ready to leave La Guaira again. This was true even though the sailing time from La Guaira to Veracruz was less than a month. Caraqueños could not ship to Spain on their own account because of the Guipuzcoana monopoly; thus, while the quantity of cacao grown on their haciendas steadily increased, the alternativa kept the Veracruz trade bottled up in the colony.

In the 1730s and 1740s, the principal opponents of the Guipuzcoana Company and advocates of the customary privileges of the elite were a Caracas marquis, a count, and a kinsman of the count. The Marqués del Toro (until his death in 1742), the Conde de San Javier, and his cousin don Francisco de Ponte y Mijares took their case to Spain, residing at court for a number of years while they carried on a paper war of major importance for Caracas. Dismissed by attorneys for the Guipuzcoana Company as self-interested managers of the traditional trade, they presented arguments that demonstrated to the Council of the Indies the damage done to commerce and cacao agriculture by the company and the alternativa. In 1734, Gov. Martín de Lardizábal, in an effort to both eliminate conflict and retain the alternativa, established quotas, twenty thousand fanegas for New Spain and thirty thousand fanegas for Spain and the Canaries, on the basis of an estimated sixty thousand fanegas annual production, with local consumption to account for the remaining ten thousand fanegas. In a memorial presented to the Council in January 1746, the Conde de San Javier and Francisco de Ponte pointed out that it was thought by some that production had been underestimated at sixty thousand fanegas in 1734, and that by 1740, a more accurate figure would have been ninety thousand fanegas of annual harvest. Since Lardizábal had made his allotments, many new haciendas had been brought to harvest; the entire valleys of Curiepe, Panaquire, and Araguita had begun to produce in the interim; and there had been great expansion in other Tuy valleys such as Capaya, Mamporal, and Caucagua. Yet in no year since 1740 had the quota of twenty thousand fanegas been sent to New Spain; fewer than nine thousand fanegas were sent in 1741 and not even seven thousand fanegas in 1743 (Graph 10.3). Furthermore, the company had failed to fill its allotment in any year after 1740, when forty thousand fanegas were sent to Spain.

One clear implication to be drawn from this information, although the petitioners did not make the point, was that most of the Caracas cacao harvest was probably traded illegally. By insisting on the alternativa, the company, far from controlling contraband as it claimed, was in fact giving Caraqueños good reason to take their cacao business to smugglers. San Javier and Ponte did present the view that many cosecheros were unwilling to sell their beans to the company. Since planters refused to trade when it was a company ship's turn to take on cargo, preferring to wait to consign their cargoes on a privately owned vessel, the company ships were filled only very slowly, and the legal export of cacao from the province came to a virtual standstill. The bottleneck created by the alternativa caused a dramatic increase in cacao beans stored in planters' Caracas and La Guaira warehouses,

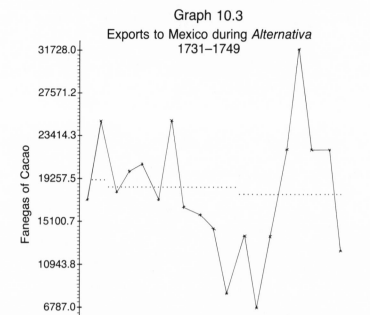

Graph 10.3
Exports to Mexico during *Alternativa*
1731–1749

Source: Eduardo Aroila Farias, *Economia colonial de
Venezuela* (Caracas, 2d. ed., 1973), 2 vols.,
I:153–57.

as cosecheros waited for the chance to ship on their own account to New
Spain. With such an extraordinary abundance of beans available for sale, the
local price paid for cacao fell to record low levels (Graph 10.4). There was
so much cacao that most planters, according to one observer, "found themselves obliged to sell their cacao while it was still in flower" at
whatever price they could get for it.[21] This was made all the more disturbing
because while the alternativa policy brought the price paid in Caracas down
to nine and then eight pesos, in Veracruz, where the demand for beans had
far outreached the now-restricted supply, would-be buyers were willing to
offer fifty pesos and more per fanega. In the graphic metaphor of a frustrated
cabildo, this constrictive policy had made the legal cacao trade "a throat too
small for the vomit of the great stomach that is this province."[22]

The excessive supply of cacao on hand was only part of the low-price
problem. New Spain had always been Venezuela's principal source of circulating specie, but the decrease in the quantity of cacao for sale at Veracruz

Graph 10.4

Minimum Cacao Price Paid During *Alternativa* 1731–1749

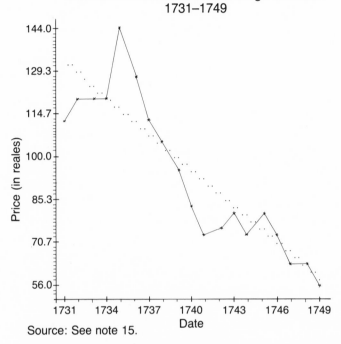

Source: See note 15.

meant that there was less silver coin to bring back across the Caribbean. Mexican merchants, who had traditionally advanced cash for the purchase of Caracas cacao,[23] were now reluctant to tie up their investments for as long as two years in a market brought to stagnation because ships bound for New Spain had to load cargoes on an alternating basis with Guipuzcoana Company ships. Therefore, even though the demand for cacao in Veracruz was strong, Mexican cacao buyers were willing to part with fewer of their pesos to acquire the beans. These interrelated factors, the excess of cacao in Caracas warehouses and the shortage of coin to pay for its purchase, caused prices to come crashing down. San Javier and Ponte pointed out that low prices were ruinous to many, especially in Caracas, *la capital,* where the lack of cash made business of all kinds difficult, where even artisans had been forced to leave their crafts and take up subsistence agriculture in the countryside. On the haciendas slaves who ran away or died could not be replaced, and there was no cash to pay wage labor as a substitute. The best that could be done, under the circumstances of torpid trade and low prices, was to "keep the slaves busy, without expecting to get any benefit whatever from them or from one's *árboles de cacao*."[24]

The Guipuzcoana Company made no great effort to counter the criticisms directed at it by Toro, San Javier, Ponte, and others. Probably it was secure that its license guaranteed royal support, and perhaps it was expected that there would always be some resistance to its operation from Caracas growers. Company spokesmen and influential friends of the company did try to discredit Toro and the other critics by claiming that they argued only on the basis of self interest. In 1739 an attorney for the company claimed that the Marqués do Toro and the Conde de San Javier were "the only, or at least the principal, merchants, who for themselves and for their commission agents in Vera Cruz resist the Company." They did not want competition of any sort in the cacao trade which they had dominated for many years. And in February 1745 the Basque governor Gabriel de Zuloaga questioned the disinterestedness of the Caracas cabildo, which a month earlier had described commerce under the company and the alternativa as a "throat too small" for the great productivity of the province. Most of the officers elected to the town council in 1745, Zuloaga claimed, were members "of the family Solorzano, which is the family of the Conde [de San Javier]."[25]

In fact opposition was widespread. Caraqueños expressed their objections in terms of the alternativa and prices, and the company's policies and the results of those policies did create immediate hardships for many hacienda owners and others whose livelihoods depended on the exchange of cacao for silver coin. But for the Caracas elite these immediate difficulties were the more intolerable because they touched a deeper problem, a more serious aggravation, which was felt only by the colony's oldest and most prestigious families. For several successive generations, in some cases as many as four generations by the 1740s, steadily expanding cacao production had allowed similarly rapidly expanding elite families the means to sustain the level of material wealth and social standing that their great-grandparents and grandparents had enjoyed. For these Caraqueños the Tuy River boom of the 1720s and 1730s was the regular continuation of a remarkable process of expansion that had gone on without much variation since the 1670s. But by the 1740s, especially after the importation of African slaves came to a virtual stop in 1738, there are indications that the cacao economy could no longer keep pace with the demographic growth of some Caracas elite families.[26] Nowhere in the documentation does the fear of downward social mobility appear stated explicitly; however, a conspicuous theme in the literature of protest is that the Guipuzcoana Company's policies were harmful to families, to elite families, in particular, and especially to elite families that were headed by elderly parents and at the critical juncture when one generation gives way to the next. In this sense there were no individuals who were more vulnerable or more worthy of royal attention and protection than Caracas's elite widows, and it was perhaps for this reason that these women authored and were the first to sign the protest memorials sent from the city to the Council of the Indies in the 1740s.

THE ENGLISH ASIENTO

Besides prices and ships' cargoes there was one other particular, for the most part overlooked by historians, which deeply troubled Caraqueños. With the outbreak of the War of Jenkin's Ear in 1739, the English South Sea Company ended its slaving operations in Spanish America,[27] and in Caracas, slaves, which had been available in abundance for some time, were suddenly in very short supply. Already in January 1741, the eleven elite widows who wrote to the Council of the Indies in protest of the Guipuzcoana Company made reference to the problem. They complained that the company demanded exorbitant amounts ("20, 25 and more" fanegas of cacao), three times what the English had charged, for each of the few slaves it brought to Caracas for sale. The end of the English asiento, which had operated with considerable success and profit in Caracas, contributed directly to the general aggravation which resulted in León's rebellion in 1749.

One of the most important factors for an understanding of the social and political tension that troubled Caracas in the 1730s and 1740s is that much of the expansion of the Caracas cacao industry had already taken place before 1720, well before the creation of the monopoly Guipuzcoana Company in 1728 and the arrival of the first company ships in 1730.[28] The number of cacao trees growing in the province had increased more than seven times, from less than 0.5 million in 1684 to more than 3 million in 1720, a rate of about 75,000 additional trees per year. Thereafter, from 1720 to 1744, the number of trees increased to more than five million, again at a rate of about 75,000 trees per year. This constant rate of expansion from 1684 to 1744 suggests that the arrival of the Guipuzcoana Company in 1728 did not influence the growth of the cacao production in any significant way. In fact, as the map showing the location of these trees in the Caracas province makes clear, almost all of the expansion after 1720 took place in the Tuy River (Figure 10.1), and production in this frontier zone was if anything

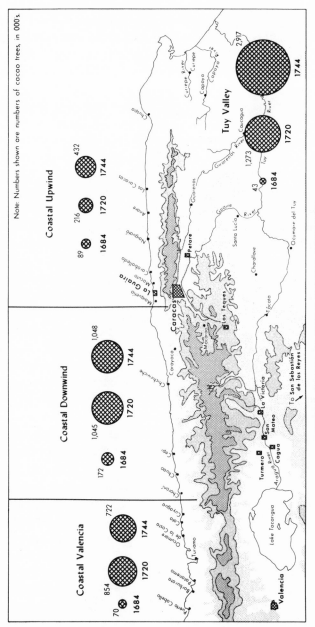

**CACAO TREES IN THE CARACAS PROVINCE,
1684, 1720 AND 1744**

Fig. 10.1

constrained by the official policy of requiring that cacao be carried by expensive mule transport to Caracas.

During the early part of the century the expansion of cacao agriculture both financed and to a considerable extent depended upon the importation of African slave labor. From 1715 to 1728 the South Sea Company sold a modest number of slaves in Caracas, about 100 individuals per year on the average. After 1728, temporary cessation of the chronic hostilities between England and Spain marked the beginning of the South Sea Company's best slave trading years in Spain's American colonies. In Caracas sales increased considerably, and for the eleven years from 1729 to 1739 more than 350 slaves were sold there annually on the average. This decade of booming slave imports coincided with the first decade of operations for the Guipuzcoana Company, and the English monopolists who controlled the supply of labor to the colony found themselves in constant competition with those northern Spaniards who held monopoly rights to the colony's commerce with Spain.[29] The Basque traders were not slavers, however, and after the end of the asiento in 1739 the Guipuzcoana Company proved singularly unable (or unwilling) to market African slaves in Venezuela. No more than about 350 African slaves were sold by the company in the colony during the entire half century after 1739.[30]

The 1730s were years of generally high cacao prices, especially during the early years of the decade, total exports were greater than at any previous time, and the Caracas cacao planters found themselves in the fortuitous position of receiving more money for their beans just at the time when more African slaves were made available for purchase at the English factory in La Guaira. The minimum price paid for cacao at Caracas rose steadily from a low of eight pesos in 1724 to a high of eighteen pesos in 1735, and during this same period total cacao exports increased by about eight thousand fanegas per year on the average. Simultaneous to these upward patterns, the South Sea Company's sales in Caracas increased from less than two hundred slaves in 1724 to more than five hundred in each of the years from 1731 to 1733. The attraction of the Caracas market is evident in the fact that the Caracas share of South Sea Company business in all the Spanish American ports where it had factories, never more than 5 percent of the total number of slaves sold before 1727, had reached about 25 percent by 1737 and 1738.[31] The nature of the relationship between prices and slave sales would seem to have been a simple matter of higher prices and expanding cacao production resulting in greater buying capacity for Caracas planters, a situation which the English slave sellers took to their advantage. But the possibility also exists that the presence of substantial numbers of slaves for sale by the South Sea Company helped keep Caracas cacao prices high until the late 1730s.

Three distinct factions competed with one another to profit from cacao for export: Caracas elites, who were also planters, with commercial connections of their own in New Spain and an exemption from the Basque monopoly to trade there; the Guipuzcoana Company, with its exclusive rights to carry cacao to Spain; and the foreigners' South Sea Company, which could take cacao in exchange for slaves. A remarkable document prepared by a South Sea Company account in 1733 demonstrates just how handsomely profitable the commercial sale of Caracas cacao in these distant ports could be. The proceeds from the sale of 600 blacks in Caracas, after transportation costs and Spanish duties had been paid, would be approximately 24,000 pesos. If, however, payment for the six hundred slaves were taken in cacao, which the South Sea agent generously rated at 23 pesos the fanega in Caracas (the price did not exceed 18 pesos in 1733), and if this quantity of cacao were then transported to Veracruz, where the agent believed it could be sold for 40 pesos the fanega (its price there was probably somewhat higher), then the profit to be made after additional shipping and duty had been paid would be about 51,350 pesos.[32]

This estimate indicates that value of Caracas cacao increased by more than 100 percent in the Caribbean crossing, and the profits to be made by carrying the beans across the Atlantic were similarly high. The Guipuzcoana Company paid its stock holders dividends of 20 percent on their investment no fewer than five times from 1735 to 1739.[33] With such profits to be made, the competition to acquire cacao created a market favorable to cacao producers, which is to say a market in which high prices were paid for planters' beans. Until their contract was ended the English asiento, factors were probably the preferred export merchants in Caracas, exchanging as they did their much sought after human commodity at a competitive rate for cacao. That the demand for slaves on the part of the Caracas planters paralleled the desire of the South Sea Company to acquire cacao is reflected in the fact that in Caracas, the *asientistas* did not have to resort to credit in order to sell their slaves. In 1736, Spanish Americans owed the South Sea Company more than three-quarters of a million pesos for slaves purchased on credit, but none of this debt was located in Caracas.[34] Thus the termination of the English contract in 1739 was doubly difficult in Caracas, because at one blow both the colony's basic source of labor was lost, and a major competitor for the purchase of the region's cacao was removed. In the 1740s, the Guipuzcoana Company, free from the rivalry of the English slave merchants, had no need to pay competitive prices for the cacao that it bought, because cargoes for its ships could be acquired by means of the obligatory alternativa loading system. Already in 1741 the minimum price for cacao was at nine pesos, lower than it had been since 1726, and by the end of the decade it would reach the unprecedented low of seven pesos per fanega.[35]

The history of the South Sea Company in Caracas had one other important consequence that contributed directly to the unrest of the 1740s and the uprising of 1749. During the 1730s, the asiento sold more slaves in Caracas (3,683) than it did in Havana (2,874), Veracruz (1,353), or Campeche (737). Caracas and these ports were only minor markets for the English slavers in comparison with Cartagena (5,043 slaves sold from 1730 through 1736), Buenos Aires (6,473 sold from 1730 through 1738), and Porto Bello/Panama (9,168 slaves sold from 1730 through 1738).[36] Whereas these latter ports served as redistribution centers for the nefarious trade, providing slaves for the entire Pacific coast and the Andean highlands in addition to their more immediate hinterlands, from Caracas there was only one destination for the great majority of Africans imported during the 1730s: the burgeoning cacao haciendas then being planted on the banks of the Tuy River and its several tributaries.

The first parish register for the rich cacao valley of Caucagua, located about halfway between Caracas and the mouth of the Tuy, is dated 1727, which indicates that much of the planting of cacao in the Tuy valley coincided with the South Sea Company's best years in Caracas. By contrast, most of the haciendas in the Lower Tuy, such as those established by Canary Islanders in the vicinity of Panaquire (first parish register dated 1738), were begun during the late 1730s and thereafter and were consequently developed for the most part after the slave trade had collapsed. As a result, from Caucagua upstream, labor on Tuy cacao haciendas was predominantly slave labor, while downstream from that point, many of the newer and smaller cacao groves were commonly worked by their owners, who only occasionally had the assistance of a small gang of slaves. Most of the immigrants who actually settled the Lower Tuy, many of them recently arrived in the 1720s and 1730s from the Canary Islands, had no slaves and therefore had to depend on their own labor first and then the Atlantic slave trade and the English asiento to provide them with African workers. After 1728, the supply of slaves to Caracas increased as the price paid for cacao beans rose, but this coincidence, which lasted less than a decade, really favored only elite growers who then owned fruit-bearing trees on established haciendas in the Upper Tuy or along the Caribbean coast, and who therefore had cacao beans already in hand, ready to exchange for slaves.

High cacao prices were not much more than an incentive, although evidently a powerful one, to the Tuy River frontiersmen who, by planting their land themselves, could only hope that this concurrence of favorable conditions would continue until they had harvested a cacao crop and were able to buy a slave or two with their profits. The removal of the South Sea Company put an end to this hope. Frustrated by this, angered by the declining price paid for cacao in Caracas, irritated by the high cost of obligatory mule transport from the lower Tuy, and finally provoked into action by the replacement of Juan Francisco de León as teniente in Panaquire by an agent of the Guipuzcoana Company, in the spring of 1749 the Isleño planters of the Tuy reached the point where they were more than susceptible to the ill-fated suggestion, put to them by the colony's elite, that they should march to Caracas and demand an end to the Basque monopoly.

NOTES

1. Archivo General de Indias (hereinafter AGI) (Seville), Santo Domingo, leg. 786.

2. The 1744 memorial is in AGI, Santo Domingo, leg. 787. The 1744 *padrón* of cacao haciendas was made at the request of Gov. Gabriel Joseph de Zuloaga. Archivo General de la Nación, Caracas, Sección Diversos, XXVII, fols. 348–61. Haciendas were listed by location, owner, and number of trees.

3. Zuloaga to the king, 1 Jan. 1745, AGI, Caracas, leg. 418.

4. León's statements made in a conversation with the lieutenant governor, Domingo Aguirre y Castillo, cited in José de Armas Chitty and Manuel Pinto C., eds., *Juan Francisco de Léon. Diario de una Insurgencia* (Caracas, 1971), 67.

5. Chitty and Pinto, *Juan Francisco de León*, 80.

6. Chitty and Pinto, *Juan Francisco de León*, 67.

7. Ricardos to the Marqués de la Ensenada, 11 Sept. 1751, AGI, Caracas, leg. 421.

8. Arístides Rojas, *Estudios Históricos* (Caracas, 1891), 268. The Spanish text of the plaque is as follows:

Esta es la Justicia del Rey nuestro Señor, mandada hacer por el Excmo. señor Don Phe. Ricardos Tne. General de los Exceros. de Su Majestad su Govr. y Camp. General desta prova. de Caracas, con Francisco León, amo de esta casa, por pertinaz, rebelde y traidor á la Real Corona y por ello Reo. Que se derribe y siembre de sal pa. perpetua memoria de su Infa.

9. AGI, Caracas, leg. 368. Decree by Ricardos, 25 Apr. 1753; Caracas cabildo to the Marqués de Ensenada, 28 May 1753.

10. AGI, Caracas, leg. 57. Royal order to Ricardos, Buen Retiro, 6 Mar. 1751.

11. The company was ordered or persuaded to offer stock to Caracas residents at its 1752 meeting in Guipúzcoa by d. Julián de Arriaga, minister of the Council of the Indies, who had witnessed the León rebellion firsthand. He had been sent to Caracas from Santo Domingo at first word of the rebellion and had served as governor from November 1749 until Ricardos arrived in 1751. This information is cited in Jules Humbert, *Los orígenes venezolanos* (Spanish edition, Caracas, 1976; original edition, *Les origines vénézuéliennes*, Bordeaux, 1905), 112.

12. *La Gazeta de Caracas,* 20 Sept. 1811. Arístides Rojas gives the subsequent history of this copper tablet in *Estudios Históricos,* 267–73.

13. From the beginning of the century, Caracas showed no affection for the Bourbon regime. Many elites, including the Isleño governor, Ponte y Hoyo, aided the short-lived conspiracy of Bartolomé de Capocelato, the Conde de Antería, agent of the Habsburgs, who visited the colony during the War of the Spanish Succession in an effort to persuade its residents to declare for the House of Austria. Analola Borges, *La Casa de Austria en Venezuela durante la guerra de Sucesión Española (1702–1715)* (Santa Cruz, Tenerife, 1963). The history of cabildo opposition to royal authority in the first half of the eighteenth century is given in my *The Colonial Elite of Early Caracas: Formation and Crisis, 1567–1767,* chap. 5 (University of California Press, 1989).

14. Lucas Guillermo Castillo Lara, *La aventura fundacional de los isleños* (Caracas, 1983), esp. chaps. 2–4.

15. Estimates of elite wealth are made in *Early Caracas,* chap. 5.

Price data are from Roland D. Hussey, *The Caracas Company, 1728–1784* (Cambridge, Mass., 1934), 319. In most of the years from 1701 to 1749, several different prices were paid for Caracas cacao, and Hussey cites a minimum and maximum price for each year. There is no record of how much cacao was sold at a given price, however, and in order to determine which price (minimum, maximum, or mean) was the price most often paid for cacao, some statistical estimates were made. In the first place, the difference between minimum and maximum price in any given year from 1701 to 1749 was usually small, with a mean difference for the half-century of only one and a half pesos. In twenty-three of forty-nine years, the difference between the maximum and the minimum price paid for a fanega of cacao was one peso or less, although in thirteen other years, the difference ranged from four to a maximum of six pesos. Two distinct measures indicate that the minimum price was the price most commonly paid for Caracas cacao.

One method was to compare price curves with receipts of the royal treasury. There are aggregate data for the income of the royal treasury in Caracas for a twenty-year period, 1730 to 1749, in Eduardo Arcila Farías, *Economía colonial de Venezuela,* 2 vols. (2d ed., Caracas, 1973), 1:305. Because a major part of the treasury income came from taxes on cacao exports, the statistical correlation between treasury receipts for the years 1730 to 1749 and minimum, maximum, and mean cacao prices paid during those years can serve as a measure of which price was most likely to have been paid most often. Comparison of the coefficients indicates that the minimum price correlates most closely: minimum price: R = .47; mean price: R = .41; maximum price: R = .29.

A second measure was provided by church tithe records, also for a period of twenty years, 1724 to 1743, for three coastal valleys. The three valleys, Ocumare, San Esteban, and Guaiguaza, were given entirely to cacao farming, and they had reached their capacity for expansion by 1720. Therefore, with production of cacao at a generally constant rate in these valleys, the tithe collected there would presumably vary most closely in correlation with the current price paid for the cacao. The correlation coefficients for the price curves and the curve of the sum of the tithes for the three valleys also indicate that it was the minimum price that was most often paid for cacao from 1724 to 1743: minimum price: R = .53; mean price: .41; maximum price: .30. The tithe data are from the archive of the Registro Principal, Caracas, Civiles, 1744 R.

16. Demetrios Ramos Pérez, "La política del Marqués de la Ensenada—asesorado por el exvirrey Eslava—en relación con el levantamiento contra la Guipuzcoana," in *Estudios de Historia Venezolana* (Caracas, 1976), 673. According to Ramos (665) it was Eslava who first suggested that principal Caracas planters and merchants be invited to purchase shares in the Guipuzcoana Company, as had been done with the recently created Havana Company.

17. This is my understanding of the custom of tercio buque. Several aspects of the process of taking on cargo remain unclear. Once a ship's captain had received a royal license to receive cargo, both cosecheros and merchants must have appeared to register the cacao they wanted to export. An agent of the royal treasury probably figured their tax obligations at this point. What is unknown is the method by which it was decided who would get the opportunity to ship when there was more cacao for export than the ship could carry. When there was more cosechero cacao for export than could be accommodated in the hacienda owners' tercio buque, how was it determined whose cacao would be loaded and whose cacao would necessarily be sold to merchants or to the ship's captain? Did the ship's supercargo accept cacao for these reserved portions of the ship on a first-come, first-served basis? Did the governor or the royal treasury have any supervisory role in this, and, if so, was this one reason why the cabildo was eager to govern in the absence of the governor?

18. See Analola Borges, *Alvarez Abreu y su extraordinaria misión en Indias* (Santa Cruz, Tenerife, 1963).

19. AGI, Santo Domingo, leg. 787.

20. In June 1742, word reached Caracas that the common price paid for cacao at Veracruz was fifty-two and one-half pesos; in Caracas the price then ranged from nine and one-half pesos to fourteen and one-half; Gov. Gabriel de Zuloaga to the king, 26 Feb. 1745, AGI, Santo Domingo, leg. 786.

21. Letter of Julián de Arriaga (interim governor of Caracas from 1749 until the

arrival of Ricardos in 1751) to the factors of the Guipuzcoana Company, 29 Mar. 1750, cited in Demetrio Ramos Pérez, *Estudios de Historia Venezolana*, 655.

22. Cabildo to the king, Jan. 1745, AGI, Santo Domingo, leg. 786.

23. Examples of Mexican investments in Caracas cacao are included in a Guipuzcoana Company document that lists the ships either lost at sea or taken by enemy corsairs while traveling between Veracruz and La Guaira from 1733 to 1739. In 1733, the frigate of Gerónimo López Barroso, "uno de las del trajín de la Vera Cruz," sank in the Bermuda Canal with 25,000 pesos lost to Caracas and New Spain investors; in 1734, the frigate of Pedro de Arrieta sank off Grand Cayman with cacao worth 150,000 pesos, much of it purchased by New Spain merchants; in 1734, the frigate of Gabriel de Bezama was lost near the island of Arenas, fifty leagues from Campeche, with 10 percent of its cargo silver coin for Caracas; and in 1738, a frigate bound for Caracas was taken near the island of Tortugilla with 100,000 pesos in cash and Mexican merchandise. Interested in discrediting the traditional trade, the company also gave examples of unscrupulous or inept individuals who had stolen or misspent cash intended for the purchase of Caracas cacao. In 1736, Pedro Ariztoy, maestre, could not account for 12,000 pesos he had been given in Veracruz by Andrés González for "the purchase and return of cacaos"; the previous year, Capt. Lorenzo Hernández de Santiago, vecino of Caracas, was jailed in Veracruz for the loss of 50,000 pesos he had received for the same purpose. The directors of the Royal Guipuzcoana Company to the Council of the Indies, 17 Mar. 1739, AGI, Santo Domingo, leg. 786.

24. The published broadside is entitled: "Segundo Memorial del Conde de San Xavier y de Don Francisco de Ponte en nombre de los vecinos, cosecheros y cargadores a Nueva España" (Madrid, 1746). The observations about the reluctance of New Spain merchants to invest in the cacao commerce and the flight of residents from Caracas to the countryside as a result of difficulties caused by the lack of capital were made in the first memorial (Madrid, 1745). Copies of these are in AGI, Santo Domingo, leg. 786.

25. The directors of the Royal Guipuzcoana Company to the Council of the Indies, 17 Mar. 1739; Governor Zuloaga to the king, 26 Feb. 1745, AGI, Santo Domingo, leg. 786.

26. I explore this theme in *Early Caracas*, chap. 6.

27. The best discussion of Anglo-Spanish diplomacy and the American trade during this period is Geoffrey J. Walker, *Spanish Politics and Imperial Trade, 1700–1789* (Bloomington and London, 1979), chap. 8.

28. The company was established by royal cédula dated 25 Sept. 1728, and the first company ships arrived at Puerto Cabello on 4 Sept. 1730.

29. Arcila Farías, *Economía colonial de Venezuela* 1:248–50.

30. Colin A. Palmer, *Human Cargoes: The British Slave Trade to Spanish America, 1700–1739* (Urbana, 1981), chap. 6. The Guipuzcoana Company's record as slave trader is mentioned in Hussey, *The Caracas Company*, 172–74.

31. Palmer, *Human Cargoes*, 102–10.

32. Palmer, *Human Cargoes*, 170.

33. Hussey, *The Caracas Company*, 321.

34. Palmer, 126–27.

35. In fact, the South Sea Company had already begun to fail to meet the Caracas demand for slaves some years before its operations were brought to a close by the outbreak of the War of Jenkins's Ear. After selling more than four hundred blacks in 1730 and more than five hundred from 1731 through 1733, fewer than one hundred slaves were sold in 1734, and more than three hundred slaves would be sold in only two of the remaining five years of company operation. Cacao prices seem to have responded sensitively to the weakening of the slave supply, and as early as 1736, they had begun their descent toward the record low levels that would result in León's rebellion. When the South Sea Company ceased operations in 1739, however, the minimum price paid for cacao was still at twelve pesos, the lowest minimum price paid in a decade, but a price equal to the mean price paid during the eighteenth century up to that date.

36. Palmer, *Human Cargoes*, chap. 6.

Price Movements in Brazil Before, During, and After the Gold Boom, with Special Reference to the Salvador Market, 1670–1769

Dauril Alden

AFTER MORE THAN A CENTURY OF DISAPPOINTMENT, THE QUEST FOR PRECIOUS wealth in Brazil was crowned with success in the 1680s when the first major gold deposits were discovered a few hundred miles north of Rio de Janeiro. Between about 1695 and 1755, vast quantities of ore were extracted from half a dozen Brazilian captaincies, most notably Minas Gerais, Goiás, and Mato Grosso. It is estimated that the average yearly bullion yield from these three administrative units rose from 1,470 kilograms (1700–1705) to a peak of 15,760 kilograms (1750–54) before beginning its inevitable spiral downward.[1]

Inevitably such an outpouring of gold must have had considerable impact upon price movements in major Brazilian markets, but earlier studies of price movements in colonial Brazil have not been particularly informative on this point. The first, published half a century ago by Alfredo de Escragnole Taunay, the prolific, popular Paulista historian, provided some useful information concerning prices in seventeenth- and eighteenth-century São Paulo extracted from the steward's book of a Benedictine monastery.[2] Taunay's study, however, failed to conform to accepted canons for the preparation of systematic price series. The same was true of Francisco Rodrigues Leite's 1963 article, which offered additional data concerning seventeenth-century Paulista prices derived from inventories, wills, and price regulations enacted by the municipal council (*câmara*) of São Paulo.[3]

Significant advances in technique were evident in the work of the Bahian scholar Katia Maria de Queiros Mattoso and that of the North American Harold B. Johnson, Jr., both of whom published in the early 1970s.[4] Queiros Mattoso used local archives to measure cycles and price trends of a limited number of commodities in Salvador, Brazil's administrative capital, leading port, and chief cane sugar producer, between 1750 and 1830. Johnson did the same for the larger number of goods available in Rio de Janeiro, Salvador's rival and successor, from 1763 until 1830. None of these writers was, however, primarily concerned with price behavior during Brazil's golden age.

The most famous contemporary gloss concerning such activity during the era itself comes from the quill of a Tuscan-born Jesuit, Giovanni Antonio Andreoni, better known by his pseudonym, André Joâo Antonil. In his classic analysis of the sources of Brazil's wealth, first published in 1711, Antonil bemoaned "these excessively high prices that were current in the Mines, [which] were the reason why the price of other things increased so much elsewhere . . . in the ports and cities and towns of Brazil . . . and why the inhabitants suffer from great lack of provisions, which are almost all taken and sold where they give the most profit.[5] Was Antonil correct in his indictment? Was the upward movement in prices throughout Brazil simply a response to the exceptional demands of the interior mining camps? Were price levels of locally produced commodities as seriously affected as imported goods? Did Brazil suffer from a continuous inflationary spiral for more than a half-century, as some writers imply?[6] At the end of the boom, were price levels generally higher, lower, or approximately the same as when the boom began?

This essay attempts to provide some answers to these questions by focusing primarily upon the behavior of prices of locally produced and imported foodstuffs in the key market of Salvador between the 1670s and the late 1760s. The study starts before the bullion boom began and ends after its conclusion. In addition, the essay offers some comparisons between price levels prevailing in Salvador and those in several other parts of Brazil during the period.

The analysis of Salvadorean prices offered here relies upon several types of sources. The most important are those of the archives of the Santa Casa de Misericórdia of Bahia, the most characteristic charitable institution of the Portuguese empire. Some light is cast by four surviving registers of expenses (*livros de despezas*) which incompletely span the years 1672–1709. Far more illuminating, however, are the *maços* or *pacotes de despeza* series of monthly receipts.[7] They begin in 1702 and continue, in different form, until today. I examined the first 115 bundles, which contain two types of documents of interest to the price historian. The first are the authenticated monthly expense accounts of the chief steward of the Holy House, who bought supplies for its hospital and for prisoners confined to the city jail. The second are the monthly records of expenses incurred on behalf of the Santa Casa's women's shelter (*recolhimento*).

Two other sources fill in some of the gaps in the Santa Casa's documentary series. The first is a unique account of purchases and sales made by a local planter-merchant for a newly established Italian Capuchin house while it was being constructed in Salvador between 1709 and 1725.[8] The second consists of surviving fragments of the expenditures of the Bahian nunnery of Santa Clara do Desterro, founded in 1677.[9] Such fragments, kindly made available by Dr. Susan Soeiro, include one bound volume for the years 1726–32 and loose pages of an account book for the years 1751–69.

Three other groups of material offer important supplemental information. The first is the published correspondence of commission agents of a Lisbon merchant who traded with various parts of Brazil during the golden age.[10] The second consists of the annual economic reports and various other dispatches prepared by Bahian viceroys for the crown. Last are the resources of the municipal archives of Salvador. They include reports by the local câmara to the viceroy and to the crown, the council's periodic price regulations (*posturas*), a shipping register, and a register of weekly beef prices prevailing at the municipal abattoir. In varying degrees, each of these sources helps to illuminate the behavior of prices in colonial Brazil's leading city.

The city of Salvador, founded in 1549 and the administrative center of Brazil until 1763, is situated along the eastern shore of the broad and deep Bay of All Saints. By the early eighteenth century, the city had spread along the narrow beachfront and the adjoining heights from the entrance bar northward for a distance of four or five leagues (about twenty kilometers).[11] When the English sailor William Dampier visited Salvador in 1699, he guessed that it contained about two thousand houses, suggesting a population of some 10,000 persons.[12] If ecclesiastical counts made in 1706 and 1718 are to be trusted, Dampier was only half-right, for they show the number of persons of confessional age in the city to have been between 18,000 and 21,000.[13] Two other estimates made in the late 1750s indicate between 32,000 and 37,000 persons within the city limits and another 60,000 dwelling on plantations and farms and in small towns around the bay.[14] Other clusters existed in the subordinate captaincy of Sergipe (northeast of the capital), another along the south coast, especially in the Ilhéus district, and another in the interior. A census of 1780, the most complete of a series extending over a quarter-century, indicates a total enumerated population for Salvador and its dependencies of 288,000, or about 19.2 percent of the recorded population of Brazil.[15]

Until successfully challenged by Rio de Janeiro in the late eighteenth century, Salvador was both Brazil's most populous city and its economic center. The Capuâme livestock grounds, situated about forty kilometers north of the city, received hundreds of cattle a week, the survivors of long drives that originated in ranches along the São Francisco River and in the interior cattle barony of Piauí. Thirty or more ships a year brought wines, brandies, wheat, olive oil, codfish, cloth, iron, steel, hardware, and luxury products from Lisbon and Porto, and returned to the Portuguese kingdom with thousands of chests of sugar, hides, and rolls of tobacco. More than a score of vessels sailed each year to the Mina coast to replenish Bahia's slave population. The urban waterfront was serviced daily by as many as forty small craft (*barcas, lanchas, saveiros*) that supplied the city with fresh quantities of fish, manioc, beans, corn, and other foodstuffs produced within the captaincy. From the capital's warehouses, goods were transported by land and water to interior markets, especially the gold camps of Minas Gerais and Goiás, but also to the cattle stations of interior Pernambuco and adjacent Piauí. Salvador was thus a vital center of the Brazilian economy.[16]

In order to measure the behavior of prices in the Bahian market, I have selected five locally grown foodstuffs—white cane sugar, beef, manioc, white beans, and hens; six commodities imported from Europe—wheat, olive oil, salted cod, rice, vinegar, and wine; and one from Africa—slaves. Cane sugar was, of course, Bahia's dominant crop from the captaincy's sixteenth-century inception. Most of it was exported to the Iberian peninsula, but about 10 percent of the crop was locally consumed. In the 1680s, there were about a hundred mills (*engenhos*) in the captaincy, the most important being those situated in the north and west of Salvador in the fertile periphery of the Bay of All Saints; others were located at considerable distances in the drier backlands north and west of the bay, in the northeast, and along the south coast. By Antonil's time, the number of mills had increased to 146, and by the late 1750s, there were between 172 and 180 engenhos in the captaincy.[17] As Dr. Rae Jean Flory perceptively observes, however, "The number of functioning engenhos varied from season to season in response to climatic conditions, the availability of slaves, the financial status of individual owners, and other factors."[18] The level of the captaincy's yearly exports therefore varied markedly from a low of five to a maximum of fifteen thousand chests, each weighing in excess of five hundred kilograms in this period.[19]

The researches of Frédéric Mauro and Vitorino Magalhães Godinho have demonstrated convincingly that Brazil's sugar industry, the mainstay of its economy since about 1570, was in the doldrums a century later.[20] One barometer of the sugar crisis, whose effects were felt throughout the entire Atlantic world, is the Lisbon wholesale price, which fell 33 percent between

1659 and 1668 and tumbled another 11 percent between 1668 and 1688.[21] Bahian cane sugar prices continued to be depressed throughout most of our period. Even recurrent droughts (secas), which reduced harvests by half and caused many transports to lay over for a second season because of the lack of sufficient cargoes, rarely boosted prices.[22] The five-year drought of the 1690s did eventually drive up the price briefly, but it fell back quickly and did not advance again until the 1710s, when commodity prices in Bahia were generally high. Sugar prices declined during the 1720s, but rose sharply in 1736 after a two-year seca. They then quickly dropped again before moving upward during the 1740s, when maritime warfare in the Caribbean inter-rupted competing supply lines to Europe. Sugar prices in Bahia rose again, but less confidently, during the Seven Years' War (1756–63); thereafter they descended to a level fewer than ten index points higher than what had prevailed during the years 1678–98 (see Table 11.1).

Some years ago, J. H. Galloway, a historical geographer, published a provocative essay in which he challenged conventional wisdom and argued that the sugarcane industry of the Brazilian Northeast did not experience a serious crisis until the early 1730s.[23] The evidence summarized here does not support that contention. On the contrary, it demonstrates that through-out the late seventeenth and early eighteenth centuries, the industry was continually beset by rising costs and generally low returns. The first blow to planters was the crown's drastic, 20-percent currency devaluation in 1688,[24] but the most persistent burden thereafter was the constantly escalating cost of fresh slaves.

During the golden age, every sector of the Brazilian economy bid up the price of slaves. In an oft-quoted passage, Antonil wrote that "the slaves are the hands and feet of the sugar planter, for without them it is neither possible to maintain or to increase the productivity of the plantation nor to operate its mill."[25] Not only were blacks the backbone of the sugar industry, they were also required to serve on the tobacco and manioc farms, on the backland gold washings and livestock ranches, on the seaport docks, and in the homes of the elite.

Thousands of slaves entered Salvador and its sister ports in the State of Brazil—Recife and Rio de Janeiro—each year.[26] Perhaps a third of the 439,000 whom Philip D. Curtin estimates to have reached those ports between 1701 and 1730 passed through Salvador.[27] There is good evidence that between 1728 and 1748 more than 5,000 a year did so.[28] Most of these slaves were from the Mina coast, the source of 54,566 chattels who arrived in Salvador between 1750 and 1755, when the slave trade to that city reached its apparent

Table 11.1

White Sugar, 1675–1768
(100 = 1,645 réis/arroba)

N.B. In this and in succeeding tables percent prices and index numbers in parentheses represent an upward adjustment of 20 percent for prices recorded or set before the currency reform of 1688 in order to make the series consistent. Blank or missing years unavailable. Except as noted, reference base is 1747–51.

Year	Price in rs.	Index No.	Year	Price in rs.	Index No.
1675	(1356)	(82.4)	1701	1800	109.4
1676	(1112)	(67.6)	1702	1600	97.3
1677	(1206)	(73.3)	1703		
1678	(1200)	(72.9)	1704	1500	91.2
1679	(1200)	(72.9)	1705	1550	94.2
1680	(1392)	(84.6)	1706	1525	92.1
1681			1707	1305	79.3
1682			1708	1150	69.9
1683	(1392)	(84.6)	1709	1350	82.1
1684			1710	1300	79.0
1685			1711		
1686			1712	1600	97.3
1687			1713	1280	77.8
1688	(1020)	(62.0)	1714	1760	106.9
1689	(864)	(52.5)	1715	2050	124.6
1690			1716	2000	121.58
1691	1200	72.9	1717	2100	127.6
1692	1200	72.9	1718	1920	116.7
1693			1719	1920	116.7
1694			1720	1920	116.7
1695	1600	97.3	1721	1350	82.0
1696			1722	1550	94.2
1697	1500	91.2	1723	1550	94.2
1698	1264	76.8	1724	1500	91.2
1699	2200	133.4	1725	1710	104.0
1700			1726		

Table 11.1 (continued)

Year	Price in rs.	Index No.	Year	Price in rs.	Index No.
1727			1748	1922	116.84
1728	1663	101.0	1749	1872	113.79
1729	1575	95.7	1750	1327	80.66
1730	1457	88.57	1751	1152	70.03
1731	1530	93.0	1752		
1732	1240	73.4	1753	1600	97.64
1733	1280	77.81	1754	1472	89.48
1734			1755	1320	80.24
1735	1265	76.89	1756	1400	85.11
1736	1974	120.0	1757	1472	89.36
1737			1758	1598	97.14
1738	1066	64.8	1759	1870	113.68
1739	914	55.56	1760	1575	95.74
1740	1010	61.39	1761	1417	86.14
1741	1266	76.98	1762	1440	87.54
1742	1189	72.30	1763	1360	82.67
1743	1600	97.26	1764	1486	90.33
1744	1333	81.03	1765	1413	85.29
1745	1760	106.99	1766	1327	80.67
1746	2049	124.56	1767	1360	82.67
1747	1952	118.60	1768	1294	78.66

Sources: 1675–79, 1688–89, 1695, 1698, 1704–1706, 1718, and 1713: Arquivo da Santa Casa de Misericórdia (hereinafter ASCM), cods. 848–51; 1683, 1688, 1691, 1692, 1698, 1704–1709: Antonil, 29; 1676, 1680, 1684, 1701: Flory, 26; 1710, 1712, 1714–16, 1718–25: RE (see n. 8); 1714–15 and 1717: NC (see n. 6) 1; 1728–32: Arquivo do Convento de Santa Clara (hereinafter ASCD), Despesas, 1726–32, caixa 2 (courtesy Dr. Susan Soeiro); remaining years, ASCM, Maços de despeza (hereinafter MD).

peak for the century. Thereafter the level of imports fell to an average of 2,432 a year for the period from 1756 to 1770, reflecting the gradual exhaustion of the interior mines.[29]

Slave prices in Salvador advanced throughout the years spanned by this study (see Table 11.2). Between the 1680s and 1709, they increased by nearly 63 percent. According to Rae Jean Flory, the average values of slaves sold in Bahia's plantation zone nearly doubled between 1690 and 1725.[30] In the 1720s and 1730s, slaves were selling in Salvador for nearly 3.3 times as much as they had brought in the 1690s. Sufficient quantities were unavailable at any price because of the flourishing market in Minas Gerais where, in Antonil's time, a prime slave sold for more than 5 times the average price in Salvador.[31] Little wonder, therefore, that many Bahians remained eager to sell slaves to buyers in that premium market or that the governors-general, acting in response to pleas from Salvador's municipal council, vainly prohibited such sales and implored the crown to impose quotas to assure the sugar sector a sufficient number of slaves.[32]

According to one well-informed observer in eighteenth-century Bahia, the average slave there produced forty arrobas (580 kg) of sugar per year.[33] Graph 11.1 uses that estimate and suggests the existence of a widening gap between the price of slaves and that of sugar throughout most of the period surveyed here. It is not surprising that a royal magistrate could report toward the end of our period that "the lords of these plantations are all deeply in debt . . . and lament their impending ruin because everything they buy is so dear, including the blacks."[34]

Although many planters possessed their own sources of meat, most Bahians were obliged to purchase theirs in the open market. While imported hams and bacon and locally raised pork and lamb could be found in Salvadoran butcher shops, they were far more expensive than beef, the most readily available meat and the only type for which serial prices may be constructed from our sources.[35] Brazilian cattle were scrawny, tough beasts compared with those fat eight-hundred-pounders auctioned at the famous Smithfield market in late eighteenth-century England.[36] After being driven for hundreds of miles without a respite for fattening, stock that weighed about 147 kilograms at the ranch was sold at the Capuâme fair weighing about a third less.[37]

Table 11.3 assembles data derived from three sources. The first is a register of nearly weekly prices set at the Capuâme fair between 1714 and 1727. The second consists of the prices recorded by the Santa Casa's steward. Since better sources are lacking, the price limits decreed by the câmara during the

Table 11.2

Price of a Prime Slave, Salvador, 1659–1769

Year	Price in réis	Source	Year	Price in réis	Source
1659	49,000	1	1711	114,000	1
1670	60,000	1	1712	116,770	6
1680	50,000	1, 2	1713	90,000	5
1688	60,000	3	1723	200,000	7
1692	60,000	4	1738	200,000	8
1700	75,000	5	1742	105,000	9
1704	89,000	1	1743	120,000	9
1705	94,000	1	1754	86,400	10
1707	85,714	1	1756	100,000	11
1708	95,000	1, 5	1769	163,000	9
1709	84,000	1,5			
1710	70,000	1			

Sources:

1. Antonil, 272–273, n. 3.
2. ASCM, cod. 848.
3. Câmara (Salvador) to king, *Cartas do Senado,* 3: 63ff.
4. Câmara Coutinho to Pedro II, 4 July 1692 (see n. 24).
5. ASCM, cod. 850.
6. *NC,* 1: 124–25.
7. Câmara (Salvador) to king, 15 Nov. 1723, AMB, Cartas do Senado a sua magestade, 28:9, fls. 65ᵛ–68ʳ.
8. João Lúcio de Azevedo, Épocas de Portugal económico, 2d ed. (Lisbon, 1947), 326.
9. Courtesy of Prof. Stuart B. Schwartz, University of Minnesota.
10. Petition of procurator general (Society of Jesus) to king, ca. 1754, Arquivo Nacional da Torre do Tombo, Lisbon, Cartório Jesuítico, 68/204–205.
11. Petition of homens de negocio, Salvador, to governor-general, ca. 1756, APB, OR/56, fls. 6–26ᵛ.

Graph 11.1

Price in Salvador of a Prime Slave vs.
Price of Forty Arrobas of White Sugar, 1680–1769

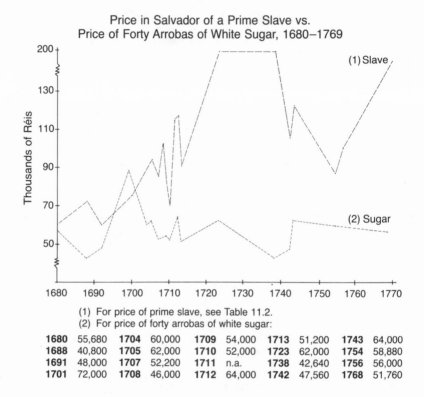

(1) For price of prime slave, see Table 11.2.
(2) For price of forty arrobas of white sugar:

1680	55,680	1704	60,000	1709	54,000	1713	51,200	1743	64,000
1688	40,800	1705	62,000	1710	52,000	1723	62,000	1754	58,880
1691	48,000	1707	52,200	1711	n.a.	1738	42,640	1756	56,000
1701	72,000	1708	46,000	1712	64,000	1742	47,560	1768	51,760

1680s and 1690s are also included as tentative benchmarks. In practice, the legally established limits were often defied, especially during the first three decades of the eighteenth century when much of the available livestock—75 percent if we may believe the câmara's complaints—was trailed through the backlands of Bahia to the mining camps of Minas where, in 1703, cattle sold for thirty to fifty times as much as at Capuâme.[38] Neither the council nor the viceroys could do much about the activities of the so-called "monopolists" (*atravessadores*) who often bought stock at the ranch gate and drove them either to the mines or slaughtered them and sold their products locally for two to three times the sanctioned price.[39]

Beef shortages in the Salvadoran market became a common occurrence during the 1710s and 1720s, when prices doubled and tripled.[40] In the mid-1720s, the câmara tried to outwit the "monopolists" when it appealed to the viceroy to authorize waivers of the well-known 1701 edict that prohibited

Table 11.3

Beef Prices, 1682–1769

(100 = 571.8 réis/arroba)

Year	Price in réis	Index number	Source	Year	Price in réis	Index number	Source
1682	(312)	(54.56)	1	1714	426	74.5	5
1683				1715	490	85.69	5
1684				1716	498	87.09	5
1685				1717	506	88.49	5
1686	(230)	(40.3)	2	1718	535	93.56	5
1687				1719	547.5	95.75	5
1688				1720	537.6	94.01	5
1689				1721	517.3	90.46	5
1690				1722	446.8	78.14	5
1691				1723	608.8	106.5	5
1692				1724	607.4	106.2	5
1693	372	65.1	3	1725	617.4	107.9	5
1694				1726	646.3	113.0	5
1695				1727	608.7	106.5	5
1696	384	67.2	3	1728	640	111.9	6
1697	372	65.1	3	1729	640	111.9	6
1698				1730	648	113.3	6
1699				1731	690	120.67	6
1700				1732	640	111.9	6
1701				1733	560	97.9	6
1702				1734	554.3	96.9	6
1703				1735	480	83.95	6
1704	400	69.95	4	1736	480	83.95	6
1705				1737			
1706				1738	531	92.86	6
1707				1739	480	83.95	6
1708				1740	529	92.5	6
1709				1741	540	94.4	6
1710				1742	521	91.11	6
1711				1743	532.5	93.2	6
1712				1744	584	102.1	6
1713				1745	533	93.2	6

Table 11.3 (continued)

Year	Price in réis	Index number	Source	Year	Price in réis	Index number	Source
1746	563	98.46	6	1758	480	83.95	6
1747	554.3	96.9	6	1759	501	87.6	6
1748	571.4	99.93	6	1760	518	90.59	6
1749	610.9	106.68	6	1761	480	83.95	6
1750	572.3	100.00	6	1762	468	81.85	6
1751	550	92.2	6	1763	509	89.0	6
1752	575	100.5	6	1764	440	76.9	6
1753	586	102.5	6	1765	442.6	77.4	6
1754	546.2	95.5	6	1766	486	84.99	6
1755	480	83.95	6	1767	474.6	83.0	6
1756	502	87.79	6	1768	472.7	82.6	6
1757	520	90.94	6	1769	472	82.6	6

Sources:
1. Atas da câmara, 5: 334.
2. Portaria, 1 July 1686, Annaes do archivo público e estado da Bahia, 7 (Salvador, 1921), 9–10.
3. Atas da câmara, 6: 209, 321, 329–30.
4. F. A. Pereira da Costa, Chronólogica histórica do estado do Piauhy desde os seus primitivos tempos até . . . 1889 ([Receife], 1909), 24.
5. "Registro de preços de gados e talhos, 1714–1727," AMB, 160.1.
6. ASCM, MD.

unfenced stock from grazing within ten leagues (about forty kilometers) of the seacoast or the mouth of any stream flowing into the Bay of All Saints. The viceroy complied and granted an impressive number of such waivers during the remainder of the 1720s and the 1730s to local planters.[41] Such exemptions and the gradual development of beef herds within the mining zones appear to have alleviated local shortages. Beef prices in Salvador peaked in the 1730s; except for years of exceptional drought, they remained relatively stable thereafter.[42]

There were, of course, many days when Bahians and other Brazilians were prohibited from eating meat and other times when they were fearful of doing so. According to the 1707 constitutions of the Archdiocese of Bahia, prohibited days included Fridays and Saturdays, the forty days between Ash Wednesday and Holy Saturday, the first three days of Rogation Week in May, and certain other occasions. Except to take care of the needs of the sick, slaughtering during Easter Week was forbidden upon threat of excommunication.[43] While such restrictions were obviously not always observed in practice,[44] an anonymous French traveler who visited Salvador in 1703 reported that "every Portuguese believes he would die if he ate lamb or beef at night."[45] An alternative, albeit an expensive one, was fowl.

Locally available fowl included ducks, turkeys, and chickens. When the English sailor Dampier visited Salvador in 1699, he observed that "the chief [fowl] beside their Ducks are Dunghill-Fowls, of which they have two sorts; one . . . much the size of our Cocks and Hens, the other very large; . . . when . . . full grown and well feathered, they appear very large . . . as indeed they are; neither do they want for Price, for they are sold . . . for half a Crown or three shillings apiece, just as they are brought first to Market out of the Country, when they are so lean as to be scarce fit to eat."[46] Unfit or not, chickens were undeniably expensive in eighteenth-century Salvador. If we may assume that a full-grown hen (*galinha*) dressed at about 900 grams, the price was ten to twenty times greater than for an equivalent amount of beef. For a young pullet (*frango*), the price was 40 percent less. Since the Middle Ages, chicken has been commonly prescribed for the infirm. The Santa Casa bought considerable quantities of hens and fryers for its hospital and the Poor Clares did so for their convent. Prices remained high until about 1730 but softened thereafter. Eggs, of which the Santa Casa regularly purchased more than two thousand a month, followed a similar pattern.[47]

One analyst of the Brazilian diet has concluded that during the colonial period "vegetables were rarely eaten, and those which were, always were cooked."[48] He is only partially correct. Most vegetables certainly were cooked, but Salvadoran markets regularly offered red, white, and black beans; chickpeas; cabbages; squashes; and lettuce.[49] Though most are mentioned in our institutional sources, the only one for which adequate serial data exist during this period is white beans. They averaged 886.8 rs. per *alqueire* (about 30 kilograms) between 1747 and 1751, but their price varied from a high of 2,560 rs. (1716) to a low of 480.8 rs. (1761).[50]

Such vegetables were supplements to manioc, the traditional poor person's staple in colonial times and one still widely consumed. Manioc comes from a bushy perennial whose starchy roots may be boiled, roasted, or, more commonly, ground to yield several grades of flour (*farinha de mandioca, farinha de terra,* or simply *farinha*) used for porridges, soups, and especially bread. In the form of flour, manioc offers about as many calories per one hundred grams as wheat, but it provides significantly fewer proteins and vitamins.[51] Yet its availability was as vital to the diet of the ordinary Bahian as wheat was to members of the elite. A government study of food consumption rates in the Amazon in the 1950s indicated that the average person consumed between one and three hundred grams of manioc flour per day, i.e., between 3.31 and 9.06 kilograms per month.[52] Consumption levels in eighteenth-century Bahia must have been much higher. In 1718, the governor of Rio de Janeiro reported that the monthly manioc ration for soldiers in his garrison was about three-quarters of an alqueire and that seems to have been the standard military ration for the rest of the century.[53] Since enlisted men were drawn from the lower classes, it is reasonable to assume that the level of consumption by the ordinary Bahian was about the same, i.e., about 20 kilograms per month.

By the 1710s, close to 3,050 metric tons of manioc entered Salvador a year, an amount destined to treble during the course of the century.[54] Such manioc came from various sources: the marginal uplands around the bay, especially the township of Maragogipe in the west; that of Jaguaripe in the south; several islands within the bay; the Rio Real district to the northwest; and the south coast, especially the townships of Boipeba, Camamú, and Cairú. Although manioc farmers (roceiros) occupied a humble status when compared to the great sugar lords, many were small slaveholders and longtime rivals of the planters. By the 1680s, some farmers near Maragogipe were shifting to more profitable crops, especially tobacco, just as today Brazilian farmers are shifting from beans and manioc to cane sugar to cash in on Brazil's celebrated gasahol program. Today the price of beans and manioc soars as a result. The same was true in Bahia during the late seventeenth and early eighteenth centuries, when authorities confronted disturbing scarcities and alarming price rises, conditions that became endemic to Salvador for decades (see Table 11.4 and Graph 11.2).[55]

As they confronted such conditions, both the câmara and the captaincy's senior royal officials vainly sought effective remedies. Governors-general unsuccessfully attempted to restrict certain lands to manioc production. Each planter and merchant active in the slave trade was enjoined to plant five hundred covas, or hollows, of manioc for every slave he possessed. The câmara repeatedly fixed, then reluctantly increased, legal prices of manioc in order to attract sufficient supplies to the capital. It tried (but failed) to secure a regulation requiring all fleets from the kingdom to carry sufficient biscuit for their return trips. Governors'-general sharply rebuked militia commanders who failed to compel farmers in their districts to boost manioc plantings. One governor-general even sought to prohibit the export of manioc to other captaincies but the crown overruled him. A successor employed a different tactic: he ordered militia officers to beach suspected boats, remove their

Table 11.4

Manioc Flour and Wheat Flour, 1674–1769
Manioc—100 = 507.1 réis/alqueire
Wheat—100 = 1,514 réis/arroba

Year	Manioc		Wheat	
	Price	Index Number	Price	Index Number
1674	(192)	(37.86)		
1675				
1676				
1677				
1678				
1679	(192)	(37.86)		
1680				
1681				
1682	(307)	(60.58)		
1683				
1684				
1685				
1686				
1687				
1688	(1,200)	(236.0)		
1689			(1,241.8)	(82.0)
1690				
1691				
1692				
1693				
1694				
1695				
1696				
1697	400	78.8		
1698	480	94.6		
1699				
1700	1,120	220.8		
1701				
1702				
1703				
1704	512	100.9	2,022	133.5

Table 11.4 (continued)

	Manioc		Wheat	
Year	Price	Index Number	Price	Index Number
1740	438.5	86.47	1,765	116.57
1741	530	104.5	2,144	141.6
1742	557.5	109.9	2,055	135.7
1743	476	93.87	1,298	85.7
1744	396.8	78.25	1,456	96.2
1745	450	88.74	1,540	101.7
1746	400	78.88	1,477.5	97.59
1747	365.6	72.1	1,578	104.2
1748	509	100.37	1,526	100.79
1749	733	144.55	1,634	107.9
1750	563.9	111	1,497	98.87
1751	364	71.78	1,335	88.2
1752	397.7	78	1,507.5	99.57
1753	548	108.1	1,418.6	93.7
1754	502.6	99	1,420	93.79
1755	326	64.28	1,150	75.95
1756	347	68.4	1,244	82.2
1757	474.6	93.59	2,107.5	139.2
1758	491.7	96.96	2,173	143.5
1759	403.8	79.6	2,020	133
1760	381.96	75	1,982	130.9
1761	324.9	64.1	1,572	103.8
1762	386	76	1,432.8	94.6
1763	484	95.4	1,905.5	125.85
1764	500	98.59	2,240	147.95
1765	306	60	2,080	137.4
1766	361.75	71	1,560	169.1
1767	411	81.1	2,560	169.1
1768	280	55	3,840	253.6
1769	250	49		

Sources:

Manioc: 1670, 1679, 1682: *Atas da câmara*, 5; 1688: ASCM, cod. 849; 1697–98: *Atas da câmara*, 6: 345, 352–54; 1700, 1704–1705, 1708: ASCM, cod. 850; 1711, 1716–23: RE; 1716, 1724–25: ASCM, MD; 1726–32: ASCD, Despesas, 1726–32; 1728–69: ASCM, MD.

Wheat: 1689: ASCM, cod. 849; 1704–1705: ASCM, cod. 850; 1707: *NC*, 1. 1710, 1712–13: RE; 1716–63: ASCM, MD; 1764–65: ASCD, caixa 2; 1766–67: ASCM, MD; 1768, ASCD, caixa 2.

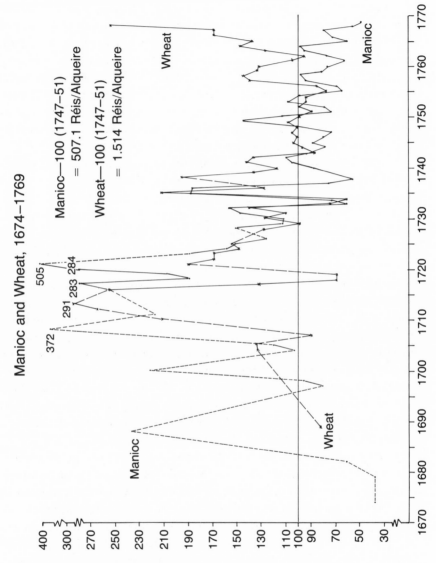

Graph 11.2

Manioc and Wheat, 1674–1769

Manioc—100 (1747–51)
= 507.1 Réis/Alqueire

Wheat—100 (1747–51)
= 1.514 Réis/Alqueire

rudders and sails, and dispatch to the municipal jail all persons suspected of running manioc to rival Rio de Janeiro. A later viceroy ruefully admitted that "experience" had demonstrated the futility of all such measures; manioc was still being exported to more profitable markets outside of Bahia, just as Antonil had said. Shortages persisted until the late 1730s, as did the perennial complaints of the câmara against shadowy, nefarious "monopolists" and greedy farmers. Thereafter, however, the price of manioc began to fall rather steadily, presumably as a consequence of the increased ability of other captaincies to satisfy their own requirements out of enhanced local production. By the late 1760s, the price of manioc in the Salvador market, like that of sugar, returned to about the level of the 1680s.[56]

Fish was another important local food source. Curiously, a Capuchin father who stopped at Salvador en route to the Congo in the early 1680s found "fish . . . extremely dear in this country, for there being but very few that apply themselves to catching it."[57] Either he was ill informed or the taste for seafood grew rapidly, for about 1702 a French traveler who visited the capital reported that "the Portuguese eat much fish. There hardly exists an inhabitant who does not possess a canoe and a black fisherman whom they send out to fish every day."[58] Those who lacked such servile labor were obliged to purchase their fish in local markets whose supply was allegedly controlled by the ubiquitous engrossers. In 1761, the viceroy, in response to a complaint from the council, issued an edict declaring that the current practice of buyers ("*vendelhões e atravessadores*") who boarded the boats as soon as they were in and purchased their entire catch at high prices was prejudicial to the consumers. He ordered fishermen to sell only to retailers. Their shops were to be open for business at 6:00 AM, but stocks unsold by noon could be purchased by other merchants. Those who violated these stipulations were threatened with six months in jail and a heavy fine (50,000 rs.).[59]

During the eighteenth century, the câmara attempted to regulate seasonal prices of thirteen kinds of local fish.[60] Several types, including tunny (*atum*), "*vermelhos*" (perhaps Lutjanus aya), and herring (*arenques*) are mentioned in our institutional sources, but the most common local fish recorded there was the *garoupa*, or grouper, a large fish found in abundance throughout the Atlantic and sold in the capital either fresh or dried.[61] Significantly, purchases of whale meat, a staple of the lower classes, are unrecorded in the accounts of the three houses studied here.[62]

By contrast, the Capuchin friars and the inmates of the Santa Casa's women's shelter consumed considerable quantities of salt cod, as did all Bahians, for it was central then, as it is today, to the Portuguese diet. The time had long since passed when intrepid Portuguese fishermen ventured across the Atlantic to the banks of Newfoundland to fetch cod for the home market. Since the early seventeenth century, their place was occupied by English and English North American fisherman who found the Iberian peninsula a lucrative market for their catches.[63] In 1707, one informant estimated that Spain and Portugal purchased cod worth £130,000 a year; by 1729–30 Portugal's share of the Newfoundland catch was estimated at between 50,000 and 80,000 quintals (3,197 to 5,115 metric tons) a year.[64] In 1742 the two leading Portuguese ports, Lisbon and Porto, were the destinations of 45.2 percent of the 121,365 quintals (7,760.5 metric tons) of cod that British ships carried to Europe.[65]

Throughout the colonial period, Brazil remained a major market for reexported cod. In 1653, the Overseas Council, the chief governing body for the Portuguese empire, estimated that the state of Brazil took an estimated 607.5 metric tons of cod a year, of which 42 percent went to Salvador. It advised the king that "codfish is a commodity that could be sent there in unlimited quantities because it is the staff of life of everyone."[66] At the end of the eighteenth and beginning of the nineteenth centuries, Salvador's cod imports averaged 443.8 metric tons, but they may well have been higher during the middle years of the eighteenth century.[67] Fish prices, including cod, were inflated during the 1710s, 1720s, and 1730s, mirroring advances on the Newfoundland banks, but they declined after the early 1740s for the balance of the period.[68]

Wheat was another vital imported foodstuff. As in Spanish America, it was the preferred type of flour among members of the Brazilian elite, even though it cost three times as much as manioc in Salvador during our period. In the seventeenth century, wheat was grown in São Paulo but was seemingly not shipped to other parts of Brazil.[69] Brazil's future granary, Rio Grande do Sul, did not export wheat to other parts of the littoral until the late eighteenth century.[70] Perforce, Salvador, like other Brazilian cities, was dependent upon shipments from the kingdom. Portugal itself, however, was rarely self-sufficient in wheat. Indeed, Magalhães Godinho has argued persuasively that one of the fundamental facts about Portugal's economic history during the early modern period was its chronic deficit in grains.[71] That deficit became especially acute during the golden age and in some years reached as high as 50 percent. Although Italian and Baltic wheat had helped to overcome Portugal's shortfall in the past, England and its North American colonies became the major suppliers in the eighteenth century. After cloth, wheat became one of the most lucrative British exports to Portugal, and beginning in 1710, a substantial portion of the Middle Colonies' wheat exports went to Lisbon via Philadelphia.[72]

It is not easy to determine what share of Portugal's domestic or imported stocks of wheat were sent to Brazil. In the 1650s, the Overseas Council calculated that 854 metric tons were sent there annually, of which 363.4 (42.5 percent) went to Salvador. The only other data on Salvador's imports that we possess date from the last years of the eighteenth and first years of the nineteenth century, when peninsular exports to the city had fallen to 197 metric tons or 54.3 percent of the estimated level of the midseventeenth century.[73]

The behavior of wheat prices in Salvador was very different from that of cane sugar, for example, and at the beginning of our period, closely reflected prices prevailing in the key Évora market situated about 160 kilometers southeast of Lisbon. The August price there stood at 150 rs. per alqueire in 1687–90, then jumped to 290 in 1691, climbed to 340 by 1694, fell briefly to 200 before advancing to 400 in 1700, then dropped to 230 in 1701 before resuming its upward advance to 380 in 1704. By 1708, it stood at 500 and the following year reached 600 before falling back to 400 in 1712 and to 350 in 1714.[74] Similar fluctuations are evident in Graph 11.2, where it is apparent that wheat prices in Salvador continued to soar until 1718 and that after a brief and sudden drop, perhaps occasioned by a not uncommon local glut, they resumed their upward movement in 1721. Such high levels were doubtless more reflective of abnormally heavy demand within Brazil than they were of the general movement of North Atlantic prices during the decade.[75] Along with manioc flour, wheat prices gradually fell in Salvador during the late 1720s, only to march upward again during the early 1730s, reflecting price advances in the Middle Colonies.[76] Prices were much lower during the 1740s and 1750s until immediately after the Lisbon earthquake in 1755, when they resumed an advance that continued, with one brief interlude, to the end of the period, ending about as high as they had been in the mid-1710s.[77]

Rice was another grain Salvador obtained from Portuguese suppliers. Although the lower classes in Brazil relied upon unhusked wild rice found in many parts of the colony, members of the elite depended upon polished rice that cost twice as much and was imported. Since Portugal did not grow rice itself, it came from northern Italy and, especially after 1730, from South Carolina.[78] The Lisbon price began to advance in the 1690s and more than doubled between 1699 and 1709, after which it declined by more than one hundred index points during the next two decades before advancing significantly in 1734 and 1747. Salvadoran prices (1,359 rs. per *sírio* in the base period, 1747–51) generally displayed a similar pattern. With the exception of 1764, when stocks may have been abnormally low, prices tended to be consistently lower from the late 1740s until the end of the period.[79]

Olive oil, a source of illumination as well as an important ingredient in food preparation and a traditional Portuguese export since Roman times, was also a prominent Salvadoran import. During the second half of the seventeenth century, the port took between two and three thousand barrels per year (sixteen to twenty-four hundred hectoliters), an amount that fell by 52 percent between 1700 and 1731, reflecting scarcities, exceptionally high prices, and perhaps the increased use of locally available fish oil, which generally cost only a fourth as much.[80] The Lisbon price of olive oil began to advance during the latter half of the 1670s and continued to do so for a decade. After falling briefly during the late 1680s, prices resumed their upward climb throughout the 1690s and early 1700s. Declining by about 25 percent in 1705–1709, they jumped by 60 percent between 1710 and 1714, when they stood (in nominal values) nearly 74 percent higher than in the 1670s. Over the next two decades, they gradually fell back until, by the late 1720s, they stood close to the level of the 1670s.[81] The pattern of oil prices prevailing in Salvador mirrors such fluctuations. Prices peaked immediately after the War of the Spanish Succession (1702–13), as they did in Lisbon. The later highs in the mid-1730s and mid-1740s reflect local scarcities caused by irregular and late fleet sailings from Lisbon.[82] After the Lisbon earthquake, prices began to climb and generally remained high for the balance of the period.

The port of Salvador also imported brandy, wine, and vinegar, mostly from the kingdom, though some came from the Atlantic islands. According to a surviving shipping register, between 150 and 870 pipes (600 to 3,480 hectoliters) of brandy (*aguardente do reino*) annually entered the Bay of All Saints between 1700 and 1714.[83] Unfortunately, it is impossible to reconstruct the movement of imported brandy prices for much of our period, since neither the Capuchins, the Poor Clares, nor the Santa Casa procured it. Beginning in 1736, however, imported brandy appears in the records of the Santa Casa, but prices generally remained high except during the late 1740s through the late 1750s, after which they moved steadily upward. Significantly, about 1750 the Santa Casa also began to purchase second-grade locally produced brandy, generally termed *aguardente de cabeça,* and relied upon it exclusively during the 1760s.[84] The same register reveals that Salvador obtained impressive quantities of wine from both the kingdom and the Atlantic islands—as much as 9,088 hectoliters per year in the period from 1700 to 1715. Although the Capuchins were remarkably steady imbibers, wine was not regularly served in the facilities of the Poor Clares and those of the Santa Casa, so we cannot trace its price movement beyond the mid-1720s. We can, however, employ as a surrogate wine vinegar, which the Santa Casa regularly bought. Figure 5 demonstrates a reasonable fit between the available prices for all three liquids and indicates that wide fluctuations in price were characteristic of each.

The data presented here raise the obvious question of how typical Salvador's prices were of levels prevailing in other parts of Brazil during the age of gold. One student of price movements has recently asserted that "all price historians search for data that covers more than a few years, are generally reliable, and include more than a single region."[85] Searching for comparable data is one thing; finding them is another. Except for Queiros Mattoso's and Johnson's essays, which begin late in our period, I know of no other systematic published studies of price movements in Brazilian communities spanning these years; and I am unaware of archival sources that would confirm them.

Tables 11.5 and 11.6 are at least suggestive of responses to the question. They display prices current for common consumables in Salvador and several other markets at two points in time—during the balmy days of the mid-1720s, when major bullion deposits were still being discovered and when older ones continued to yield bountifully; and between 1755 and 1763, when the boom had already passed in all producing regions. Table 11.5 indicates prices of foodstuffs in Salvador and its rival port, Rio de Janeiro, and in two gold camps, Sabará, which had been functioning for about two decades, and Cuiabá in southern Mato Grosso, where important gold placers had recently been found. As was true in Antonil's time, prices in the camps were astronomical by littoral standards: they ranged from 44 percent to twelve times greater in Sabará and from nearly ten to almost eighteen times greater in Cuiabá. Such differentials, the consequences of increased water and land transportation costs, extreme scarcities, and greed, lessened with the passage of time. Table 11.6 compares market prices in the two ports with those in three other towns—Oeiras, formerly Mocha, capital of the newly formed subcaptaincy of Piauí and a community of 1,120 persons (not counting slaves) in 1762; Belém do Pará, gateway to the Amazon, whose population reputedly was about 6,500 in 1749; and São Paulo, whose population was close to 20,000 in the 1760s—and the saltpeter mining district of Montes Altos, some 640 kilometers northwest of Salvador near the São Francisco River.[86]

Table 11.5

Salvador Prices Compared with Those Elsewhere in Brazil, ca. 1725

(in réis)

Commodity	Unit	Salvador	Rio de Janeiro	Sabará Minas Gerais	Cuiabá Mato Grosso
Bacon	453.6 gm	140[a]	160[d]		
Beans, white	30 kg	960			18,000
Brandy, imported	2.66 l	2,240[b]	2,015		21,136
Codfish	14.75 kg	2,022.5[c]	4,100		
Manioc	30 kg	733	1,280[b]	15,000	
Olive oil	2.66 l	555.5	611.6	833.3	7,500
Sugar	14.75 kg	1,170	1,513		
Vinegar	2.66 l	200	333.3	555.5	
Wheat	14.75 kg	2,325	2,225	15,000	

[a]1722–23 ave.　[b]1724　[c]1722 and 1728 ave.　[d]1723

Sources: Salvador: RE, ASCM, MD; Rio de Janeiro: *NC,* 1, cccix; 2: 192, 348, 420, 465, 474, and 550; Luís Vahia Monteiro to Overseas Council, 13 July, 1725, ANRJ, Cod. 80, Vol. 2, f. 11; Sabará: *NC,* 1: 249–50; Cuiabá: *NC,* 4: 5–6. N.B. The values for Cuiabá are expressed in drams of gold, here converted at 1: 1,500 réis.

Prices were evidently lower in the traditionally impoverished peripheries, São Paulo and Belém, than in the seaports, but the differentials between levels attained in Salvador and Rio de Janeiro and the two backland districts were not as great as was the case a generation earlier. Prices in Montes Altos were between one and four and a half times greater than the levels in Salvador; those in Oeiras were between one and five times as much.[87] While the statistical fits in these tables are not as precise as one would like, they suggest that Salvador's prices, which were generally somewhat less than those in Rio de Janeiro,[88] were among the lowest in Brazilian markets for which such information is available.

We may conclude by responding to the questions posed at the outset of this essay. First, it seems clear that the upward movement of prices in Salvador, and probably elsewhere in Brazil, during the last two decades of the seventeenth century was not simply a response to the exceptional demand created by the sudden flow of population from the Iberian peninsula to the

Table 11.6

Salvador Prices Compared with those Elsewhere in Brazil, ca. 1755–63

(in réis)

Commodity	Unit		Salvador[a]	Rio de Janeiro[b]	Montes Altos, Bahia[c]	Oeiras, Piauí[d]	Belém do Pará[e]	São Paulo[f]
Bacon	453.6	gm	55.9	60			45.5	22.5
Beans, white	30	kg	764.6	580				400
Beef	14.745	kg	495				200	240
Brandy, local	2.66	l	606	640	1,186			160
Manioc	30	kg	402	627		960	400	480
Olive oil	2.66	l	1,488.6	1,140	4,800	4,800	166	700
Rice, imported	30	kg	736.9	1,280			1,100	880
Sugar	14.745	kg	1,494	960?	4,800			2,400
Vinegar	2.66	l	704	220	1,258	4,320		320
Wheat	14.745	kg	1,731.8	3,584	9,600	10,240		2,560

[a] 1755–63 ave.   [b] 1763   [c] 1755   [d] 1759   [e] 1758   [f] 1760

Sources: Salvador: ASCM, MD; Rio de Janeiro: Johnson, "Money, Wages, and Prices," 268–81; Montes Altos: "Conta da despeza q. se fez p.ª o exame do salitre na socavação da serra dos montes altos . . . ," 2 Oct. 1755, APB/OR/54, fls. 424–25; Oeiras: Henrique António Gallucio to governor, Maranhão, 12 Nov. 1759, Biblioteca e Arquivo Público do Pará, cod. 11, No. 62; Belém; encl. in Miguel de Bulhões e Sousa (bishop, Pará) to Tomé Joaquim da Costa Corte Real (colonial secretary), Belém, 23 Feb. 1759, AHU/PA/Pará, cx. 16; São Paulo: Taunay, "O preço da vida em S. Paulo," 402–403.

Brazilian littoral and from there to the interior mining camps. Prices of beef, manioc, olive oil, wheat, and vinegar began to advance *before* the opening of the gold fields. Second, what triggered a general rise in prices in Brazil was the devaluation of 1688, which partly drained the colony of specie and produced an immediate, disproportionately large increase in the prices of both local and imported products.[89] Third, prices continued to climb most rapidly between the early 1690s, that is, before large numbers of newcomers reached the mining zones, and the early 1720s. Unfortunately we do not possess adequate statistical evidence to chart precisely the extent of the surge during the first two of those decades, but there is an abundance of contemporary testimony that corroborates Antonil's insistence that Brazil had become a land of grave scarcities and exceptionally high prices.[90] Complaints of scarcities in Salvador diminished in the 1730s, when supplies caught up with demand and price levels began to moderate. Fourth, the shortages of imported goods after the Lisbon earthquake contributed to a renewed advance in the prices of imported products in the late 1750s, but so did the rising price trends in the external supplier markets, where the levels attained during the 1760s were influenced by the Seven Years' War. Fifth, with the exception of a few years in the 1710s and 1720s when adverse weather and exceptionally strong demands from interior markets created shortages of local products in Salvador, the composite indices of the prices of its internally produced foodstuffs and those that came from abroad usually moved in concert until the earthquake. After 1755, the index of imported goods generally moved upward while that of locally grown foodstuffs continued downward, in some cases returning to late seventeenth-century levels (see Appendix). Further studies may reveal the extent to which these findings, determined primarily with respect to Salvador, also apply to other Brazilian markets in this period.

Appendix

Combined Indices of Local and Imported Products in the Salvador market, 1710–69

	Local Products						Imported Products						Combined Means
Year	Beef	Hens	Manioc	White Beans	White Sugar	Arithmetic Means[a]	Olive Oil	Rice	Salt Cod	Vinegar	Wheat	Arithmetic Means[b]	Combined Means
1710					79.02				136.14	78.19	211.36		
1711			216.91	162.38			168.39	188.37	113.45	141.92			
1712				144.34	97.26			135.39		144.60	264.20		
1713					77.81		222.40	153.05	158.83	108.88	290.62	194.68	
1714	74.50				106.99		209.69		113.45	114.60			
1715	85.69				124.62					83.26			
1716	87.09	212.62	254.97	288.67	121.58	188.08	127.09		111.63	133.89	256.36		
1717	88.49		283.96		127.65		114.38		159.73	115.15	132.10		
1718	93.56		189.31		116.71		116.23		166.54	92.38	68.69		
1719	95.75		207.05		116.71		114.66		133.32	75.28	68.69		
1720	94.01		283.96		116.71		117.55		147.48	131.14			
1721	90.46		504.83		82.06		114.38		159.73	115.92	190.22		
1722	78.14				94.22		95.32	147.16	159.73	160.68	169.08	143.06	
1723	106.47		189.31		94.22		95.32		119.12	135.01	169.08		
1724	106.22	179.12	157.75	169.14	91.18	131.07	118.38			85.74	147.95		
1725	107.97	146.60	152.43	108.25	103.95	118.15	127.08			86.25	153.56		
1726	113.02		126.20										
1727	106.45												
1728	111.92	130.15	150.66	96.19	101.09	114.96	79.65	94.18	64.36	71.64	128.56	93.51	104.23
1729	111.92	148.84	112.79	124.15	95.74	111.15	84.21	117.73	82.22	101.49	98.15	100.39	105.77
1730	113.33	129.83	112.40	113.77	88.57	111.65	68.34	188.37	97.24	131.13	127.27	128.78	120.21
1731	120.67	120.10	146.71	133.62	93.00	123.50	103.45	128.84	111.36	112.53	108.71	113.38	118.44
1732	111.92	123.71	157.75	99.23	75.37	111.07	134.20	131.71	102.46	107.46	140.02	125.85	118.46
1733	97.93	118.56	60.15	117.27	77.81	88.29	86.67			92.53	75.30		
1734	96.94	126.61	71.58	92.80			112.04		174.26	115.67	59.44		
1735	83.95	142.40	189.31	154.83	76.89	126.25	169.61	153.05		119.40	211.36	163.35	144.80
1736	83.95	126.29	186.55	108.59	120.00	124.77	157.97	188.37	57.58	107.46	127.41	145.30	135.04

Year													
1737	92.86	105.83	75.43	90.21	64.80	75.26	100.65	80.94	261.39	131.13	204.75	133.75	86.83
1738	83.95	103.09	55.22	88.18	55.56	74.09	118.20	61.81	46.47	107.46	131.63	99.56	90.47
1739	92.51	106.31	72.17	84.69	61.39	77.29	97.36	65.31	79.41	126.12	116.57	103.65	102.74
1740	94.44	93.42	86.47	68.79	76.98	84.88	106.60	117.73		125.37	141.61	120.60	104.90
1741	91.11	104.06	104.52	63.59	72.28	97.65	97.69	94.55	94.39	118.35	135.73	112.15	94.04
1742	93.13	105.67	109.94	117.27	97.26	98.43	99.95	79.15	108.91	88.05	85.73	89.65	96.57
1743	102.13	91.97	93.87	109.44	81.03	85.65	105.68	83.37		131.13	96.17	107.49	
1744	93.21	90.21	78.25	81.19	106.99	107.90	119.29		87.13	77.61	101.72		94.02
1745	98.46	114.05	88.74	142.65	124.56	99.83	190.12	79.22	72.60	77.61	97.59	88.21	94.88
1746	96.94	118.56	78.88	97.43	118.60	98.36	98.41	83.30	98.02	83.58	104.23	91.40	110.93
1747	99.93	101.48	72.10	105.79	116.84	112.75	94.50	118.47	108.91	95.52	100.79	109.11	110.71
1748	106.68	115.21	100.37	133.85	113.79	115.43	121.67	106.17	112.54	101.49	107.93	105.98	93.93
1749	100.01	96.33	144.55	96.69	80.66	90.17	108.34	93.16	85.40	111.94	98.87	97.69	89.49
1750	96.19	94.39	111.02	68.98	70.03	83.18	86.81	98.89	95.12	107.46	88.18	95.80	
1751	100.55	92.46	71.78	94.72			88.66	97.13		124.18	99.57	110.25	104.83
1752	102.48	104.38	78.43	121.78	97.64	102.30	120.14	97.71	103.47	131.13	93.70	107.35	97.34
1753	95.52	101.74	108.06	101.04	89.48	90.64	106.87	92.13		131.13	93.79	104.03	81.35
1754	83.95	99.23	99.11	78.48	80.24	76.51	99.09	92.71	87.13	89.55	75.95	86.18	86.45
1755	87.79	95.30	64.28	77.58	85.11	83.95	86.53	84.37		89.25	82.17	88.95	97.50
1756	90.94	98.80	68.43	94.49	84.36	87.14	100.02	86.17	87.13	99.10	139.20	107.86	101.11
1757	83.95	92.04	93.59	79.68	97.14	86.06	106.97	78.95		119.40	143.52	116.16	108.37
1758	87.61	94.57	96.96	66.19	113.68	95.38	122.78	92.89		135.97	133.42	121.36	100.47
1759	90.59	93.00	79.63	100.59	95.74	88.53	123.16	98.60		119.40	130.91	112.41	84.48
1760	83.95	87.95	75.32	92.47	86.14	72.09	100.72	88.30		104.47	103.83	96.88	90.95
1761	81.85	87.30	64.07	54.22	87.54	83.39	90.92	102.87		95.52	94.64	98.51	105.38
1762	89.02	76.67	76.12	88.07	82.67	97.45	100.73	129.13		93.43	125.85	113.32	103.87
1763	76.95	100.99	95.44	122.69	90.33	96.37	104.87	89.40		107.46	147.95	111.36	92.30
1764	77.40	89.88	98.59	119.63	85.89	84.05	100.65	72.59		86.56	137.38	100.55	111.10
1765	84.99	78.29	60.34	112.59	80.67	89.47	105.68	106.08		98.50	169.09	132.74	101.77
1766	83.00	75.06	71.33	120.88	82.67	81.07	157.27	73.95		107.46	169.09	122.47	114.86
1767	82.67	71.19	81.05	77.58	78.66	96.14	139.37	96.84		89.55	253.63	133.58	
1768	82.55	74.74	55.22	91.45			94.29	55.92		80.00			
1769		83.76	49.29	79.80			106.94		101.65				

aHens not included   bCod not included

NOTES

1. Virgílio Noya Pinto, *O ouro brasileiro e o comércio anglo-português* (São Paulo, 1979), 114–15. See also Charles R. Boxer, *The Golden Age of Brazil: Growing Pains of a Colonial Society* (Berkeley, 1962); and A. J. R. Russell-Wood, "Colonial Brazil: The Gold Cycle, c. 1690–1750," *The Cambridge History of Latin America* (hereinafter *CHLA*), ed. Leslie Bethell (1984), 2: 547–600.

2. Alfredo de Escragnole Tauney, "O preço da vida em S. Paulo em fins do século xvii e em meiados do século xviii," *Annaes do Museu Paulista*, 3 (1927), 391–405.

3. Francisco Rodrigues Leite, "Preços em São Paulo seiscentista," *Annaes do Museu Paulista*, 17 (1963), 43–[120].

4. Katia M. de Queiros Mattoso, "Conjoncture et société au Brésil a la fin du xviiie siecle. Prix et salaires a la veille de la revolution des alfaiates,—Bahia 1798," *Cahiers des Ameriques Latines*, 5 (1970), 3–53; Harold B. Johnson, Jr., "A Preliminary Inquiry into Money, Prices, and Wages in Rio de Janeiro, 1763–1823," in D. Alden, ed., *Colonial Roots of Modern Brazil* (Berkeley, 1973), 230–83. Although restricted to printed sources, Mirceu Buescu, *300 anos de inflação* (Rio de Janeiro, 1973) is useful.

5. André João Antonil, *Cultura e opulencia do Brasil por suas drogas e minas*, ed. and trans. Andrée Mansuy (Paris, 1965), Pt. 3, ch. 7.

6. Cf. Boxer, *Golden Age*, s.v. index "Price rises and price fluctuations"; E. Bradford Burns, *A History of Brazil* (New York, 1970), 63; Hubert Herring, *A History of Latin America*, 3d ed. (New York, 1968), 228. Pinto, *O ouro brasileiro*, 42–43, cites some exceptionally high prices, but does not make any general inferences as to their persistence. As Luis Lisanti observes, "Pouco ou quase nada se conhece acerca do movimento do preços no Brasil, para a primeira metade do século xviii." Luis Lisanti ed., *Negócios coloniais (Uma correspondência comercial do século xviii* (5 v., [São Paulo], 1973), 1; cdlxxxiv (hereinafter cited as *NC*).

7. I am indebted to the former provedor, Victor Gradin, for special permission to conduct research in the archives of the Santa Casa and especially to Neusa Rodrigues Esteves, the archives' exceptionally able and charming head, for directing my attention to the maços, whose existence was unknown to A. J. R. Russell-Wood, whose statement that his bibliography "represents a complete catalogue of pre-1755 documents in these archives" is inexact. A. J. R. Russell-Wood, *Fidalgos and Philanthropists: The Santa Casa da Misericórdia of Bahia, 1550–1755* (Berkeley, 1968), 386–90.

8. Joseph Abreu Vianna, "Despeza que faço com os R^{dos} P^{ez} Capuxos da Piedade com sindico que sou do d° hospicio," and "Receyta daz esmollaz que os devotoz de Nossa Senhora da Pied^e fazem ao[s] religiozos capuchinos do d° hospicio de que eu Joseph A^u Vianna sou sindico," ca. 14 June 1725, and related documents (hereinafter cited as RE). Arquivo Histórico Ultramarino, Lisbon, *Papeis Avulsos* (hereinafter AHU/PA), Bahia, 1st ser. não catalogada, *caixa* (hereinafter cx.) 33. I am indebted to Mr. Sheridan T. Grippen, former graduate student, Department of History, New

York University, for having called my attention to these documents. For a bibliographical introduction to the role of the Capuchins in Bahia, see Fr. Martin de Nantes, *Relation succincte & sincère de la mission du père Martin de Nantes, predicateur Capuchin, . . . dans le Brésil,* fasc. ed. with notes by Frédérico G. Edelweiss ([Bahia, 1952]), [Pt. 2], [43]–44. Except for a reference to the French Capuchins in Maranhão, 1612–15, Father Cuthbert, *The Capuchins: a Contribution to the History of the Counter-Reformation* (2 v., New York, 1929), ignores his order's role in Brazil.

9. Susan A. Soeiro, "A Baroque Nunnery: The Economic and Social Role of a Colonial Convent: Santa Clara do Desterro, Salvador, Bahia" (Ph.D. diss. New York University, 1975) and "The Social and Economic Role of the Convent: Women and Nuns in Colonial Bahia, 1677–1800," *The Hispanic American Historical Review* (hereinafter *HAHR*), 54 (1974), 209–32.

10. See note 6 and Dauril Alden, "Vicissitudes of Trade in the Portuguese Atlantic Empire during the First Half of the Eighteenth Century: A Review Article," *The Americas,* 33 (1975), 282–91. Mr. Bill Donavan, a graduate student under the supervision of Professor Russell-Wood at Johns Hopkins University, is currently completing an analysis of the activities of the merchant, Francisco Pinheiro, on the basis of archival work in Portugal and Brazil.

11. For visual depictions of colonial Salvador, see Robert C. Smith, "Some Views of Colonial Bahia," *Belas Artes: Revista e Boletim da Academia Nacional de Belas Artes,* 2d ser., 1 (Lisbon, 1948), 31–47, and Nestor Goulart Filho, *Evolução urbana do Brasil* (São Paulo, 1968).

12. William Dampier, *A Voyage to New Holland,* ed. James A. Williamson (London, 1939), 35.

13. The 1706 count is mentioned in Archbishop of Salvador to Diogo de Mendonça Corte Real, 30 Aug. 1755, *Anais da Biblioteca Nacional* (Rio de Janeiro (hereinafter *ABNRJ*), 31 (1913), 131, while that of 1718 appears in the "Discertaçoens da historia eclesiastica do Brasil que recitou na academia brazilica de esquecidos o Reverendo Padre Gonçalo Soares de França no anno de 1724," Biblioteca da Sociedade de Geographica de Lisboa, Res. 43-C-147, fls. 87–123. Internal evidence makes it clear that the data were collected six years earlier.

14. "Relação topagraphica da cid.ᵉ do Salvador da B.ᵃ de todos os S.ᵗᵒˢ e seu t[e]ʳ[m]° q. fes o mediador das obras da cidade Manoel de Oliv.ʳᵃ e Mendes 1757," Arquivo Municipal da Bahia (hereinafter AMB), Cartas do senado a sua magestade (hereinafter CSSM), 1742–1822, fls. 73ʳˑ–78ᶠˑ Cf. José António Caldas, "Noticia geral de toda esta capitania da Bahia desde o seu descobrimento até o prezente anno de 1759," fasc. ed. (Salvador, 1949), fls. 66–67.

15. Dauril Alden, "The Population of Brazil in the Late Eighteenth Century: A Preliminary Survey," *HAHR,* 43 (1963), 199; *ABNRJ,* 32 (1914), 480. For other descriptions of eighteenth-century Salvador, see Boxer, *Golden Age,* 127–31 (where the population estimate given is inflated, as it is in Russell-Wood, *Santa Casa,* 260).

16. Although this paragraph rests upon many of the primary sources cited in

this essay, confirmation of the statements it contains may be found in Boxer, *Golden Age*, 126–61. In recent years, the socioeconomic history of eighteenth-century Bahia has been the focus of three fine dissertations: Rae Jean Flory, "Bahian Society in the Mid-Colonial Period: The Sugar Planters, Tobacco Growers, Merchants, and Artisans of Salvador and the Reconcavo, 1680–1725" (Ph.D. diss. University of Texas, 1978); Catherine Lugar, "The Merchant Community of Salvador, Bahia, 1780–1830" (Ph.D. diss., Stony Brook, 1980); and Soeiro (see note 9). John Norman Kennedy, "Bahian Elites, 1750–1832," *HAHR*, 55 (1973), 415–39, remains the only published fragment of a promising but never finished dissertation.

17. Two seminal studies of the Bahian sugarcane industry are Stuart B. Schwartz, "Colonial Brazil, c. 1580–c. 1750: Plantations and Peripheries," *CHLA*, 2: 423–99, and Schwartz and Ward J. Barrett, "Comparación entre dos economías azucareras coloniales: Morelos, México y Bahía, Brasil," in E. Florescano, ed., *Haciendas, latifundios y plantaciones en América Latina* (Mexico City, 1975), 532–72. Professor Schwartz's long-awaited monograph on the colonial sugar industry of Brazil is in press.

18. Flory, "Bahian Society," chaps. 2–3, is an excellent introduction to the state of the sugar industry in the captaincy during the period 1680–1725.

19. This statement is based on an analysis of cargo remittances from Bahia to Portugal that forms part of an ongoing study of fleet movements between the kingdom and the state of Brazil, 1649–1766.

20. Fédéric Mauro, *Le Portugal et l'Atlantique au xvii*ᵉ *siècle 1570–1670: Étude économique* (Paris, 1960), esp. 233–34; Vitorino Magalhães Godinho, "Portugal, as frotas do açucar e as frotas do ouro (1670–1770)," reprinted in Vitorino Magalhães Godinho, *Ensaios* (Lisbon, 1968), 2: 295–315, esp. 300ff.

21. For Lisbon prices, see Magalhães Godinho, *Ensaios*, 300–301; for Amsterdam prices during this period, see N. W. Posthumus, *Inquiry into the History of Prices in Holland* (Leiden, 1946), 1: 119–20, 134–35, and (Leiden, 1964), 2: 276–79, 664. Prices of sugar in the Lima market fell even more drastically, some 73.4 percent between 1678 and 1753. Nicholas P. Cushner, *Lords of the Land: Sugar, Wine and Jesuit Estates of Coastal Peru, 1600–1767* (Albany, N.Y., 1980), 116.

22. Secas occurred in 1671, 1673, 1683, during much of the 1690s, and again in 1724, 1728, 1733, 1736, 1739, 1742, and 1746. In 1683, the always-pungent Jesuit António Vieira wrote: "A novidade do açucar, sendo o de Pernambuco muito florescente, foi aqui notavelmente menor que em outros anos . . . e assim dizem que vai esta frota mais carregada de queixas que de caixas." To Roque da Costa Barreto, Bahia, 23 June 1683, in João Lúcio de Azevedo, ed., *Cartas do Padre António Vieira* (3 v., Lisbon, 1925–28), 3: 468. For undocumented references to the eighteenth-century droughts, largely confirmed by the manuscript materials consulted for this study, see Frédéric Mauro, *Le Brésil a la fin du xviii*ᵉ *siècle* (Paris, 1977), 195.

23. J. H. Galloway, "Northeast Brazil 1700–50: The Agricultural Crisis Reexamined," *Journal of Historical Geography*, 1 (1975), 21–38.

24. On the currency devaluation see Carl A. Hanson, *Economy and Society in Baroque Portugal, 1668–1703* (Minneapolis, 1981), 149–59; cf. Godinho, "Portugal, as frotas do açucar," 303. For its effects upon goods regularly procured by planters, see António Luis Gonçalves da Câmara Coutinho (governor-general) to Pedro II, Bahia, 4 July 1692, *Documentos históricos* (hereinafter *DH*), 33 (Rio de Janeiro, 1936), 430–40, esp. 435; excerpted in Mansuy, *Cultura,* 272, n. 3.

25. Mansuy, *Cultura,* 120.

26. Until the legal end of Indian slavery in 1757, very few Africans were imported by the north coast ports of São Luís do Maranhão and Belém do Pará, which served the state of Maranhão situated northeast of the Brazilian hump.

27. Philip D. Curtin, *The Atlantic Slave Trade: A Census* (Madison, 1969), 205–10.

28. Conde de Atouguia (viceroy) to crown, 17 Sept. 1753, Arquivo Público do Estado da Bahia (hereinafter APB)/Ordens régias (hereinafter OR)/49/fls. 41^r–44^r.

29. Dauril Alden, "Late Colonial Brazil, 1750–1808," *CHLA,* 2: 611.

30. Flory, "Bahian Society," 67, Table 3.

31. Mansuy, *Cultura,* 386.

32. Mansuy, *Cultura,* 32–34; Manoel Cardoso, "The Brazilian Gold Rush," *The Americas,* 3 (1946), 137–60, at 151; câmara (Salvador) to king, 12 Aug. 16[88], Prefeitura do município de Salvador, *Cartas do Senado,* 3 (Salvador, n.d.), 62. The câmara reminded the king that "O Brasil[,] Senhor, desde o seu nascimento se sustentou sempre em duas collumnas . . . Tobacco e . . . o Asucar . . . Tobacco aruinouçe já alguns annos, . . . e [a]gora se aruinar a do asucar ficara perdido o brasil todo, porque para todos se acabaram as collumnas." Câmara (Salvador) to king, 15 Nov. 1723, AMB, CSSM, 28:9, fls. 65^v–68^r, and Vasco Fernandes César de Menezes (viceroy) to same, 23 Oct. 1723, APB/OR/17/8, in which the viceroy lamented "a inexplicavel mizeria em q. hoje se vem os senhores de engenho a respeito do abatimento dos asucares e do excesso do vallor dos negros. . . ."

33. José da Silva Lisboa to Dr. Domingos Vandelli, 18 Oct. 1781, *ABNRJ,* 32: 502.

34. José Mascarenhas Pacheco Pereira Coelho de Melo to Tomás Joaquim da Costa Corte Real (colonial secretary), 23 Dec. 1758, *ABNRJ,* 31: 321.

35. Strangely, the Santa Casa made several large purchases of lamb in October 1699, when the average price was 191.5 rs./453.6 gms (6,128 rs/arroba), but no other entries appear for lamb during later years. ASCM, cod. 848. The câmara set the maximum price for pork (*carne de porco*) at 1,920 rs./arroba, compared with only 1,280 rs./arroba for carne de porca and 384 rs./arroba for beef. AMB, Livro das posturas da câmara municipal, 1696, f. 15^r; the 1726 municipal price regulations raised the two categories to 2,560 rs. for the male and to 1,920 rs. for female pork. AMB, Livro de posturas, 1650–1787, f. 107^v. My distinguished colleague Vernon Carstensen has astutely suggested that carne de porco may have referred to barrows, i.e., castrated males, rather than to boars. The 1716 regulations by the council

established lamb prices at 1,920 rs./arroba, nearly four times the actual market price for beef. Posturas do senado da câmara da Bahia . . . 1716, Arquivo Nacional, Rio de Janeiro (hereinafter ANRJ), cod. 90.

36. Rosamond Bayne-Powell, *Housekeeping in the Eighteenth-Century* (London, 1956), 67.

37. Luiz R. B. Mott, Fazendas de gado do Piauí (1697–1762 [sic for 1772], *Anais do viii simpósio nacional dos professores universitários de história* (São Paulo, 1976), 366. Cattle slaughtered in Rio de Janeiro in the 1790s averaged only 98.6 kilograms. "Almanaques da cidade do Rio de Janeiro para os anos de 1792 e 1794," *ABNRJ*, 59 (1937), 351; António Duarte Nunes, "Almanac histórico da cidade de S. Sebastião do Rio de Janiero, composto por Antonio Duarte Nunes, Tenente de Bombeiros, para o anno de 1799 acompanhado de um mappa da força maritima e terrestre de Douguay Trouin," *Revista do Instituto Histórico e Geográfico Brasileiro* (hereinafter *RIHGB*), 21 (1858), 173.

38. Mansuy, *Cultura,* 382.

39. Mansuy, *Cultura,* 484. As early as 1694, the câmara protested against such "robbery." Câmara to king, 16 Oct. 1703, *Cartas do senado,* 5: 62–63, referring to a memorial of 3 July 1694. In 1723, the câmara identified one such culprit, Domingos de Oliveira Lopes, a Portuguese-born hoemaker-turned-merchant, câmara to king, 23 Oct. 1723, *Cartas do senado,* 65–67. The câmara's further complaints against beef engrossers are registered in its *memórias* of 14 Jan. 1719, AMB, 28: 9, fls. 50^r–52^r, 10 Sept. 1718, AMB, Ofícios ao governo, 1712–37, f. 35^r, and 14 Nov. 1725, AMB, Ofícios ao governo, 1712–37, f. 149^r, and 17 Nov. 1722, Ofícios ao governo, 1712–37, f. 92^v, the last of which indicates that two of the mostly unnamed contrabandists had been caught and jailed.

40. Câmara to viceroy, 14 Sept. 1726, AMB, Ofícios ao governo, 1712–37, f. 175^v. The viceroy attributed the continued beef shortage partly to "the bad government and underdevelopment of the land" and partly to the superior attractions of the Minas market. Conde de Sabugosa to Diogo de Mendonça Corte Real, 7 May, 1726, APB/OR/20/135.

41. The codice Ofícios ao governo, 1712–37, AMB, contains a large number of proposed waivers endorsed by the câmara to the viceroy. Such proposals were to permit planters to acquire fifty to one hundred so-called "wild cattle" from the backlands, ostensibly to graze on their estates, but probably for sale in the urban market.

42. In 1754, for example, the câmara reported a beef scarcity had followed the previous year's seca in the backlands. Câmara to viceroy, 20 Apr. 1754, AMB, Ofícios ao governo, 1730–68, 111: 3, no. fol. Major droughts that account for some of the beef price jumps during the period include those of 1710–11, 1723–27, 1734–37, and 1744–45. António José de Sampaio, *A General Description of Piauhy* (Rio de Janeiro, 1905), 70–75. The seca of the mid-1730s was especially severe and was responsible for the loss of many animals along the São Francisco

River and the abandonment of some ranches. Conde de Galveas (viceroy) to king, 30 Mar. 1736, APB/OR/32/122.

43. *Constituçoens primeyras do arcebispado da Bahia . . . celebrou em 12 de junho . . . de 1707* (Lisbon, 1719), Bk. 2, tit. 6, pars. 408–11, and tit. 20.

44. E.g., the treasury superintendant of Rio Grande de São Pedro in southernmost Brazil reported that many *gaúchos* ate meat every day, including those forbidden, and that it was impossible to prevent them from doing so. Nevertheless the crown directed the governor to see that the military garrison there was served only fish on restricted day. Carta régia to Gomes Freire de Andrada, 1 June 1753, ANRJ, 63, 2, 159ᵛ.

45. Gilberto Ferrez, tr. and ed., "Diário anônimo de uma viagem às costas d'Africa e as Indias espanholas[:] O tráfico de escravos (1702–1703)," *RIHGB*, 267 (1965), 24.

46. Dampier, *Voyage*, 52–53.

47. Hen prices peaked at 660 rs. each in 1716 and dropped to a low of 221 in 1767. The highest recorded price for fryers was 240 rs. (1724) and the lowest was 61.8 (1767). The price per dozen eggs varied from a high of 162.8 rs. (1734) to a low of 88 rs. (1765). Serial prices for each are available from the author.

48. Warren R. Fish, "Changing Food Use Patterns in Brazil," *Luso-Brazilian Review*, 15 (1978), 70–89, at 76.

49. Such vegetables are mentioned in the "Recyta daz esmollaz" (note 8), the ASCM/MD series, and the various municipal price regulations previously cited.

50. A series of white bean prices beginning in 1711 but broken until 1728 and complete from that point until 1769 is available from the author. Concerning the definition of the alqueire, see note 53 below.

51. Charlotte Chatfield, "Food Consumption Tables—Minerals and Vitamins for International Use"(United Nations, Food and Agricultural Organization, Nutritional Studies, 11 [Rome, March, 1954]), 10–12.

52. Fish, "Changing Food Use Patterns," 81, and sources cited there.

53. Antonio de Brito de Menezes to king, Rio de Janeiro, 7 Mar. 1718, ANRJ, Cod. 80, vol. 1, f. 16ᵛ·; Silva Lisboa to Vandelli, 18 Oct. 1781 (cited in note 33), 503.

The alqueire was a unit of dry measure used to record volumes of grain. The Lisbon alqueire was 13.8 liters, but the Brazilian alqueire is usually taken to have been 2.5 times larger or 34.5 liters, i.e., 41.25 kilograms. For contemporary definitions, see Ambrosio Fernandes Brandão, *Diálogos das grandezas do Brasil,* ed. Rodolfo Garcia (Bahia, 1956), 214, and anon. "Relação das capitanias," *RIHGB*, 62: 1, 17. In southern Bahia, manioc was sold by the sírio, a common measure for rice, about 1.75 Bahian alqueires. I suspect that the Bahian alqueire of colonial times was about the weight of the modern alqueire do Pará (about 60 kilograms). Aurélio Buarque de Holanda Ferreira, *Novo dicionário da língua portuguesa* (Rio de Janeiro, ca. 1977), 74. This is the equivalence used in this essay.

54. An estimate based upon the average yearly receipts of manioc in the public granary (*celeiro público*) from 1786, the first full year after its establishment in the former Jesuit *fazenda do tanque* east of Salvador, through 1800 and reduced by two-thirds to approximate the amount of manioc needed when the city was a third of its size at the end of the eighteenth century. See "Mappa dos generos, que pagarão a contribuição de 20 réis por alqueire . . . 9 de setembro de 1785, até 31 de dezembro de 1834," Ignacio Accioli de Cerqueira e Silva, *Memorias históricas e politicas da província da Bahia*, ed. Braz do Amaral (6 v., Salvador, 1919–40) (hereinafter *MHB*), 3: facing p. 14.

55. The best contemporary descriptions of manioc farming in Bahia are Silva Lisboa to Vandelli, 18 Oct. 1781, 503, and Luiz dos Santos Vilhena, *Recopilação de notícias soteropolitanas e brasílicas.* . . . , ed. Braz do Amaral (2 v., Salvador, 1921), 1: 205–208. See also Flory, 163–66.

56. This paragraph rests upon a reading of all available correspondence by the governors-general of Bahia and its câmara between the 1680s and 1760, most of which is to be found in AMB/CSSM and APB/OR.

57. Jerom Merolla da Sorrento, "A Voyage to Congo and Several other Countries (1682)," comp. A. Churchill, *Voyages* (London, 1722), 1: 599.

58. Ferrez, "Diário anomino," 24.

59. Bando of 11 Apr. 1761, Bahia, Biblioteca Nacional, Rio de Janeiro (hereinafter BNRJ), II-33, 34, 1 #24.

60. "A Bahia de outros tempos: As posturas do senado da câmara em 1785," *Revista do Instituto Geographico e Histórico de Bahia*, 4 (1897), 47–72, at 54–55.

61. Whether the groupers sold in Salvador were rock hinds (Epinephelus ascensionis [Osbeck]) or yellowfins (Mycteroperca venosa [Linn.]) cannot be determined. John White, first English governor of Virginia, was perhaps the first artist in the New World to depict them. Paul Hulton, *America 1585: The Complete Drawings of John White* (Chapel Hill, 1984), plates 22 and 23.

62. E.g., in 1721 the *Gazeta de Lisboa* reported "não tem havido este ano pesca de baleas com grande prejuizo deste povo (i.e., those of Bahia), porq. he o principal sustento dos pobres & dos escravos." M. Lopes de Almeida, comp., *Notícias históricas de Portugal e Brasil* (2 v., Coimbra, 1961–64), 1: 65.

63. Harold A. Innis, *The Cod Fisheries: The History of an International Economy* (New Haven, 1940). The importance of cod imports is clear from J. A. Pinto Ferreira, *Visitas de saude: As embarcações entradas na barra do Douro nos séculos xvi e xvii* (Oporto, 1977).

64. H. E. S. Fisher, *The Portugal Trade: A Study of Anglo-Portuguese Commerce, 1700–1770* (London, 1971), 17–18.

65. Innis, *The Cod Fisheries,* 70–71, 118, and 180.

66. Consulta of 1 Aug. 1653, AHU/Conselho Ultramarino/consultas mixtas, cod. 15, fls. 54^{r}–55^{v}.

67. "Mapa das importações que fez Portugal sobre a Bahia . . . 1798," and 1799, 1800, 1803–1805, BNRJ, I-17, 12, 3, #s 3, 7, 15, and 20.

68. Innis, *The Cod Fisheries,* 149, 159. From the late 1680s, the price of an arroba of codfish in Salvador rose from 1,400 rs. to an average of 3,078 rs. (1709–21) and reached an apparent peak of 5,760 rs. (1738) before beginning a long descent. ASCM/MD and "Recyta daz esmollaz."

69. We will be better informed when John Monteiro, a graduate student at the University of Chicago, completes his dissertation on seventeenth-century Paulista agriculture.

70. Alden, "Late Colonial Brazil," 642.

71. Vitorino Magalhães Godinho, *Prix et monnaies au Portugal 1750–1850* (Paris, 1955), 147.

72. For wheat shipments to Portugal from the British Isles, see Fisher, *The Portugal Trade,* 17; for Philadelphia, Anne Bezanson, Robert D. Gray, and Miriam Hussey, *Prices in Colonial Pennsylvania* (Philadelphia, 1935), 9, 11, 23, 29, 35–36, 45, and 60. In 1741, one Philadelphia merchant worried that the prospect of the passage of a corn bill in England would "affect our province if it should pass or prohibit our trade to Portugal which we look on as very valuable and as it is the chief means by which we pay our debts in England. . . ." Between 1734 and 1740, 158 vessels sailed from Philadelphia to Portugal, and another 36 ventured to the Azores and Madeiras, mostly loaded with grain. Bezanson, et al., *Prices,* 29.

73. See notes 66 and 67. Here and throughout the discussion of wheat the alqueire is assumed to be that of Lisbon and to have weighed about 16.5 kilograms. See A. H. de Oliveira Marques, *Introdução à história da agricultura em Portugal,* 2d ed. (Lisbon, 1968), 183.

74. Vitorino Magalhães Godinho, "Preços e conjunctura do século xv ao xix," in J. Serrão, ed., *Dicionário de história de Portugal* (4 v., Lisbon, 1971), 4: 508.

75. While Philadelphia prices remained high during the 1710s (Bezanson et al., *Prices,* 9), London prices, after stabilizing at an index number of 171.5 (using the reference base of 1747–51 as 100), fell gradually but steadily during the decade and by 1717 were only 54 percent of their 1710 level. William Beveridge, *Prices and Wages in England from the Twelfth to the Nineteenth Century* (London, 1939), I: 567, ser. A.

76. Bezanson et al., *Prices,* 23–25. For Lisbon prices at this time see Magalhães Godinho, *Prix,* 76–77.

77. Wheat prices in Rio de Janeiro were likewise exceptionally high during the 1760s (Johnson, "Money, Prices, and Wages," 255, 276), reflecting prices in Evora (45 percent higher than during 1747–51), Porto (12 percent greater), and Bragança (59 percent higher). Godinho, *Prix,* 152–53. Philadelphia prices in the 1760s ranged from 20 to 37 percent greater than during the same base period (Bezanson et al., *Prices,* Table 1), while Winchester College prices peaked at 78 percent above the reference period in 1767, though London prices averaged 28 percent higher during

the years 1764–69 than during the same reference period. Beveridge, *Prices and Wages*, 1: 82 and 567, ser. A.

78. Violet M. Shillington and A. B. Wallis Chapman, *The Commercial Relations of England and Portugal* (Rpt.; New York, 1970), 243. At the beginning of the 1770s, 24,000 quintals of rice annually entered Portugal from England and an additional 17,413 came directly from Charleston. Fisher, *The Portugal Trade*, 42, 129. Foreign rice imports were barred by the crown in 1781 in order to protect new Brazilian "Carolina" rice production whose origins are discussed in Dauril Alden, "Manoel Luís Vieira: An Entrepreneur in Rio de Janeiro During Brazil's Eighteenth-Century Agricultural Renaissance," *HAHR*, 39 (1959), 521–37, and whose growth is examined in Alden, "Late Colonial Brazil," 639–42.

79. For Lisbon prices, 1667–1750, see Magalhães Godinho, "Preços e conjunctura," 506. I have recalculated them on the basis of the 1746–50 average of 453 gm = 37 rs. For similar fluctuations in English prices, see Beveridge, *Prices and Wages*, 1: 292 and 432. A somewhat broken series of rice prices in Salvador, 1711–69, is available from the author upon request.

80. Besides the source cited in note 66, the estimates employed here are based on statements by the câmara in 1673 and 1694 (*Atas da câmara*, 5: 116 and 6: 249–59), and an analysis of a surviving ship register, "Entrada de navios, 1699–1728," AMB, cod. 56.1. Imports around the turn of the nineteenth century averaged 1,294 hectoliters. See note 67.

81. Magalhães Godinho, "Preços e conjunctura," 505. The drastic increase in olive oil prices was the subject of complaints by the Lisbon câmara on more than one occasion. See câmara to king, 16 Nov. 1689, and câmara to king, 3 Oct. 1712, Eduardo Freire de Oliveira, ed., *Elementos para a história do município de Lisboa*, 9 (1896), 159, and 11 (1899), 11.

832. Conde de Sabugosa to king, 2 June 1734, APB/OR/30/55; câmara to viceroy, 8 July 1735, AMB, Ofícios ao governo, 1730–68, f. 38ᵛ; António Guedes Pereira to Conde das Galveas, 28 Mar. 1746, APB/OR/43/98.

83. See note 80.

84. There were thirty-nine distilleries (*alambiques*) within the city and its environs and another thirty-two elsewhere in the Bay of All Saints by the 1750s. Caldas, "Noticia geral . . . da Bahia," 445–48. Many of those stills were tied to African markets through the slave trade between Bahia and the Mina coast.

85. Richard L. Garner, "Price Trends in Eighteenth-Century Mexico," *HAHR*, 65 (1985), 281.

86. "Cenço das casas proprias e de aluguer q. occupa os moradores da cidade de Oeiras . . . ," Sept. 1762, Arquivo Nacional da Torre do Tombo, Lisbon, Ministerio do Reino, maço 601; Francisco Bernardino de Sousa, *Lembranças e curiosidades do valle de Amazonas* (Pará, 1873), n.p.; Maria Luiza Marcilio, *La ville de São Paulo: Peuplement et population 1750–1850* (Rouen, [1968]), 119.

87. The "Memoria dos preços communs a que no Matto Grosso sao' vendidos os

generos molhados e secos," n.d. ca. 1772, AHU/PA/Pará, cx. 33, indicates price levels there were two to three times greater than those in Salvador.

88. Serial prices for Rio de Janeiro for part of our period have been compared with those in Salvador with respect to cod, wheat, wine, and olive oil. The results are available on request from the author.

89. In addition to the key dispatch from Câmara Coutinho to Pedro II (see note 24), that evidence includes câmara (Salvador) to Câmara Coutinho, July 1692; Câmara Coutinho to king, 22 and 28 July 1693, DH, 34 (1936), 73–76, 151–53, 171–72, and a series of vivid accounts by António Vieira to various prominent persons in Portugal between 1688 and 1692. Cartas, 3: 545, 550–51, 611–12, 617, 628, and 635–41.

90. The evidence, too extensive to be cited here, includes reports from the papal nuncio in Lisbon to Rome, the Dispatches of French consular and diplomatic officials in Lisbon, the statements of commission agents, complaints by the câmara of Salvador, and various state-of-the-economy reports prepared by the governors-general.

THE MARKETS OF LATIN AMERICAN EXPORTS, 1790–1820

A Comparative Analysis of International Prices*

Javier Cuenca-Esteban

IT IS A WELL-KNOWN PREDICTION OF THE THEORY OF INTERNATIONAL TRADE that the free flow of commodities under the motive of profit maximization tends to equalize prices across countries. Goods that are relatively cheap to produce in any given country will be exported until price differentials across national borders are eliminated. If the focus is narrowed to goods exported from one producing area to several nonproducing countries, the tendency towards price equalization in the latter still holds as the goods seek the markets where prices are higher. When applied to the real world, the theory can be altered to allow for differential transport costs and tariff barriers that lead to less than full equalization of prices. Further departures from the underlying tendency are naturally expected from such distortions as trading restrictions, speculations, and warfare.

The international market conditions confronting Latin American exports during the Napoleonic period richly illustrate the potential impact of major trade distortions while providing a testing ground for a wide range of theoretical predictions. Since the goods exported were in most cases agricultural products with low elasticities of demand, unpredictable shifts in supply were bound to trigger wide fluctuations in prices even during peacetime. The advent of war in the 1790s, and in particular the sequence of naval conflicts and shifting alliances that followed, severely strained the delicate mechanism by which goods from several colonial areas, subject to quasi-monopoly controls, were shipped to European markets via their respective home countries, their allies, and neutral nations. So long as supply shortages were confined to small consuming areas, local prices might rise dramatically with no sizeable effects elsewhere. Even then, however, expectations of generalized warfare or punitive actions against allies and neutrals could trigger an inflationary bubble in world prices. If a large consuming area were effectively cut off from the lines of provision, while world supply was held up by growing productivity, speculation, and wide profit margins in neutral imports from the affected colonies, prices would soar in the closed markets and fall elsewhere. In either case, the return of peace would tend to realign prices at common levels that might remain severely depressed by the momentum in world supply acquired during the war.

This essay draws on data from major recipient countries to attempt an explanation of price trends and divergence in terms of changing conditions of supply and demand. Limitations of coverage and gaps in the sources have made it necessary to restrict the joint analysis of prices and trade flows to sugar, coffee, cocoa, indigo, logwood, and hides imported into Britain, the United States, France, and Spain in the period 1790–1820. It will be shown that mounting world production in the 1790s, fueled by supply disruptions and speculative demand, acquired a dynamic of its own after the turn of the century. The price cycle of 1794–1802 set the pattern for a recurrent sequence of inflation and deflation in the open markets that would perpetuate over-supply conditions through much of the subsequent two decades. The deflationary pressure of swelling supplies on prices was compounded in the 1800s by market contraction, as naval and Continental blockades effectively impeded the flow of colonial goods into large consuming areas under French control. The resulting pattern of severe inflation in the blockaded markets, and falling prices through the short-term cycles elsewhere, will be explained in terms of such related variables as import and reexport quantities, the nature of each country's connection to the sources of production, the relative sizes of domestic markets, and the overall balance of world supply and demand in selected subperiods. The analysis of price differentials across recipient countries will be presented as a series of case studies incorporating increasing orders of complexity.

The price evidence for six major Latin American commodities testifies to the stabilizing effects of trade and the disruptive impact of warfare. Graph 12.1 displays four Paasche indices, all equally weighted with the overall import quantities of each good, and with a common base in 1804—a central year when average prices in British currency in the four recipient countries came within 10 percent of the overall mean.[1] Price convergence is most apparent in the mid-1790s, when the averages for Britain, the United States, and Cadiz remained for several years at roughly similar levels relative to 1804. This general tendency was to reemerge, despite lingering disparities and postwar readjustments, during the Truce of Amiens (1802–1803) and in the mid- and late 1810s. In Britain and in the United States, where the

Graph 12.1

Prices of Six Commodities
(all indices equally weighted with the total values imported
by four countries at 1804 prices)

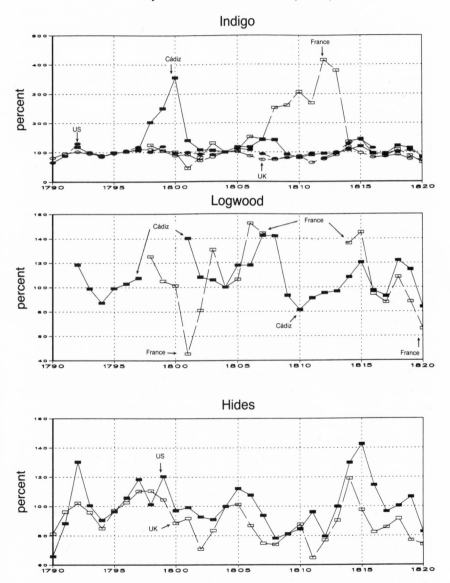

lines of access to major producing and consuming areas remained relatively open through much of the period, prices tended to fluctuate in unison or with one-year lags at roughly similar levels. Against this pattern of convergence, the periods of severe inflation at Cadiz and in France may be regarded as exceptions to a well-defined general trend.

The supply conditions underlying this general trend are outlined in Graph 12.2. The three series displayed in the first panel incorporate various combinations of import and reexport values of the six commodities in common sterling units at 1804 prices. The subseries of *retained imports* is the overall summation of import minus reexport values at the four recipient countries. The values *reexported to the rest of the world* include all documented reexports, but have been made net of trade flows within the four countries and of French imports from without, in an effort to avoid double counting. The aggregate of retained imports and reexports, labeled *total imports,* may be viewed as a rough proxy for world production distributed through the four nations under consideration. The country breakdowns of retained imports are given in the middle panel, and the two indices that most clearly convey the general trend in prices are displayed below to facilitate comparison with the trade series.

With a number of qualifications regarding gaps and omissions in the trade series,[2] the general picture conveyed in Graph 12.2 is one of pronounced and sustained expansion in total imports of the six commodities, with wide swings in the pattern of distribution and in the course of prices in the open markets of Britain and the United States. The real value of total imports in the four recipient countries more than doubled in the period 1792–1802 and hovered over the 1802 level through much of the subsequent decades. The expansion of the 1790s was clearly associated with a rise in the reexport trade that culminated in the "Hamburgh speculation" of 1796–99.[3] As the volume of reexports to the rest of the world leveled off and declined after the turn of the century, however, the continued flood of supplies accumulated as retained imports in Britain and in France. The pattern of distribution subsequently altered in favor of reexports at the expense of France, but on the whole, the volume of retained imports remained strong through the last two decades, and the large British share significantly increased during the Continental Blockade (1807–12). The supply conditions thus outlined, and other considerations to be discussed in connection with relevant subperiods, suggest a broad interpretation of price trends in the open markets that would place an upswing in the 1790s and a prolonged downswing thereafter to 1820, with increasingly pronounced deflation through the short-term cycles in the period 1799–1812.

Graph 12.2

Six Commodities
Imports, re-exports, and prices at four recipient countries
Values in thousand £ sterling at 1804 prices
(comparable French data for 1790–96 not available)

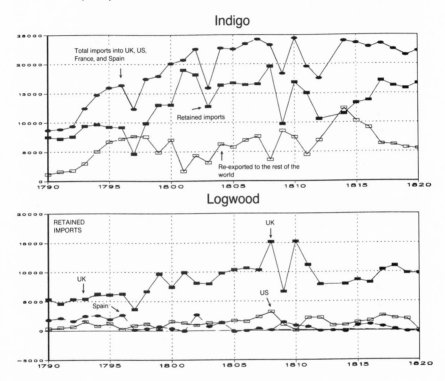

Indigo

Logwood

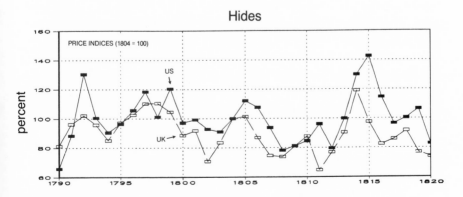

Hides

The expansion of world production at rising prices in the 1790s is largely explained by supply disruptions and speculative demand. The collapse of sugar imports from St. Domingue after 1791 fostered production elsewhere under the stimulus of rising prices and profit expectations. Such was the spread of the resulting sugar boom in Cuba that by 1798 tobacco leaf had to be imported from Virginia.[4] On the demand side, sugar consumption in England had been stimulated by a tax cut on tea since 1784.[5] This was the period when coffee finally became an article of general consumption, particularly among the British middle classes.[6] The rise in British exports, which reached boom proportions at the end of the decade, also stimulated demand for industrial raw materials, including indigo, logwood, and hides. By far the strongest and most general influence behind rising prices, however, was the feverish speculation in West Indian commodities that centered in Hamburgh from 1796 onward in expectation of prolonged naval warfare.

The speculative upswing of the 1790s brought about its own demise well ahead of the return of peace in 1801–1802. The price increases that stimulated colonial production also curbed purchasing power and sales at recipient countries, until supply caught up with demand and the inflationary trend was reversed. The first significant accumulation of stocks has been attributed to the closure of Swiss and Italian markets upon their occupation in 1798.[7] In England, the average prices of the six commodities under consideration had already peaked in 1797–98 and tumbled down thereafter to an absolute trough in 1802. Here the cycles in individual commodities most clearly reflect well-known conditions of local demand at the turn of the century, with the prices of indigo and hides being held up by the investment boom, while those of sugar and coffee peaked earlier and declined further under the likely pressure of falling real wages in 1801–1802.[8] As will be noted in Section II, the downturn in the United States was delayed until 1800 through relatively tight control of the tide of imports, thus setting a pattern by which fluctuations in U.S. prices would tend to follow those in their British counterparts with a one-year lag. In France, where supplies kept pouring in via Hamburgh and Amsterdam, prices were already falling in 1799 and sank to the lowest recorded levels in 1801. At the other end of the spectrum, prices at the blockaded port of Cadiz soared to unprecedented heights in 1798–1800.

The cycle of 1794–1802 set the pattern for a recurrent sequence of inflation and deflation that would perpetuate oversupply conditions through much of the subsequent decades. By the turn of the century, growth in colonial production had acquired a dynamic of its own, notably in tropical crops with long periods of gestation, including sugar, coffee, and cocoa. Had the Truce of Amiens been prolonged, the process of adjustment to inelastic and probably sluggish demand might have run its course through price and income effects at recipient markets. As it was, the expansionary impact of falling prices, and growing demand in Continental Europe as war resumed in 1803, took the slack of dwindling supplies and launched a new phase of inflation that in turn stimulated production. In the decade 1802–11, overall supply remained on the average at record levels, while demand lagged behind once Continental markets were closed and Spain regained direct access to the Indies in 1808. As a result, peaks in prices were increasingly lower and troughs much deeper than they had been in the 1790s. Under the triple impact of the Continental Blockade, the British Orders of Council that provoked the U.S. embargo of 1808, and the end of the Latin American boom that flooded the open markets in 1809–10, the bottom was reached in England in 1811 while French prices soared to unprecedented heights. Despite war-related inflation and short-lived speculation in 1814 and in 1817,[9] overall conditions remained mildly deflationary to the end of the period in 1820.

In analyzing the course of prices in individual recipient countries, it is useful to group the economic forces at work under the operational concepts of supply and demand. Fluctuations in *supply* and in *foreign demand* are roughly measured, respectively, by the values of retained imports and reexports at constant prices. In the absence of reliable annual evidence on consumption and national income in most cases, shifts in *domestic demand* must be inferred from documented changes in other variables and from theoretical considerations regarding price and income effects. Within this conceptual framework, the analysis will be presented as a series of case studies incorporating increasing orders of complexity. Since France was a large and terminal consuming market of colonial goods with minimal reexport activity, its import volumes are good proxies for domestic supplies and should be inversely correlated with prices on the simplifying assumption of stable domestic demand. The case of Spain represents intermediate conditions where the pull of foreign demand may have become a major determinant of prices in periods of free access to colonial supplies. For the United States, reexports always were a dynamic component of demand and indeed the main reason for the trade's existence. Here, as in the larger home market of Britain that was also fully exposed to world conditions of supply and demand, the primary influence on prices must be sought in the excess of retained imports over domestic consumption and stocks.

The course of French imports and prices is fully documented for the six major Latin American commodities from 1798 onward, but for the years 1790–96, no French figures have been found, and for 1797 only import values are available (see Graph 12.3, first panel, where a weighted average of the six prices at Amsterdam is also displayed).[10] Partial evidence from non-French sources inconclusively points to severe shortages and consequent inflation in the country after the loss of St. Domingue in 1791. The United States did step up reexports of colonial food crops to France, particularly during the Franco-Spanish war (1793–95) and again in 1797; even at the peaks of U.S. reexports of sugar and coffee in 1795 and 1797, however, the respective quantities were less than a fourth of those imported by France directly from its colonies in the documented years 1787–89.[11] Supplies from Spain in 1792 appear to have been even less substantial.[12] The magnitude of French imports from northern Europe in the early and mid-1790s must remain a matter of speculation. Since France was a large market for tropical crops and dyes by virtue of its population and textile industry, local shortages should have exerted considerable upward pressure on prices in neutral nations and client states. The pull of French demand from northern Europe is evidenced by steadily rising prices of the six commodities at the Amsterdam Exchange through much of the decade, despite substantial imports from the United States into both Hamburgh and Holland.[13] The latter country possibly became the leading supplier of colonial goods to France as early as 1792, as it would remain through 1798–1809, but such imports as did come from Holland in the 1790s were increasingly more expensive from 1795 to 1799. The most plausible picture is then one of rising French prices in the mid-1790s until 1798.

Throughout the documented years 1798–1820, the expected inverse correlation of French prices with import quantities is unmistakable. The fourfold rise in imports from Holland and northern Europe in 1798–1801, triggered as it must have been by the closure of normal channels of supply since the onset of naval hostilities with England, appears to have driven average prices well below international levels by 1801. The mild recovery of prices before the import correction of 1803, and in particular the nearly stable levels of 1803–1805 despite sharply rising supplies, may be partly explained by growing domestic demand as the result of falling prices and to mounting reexports to countries favorably affected by the Truce of Amiens. Resumption of generalized war in 1804, and the shifts of international

Graph 12.3

France
Six commodities
Import values and prices
(import values in thousand £ sterling at 1804 prices)

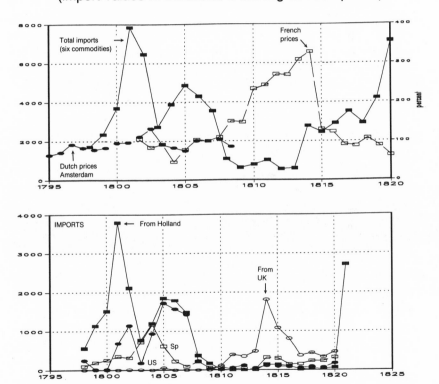

alliances and commercial policies that followed, brought dramatic changes in the level and composition of French imports of colonial goods. Since 1798 at least, Holland had been by far the largest single supplier, closely followed by Spain in 1803 and by the United States in the following three years (see Graph 12.3, lower panel). Imports from Spain sharply declined with the resumption of naval war in 1804 and virtually dried up after 1808, when Spain became an ally of England during the peninsular War of Independence (1808–1813). Meanwhile, in 1804–1807, Holland appears to have become heavily dependent on U.S. supplies of colonial goods.[14] Pres. Thomas Jefferson's 1808 embargo consequently dealt a severe blow to French imports by simultaneously cutting supplies from both the United States and northern Europe. Soaring import prices well above international levels in 1808–1813 testify to the effectiveness of Napoleon's Continental System insofar as colonial goods are concerned. The French statistics record moderate imports directly from the colonies in 1810 and indirectly from Britain under special licenses in 1811–13. A short-lived surge in the latter played a decisive role in bringing down French prices in 1814, but overall supplies appear to have remained short of demand through 1814–15. It was not until direct trade with the French colonies was fully restored in 1816 that French prices came down to international levels.

Fluctuations in Spanish prices are less intelligible for lack of strictly comparable and comprehensive evidence on imports and reexports. Price quotations at major Spanish ports frequently appear in contemporary sources, but only for Cadiz has it been possible to reconstruct continuous series through 1820 from manuscript sources extant in the Archivo General de Indias. The prices of the six major colonial goods at Cadiz did fluctuate inversely with retained imports in the documented years (see Graph 12.4), but there is reason to believe that shifts in foreign demand also played significant roles on at least three occasions. The decline in Spanish prices during the Franco-Spanish war of 1793–95 may be partially attributed to the closure of French markets, which had absorbed more than one-third of Spain's colonial imports in 1787–89.[15] For the second half of the 1790s, evidence on other Spanish ports and on foreign countries' trade with Spain allows for informed speculation as to market conditions in the entire country. Before 1797, Cadiz had been by far the largest recipient of colonial goods and had acted as a distributing center for other Spanish regions and European countries. The first naval war with England (1796–1801) virtually stopped direct communications with the Indies and forced Spain to open colonial ports to neutral ships in May 1797. Total imports accordingly began to

Graph 12.4

Spain
Six commodities
Imports, re-exports, and prices
(trade values in thousand £ sterling at 1804 prices)

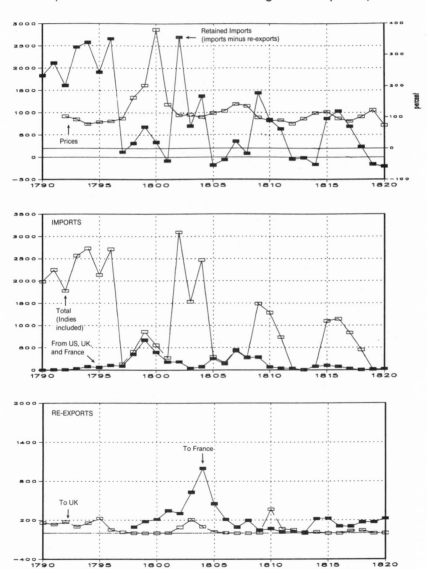

recover from near collapse in 1798–1800, but those from the United States remained well below normal supplies from the Indies into Cadiz in years of peace (cf. scales in upper and middle panels).

One contributing circumstance to this poor response was Spain's premature suspension of neutral trade in 1799. The price evidence confirms what little is known about import levels and their geographical distribution. At Cadiz, where naval blockades were frequent during these years, prices soared by 1800 to nearly four times the level reached in 1804. Elsewhere in Spain, inflation was far less substantial, particularly in sugar and coffee, which were in relatively plentiful supply by 1800. At any rate, the Spanish hyperinflation of 1798–1800 stands in sharp contrast to contemporary conditions in France, where imports from northern Europe had been driving prices down since 1799 at least. When Spanish prices collapsed in 1801, they remained well above French levels, as one-third of the supplies from the Indies into Cadiz were reexported to the neighboring country (cf. scales in middle and lower panels). The second naval war with England (1804–1808) again brought shortage conditions to Spain, but, in contrast to the 1790s, imports from foreign countries at sharply falling prices appear to have moderated inflationary pressures. One surprising feature of this period is the rise of British reexports of colonial goods to Spain. The alliance with Britain against Napoleon in 1808 once again turned shortage into surplus at Cadiz, with moderate supplies from the Indies in 1809–11 now outpacing weakened demand from the closure of French and French-occupied markets. Judging from the price evidence at Cadiz, supply conditions in unoccupied Spain remained favorable through the War of Independence (1808–13) until French markets were opened again in 1814–15. By then, however, a weakened country clinging to a shrinking empire could no longer sustain even a modest role as a carrier of colonial commodities.

The analysis of Spanish prices has stressed the role of shifts in foreign demand in 1793–95, 1802–1804, and 1809–15. For the United States, reexports always were a dynamic component of demand and indeed the main reason for the trade's existence (see Graph 12.5). Imports of four major Latin American commodities always kept ahead of reexports, but surplus margins were at times tiny and frequently unsteady. Under such circumstances, the key variable that governed cycles in price levels was the excess of retained imports over domestic consumption and stocks. So long as home demand was relatively small and inelastic, fluctuations in retained imports of a single commodity could dramatically affect average home prices despite the absence of major trade distortions such as those experienced by France and by Spain.

Graph 12.5

United States
Four commodities
Imports, re-exports, and prices
(trade values in thousand £ sterling at 1804 prices)

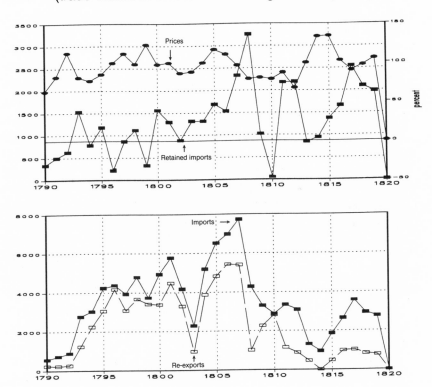

One such instance occurred in 1790–91, when the entire imports of sugar were reexported. The resulting surge in domestic prices by 1791–92 probably triggered its own correction by cutting home sales and stimulating imports. By 1793, however, the pull of demand from war-trodden Europe was beginning to override domestic market conditions. Reexport values at 1804 prices mounted steadily to £4.5 million from 1793 to 1796 and fluctuated thereafter around £4 million until 1802. The course of prices during this period suggests that, once stocks were cleared in 1794–95, the £1 million mark in retained imports for domestic consumption held the balance between inflation and deflation (see upper panel). The upward trend in prices to 1799, while home supplies appear to have fallen short of demand, was reinforced in 1796 by sagging imports, possibly related to expectations of lasting peace in Europe. As it was, foreign demand remained strong after 1797, but not so strong as to warrant the flood of imports that followed at the turn of the century. By 1800, deflation had set in as retained import values rose and remained, on the average, well above £1 million through the Truce of Amiens and beyond. The price increases of 1804 and 1805 may be attributed, in part, to the holding of stocks in anticipation of renewed warfare, and in part to expanding markets in the increasingly prosperous northeastern United States.

Meanwhile, foreign demand from the belligerent parties was mounting, but imports once again outpaced reexports with consequently falling prices after 1805. The export embargo of 1808 simply deepened and prolonged surplus conditions and deflation at home despite a major import correction in 1808–10 and rising reexports of sugar and coffee to Spain and northern Europe in 1809–10. By 1811, stocks appear to have run out and imports were again rising, but home supplies proved excessive by 1812 in the face of declining exports. The decisive fact during the 1810s is that Spanish and French markets of colonial goods had been irretrievably lost, partly to Britain, but also to Spain itself since 1810 and to France's own shipping after 1815. Against this background of moderate reexports since 1811, the balance of import supplies and home demand became the major determinant of prices. The sharp contraction of imports during the War of 1812 (1812–15) predictably drove prices to unprecedented heights. At the moderate prices prevailing after 1815, the home market proved capable of sustaining twice the level of Latin American supplies it had absorbed during the 1790s.

The British case resembles that of the United States, in that both countries were large carriers of colonial goods operating within a free-trade area. Since both nations were exposed to similar conditions of world supply and demand, it is not surprising to find that trends and cycles in their respective local prices closely approximated one another (see Graph 12.6, first panel). Observed disparities of timing and degree can be explained in terms of price and income effects on world supply and demand, the nature of each country's connection to the sources of production, and the relative sizes of the domestic markets involved. As has been noted, rising prices during the feverish speculation of the mid- to late 1790s stimulated colonial production and curbed purchasing power and sales at recipient markets, until the inflationary trend was reversed. Since the British home market was much larger and supplies could be more readily drawn from a growing and captive colonial area, British prices eventually rose at a slower rate and peaked in 1797–98, well before their U.S. counterparts. By the turn of the century, growth in colonial production had acquired a dynamic of its own, notably in tropical crops with long periods of gestation. Britain, by the nature of its imperial connections, could not effectively stem the flood of supplies until 1803, while the United States had simply cut imports a year earlier. Thus, the very momentum of supply that had curbed British inflation during the upturn was to prolong and deepen the subsequent downturn into 1802, when deflation in the United States was already leveling off. At this point, the expansionary impact of collapsing prices on Britain's larger market took the slack of dwindling supplies and launched a new phase of inflation, well before U.S. prices began to rise under the pull of foreign demand. A pattern had thus been established by which fluctuations in British prices would precede those in their U.S. counterparts, but the upswings would become progressively milder and the downswings would be steeper. In this respect, the cycles of 1802–1807 and 1807–12 were mirror images of that of 1794–1802, with the one significant difference that Jefferson's embargo deepened the downturn in U.S. prices in 1808. By the eve of the War of 1812, Britain had captured additional sources of supply in Spanish America at the expense of the United States, while the balance of the latter country's exports was turning strongly in favor of domestic staples. The differential impact of the war on prices is explained by persistent blockades of major North American ports, while Britain's access to West Indian markets remained unimpeded. By 1815, a significant share of colonial production had been or was being rechanneled directly to Europe via the respective home countries. In the absence of major shifts in European demand, the postwar readjustments in British and U.S. prices were a pale reflection of the cycles that had punctuated the Napoleonic period.

Graph 12.6

United Kingdom
Six commodities
Imports, re-exports, and prices
(trade values in thousand £ sterling at 1804 prices)

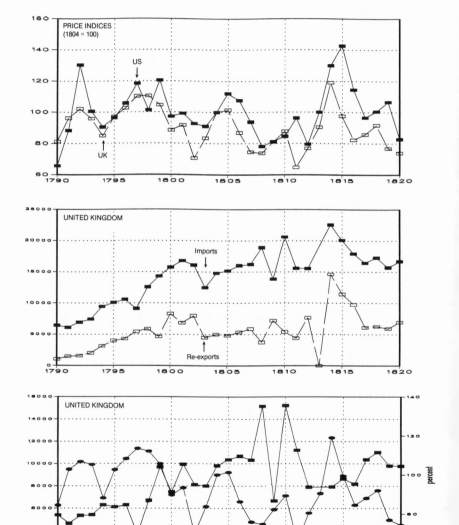

The foregoing analysis has identified a cluster of variables that together appear to have shaped, in varying degrees and in different combinations, the course of prices of six major Latin American commodities in four separate recipient countries. The overall trend of rising prices during the 1790s has been explained by supply disruptions and speculative demand, and the prolonged deflation that followed by a recurrent sequence of stimuli to world production against a background of market contraction in Continental Europe. In the large, terminal consuming market of France, import volumes broadly explain price fluctuations on the simplifying assumption of stable domestic demand. The poorly documented case of Spain represents intermediate conditions, where sharp but short-lived shifts in foreign demand were a major determinant of price levels on at least three occasions. In the United States, where home markets were also small and most imports were reexported, the decisive variable was the excess of retained imports over domestic consumption and stocks. In comparing trends and cycles in British and U.S. prices, the key variables at work appear to have been the relative sizes of domestic markets, the nature of each country's connection to the sources of production, and the overall balance of world supply and demand in relevant subperiods. The evidence presented also confirms such theoretical predictions as the tendency toward price equalization across trading nations and the pronounced instability of prices of agricultural commodities with low elasticities of supply and demand.

APPENDIX

The statistical foundation of this paper ranges from prices and international exchange rates to import and reexport quantities of six colonial commodities in five different countries. Many of the figures derive from primary sources and are here presented and used for the first time. Most have been selectively compiled and processed for the specific purposes detailed in the text.

The new series of Spanish prices were compiled from *Correo mercantil de España y sus Indias* (Madrid, 1792–1808: monthly or bimonthly price lists from Cadiz and Málaga, 1792–1803; Cadiz prices missing in 1800) and from Archivo General de Indias, Consulados, libs. 1130, 1132, and 1134 (biweekly) quotations in *Libros de precios corrientes de la Lonja de Corredores de Cádiz,* 1803–1820). All annual series were calculated as simple averages of the first quotations of each month whenever possible; comparisons of these monthly series with random samples of exhaustive quotations showed little significant variation at the annual level. "On board" quotations were converted into "on land" prices with rates implicit in the double entries that appear in Archivo General de Indias, Consulados, lib. 1134 (1819–20), passim. Units of measurement are not always directly comparable in the early returns printed in the *Correo mercantil*, particularly in those of Málaga. All coinage denominations and weights and measures were homogenized with those in the later years with the aid of information and rates given in T. de Marién y Arróspide, *Tratado general de monedas, pesos, medidas y cambios de todas las naciones, reducidas a las que se usan en España*, 2 vols. (Madrid, 1789), 1: 2–3, and in *Almanak Mercantil o Guía de comerciantes* . . . (Madrid, 1795–1807), passim. The annual estimates adopted for the present paper are given in Table 12.1.

The preparation of comparable price series for other countries was far less elaborate. Annual averages at several French ports from 1798 to 1821 are given, from original sources, in A. Chabert, *Essai sur les mouvements des prix et des revenus en France de 1798 a 1820*, 2 vols. in 1 (Paris, 1945–49): relevant series in 1: 128–29, 134–35, 141, 142, 146, and 221. Chabert's own indices were found defective and had to be rejected; the adopted series are those from either Bordeaux or Beaucaire, with occasional interpolations from parallel data for the respective commodity at other French ports. Amsterdam prices also are readily available in annual averages in N. Posthumus, *Inquiry into the History of Prices in Holland*, 2 vols. (Leiden, 1946, 1964), 1: 130, 196–97, 356–57, 417–18, and 419–20; the adopted series end in 1806 for lack of adequate coverage in later years. The British series were derived from the monthly quotations of "in bond" prices (that is, no duty added) given in the microfilmed supplement to A. Gayer, W. Rostow, and A. Schwartz, eds., *The Growth and Fluctuation of the British Economy, 1790–1850*, 2 vols. [microfilmed supplement] (Oxford, 1953), 674, 676, 690, 692, 703, and 729. The U.S. series were derived from selected tables of monthly price relatives in A. Bezanson, R. Gray, and M. Hussey, *Wholesale Prices in Philadelphia 1784–1861*, 2 vols. (Philadelphia, 1936), 1: 42–44, 47, 93–94, 99–100, 132, and 224; the conversion procedure from relatives into actual prices per unit is explained in 2: xxxviii. As noted in the text, all U.S. prices were averaged by fiscal years commencing 1 October to allow for time lags between entries at home customs—also given by fiscal years—and the sales of reexported cargoes in Europe. The resulting averages were then reduced by deduction of official annual rates of specific duty on each commodity in each year, so as to approximate as closely as possible the actual "in bond" prices upon arrival at U.S. ports. The rates of specific duties were compiled from the sources listed in J. Cuenca Esteban, "The United States

Table 12.1. Current Prices at Cadiz

Year	Cocoa (Caracas) pesos/fanega	Cocoa (Guayaquil) pesos/fanega	Coffee quartos/libra	Hides (Cueros al pelo) reales plata/35 libras	Indigo ("Corte") reales plata/libra	Indigo ("Flor") reales plata/libra	Indigo ("Sobre") reales plata/libra	Logwood (Palo de Campeche) pesos/quintal	Sugar (Azucar terciada) reales plata/arroba	Sugar (Azucar blanca) reales plata/arroba
1792	44.3	33.3	34.0	45.0	20.0	27.8	24.5	1.9	42.7	48.7
1793	52.7	44.4	46.8	41.7	18.3	26.7	23.3	2.2	36.8	43.6
1794	50.4	48.1	48.6	42.3	16.5	25.9	21.9	2.2	36.6	42.8
1795	56.0	45.2	51.0	43.8	18.1	27.6	23.7	3.3	47.3	54.3
1796	55.4	37.1	52.5	46.3	18.2	28.2	24.5	4.6	52.4	58.5
1797	72.5	45.8	64.5	56.1	19.4	30.7	25.8	5.9	60.5	66.8
1798	91.3	77.8	88.5	68.7	22.3	36.5	30.5	7.4	97.2	104.8
1799	115.6	97.3	93.3	91.9	32.0	52.8	44.7	13.1	111.1	117.2
1800	173.7	120.2	97.4	85.5	46.7	76.9	62.3	10.0	136.3	142.3
1801	83.3	51.4	57.7	73.1	23.5	31.9	28.5	6.7	43.7	57.6
1802	51.7	32.0	42.5	57.1	17.6	26.8	23.0	3.8	37.5	46.3
1803	74.2	40.1	44.9	48.7	18.9	29.8	24.3	5.9	35.6	41.8
1804	77.9	40.2	51.9	41.4	18.9	27.5	23.5	6.4	34.3	42.7
1805	102.4	63.9	79.2	39.4	23.1	30.0	27.1	8.5	37.8	51.4
1806	83.4	59.4	57.0	41.0	25.6	31.3	28.8	8.1	35.6	47.9
1807	73.1	60.2	57.9	48.3	29.5	35.1	32.5	7.4	45.2	54.3
1808	72.2	52.0	58.4	58.6	26.0	33.0	29.8	7.6	41.5	50.5
1809	58.6	41.8	36.7	44.2	17.8	25.3	21.6	5.0	28.7	37.0
1810	44.5	26.5	32.3	34.0	16.7	24.3	21.7	4.7	23.5	31.4
1811	42.3	22.8	27.2	32.2	12.5	22.9	18.2	3.4	25.7	33.0
1812	39.4	19.2	18.3	32.7	9.5	18.8	14.9	2.7	28.6	34.4
1813	41.7	20.3	15.7	40.8	10.5	20.7	16.8	2.6	33.9	38.9
1814	77.3	27.8	27.4	64.3	14.5	24.3	20.0	4.5	33.3	49.2
1815	85.3	36.1	26.7	69.5	13.4	24.5	19.8	4.8	45.6	58.0
1816	64.2	34.1	26.6	72.4	13.1	23.5	19.5	3.2	41.0	47.0
1817	63.6	27.1	28.9	68.1	10.5	22.8	17.9	2.5	36.1	43.1
1818	66.2	26.1	47.0	66.3	13.0	24.1	19.3	2.1	40.3	47.4
1819	64.8	27.9	45.7	56.9	13.1	23.6	19.6	2.2	38.4	45.5
1820	56.4	27.8	44.5	62.9	13.1	23.5	19.3	2.2	27.8	34.3

Sources and procedures: See the Appendix.

Balance of Payments with Spanish America and the Philippine Islands, 1790–1819. Estimates and Analysis of Principal Components," J. Barbier and A. Kuethe, eds., in *The North American Role in the Spanish Imperial Economy 1769–1819* (Manchester, 1984), 204, n. 116 (see also Tables 12.2 to 12.5 herein).

International comparisons of prices and trade values require conversion into a common unit, such as the pound sterling, with rates of exchange (see Table 12.6 herein). The dollar-sterling series developed for this paper is based on J. White's rates from the actual transactions of two large trading houses of Baltimore with bills of exchange, which are reprinted in *International Monetary Conference, Senate Executive Document no. 58*, 45th Cong., 3rd sess. (Washington, D.C., 1879), 634–41. Annual averages of White's monthly quotations were corrected for their sixty-day interest component with L. Officer's proposed methodology as explained in "Dollar-Sterling Mint Parity and Exchange Rates, 1791–1834," *Journal of Economic History* 43 (1983): 600. The author is indebted to Professor Officer for advice on the choice of correction for the present purposes. All other rates of exchange are based on monthly quotations compiled and processed from Wetenhall-Castaign's *Course of the Exchange:* London on Paris, on Cadiz, on Amsterdam, and on Hamburg. The few gaps in the first three series were interpolated with estimates derived from the London-Hamburg rates and from the relevant monthly or quarterly quotations from the Amsterdam Exchange as given in Posthumus, *Inquiry,* 1: 610–14. Conversions into common units were facilitated by reference to the Spanish sources cited above and to J. McCusker, *Money and Exchange in Europe and America, 1600–1775. A Handbook* (Chapel Hill, N.C., 1978), passim.

Many of the import and reexport quantities are available in well-known primary sources, but most have required considerable elaboration. The British figures were compiled from the *Ledgers of Imports and Exports:* Public Records Office (London), Customs 17 (vols. 12–30), Customs 4 (vols. 5–7), Customs 14 (Scottish Ledgers: vols. 22–23), Customs 5 (vols. 2–9), and Customs 11 (vols. 1–11). Prize goods were added wherever they appeared in separate lists. The figures for 1809–11 had to be added up almost from scratch and the entries are probably incomplete; no data at all are available for 1813. The U.S. quantities of imports and reexports were compiled and processed from the sources listed in Cuenca Esteban, "United States Balance of Payments," p. 203, n. 104. The quantities imported into Cadiz are those compiled in the Archivo General de Indias by A. García Baquero González:

Table 12.2. French Prices

Year	Cocoa fr/lb	Coffee (Martinique) fr/lb	Hides (a poil) fr/lb	Indigo fr/kg	Logwood (Campeche) fr/kg	Sugar (Martinique) fr/lb
1798	2.2	2.9	0.6	16.0	145.0	2.1
1799	1.5	2.6	0.8	13.0	100.0	1.7
1800	1.6	2.3	0.8	16.0	100.0	1.8
1801	1.0	1.4	1.0	13.0	58.0	1.4
1802	0.9	1.2	1.0	14.0	44.0	0.7
1803	1.4	1.4	1.0	16.0	90.0	1.1
1804	1.3	2.0	0.9	22.0	50.0	1.1
1805	2.7	2.7	1.0	24.0	60.0	1.5
1806	2.7	2.4	2.2	38.0	76.0	1.3
1807	2.4	2.9	2.6	30.2	47.0	1.5
1808	2.0	4.2	2.8	33.5	190.0	1.5
1809	2.5	4.0	2.8	33.5	200.0	2.0
1810	4.0	4.1	3.0	36.0	72.0	3.4
1811	3.7	4.0	3.0	33.6	168.0	3.7
1812	3.7	4.1	3.4	33.7	183.0	4.4
1813	3.6	3.6	3.3	44.8	205.0	3.9
1814	3.6	1.4	2.3	27.7	70.0	1.3
1815	2.7	1.4	2.0	23.1	37.7	1.6
1816	2.2	1.4	1.8	17.5	33.5	1.4
1817	2.0	1.0	2.0	18.5	35.5	1.1
1818	2.2	2.2	2.2	23.0	31.5	1.0
1819	2.2	2.1	2.3	22.0	32.5	0.9
1820	2.0	1.9	2.4	22.5	36.5	1.0

Sources and procedures: See the Appendix.

Table 12.3. Dutch Prices

Year	Cocoa (Surinam) guld/lb	Coffee (S. Domingo) guld/lb	Hides (B. Aires) guld/lb	Indigo (Guatimalo) guld/lb	Logwood (Yellow Wood) guld/100 lbs	Sugar (Surinam) guld/lb
1790	0.26	0.48	0.42	6.00	4.38	0.23
1791	0.27	0.42	0.42	6.25	6.54	0.27
1792	0.37	0.56	0.42	6.25	7.29	0.36
1793	0.44	0.55	0.42	6.36	7.42	0.36
1794	0.56	0.57	0.39	6.67	6.46	0.35
1795	0.62	0.70	0.39	6.57	7.00	0.37
1796	0.65	0.80	0.37	6.39	8.67	0.49
1797	0.72	0.87	0.40	6.25	13.10	0.51
1798	0.79	1.10	0.41	6.79	35.00	0.62
1799	0.91	1.24	0.48	7.25	35.75	0.68
1800	0.82	0.86	0.45	7.25	18.63	0.36
1801	0.69	0.72	0.45	6.75	8.69	0.36
1802	0.55	0.53	0.40	6.56	7.13	0.25
1803		0.89	0.41	6.39	11.00	0.37
1804		1.00	0.35	7.00	12.00	0.41
1805		0.99	0.35	7.32	13.75	0.38
1806		0.91	0.39	8.50	9.00	0.28

Sources: See the Appendix.

Table 12.4. British Prices

Year	Cocoa (Grenada) sh/cwt	Coffee (Jamaica) sh/cwt	Hides (B. Aires) d/lb	Indigo (Caracas) sh/lb	Logwood (Campeche) L/ton	Sugar (Brown Jamaica) sh/cwt
1790	48.2	83.0	7.1	7.8	8.4	46.4
1791	56.8	70.7	6.5	8.7	7.7	57.5
1792	62.9	97.4	5.5	8.8	8.8	58.8
1793	79.2	85.7	5.7	9.0	10.2	57.7
1794	104.1	87.8	7.8	8.4	11.0	46.0
1795	87.5	100.2	5.4	8.3	16.4	60.4
1796	93.3	109.1	5.9	6.5	17.4	66.2
1797	102.5	117.7	6.5	8.4	19.3	65.5
1798	99.5	138.2	7.5	8.6	27.8	62.1
1799	106.3	147.1	9.3	8.6	34.9	51.9
1800	98.7	120.4	8.6	8.4	23.7	41.8
1801	107.3	111.3	8.8	8.8	22.5	47.8
1802	84.3	85.8	7.3	9.0	17.3	32.5
1803	84.3	115.0	8.5	9.3	26.9	37.3
1804	128.2	134.9	7.8	9.7	25.7	48.8
1805	136.5	143.3	7.4	10.6	25.2	46.8
1806	108.3	128.8	6.9	10.6	21.5	37.1
1807	95.0	107.4	6.9	8.8	17.9	29.1
1808	85.5	83.1	6.4	8.1	17.4	35.0
1809	81.4	98.8	6.6	7.7	19.8	43.3
1810	78.8	81.7	8.9	10.1	36.8	46.6
1811	68.4	45.2	5.4	8.8	19.3	37.3
1812	56.8	43.1	6.6	8.2	16.1	43.5
1813	67.8	70.4	7.3	9.3	19.1	59.8
1814	104.7	91.8	9.5	10.0	23.5	73.7
1815	86.9	78.1	9.4	8.4	17.4	58.4
1816	76.4	69.8	7.9	7.4	10.6	44.8
1817	75.0	81.5	8.0	7.8	10.1	46.6
1818	84.5	121.7	7.5	8.1	9.8	46.2
1819	109.5	107.7	7.4	7.4	8.8	36.2
1820	105.0	118.4	7.4	6.9	7.7	33.3

Sources and procedures: See the Appendix.

Table 12.5. U.S. Prices

Year	Cocoa (Island & Caracas) $/lb	Coffee (Havana base) $/lb	Indigo (East Indies) $/lb	Sugar (Havana brown) $/lb
1790	0.07	0.16	1.42	0.05
1791	0.07	0.13	1.29	0.08
1792	0.11	0.15	1.26	0.13
1793	0.11	0.14	1.36	0.10
1794	0.09	0.15	1.74	0.10
1795	0.12	0.16	1.44	0.10
1796	0.14	0.19	1.44	0.11
1797	0.13	0.21	1.25	0.12
1798	0.14	0.19	1.13	0.10
1799	0.16	0.24	1.10	0.10
1800	0.20	0.20	1.17	0.09
1801	0.19	0.20	1.16	0.09
1802	0.15	0.16	1.44	0.09
1803	0.14	0.20	1.90	0.08
1804	0.18	0.23	1.83	0.08
1805	0.18	0.26	1.49	0.09
1806	0.17	0.28	1.64	0.09
1807	0.15	0.25	1.68	0.07
1808	0.12	0.21	1.45	0.06
1809	0.16	0.19	1.52	0.06
1810	0.14	0.17	1.49	0.07
1811	0.11	0.13	1.39	0.08
1812	0.05	0.07	1.33	0.06
1813	0.07	0.10	1.58	0.10
1814	0.12	0.15	1.93	0.14
1815	0.18	0.21	2.11	0.18
1816	0.18	0.19	1.71	0.14
1817	0.13	0.14	1.29	0.10
1818	0.12	0.20	1.34	0.09
1819	0.11	0.23	1.41	0.09
1820	0.10	0.20	1.32	0.07

Sources and procedures: See the Appendix.

Table 12.6. Exchange Rates

Year	Reales de vellon/ Pound St.	Francs/ Pound St.	Guldens/ Pound St.	Dollars/ Pound St.
1790	113.15	27.60	11.66	
1791	101.12	30.60	11.63	4.58
1792	98.16	40.35	11.12	4.49
1793	106.39	67.55	11.78	4.54
1794	119.00	46.88*	11.96	4.78
1795	122.85	—	12.04	4.55
1796	126.06	23.95*	11.86*	4.31
1797	147.52	26.52*	12.92*	4.46
1798	114.22*	27.42*	13.31*	4.41
1799	111.64*	25.56*	12.99*	4.16
1800	89.93	22.67*	11.56*	4.58
1801	91.50	22.77*	11.55*	4.41
1802	97.71	23.99	9.83	4.51
1803	100.64	24.75	10.90	4.57
1804	104.94	25.55	11.33	4.58
1805	108.08	25.96	11.31	4.37
1806	95.31	24.82	10.98	4.46
1807	93.27	24.55	10.87	4.45
1808	88.37	23.55	10.61	4.65
1809	91.41	20.75	9.60	4.60
1810	87.94	20.90	9.76	4.33
1811	78.60	18.26	8.66	3.84
1812	76.36	19.39	9.09	3.64
1813	73.21	19.58	9.24	3.77
1814	81.14	21.61	9.83	4.27
1815	90.65	21.81	10.15	4.93
1816	105.99	25.48	11.79	5.25
1817	101.21	24.97	11.57	4.63
1818	92.22	24.45	11.10	4.53
1819	95.44	24.82	11.63	4.54
1820	104.12	25.83	12.18	4.55

*Data interpolated with indirect quotations via Hamburgh and Amsterdam, as explained in the Appendix.

Sources and procedures: See the Appendix.

Comercio colonial y guerras revolucionarias (Seville, 1972), Segunda parte, passim.

All other import and reexport quantities had to be derived by division of trade values by current prices. The French values were compiled from Archives Nationales (Paris), F[12], no. 251, *Tableaux imprimés des importations et exportations,* 1787–89, 1797–1821. Import and reexport quantities also given in this source after 1816 differ little from those derived by division of values by prices. For a detailed analysis of French official valuations and current prices, see Javier Cuenca-Esteban, "Fundamentos para una interpretación de las estadísticas comerciales francesas de 1787–1821, con referencia especial al comercio franco-español," in *Hacienda Pública Española,* 97 (1988): 44–76. The Spanish import values from 1792 to 1796 are those compiled by J. Fisher: "The Imperial Response to 'Free Trade': Spanish Imports from Spanish America, 1778–1796," *Journal of Latin American Studies,* 17 (1985): 35–78.

NOTES

*The author wishes to acknowledge financial support from the Social Sciences and Humanities Research Council of Canada during the period of data collection in London, Paris, and Seville.

1. All sources and procedures not specifically referred to in the text or in the notes are documented and described in the Appendix.

2. French figures before 1798 are not included for lack of price evidence to deflate the extant market values, but the overwhelmingly important inflows of sugar into this country certainly declined sharply after the loss of St. Domingue in 1791. Other unavoidable omissions that are probably insignificant at the aggregate level include the U.S. figures for logwood and hides and all direct imports from the Indies into Spanish ports other than Cadiz. No attempt has been made to estimate the extent of smuggling, but the swings in supply conveyed by the official figures are sufficiently strong and well defined to warrant a broad explanation of most trends and cycles in market prices. The reader is referred to the Appendix for background and additional detail.

3. The "Hamburgh speculation" of 1796–99 is described by reference to contemporary sources in A. Gayer, W. Rostow, and A. Schwartz, eds., *The Growth and Fluctuation of the British Economy, 1790–1850,* 2 vols. (Oxford, 1953), 1: 32–35.

4. M. Moreno Fraginals, *The Sugarmill. The Socioeconomic Complex of Sugar in Cuba 1760–1860* (New York, 1976), 23. For relevant background see also pp. 17 and 41–42.

5. Gayer et al., *Growth and Fluctuation,* 1: 34.

6. Gayer et al., *Growth and Fluctuation,* 2: 965.

7. Reference to M. Wirth's analysis in Gayer et al., *Growth and Fluctuation,* 1: 34, n. 4.

8. Evidence and analysis of investment conditions and real wages during these years in Gayer et al., *Growth and Fluctuation,* 1: 35–43, 54–57.

9. See Gayer et al., *Growth and Fluctuation,* 1: 119, 146–47.

10. As noted in the Appendix, French import and reexport quantities had to be derived by division of trade values by current prices. The 1797 quantities were estimated from 1797 values at 1798 prices.

11. See again note 10: the 1787–89 quantities were estimated from extant 1787–89 values at 1804 prices.

12. Quantities of Spanish exports to France are given in *Balanza del comercio de España con las potencias estranjeras en el año de 1792* (Madrid, 1803), passim.

13. Quantities exported from the United States to Holland and to Hamburgh in the 1790s were compiled from American State Papers, *Commerce and Navigation* (Washington, D.C., 1832, 1834), vol. 1, passim.

14. American State Papers, *Commerce,* vol. 1, passim. The export quantities of sugar and coffee to most countries in the 1800s were reprinted in T. Pitkin, *A Statistical View of the Commerce of the United States of America . . .* (Hartford, 1816), 145–49.

15. See again notes 10 and 11.

CONTRIBUTORS

Dauril Alden, Professor of History, University of Washington

Kendall W. Brown, Associate Professor of History, Hillsdale College

John H. Coatsworth, Professor of History, University of Chicago

Javier Cuenca-Esteban, Associate Professor of Economics, University of Waterloo

Stanley L. Engerman, Professor of Economics, University of Rochester

Robert J. Ferry, Assistant Professor of History, University of Colorado

Richard L. Garner, Associate Professor of History, Pennsylvania State University

Lyman L. Johnson, Professor of History, University of North Carolina at Charlotte

Herbert S. Klein, Professor of History, Columbia University

José Manuel Larraín Melo, Professor of History, Pontificia Universidad Católica de Chile

Brooke Larson, Associate Professor of History, State University of New York at Stony Brook

Ruggiero Romano, Professor, Ecole des Hautes Etudes en Sciences Sociales, Paris

Enrique Tandeter, Professor, Universidad de Buenos Aires; Researcher, C.O.N.I.C.E.T. (National Scientific and Technological Research Council) and C.E.D.E.S. (Center for the Study of State and Society), Buenos Aires

Nathan Wachtel, Professor and Director of the C.E.R.M.A.C.A. (Mexican and Andean Research Centre), Ecole des Hautes Etudes en Sciences Sociales, Paris

INDEX